Advance Praise for
YouTube and Video Marketing: An Hour a Day

Once again, Greg Jarboe offers a detailed, well-researched guide for businesses wanting to get the most out of YouTube marketing. It's a must-read for anyone serious about incorporating YouTube as part of their online marketing strategy.
  —MICHAEL MILLER, author, *YouTube for Business*

In an age of too much of everything, YouTube has become an essential channel for every Marketer. It is a place to let your creativity shine through, engage a massive audience, and build a long-term platform for your company (b2c, b2c, a2z!). In his new-and-improved second edition, Greg holds your hands, whispers soothing words, points out the path, and leads you down it optimally. Buy the book, now!
  —AVINASH KAUSHIK, author, *Web Analytics 2.0* and *Web Analytics: An Hour A Day*

Greg Jarboe's breadth and depth of YouTube marketing knowledge is exceptional! I was an avid reader of the first edition of YouTube Marketing: An Hour A Day, *and now I must say that Greg's second edition is well worth the investment too. YouTube continues to explode on a regular basis, and the latest case studies are incredible. If you're eager to find out how brands are easily generating one million in sales through YouTube, or how even small companies have generated nearly three million video views and more than $130,000 in revenue, and—more importantly—how you can too, definitely pick up a copy of Greg's latest book!*
  —MARI SMITH, author, *Facebook Marketing: An Hour A Day* and *The New Relationship Marketing*

Somehow, Greg Jarboe has the ability to take the fluid, fast-paced environment of video marketing and communicates it in a clear, practical format. He makes the principles of successful video promotion easily accessible to business owners, campaign managers, marketers—[anyone who] needs to understand the critical elements of promoting a video-based campaign. Too many people have "tried it" and given up, but there is a difference between trying video marketing and doing it correctly. Greg will guide you to do it correctly the first time.

Being from Ohio, it's hard enough to compliment a Michigan native, but his insights are that good!

  —MATT BAILEY, President, *SiteLogic Marketing*; consultant; speaker; author, *Internet Marketing: An Hour a Day*

YouTube® and Video Marketing:

An Hour a Day

Second Edition

Greg Jarboe

WILEY

John Wiley & Sons, Inc.

Senior Acquisitions Editor: Willem Knibbe
Development Editor: Connor O'Brien
Technical Editor: Brad O'Farell
Production Editor: Liz Britten
Copy Editor: Judy Flynn
Editorial Manager: Pete Gaughan
Production Manager: Tim Tate
Vice President and Executive Group Publisher: Richard Swadley
Vice President and Publisher: Neil Edde
Book Designer: Franz Baumhackl
Compositor: Chris Gillespie, Happenstance Type-O-Rama
Proofreader: Kristy Eldredge and Louise Watson; WordOne, New York
Indexer: Ted Laux
Project Coordinator, Cover: Katherine Crocker
Cover Designer: Ryan Sneed
Cover Image: © Thinkstock Images / Getty Images

Dear Reader,

Thank you for choosing *YouTube and Video Marketing: An Hour a Day*. This book is part of a family of premium-quality Sybex books, all of which are written by outstanding authors who combine practical experience with a gift for teaching.

Sybex was founded in 1976. More than 30 years later, we're still committed to producing consistently exceptional books. With each of our titles, we're working hard to set a new standard for the industry. From the paper we print on, to the authors we work with, our goal is to bring you the best books available.

I hope you see all that reflected in these pages. I'd be very interested to hear your comments and get your feedback on how we're doing. Feel free to let me know what you think about this or any other Sybex book by sending me an email at nedde@wiley.com. If you think you've found a technical error in this book, please visit http://sybex.custhelp.com. Customer feedback is critical to our efforts at Sybex.

Best regards,

Neil Edde
Vice President and Publisher
Sybex, an imprint of Wiley

Acknowledgments

I could not have written this book without the help and support of many people.

First, I need to thank my wife, Nancy, for putting up with me during the past 12 months—especially when I was in the "Room of Requirement," our nickname for the room down the hall where I worked on this book evenings and weekends. To make it up, I will watch *Glee* and *The Last Word with Lawrence O'Donnell* with you for the next 12 months. And I want to thank my kids, Andrew, Brendan, and Kelsey; you've listened to me talk about YouTube and video marketing at Thanksgiving and family cookouts. I will listen to you talk about the Boston Red Sox, Massachusetts politics, and Magical Realism, as specified by the Equal Time rule. And thanks to Melanie Riccobene Jarboe, Anne Sheldon, and Vaughn Cartwright for joining our speech and debate team and receiving my frequent emails with links to videos like "7 Harry Potter Movies in 7 Minutes" from The Fine Brothers (http://youtu.be/L3AdfZ346wg) without complaining.

Next, I need to thank my business partner, Jamie O'Donnell, and my colleagues at SEO-PR: Nell Connors, Byron Gordon, Sean O'Connoll, Sergei Fyodorov, Nathan Groom, Jean Sexton, John Zukowski, Chris Halcon, Danya Abt, Adam Macbeth, and Kilo. You helped me keep my day job and watched my back during the swing shift. I'm taking all of you to Joe's Cable Car Restaurant in San Francisco the next time I visit the Left Coast.

I need to thank SEO-PR's clients. This includes Matt McGowan, Managing Director of Americas, and Angela Man, Marketing Director, Incisive Media; Tamir Lipton, Senior Director Innovation, and Mark Ribich, Senior Director Audience Development, Meredith; Eric Greenberg, Director, Marketing Programs, Rutgers Center for Management Development; Steven Gursten, Partner, and Natalie Lombardo, Public Relations Director, and Rebecca Turner, Editorial Media Assistant, Michigan Auto Law; William Valentine, Founder, and Jon Tapper, Head of Operations and Chief Compliance Officer, Valentine Ventures; Brad Heureux, CEO, Bradford Media Group; John Pasmore, CEO of Voyages North America; Carl Mehlhope, SVP, integrated sales and marketing at STACK Media; Deni Kasrel, director, Web & publications, Office of University Communications at the University of Pennsylvania; and Al Eccles, SEO manager of Yell. You've all helped me to make "Stone Soup."

I want to thank the four people who shared their success stories for this book: George Wright, the former vice president of marketing and sales for Blendtec; Arun Chaudhary, new media road director of Obama for America; John Goldstone, producer of Monty Python and the Holy Grail (1975), Monty Python's Life of Brian (1979), and Monty Python's The Meaning of Life (1983); and Michael Kolowich, Founder and Executive Producer, DigiNovations.

I want to thank the folks at YouTube and Google who helped me with my book: Kate Rose, Brian Cusack, Suzie Reider, Ricardo Reyes, Aaron Zamost, and Karen Wickre. It takes a village to teach these lessons.

I want to thank several people who shared their market research and insights. This includes Bill Tancer and Matt Tatham of Experian Hitwise, as well as Dan Piech and Stephanie Flosi of comScore. I get by with a little help from my friends.

I want to thank Mike Grehan, Marilyn Crafts, Jackie Ortez, Christian Georgeou, Jonathan Allen, and the other members of the SES Advisory Board for putting me on panels about YouTube and video marketing at SES conferences. And I should thank my fellow panelists for sharing their expertise. If I'm known as an expert on this topic, it's because I've spent less than 20 percent of my time speaking at SES and more than 80 percent listening to you.

I should thank the team at the Rutgers Center for Management Development. This includes Eric Greenberg, Jackie Scott, Peter Methot, and Jennie Fine. It also includes all the participants in the Mini-MBA Programs that I've taught. This includes the open enrollment courses in Digital Marketing and Social Media Marketing as well as the tailored programs for Johnson & Johnson and SonoSite. Teaching and learning is a two-way street.

I should thank my colleagues at Market Motive: Michael Stebbins, John Marshall, Avinash Kaushik, Matt Bailey, Bryan Eisenberg, Brad Geddes, Jennifer Laycock, Todd Malicoat, Scott Milrad, Tyler Link, and Justin Neustadter. We've been called the "Internet marketing dream team." But I can't remember why.

Finally, I should thank the folks at Sybex, an imprint of John Wiley & Sons. This includes Willem Knibbe, Connor O'Brien, Brad O'Farrell, Liz Britten, Pete Gaughan, and Judy Flynn. I have come to the conclusion that the making of books is like the making of sausages: the less you know about the process, the more you respect the result.

If I've forgotten anyone, then I hope you will forgive me. As Mel Brooks says, "God willing, we'll all meet again in Spaceballs 2: The Search for More Money."

About the Author

Greg Jarboe is president and cofounder of SEO-PR (www.seo-pr.com), which provides search engine optimization, online public relations, online video marketing, and social media marketing services. Michelle Goodall of Econsultancy in the U.K. has called SEO-PR the "U.S. online marketing agency specialising in successfully optimising seemingly anything that moves for search."

SEO-PR has produced, optimized, or promoted hundreds of YouTube videos for Bradford Media Group, Marvell Technology Group, Meredith, Michigan Auto Law, Rutgers Center for Management Development, Search Engine Marketing Professional Organization (SEMPO), Search Engine Watch, SES Conference & Expo, STACK Media, the University of Pennsylvania, Valentine Ventures, Voyages North America, and Yell.com.

According to Bas van den Beld of State of Search, Jarboe is "one of the (or the?) biggest online video experts out there." According to Virginia Nussey of the SEO Blog on Bruceclay.com, "Greg is considered an expert on everything from news search to video search to linkbait and beyond."

In addition to being the author of *YouTube and Video Marketing: An Hour a Day*, Jarboe is a contributor to Guy Kawasaki's *Enchantment: The Art of Changing Hearts, Minds, and Actions* (Portfolio, 2011). Jarboe is also profiled in Michael Miller's *Online Marketing Heroes: Interviews with 25 Successful Online Marketing Gurus* (Wiley, 2008).

Jarboe is on the faculty of the Rutgers Center of Management Development (CMD) and teaches courses in the Mini-MBA programs in Digital Marketing, Social Media Marketing, and Digital PR. He is also a member of the Market Motive faculty, which has been called the "Internet marketing dream team."

Jarboe writes for Search Engine Watch and ReelSEO. He does interviews for SESConferenceExpo's and SearchEngineWatch's channels on YouTube. He is a frequent speaker at SES and other conferences. He won the "Medallion Speaker Award" at the 2010 International Search Summit in London.

Before cofounding SEO-PR, Jarboe was vice president and chief marketing officer for Backbone Media, vice president of marketing for WebCT, and director of corporate communications for Ziff-Davis. At Ziff-Davis, he helped launch dozens of new media, including ZDTV and The Site, hosted by Soledad O'Brien, on MSNBC.

Before that, Jarboe was president of Jarboe Communications and director of marketing for *PC Computing* and director of corporate communications at Lotus Development Corporation. Prior to that, he held PR, marcom, and public affairs positions at Data General, Sequoia Systems, Stratus Computer, and Wang Laboratories.

In the 1970s, he was a radio newscaster, newspaper editor, and cohost of the *Marcie and Me* show on the public access channel of Continental Cablevision in Lawrence, Massachusetts. He won two New England Press Association awards while editor of *The Acton Minute-Man*.

Jarboe graduated from the University of Michigan in 1971, attended the University of Edinburgh, and completed all the course work for his master's at Lesley College. He lives in Acton, Massachusetts, where he has been elected to the board of selectmen.

Contents

Foreword

- Who is Greg Jarboe?
- Why should you read his book?
- Why should you read this foreword?

I'll try to answer the first two but may not have a full justification for the third.

If you read Greg's first book, you know the answer to both questions. If you didn't, you missed out and maybe you're the target audience for this foreword.

I first met Greg in 1988 when we both worked at Ziff Davis, along with a few other folks and many others you'll meet in the following chapters. At the time, Greg made an impression on me with his obvious skills, interests, and passions—for marketing, learning, and teaching. (We'll leave his politics out for the purpose of this note.) He loved to market and talk about marketing. We were all learning faster than we ever had—drinking from the proverbial fire hose. Greg had another dimension though. He took his love of marketing and learning and turned it to formal and informal conversations with his associates—tenured pros and rookies. That's the teacher part of Greg. These types of water-cooler conversations, roundtables over Friday pizza sessions, sales meetings, and customer meetings gave Greg the chance to exchange feedback in ways few of us have had the opportunity to do. Today Greg is an author, lecturer, and consultant; but what are those things really but "teacher"?

It was a time and place of great learning. Little did we know that as we worked on magazines chronicling the rise of the PC, we were actually seeing the origins of where we have arrived today. Access for everyone. One to many. One to one. Deep Insights. We were learning about audiences, the power of great content, and the value of research in refining the targeting and message and of telling the story from the marketer's perspective. All of these disciplines, skills, and terms all are relevant today; however, the platform is very different.

Did any of us really imagine that there would be singular platforms enabling super-communities of 500 million people to share their lives with each other? To share too much? To share their weekend plans? To share their favorite experiences in full sight, sound and motion? To be inspired, educated, entertained, and persuaded in an environment where 48 hours of video are uploaded every minute of every day? No, we didn't. At least I didn't.

But I'm glad I made the jump from those wonderful magazines to this wonderful world and never really looked back. Every day there is something new to learn. People ask me, "What is it like to work at Google?" My answer could be the same if I worked at any number of companies, but it's especially true here. I respond, "It's like living a new case from the *Harvard Business Review* every day... how to leverage technology, how to best service the user and marketer, how to organize assets and efforts to leverage the incredible work of our engineers." Sitting on the outside looking in, while living it, Greg is bringing you an understanding of digital video marketing that you won't get anywhere else. By focusing on YouTube, he's bringing wisdom to you on the back of the market maker.

Brands are adopting YouTube at different rates and levels of zeal. Look at what Toyota did with the Swagger Wagon campaign in support of the Siena. Challenged by recalls and sitting in the #3 spot among minivans, Toyota created a fun campaign that invited consumer participation. Check out some of the user-generated videos submitted in response to the campaign and embraced by Toyota. Heck, they involve Ford SUVs. Toyota really understands how to engage the community, participate as a member of the community, and gain additional traction across the YouTube platform and their entire social graph.

Look at how Lady Gaga is leveraging YouTube, Google, and a variety of other social and video outlets. I'd argue that Lady Gaga is as big a brand as any in the world now. She's using many of the same tactics and strategies Greg will reveal to you in this book. Whether you'll be trying to sell cars, launch a music career, market your youth sports camps, or sell your new award-winning craft beer, Greg's insights will apply just like they do for Toyota, Lady Gaga, and everyone's favorite from the last year, Old Spice.

Read the book, enjoy and learn from a really good, natural teacher of marketing, 21st century style. When you are done, apply it or use it as a frame of reference for your ongoing observations and learning. It's a book you can come back to for maybe two or three years. After that, you'll be ordering volume three in Greg's ongoing curriculum, I hope. The technology will grow and change, user habits will evolve, and marketers will embrace YouTube more fully. There will be no shortage of new challenges and lessons for Greg to describe and dissect.

I hope I answered at least two of those questions. Turn the page and open your eyes to the world of YouTube.

I'm not on a horse…

BRIAN CUSACK
Head of Display, Retail and Canada
Google

Introduction

Why should you read this YouTube book? And why should you read any step-by-step guide to video marketing? Why not shoot first and ask question later? That's what the pioneers of online video had to do.

YouTube Has Grown Dramatically

There were no YouTube books in the early days. And there wasn't a step-by-step guide to get them started in video marketing. So, innovators would create a YouTube account, upload a video, and hope to get lucky.

Several did. Among the early YouTube pioneers were Anthony Padilla and Ian Hecox, the stars of Smosh. Both members of the comedy duo are from Carmichael, California, and were born in the fall of 1987. Yes, they're that young.

On Nov. 19, 2005, they uploaded three videos to the Smosh Channel (www.youtube.com/smosh): "Mortal Kombat Theme" (which had nearly 21 million views as this was written), "Power Rangers Theme" (which had over 6.3 million views), and "The Epic Battle: Jesus vs Cyborg Satan" (which had more than 1.6 million views).

Smosh also uploaded a video in which they lip-synched and danced to the Pokemon theme song. It was one of the most viewed videos on YouTube for almost a year, but it had to be removed due to copyright infringement. According to Brad O'Farrell, the technical editor of this book, "It's the reason they're popular." I'll take his word for it because I'm not their target demographic.

One of the 182 videos on their channel, "Smosh Short 2: Stranded" (http://youtu.be/oCd_i7wW87Q), won the 2006 YouTube Award for Best Comedy. As this was written, Smosh's channel had over 821 million total upload views and more than 2.9 million subscribers, making it the #3 most subscribed channel of all time, behind RayWilliamJohnson's channel with more than 4.1 million subscribers and nigahiga's channel with over 4.0 million subscribers.

Smosh and other comedians gave the small video sharing site its early reputation as the place where any wannabe director with a video camera and an Internet-connection could upload their quirky and unusual amateur content for an audience of 18- to 24-year olds to discover, watch and share. Well, that's what YouTube was back in late 2005 and early 2006.

But other categories of original content creators started uploading more serious videos to the growing video sharing site.

For example, Peter Oakley, a pensioner from Leicester, England, uploaded his first video to YouTube on Aug. 5, 2006. Entitled "first try" (http://youtu.be/p_YMigZmUuk), the video had almost 2.9 million views as this was written.

Oakley was born in 1927. Yes, he's that old. So, the Internet Granddad decided to call his VLog (video log) geriatric1927's channel (www.youtube.com/geriatric1927).

Oakley's "geriatric gripes and grumbles" gained immediate popularity with a wide section of the YouTube community. Following one of his signature phrases, "Hello, YouTubers" or "Good evening, YouTubers," Oakley's series of autobiographical videos shared details about his life, including: he has loved motorcycles and blues music since he was a child, he served as a radar mechanic during World War II, he got a degree in fine art after turning 60 years old, and he lives alone as a widower.

In mid-2006, geriatric1927 became the most subscribed channel on YouTube with 30,000 subscribers. Oakley's rise to the #1 position took place in just over a week. As this was written, geriatric1927's channel had almost 8.9 million total upload views and more than 55,000 subscribers, making it the 19th most subscribed "Director" of all time in the United Kingdom.

Another new video was uploaded to YouTube on Aug. 14, 2006, that had less than 387,000 views as this was written. Generally, a video needs more than 500,000 to 1 million views before it is considered a "viral video." But this new video from a "Politician" became "a signature cultural event of the political year," according to op-ed columnist Frank Rich of the *New York Times*.

Here is the backstory for those of you who aren't political junkies like I am. On August 11, 2006, U.S. Senator George Allen (R-Virginia) appeared before a crowd of white supporters. His re-election campaign seemed to be a mere formality.

Allen had a double-digit lead over Jim Webb, his Democratic challenger, and some Beltway insiders were calling Allen the most likely Republican presidential nominee in 2008. S. R. Sidarth, a 20-year-old Webb campaign worker of Indian descent, was tracking Allen with a video camera.

Rich described what happened next in his column that November. He wrote, "After belittling the dark-skinned man as 'macaca, or whatever his name is,' Mr. Allen added, 'Welcome to America and the real world of Virginia.'"

On August 14, "Allen's Listening Tour" was uploaded to the WebbCampaign's channel on YouTube. According to Rich, "The one-minute macaca clip spread through the national body politic like a rabid virus. Nonetheless it took more than a week for Mr. Allen to recognize the magnitude of the problem and apologize to the object of his ridicule."

Allen claimed later that he had no idea that the word, the term for a genus of monkey, had any racial connotation. Nevertheless, it soon became clear that Senator Allen was in serious trouble. Even conservative pundits faulted him for running an "awful campaign." And in November, Allen was defeated by Webb.

Rich concluded, "The macaca incident had resonance beyond Virginia not just because it was a hit on YouTube. It came to stand for 2006 as a whole."

In other words, YouTube was already expanding into new categories five years ago. And the content on the video sharing site was quickly becoming harder to pigeonhole.

The Current Scope of YouTube

Back in July 2006, YouTube.com broke into the comScore Media Metrix Top 50 for the first time, debuting at number 40 with 16 million visitors, a 20-percent increase from June. The video-sharing site has grown dramatically since then.

According to comScore Video Metrix, 149.3 million Americans watched an average of 104 YouTube videos during 15 to 16 sessions in June 2011 for a total of 324.1 minutes. This means they watched about 6 or 7 videos during the typical 21-minute session. Averages were even higher for Canadians and slightly lower for Britons, but all were still very impressive.

Today, you will find video content in 15 major categories, from Autos & Vehicles to Travel & Events. You will find video content from nine YouTube account types, from Comedians to Sponsors. You will also find some significantly different kinds of video content, including:

- Television shows, such as *Weeds, Big Brother,* and *America's Got Talent.*

- Movies, such as *The Lincoln Lawyer, Insidious,* and *Battle: Los Angeles.*

- Trailers, such as "Harry Potter and the Deathly Hallows Official HD Trailer", "Skyline - Theatrical Trailer", and "THE NEXT THREE DAYS - Amazing Review: Now Playing".

- Contests, such as YouTube Creator Programs, Project: Report, and YouTube Symphony Orchestra 2011.

- Live Events, such as the red carpet event of *Harry Potter and the Deathly Hallows - Part 2* from Trafalgar Square in London, the Royal Wedding, and the 2011 Copa America soccer tournament.

So, what started as a video-sharing site for bedroom vloggers has evolved into the largest worldwide video-sharing community. YouTube not only provides a forum for people to connect, inform, and inspire others across the globe, it also acts as a distribution platform for original content creators and advertisers large and small.

During 2010, more than 13 million hours of video were uploaded to YouTube. And as this was written, 48 hours of video were uploaded every minute, resulting in nearly 8 years of content uploaded every day. This means users upload the equivalent of 240,000 full-length films every week—or, more video is uploaded to YouTube in one month than the three major television networks in the U.S. have created in 60 years.

Tens of millions of people have created YouTube channels. There are thousands of full-length movies and thousands of full-length TV episodes on the online video site. As this was written, 10 percent of YouTube's videos were available in HD. This means YouTube has more HD content than any other online video site.

In 2010, YouTube reached over 700 billion playbacks. As this was written, over 3 billion videos were viewed a day. YouTube mobile got over 320 million views a day, up 300 percent year over year, representing 10 percent of the site's daily views. And 70 percent of YouTube traffic came from outside the United States.

As this was written, 100 million people took a social action on YouTube, such as likes, shares, or comments, every week. Millions of subscriptions happened each day. More than 50 percent of videos on YouTube had been rated or included comments from the community (including some comments by haters and trolls). Nevertheless, millions of videos were "favorited" every day.

As this was written, the YouTube player was embedded across tens of millions of blogs and websites. Nearly 17 million people had connected their YouTube account to at least one social service, such as Facebook or Twitter. About 150 years of YouTube videos were watched every day on Facebook, up 250 percent year over year. And every minute more than 500 tweets contain YouTube links, up 375 percent year over year.

Created in 2007, the YouTube Partner Program now has more than 20,000 partners from 22 countries around the world. As this was written, YouTube was monetizing over 3 billion video views per week globally. Hundreds of partners were making six figures a year, and the number of partners making over $1,000 a month was up 300 percent year over year. YouTube was paying out millions of dollars a year to partners.

As this was written, 98 of *Ad Age*'s Top 100 advertisers had run campaigns on YouTube and the Google Display Network. The number of advertisers using display ads on YouTube had increased tenfold in the last year. The YouTube homepage averaged more than 18 million unique visitors and 50 million impressions per day in the U.S. YouTube Mobile (http://m.youtube.com) was the #1 video viewing mobile website in the U.S. according to Nielsen, with 7.1 million unique monthly users.

And as this was written, more than 2,000 partners used Content ID, YouTube's copyright tools, including every major U.S. network broadcaster, movie studio and record label. Content ID was scanning over 100 years of video every day and comparing that content to more than 6 million reference files (audio-only or video). More than 120 million videos had been claimed by Content ID, which enables rights holder to monetize, track, or block them. Over a third of YouTube's total monetized views came from Content ID.

So, you can learn the ins and outs of YouTube as well as pick up lots of actionable insights by reading this book. And, as Mark Twain once observed, "A person who won't read has no advantage over one who can't read."

The Ever-Changing Online Video Market

YouTube has grown dramatically during the past five years. At the same time, the market for online video has also been changing constantly.

On July 26, 2011, Kathleen Moore of the Pew Internet Project wrote a report that said the use of video-sharing sites such as YouTube and Vimeo had jumped from 33 percent of online Americans in December 2006 to 71 percent in May 2011. The use of video-sharing sites on any given day had also jumped from 8 percent to 28 percent in the same period.

Pew also found that Internet users in rural areas are now just as likely as users in urban and suburban areas to have used these sites, and online African-Americans and Hispanics are more likely than Internet-using whites to visit video-sharing sites. In addition, 81 percent of parents in the survey reported visiting video sharing sites, compared with 61 percent of the nonparents.

According to Moore, "The rise of broadband and better mobile networks and devices has meant that video has become an increasingly popular part of users' online experiences." She added, "People use these sites for every imaginable reason—to laugh and learn, to watch the best and worst of popular culture and to check out news. And video-sharing sites are very social spaces as people vote on, comment on, and share these videos with others."

Reading a step-by-step guide can also show you how to craft video marketing strategies that deliver—even in this rapidly changing channel. However, the key is finding a guide that recognizes each step is more like a riverboat landing along the Mississippi River and less like a train station along a railroad track.

Twain understood this, too. I recently reread his book, *Life on the Mississippi* (1883), and found a couple of lessons that YouTubers and others in the online video market would benefit from learning sooner rather than later.

In Chapter 1 of *Life on the Mississippi*, Twain says the river "is in all ways remarkable." As a pilot's apprentice on a riverboat in 1857, he had to learn "this troublesome river *both ways*"—because the Mississippi was a different river coming upstream than it was going downstream when "a boat was too nearly helpless, with a stiff current pushing behind her."

Twain added, "The Mississippi is remarkable in still another way—its disposition to make prodigious jumps by cutting through narrow necks of land, and thus straightening and shortening itself. More than once it has shortened itself thirty miles at a single jump! These cut-offs have had curious effects: they have thrown several river towns out into the rural districts, and built up sand bars and forests in front of them. The town of Delta used to be three miles below Vicksburg: a recent cutoff has radically changed the position, and Delta is now *two miles above* Vicksburg."

This brings us to another lesson that video marketers, local retailers, *Ad Age* 100 advertisers, and YouTube Partners should learn. Since "the Mississippi changes its channel so constantly," who can successfully navigate their way up and down this troublesome river?

According to Twain, it was the riverboat pilots—especially the ones who shared information and observations with their peers. Twain could have been describing YouTubers when he wrote, "all pilots are tireless talkers, when gathered together, and as they talk only about the river they are always understood and are always interesting."

According to Twain, "Fully to realize the marvelous precision required in laying the great steamer in her marks in that murky waste of water, one should know that not only must she pick her intricate way through snags and blind reefs, and then shave the head of the island so closely as to brush the overhanging foliage with her stern, but at one place she must pass almost within arm's reach of a sunken and invisible wreck that would snatch the hull timbers from under her if she should strike it, and destroy a quarter of a million dollars' worth of steam-boat and cargo in five minutes, and maybe a hundred and fifty human lives into the bargain."

So, what are the lessons that we can learn from Twain's memoir detailing his days as a steamboat pilot on the Mississippi River before and after the American Civil War?

First, we can learn an important lesson about video marketing. No form of marketing "changes its channel so constantly" as video marketing does. That's why it's silly to suppose that someone can make the trains run on time in this marketing channel.

It makes a lot more sense to imagine that video marketing is like the Mississippi River. It might also help a marketer, consultant, or small business owner explain why the YouTube rankings for the town of Delta's video have "radically changed" from three spots "below Vicksburg" to two spots "*above* Vicksburg." In YouTube, it is perfectly normal to observe something as remarkable "in a single jump."

Second, search engine marketers, YouTube directors, and entrepreneurs can learn an important lesson from Twain's story. Much of what we knew two years ago about video marketing is now obsolete. That's why it is absolutely essential to talk with our peers—at conferences and other events—especially the people who understand the significance of measurement and have successfully navigated their way past unseen dangers in the past few months.

If fundamental change in our marketing channel isn't going to slow down in the foreseeable future, then all of us need to share information and observations to master "the marvelous precision required" to help our companies and clients pick the "intricate way through snags and blind reefs" that could "destroy a quarter of a million dollars' worth of steam-boat and cargo in five minutes, and maybe a hundred and fifty human lives into the bargain."

Are Ad Buyers Data Driven?

As I mentioned above, 98 of *Ad Age*'s Top 100 advertisers have run campaigns on YouTube and the Google Display Network. But most of them are spending significantly more of their ad budgets on Hulu. This is *not* an example of data-driven decision making.

According to comScore Video Metrix, Americans viewed nearly 5.3 billion video ads in June 2011, with Hulu generating the highest number of video ad impressions at more than 1.0 billion. But Hulu ranked ninth that month with only 26.7 million unique visitors. YouTube's audience in the U.S. was 5.6 times larger.

And Americans watched an average of 24.4 Hulu videos during less than six sessions for a total of 184.4 minutes. This means they watched about four content videos and more than six video ads during the typical 31-minute session.

Hulu's stated mission is to "help people find and enjoy the world's premium video content when, where and how they want it." But, it can be annoying to see in-stream ads, including pre-rolls, embedded within a clip that's only five minutes and 50 seconds long, And it's beyond annoying when you are forced to watch a 30-second ad that doesn't seem relevant or engaging before you can watch the "Indecision 2012: King of the Jungle" excerpt from the Daily Show with Jon Stewart:

> http://www.hulu.com/watch/260874/the-daily-show-with-jon-stewart-indecision-2012-king-of-the-jungle

Perhaps, this explains why Hulu was up for sale as this was written. An article by Brian Stelter in *The New York Times* on July 23, 2011, said, "Representatives of Google, Yahoo, Amazon, Apple and others have kicked the tires, although no clear buyer has yet emerged and Hulu has steadfastly declined to comment." He added, "But no matter who ends up spending billions to buy Hulu, the trick will be satisfying viewers."

Meanwhile, on June 30, 2011, Heineken and Google struck a multimillion-euro partnership to collaborate on digital advertising, including YouTube video and mobile ads. The Netherlands-based brewer's marketing budget is $3 billion annually, but the company's U.S. spokeswoman Tara Carraro told EJ Shultz of *Advertising Age* that Heineken only invests "about 4% of its global marketing budget for digital marketing activities."

The Data Says "YouTube"

So, what are ad buyers waiting for? When it comes to buying advertising next to YouTube's content partners, I believe that far too many ad buyers are making a distinction without a difference.

YouTube allows advertisers to hand-pick the videos they want to advertise against and provides them with a Video Targeting Tool to create their own custom bundle of YouTube videos, channels, and categories. However, far too many advertisers limit themselves to running their video ads against only "premium" video content.

But to the online video audience that advertisers want to reach, there is no "premium" video content; there is only "popular" video content. Whether it's produced by amateurs or professionals, it's all just video content to viewers.

So, why do so many advertisers limit themselves to running video ads against only "premium" video content? Does it really matter if "popular" video content was created in bedrooms, garages, or studios across the globe?

As I mentioned above, the YouTube Partner Program has grown to more than 20,000 participants worldwide. These partners include large media companies such as Universal Music Group and CBS, niche media properties such as Expert Village and Mondo Media, and members of the YouTube community who have created consistently popular videos like Michelle Phan or Justine Ezarik (ijustine).

As I also mentioned above, over three billion videos are streamed every day on YouTube. And YouTube is monetizing over three billion video views per week. But, this means only one out of seven video views is being monetized.

The majority of these video views take place on Partner Watch pages. With users spending more than three minutes watching a video on partner watch pages, it is rare to get such a truly engaged audience on the Web. So, you should engage your audience near the content they love.

Now, I understand that some advertisers might be nervous about running their advertising against unknown user-generated content. But their ads will only appear against the videos of YouTube's tried and trusted content partners. Each partner goes through a thorough vetting and is regularly checked to ensure that they are uploading appropriate content.

Although YouTube is selective about the content its partners can upload, there are still a huge variety of partners, with content to suit all users and most advertisers. And more than half of YouTube video views are for videos that are more than six months old. So, why would an advertiser want to limit themself to running ads against only scripted content?

That's why this book will look at how to use Promoted Videos, use TrueView Video Ads, build a Brand Channel, make a splash on YouTube's homepage, and advertise next to thousands of content partners, big and small. Advertising on YouTube is one of the most under-leveraged opportunities in the online video market.

And according to comScore's Dan Piech, YouTube and comScore are planning to announce YouTube Partner Reporting this summer. This new feature will break out the individual audiences for partners and their channels for the first time.

Marketers will be able to learn much more than Google Sites, driven primarily by video viewing at YouTube.com, ranked as the top online video content property in the U.S. with 149.3 million unique viewers in June 2011, followed by VEVO with 63.0 million viewers. Marketers and media planners will also be able to learn the number of unique viewers belonging to different YouTube channels, as well as the demographics of those viewers.

This will enable CBS, Machinima, Philip DeFranco and hundreds of other YouTube Partners to monetize their content in new ways by having their audiences represented to the agencies and brands that actively use Video Metrix data.

So, we're all about to learn a lot more about YouTube content partners, independent and professional, bedroom and broadcast. I wish that I could share a few highlights of the new YouTube Partner Reporting in this book, but none were available as this was written.

But, you can visit www.videometrix2.com/YouTube.html to get additional information. And maybe online video measurement that includes YouTube partners is what ad buyers were waiting for.

So, you may not find the answers to all of your questions in this book, but it will introduce you to pilots like Piech who "are always understood and are always interesting."

Competition Can Come from Anywhere

In *Life on the Mississippi*, Twain said, "I think that the most enjoyable of all races is a steamboat race." He added, "Two red-hot steamboats raging along, neck-and-neck, straining every nerve—that is to say, every rivet in the boilers—quaking and shaking and groaning from stem to stern, spouting white steam from the pipes, pouring black smoke from the chimneys, raining down sparks, parting the river into long breaks of hissing foam—this is sport that makes a body's very liver curl with enjoyment."

Every couple of years, we get to watch that kind of competition on YouTube, especially during hotly contested political campaigns like the United States presidential election of 2008. We'll take a closer look at that campaign in Chapter 10 of this book.

But Obama for America isn't the only political organization that has learned important lessons from the 2008 presidential campaign. And it often seems like more Republicans and Conservatives have read the first edition of this book than Democrats and Liberals.

During the 2010 midterm elections, all 10 of the most-viewed videos categorized as News & Politics on YouTube came from Republicans. This was an interesting departure from 2008 when "Yes We Can Obama Song by will.i.am" (http://youtu.be/2fZHou18Cdk) topped the charts.

There have also been some riveting first-past-the-post political races on YouTube, including the United Kingdom general election in 2010 and the Canadian federal election in 2011. In both cases, the Conservatives who won the most seats in the House of Commons in Parliament made more effective use of video marketing than their opponents.

Races Are Not Just Political

Now, neck-and-neck races between politicians in the News & Politics category are well worth watching. But, some of the most enjoyable of all races on YouTube are between big and small partners in other categories.

For example, Salman "Sal" Khan's cousin Nadia asked him for some math tutoring over the Web in late 2004. But they couldn't find a time to get on webcams for tutoring sessions, so Khan decided to just record his lessons and upload them to YouTube in November 2006.

But more people than just his little cousin in Louisiana started watching. Millions of other viewers found his lessons to be useful. So, Khan made some more educational videos.

YouTube made Khan a partner and started showing ads on his videos and sharing the revenue with him. In 2009, advertising was generating enough revenue for Khan that he decided to quit his lucrative job at a hedge fund and focus full time on Khan Academy (www.youtube.com/khanacademy).

YouTube hosts videos from many educators, including taped lectures from universities like the University of California, MIT, Stanford, and Carnegie Mellon. However, khanacademy's channel on YouTube had amassed more than 66.4 million total upload views as this was written, making it the most-viewed channel in the Education category on YouTube.

There is an important moral to this story: Because great content on YouTube can come from anywhere, new competitors in every category can come from anywhere, too.

As I mentioned above, the number of advertisers using display ads on YouTube increased tenfold in the last year. As more and more advertisers tap into the world's largest online video community, more and more YouTube partners will share in the revenue generated when viewers watch their videos.

As I also mentioned above, the YouTube Partner Program now has more than 20,000 partners. And hundreds of partners are making six figures a year. But this means only a small percentage of partners can afford to quit their day jobs today.

Tomorrow is another story. I expect significantly more budding filmmakers, artists, and entrepreneurs will become YouTube partners and significantly more partners will begin making enough money to quit their day jobs and become full-time content creators.

This day-by-day, step-by-step guide can help them to develop sound video marketing strategies, avoid common pitfalls, measure and analyze their results, and achieve success.

Let Me Sum Up

So, as Inigo Montoya says in *The Princess Bride* (1987), "Let me 'splain. No, there's too much. Let me sum up." YouTube has grown dramatically. The market for online video is changing constantly. The buyers of video advertising are starting to make data-driven decisions. And new competition can come from anywhere. So, as Westley says in the movie, "That doesn't leave much time for dillydallying."

Who Should Read This Book

This book is for marketers. In fact, Internet marketers, search engine marketers, brand marketers, social media marketers, business marketers, sports marketers, product marketers, event marketers, and video marketers should all read this step-by-step guide because they didn't learn about video marketing in college—because there were no courses on this topic a couple of years ago—and their marketing jobs and marketing careers are rapidly being reshaped by YouTube.

This book is also for small business owners, entrepreneurs, local retailers, and do-it-yourselfers. They should read this guide to debunk popular myths and gain actionable insights from their YouTube and video marketing efforts.

This book is for advertisers and their advertising agencies. They should read this guide because advertising on YouTube has changed dramatically in the past few years—and their advertising careers will be stunted if they don't learn how to launch an ad campaign on YouTube and tap into the world's largest online video community.

Finally, this book is also for comedians, directors, gurus, musicians, non-profits, partners, politicians, reporters, sponsors, and YouTube. They should all read this step-by-step guide to learn how to optimize and promote their YouTube videos more effectively.

What You Will Learn

This book will show you how to implement a successful video marketing strategy in a relatively new and rapidly changing field. It focuses on YouTube, which is the top online video site, but it also covers YouTube alternatives. It uses case studies and success stories from the United States, Canada, and the United Kingdom, where I've worked with a wide variety of organizations and taught a broad spectrum of individuals.

What Is Covered in This Book

The second edition of *YouTube and Video Marketing: An Hour a Day* is fully updated with new information, including the latest changes to YouTube. It is the practical, hour-a-day, do-it-yourself guide you need to understand video marketing tactics, develop a strategy, implement the campaign, and measure results.

You'll find extensive coverage of keyword strategies, tips on optimizing your video, distribution and promotion tactics, YouTube advertising opportunities, and crucial metrics and analysis. This guide can help you avoid errors, create a dynamite campaign, and break it all down in achievable tasks.

- This book shows you how to successfully develop, implement, and measure a successful video marketing strategy.

- It is written in the popular "Hour a Day" format, which breaks intimidating topics down into easily approachable tasks.

- It is thoroughly updated with the latest YouTube functionality, helpful new case studies, the latest marketing insights, and more.

- It covers optimization strategies, distribution techniques, community promotion tactics, and more.

- This book explores the crucial keyword development phase and best practices for creating and maintaining a presence on YouTube via brand channel development and customization.

- It shows you how to optimize video for YouTube and search engine visibility.

Read *YouTube and Video Marketing: An Hour A Day, Second Edition,* to give your organization or yourself a visible, vital, video presence online.

What's Inside?

This book is a nine-month program for developing, implementing, and tracking a video marketing strategy. The months are divided into weeks, and these are divvied into days that focus on tasks that are estimated to take about an hour each. Depending on your circumstances, your familiarity with the subject matter, and the sophistication of your clients and organization, it may take you more or less time to complete certain tasks. The book is divided into 11 chapters:

Chapter 1, "A Short History of YouTube," introduces you to the world's most popular online video community. Founded in February 2005, YouTube allows millions of people to discover, watch, and share originally created videos. In this chapter, you will learn why YouTube took off, how it changed the online video landscape, and when it passed some memorable milestones. You will also learn that YouTube has come a long way since Dec. 25, 2006, when a surgeon in a *New Yorker* cartoon realized, "God, this is going to be all over YouTube."

Chapter 2, "Map Out Your Video Marketing Strategy," points out that the online video market is very large, but it doesn't work like a "mass market." In this chapter, you will learn who discovers and shares new videos; what types of video they watch; where they discover new videos; when they share new videos; why so few new videos go viral; and how YouTube and video marketing works. Finally, you will learn that it's okay to admit, "I still don't have all the answers, but I'm beginning to ask the right questions."

Chapter 3, "Month 1: Make Videos Worth Watching," tells you why you should learn video production even if YouTube is designed to make producing videos as easy as possible. This encourages some people to shoot first and ask questions later. They tell others, "I figure we can blue-screen the kids in later." For those who would rather ask questions first and shoot later, this chapter will help you get ready to shoot, learn the basics of video production, get some video production tips, and help you evaluate your video advertising options.

Chapter 4, "Month 2: Create Content Worth Sharing," is about creating content that inspires, entertains, enlightens, and educates. In this chapter, you'll watch five YouTube Award winners, explore five popular YouTube videos, examine five of the most contagious viral ads of all time, and observe five of the top viral videos of 2010. After watching a lot of videos that have gone viral, you'll know how to create content worth sharing and what to tell others who believe, "Hoarding is just as human as sharing."

Chapter 5, "Month 3: Customize Your YouTube Channel," tells you the most common way people find a new video is to go to YouTube and conduct a search, or click one of the related videos. But people are just as likely to discover a new YouTube video embedded in a blog. This means YouTube should be the center, but not the circumference, of your video marketing strategy. In this chapter, you will learn how to set up a basic YouTube channel, how to become a YouTube Partner, how to create a YouTube brand channel, and how to stream live content on YouTube—although this may not stop people from making comments like, "When I was a boy, I had to walk five miles through the snow to change the channel."

Chapter 6, "Month 4: Explore YouTube Alternatives," observes that many marketers have tried to discover viable alternatives to YouTube for the past five years. And many explorers tried to discover the "Northwest Passage," a commercial sea route around North America for almost 300 years. In this chapter, you will explore other video sites, survey video hosting services, look at online video platforms, and investigate video ad networks to discover if viable alternatives to YouTube actually exist. If one does, then you'll learn why the explorer who discovers it will say, "I name this place Terra Incognita."

Chapter 7, "Month 5: Optimize Video for YouTube," shows you how to get your video found when more than 21.1 billion "expanded search queries" are conducted each month on YouTube worldwide. In this chapter, you will learn how to research keywords, optimize Video Watch Pages, optimize your Brand Channel, and optimize video for the Web. Since 48 hours of video is uploaded to YouTube every minute, if you don't optimize your video for YouTube, then you will probably be asked, "Have you tried searching under 'fruitless'?"

Chapter 8, "Month 6: Engage the YouTube Community," gives you some advice on how to behave in the largest worldwide video-sharing community. In this chapter, you will learn how to become a fully vested member of the YouTube community. You'll also learn the secrets of YouTube success, find out how to build buzz beyond YouTube, and watch online video case studies. You'll also meet the woman who said to Paul Revere as he galloped through her community, "Thanks, but what about those silver candlesticks I ordered?"

Chapter 9, "Month 7: Trust but Verify YouTube Insight," shares Galileo's advice, "Count what is countable, measure what is measurable. What is not measurable, make measurable." In this chapter, we will look at what is countable by YouTube Insight and what is measurable by TubeMogul InPlay and Google Analytics. We'll also look at other tools that make measurable what is not measurable by these tools. But we will need to continue explaining, "The chart, of course, is nonrepresentational," until currently available metrics get more robust.

Chapter 10, "Study YouTube Success Stories," answers the question, "And what's the story behind the story?" Although it is useful to measure views and ratings, how many of these "*outputs*" do you need to make the cash register ring? In this chapter, we'll study four YouTube success stories to learn how organizations have used video marketing to generate measurable "*outcomes*." And I'll interview the key individuals who were willing and able to tell me more about their YouTube success stories.

Chapter 11, "A Quick Look at the Future," recognizes that YouTube has changed dramatically over the last six years, and the rules of video marketing are now radically different too. Today, everyone involved in YouTube marketing feels like they're playing "Calvinball." In this final chapter, you will take a quick look at what has changed at YouTube in just the past year, visit a destination for insight into the zeitgeist of the world's largest video site, identify the new rules of YouTube marketing, and learn how to shape the future of a forum for people that acts like a distribution platform. Finally, you will be ready, willing, and able to say, "Enough storyboarding. Let's shoot something."

How to Contact the Author

I welcome feedback from you about this book or about books you'd like to see from me in the future. You can reach me by calling SEO-PR's San Francisco office at 415-643-8947, sending an email to greg.jarboe@seo-pr.com, or following me on Twitter at http://twitter.com/gregjarboe. For more information about SEO-PR, please visit our website at www.seo-pr.com.

Sybex strives to keep you supplied with the latest tools and information you need for your work. Please check their website at www.sybex.com, where we'll post additional content and updates that supplement this book if the need arises. Enter *YouTube and Video Marketing, Second Edition* in the Search box (or type the book's ISBN—9780470945018), and click Go to get to the book's update page.

A Short History of YouTube

1

Founded in February 2005, YouTube is now the world's most popular online video community, allowing millions of people to discover, watch, and share originally created videos. In this chapter, you will learn why YouTube took off, how it changed the online video landscape, and when it passed some memorable milestones.

Life before YouTube

"You know how it is with technology—once something becomes so ubiquitous and so universally used, it is simply impossible to imagine life without it," observed Chris Tryhorn of guardian.co.uk on August 29, 2008. Embedded in his article "Life before YouTube" is a funny video (www.youtube.com/watch?v=HWDCeEJ9ZfI) by Matt Koval. As Figure 1.1 illustrates, "YouTube in 1985 (collab)" imagines what the personal video sharing service would have looked like a human generation ago.

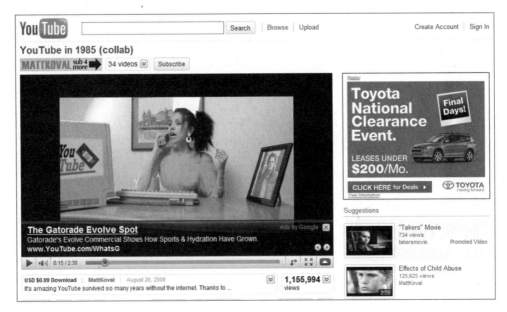

Figure 1.1 "YouTube in 1985 (collab)"

When Koval calls to submit his latest video, a woman on the YouTube staff asks, "On VHS or Betamax?"

Fast-forward from a mythical time to the real dot-com era and the first-mover advantage in online video actually belonged to Singingfish. Founded in 1999, it was one of the earliest search engines to focus on audio and video content. A public alpha version of Singingfish was unveiled in June 2000, and the company was acquired by Thomson Multimedia in November 2000.

Singingfish employed its own web crawler, Asterias, which was designed to ferret out audio and video links across the Web. It also used a proprietary system to process each of the links it discovered, extracting what little metadata it could find and then enhancing it prior to indexing.

However, Singingfish had the misfortune of going to market just as the dot-com bubble was bursting. So, even as it was being launched, Singingfish was being downsized dramatically.

AOL acquired Singingfish in October 2003 and eventually folded it into AOL Video.

Now, a first mover isn't always able to capitalize on its advantages. It often faces higher R&D and marketing costs because the first mover is creating products and markets from scratch.

That's why the title of this book isn't *Singingfish Marketing: An Hour a Day.* And it also explains why many companies pursue a fast-follower strategy.

Fast followers try to learn from the first mover what works and what doesn't. Then they try to use their resources to make superior products or outmarket the first mover. In the words of a civil war general, they try to "git thar fustest with the mostest."

For example, blinkx launched an audio and video search engine December 2004. Google launched a video search engine in January 2005. And Yahoo! launched a video search engine in May 2005.

But being fast followers didn't turn out to be a winning strategy for blinkx, Google Video, or Yahoo! Video. If it had worked, then this book would be titled *Video Search Engine Optimization: An Hour a Day.*

So why did YouTube become the world's most popular online video community? That's the question I'll answer in this chapter.

2005–2006: Early Days

The YouTube backstory is short. In fact, the Company History page on YouTube is about 400 words long, and "The Making of YouTube" video (www.youtube.com/watch?v=X2N_V2dfS1U) is only 3 minutes and 37 seconds long.

Feb. 2005: YouTube Founded

YouTube was founded in February 2005 by three former PayPal employees: Chad Hurley, Steve Chen, and Jawed Karim. According to Jim Hopkins of *USA Today* (Oct. 11, 2006), the idea for what became YouTube sprang from two very different events in 2004: Janet Jackson's "wardrobe malfunction" during the Super Bowl XXXVIII halftime show and the great Sumatra-Andaman earthquake, also known as the Asian Tsunami or Boxing Day Tsunami.

In February 2005, it was difficult to find and share online videos of either event. At a San Francisco dinner party, Karim proposed to Hurley and Chen that they create a video-sharing site. "I thought it was a good idea," Karim told Hopkins.

Within a few days, the three agreed to develop the idea and then divided work based on their skills: Hurley designed the site's interface, while Chen and Karim split the technical duties for making the site work. None of the three had strengths or interests in marketing. In May 2005, a public beta test version of YouTube went live.

Note: Later, when the cofounders divided up management responsibilities, Hurley became CEO, Chen became CTO, and Karim assumed an advisory role after leaving YouTube to get a master's degree in computer science at Stanford.

Apr. 2005: First Video Uploaded

The first video on YouTube was shot by Yakov Lapitsky and features Karim at the San Diego Zoo. As Figure 1.2 illustrates, "Me at the zoo" (www.youtube.com/ watch?v=jNQXAC9IVRw) is only 19 seconds long.

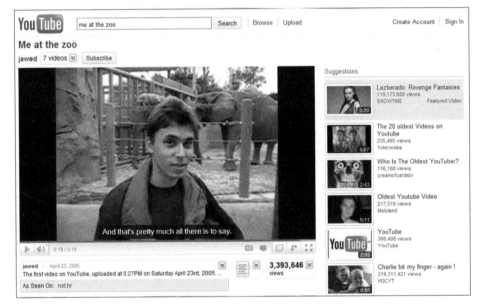

Figure 1.2 "Me at the zoo"

That video was uploaded on Saturday, April 23, 2005, at 8:27 p.m. At that time, YouTube's headquarters was above a pizzeria and Japanese restaurant in San Mateo, California.

In front of the elephants, Karim says, "The cool thing about these guys today is that they have really, really, really long, um, trunks." An annotation added more than three years later asks, "Can you hear the goat? MEEEEEEEEEEEH!"

As of today, "Me at the zoo" has over 4.8 million views.

Why is this ordinary moment so extraordinary? In spite of what Karim says, it's not the elephants or their trunks. And despite the annotation, it's not the goat.

May 2005: YouTube Beta Launched

That's why the real story is what happened next. And it's only in hindsight that we can see why YouTube went on to become the world's most popular online video community.

The beta launch of YouTube took place in May 2005 and YouTube users like Cobaltgruv (www.youtube.com/cobaltgruv) started putting up videos.

On his Channel, Cobalt, 32, says, "Hey... well I'm the crazy guy... who found youtube the second week it was out... became user 42 or something...My first intention with YouTube was to share my channel with family, and friends... then look what happened!!!"

He adds, "I'll only live once in this life... and now I'm trying to document it, and perhaps entertain your boredom. I love making films and would love to go to school for it one day. I have many other passions but this would have to be my #1 for many years now... Just another way to show who I am, and have fun doing it... even if it is to the whole world... thanks for the views!!!"

Created on May 3, 2005, Cobaltgruv's channel has over 11,000 subscribers today, and his videos have over 264,000 views.

Aug. 2005: YouTube Embeds Enabled

Although YouTube didn't spend much time or effort communicating with marketers or advertisers in 2005, the company did a great job of communicating with users. In fact, the YouTube Blog was created in July 2005 "in an effort to communicate improvements and changes."

The blog said, "We are continuously working towards our goal of making YouTube *the* digital video repository for the Internet. That said, please let us know if there's something you'd like us to address—we really, really, really do value *any* input our users send."

And in early August, the blog acknowledged that many of the changes being announced "are in direct response to your feedback."

Later that month, the blog announced, "We have added a ton of new features to our site." One of these new features enabled users to embed the YouTube video player into their own web page. "That way people can view the video on your website without even coming to YouTube!"

Nov. 2005: YouTube Secures First Round of Funding

In November 2005, YouTube received $3.5 million in funding from Sequoia Capital. In a press release, Hurley said, "Since our public preview, we are already moving 8 terabytes of data per day through the YouTube community—the equivalent of moving one Blockbuster store a day over the Internet."

Dec. 2005: YouTube Officially Launched and "Lazy Sunday" Goes Viral

YouTube was officially launched one month later. The company said its new service "allows people to easily upload, tag, and share personal video clips through www.YouTube.com and across the Internet on other sites, blogs and through e-mail."

In other words, YouTube began as a personal video sharing service, not as yet another video search engine. This strategy is called "hit 'em where they ain't." It enabled YouTube to emerge from relative obscurity shortly after December 17, 2005, when a video entitled "Lazy Sunday"—which was a copy of the Saturday Night Live skit "The Chronicles of Narnia Rap"—was uploaded to the video sharing site.

On December 27, Dave Itzkoff of the *New York Times* reported that "Lazy Sunday" had already been viewed more than 1.2 million times.

The next day, LeeAnn Prescott, who was the research director at Hitwise at the time, posted her analysis of the hot video of the past week on her Hitwise Intelligence Analyst Weblog. Visits to YouTube, where people could discover, watch, and share "The Chronicles of Narnia Rap," shot up 83 percent in one week—and surpassed visits to Google Video.

As Figure 1.3 illustrates, Prescott's examination of clickstream data for YouTube revealed the viral nature of videos: Many of the top upstream sites that sent visitors to YouTube the previous week were either community sites like MySpace or web email services.

Weekly Upstream 'Computers and Internet' sites to 'YouTube' - 12/24/05

The following list of web sites appeared in 'Computers and Internet' industry rankings by 'sessions' and delivered traffic to 'YouTube'.

Rank	Domain	More	Share
1.	MySpace	▶	11.31%
2.	Yahoo! Mail	▶	8.73%
3.	Google	▶	6.32%
4.	Xanga	▶	4.70%
5.	My Space - Mail	▶	4.25%
6.	MSN Hotmail	▶	3.39%
7.	LiveJournal.com	▶	2.19%
8.	Yahoo!	▶	1.98%
9.	Gaiaonline.com	▶	1.22%
10.	MSN	▶	1.10%

Figure 1.3 Weekly Upstream "Computers and Internet" sites to "YouTube" 12/24/05

She added, "Not surprisingly, given the nature of the video and the upstream traffic, visitors to YouTube are overwhelmingly young." For the four weeks ending December 24, 2005, 45 percent of the visitors to YouTube were in the 18 to 24 age group. By comparison, 24 percent of the visitors to Google Video and 35 percent of the visitors to Yahoo! Video Search were in the 18 to 24 bracket.

By the end of January, Prescott reported, "Since my post last month on YouTube and the SNL Chronicles of Narnia rap, YouTube has continued to gain market share against other video search sites, and since surpassing Google Video, it has also surpassed Yahoo! Video Search."

In February 2006, almost two months after "Lazy Sunday" had been uploaded to YouTube, the video was removed from the video sharing site. The YouTube staff posted this explanation on the YouTube Blog: "Hi Tubers! NBC recently contacted

YouTube and asked us to remove Saturday Night Live's 'Lazy Sunday: Chronicles of Narnia' video. We know how popular that video is but YouTube respects the rights of copyright holders. You can still watch SNL's 'Lazy Sunday' video for free on NBC's website."

The YouTube staff added, "We are happy to report that YouTube is now serving up more than 15 million videos streamed per day—that's nearly 465 million videos streamed per month with 20,000 videos being uploaded daily."

"Lazy Sunday" may have helped YouTube to take the early lead right out of the gate, but it wasn't the only video fueling the growth of the video sharing site. In fact, after "Lazy Sunday" was removed, YouTube continued to gain market share.

In other words, YouTube wasn't dependent on a single hit.

Mar. 2006: 10-Minute Limit Implemented

YouTube's growth also continued the following month, even after the video sharing site implemented a 10-minute limit for video uploads.

In March 2006, Maryrose, a YouTube staff member, posted this on YouTube Blog: "This change won't impact the vast majority of our users. We know that over 99% of videos uploaded are already under 10 mins, and we also know that most of our users only watch videos that are under about 3 minutes in length."

If most users were uploading and watching short-form video clips, then why did YouTube even bother to make the change?

Maryrose explained, "If you've followed our blog postings or any of the press articles, you know we're constantly trying to balance the rights of copyright owners with the rights of our users. We poked around the system a bit and found that these longer videos were more likely to be copyrighted videos from (TV) shows and movies than the shorter videos posted."

May 2006: Video Responses Launched

YouTube noticed that users within many of the different ecosystems on YouTube were communicating with each other through their videos. In addition to text comments and messages, users had once again created something really innovative completely on their own—video responses.

In May 2006, Maryrose said, "It's been amazing to watch our users create an entirely new mechanism for communicating with one another. However, one of the challenges with these video dialogues has been there is no way to 'link' your response back to the original video. To encourage and simplify this type of communication we just launched a new Video Response feature that will allow you to upload your own video reply while you're watching a video."

July 2006: 100 Million Mark Passed

On July 16, 2006, YouTube told Reuters that viewers were watching more than 100 million videos per day on its site, marking a surge in demand for its "snack-sized" video fare.

Since springing from out of nowhere in late 2005, YouTube had come to hold the leading position in online video with 29 percent of the U.S. multimedia entertainment market, according to the most recent weekly data from Hitwise.

MySpace, another video sharing site, had a nearly 19 percent share of the market according to Hitwise. Yahoo!, Microsoft's MSN, Google, and AOL each had 3 percent to 5 percent of the online video market. In other words, the four major video search engines had a smaller collective share than either YouTube or MySpace did alone.

In June, 2.5 billion videos were watched on YouTube. In July, more than 65,000 videos were uploaded daily to YouTube, up from around 50,000 in May.

Aug. 2006: YouTube Launches Advertising

On August 16, 2006, Bill Tancer, the general manager of global research at Hitwise, posted the chart in Figure 1.4 to his analyst weblog comparing the market share of visits to YouTube, MySpace Video, Google Video, and Yahoo! Video.

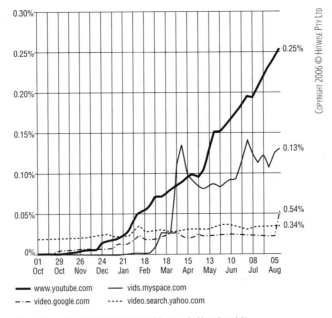

Figure 1.4 Market share of visits to YouTube, MySpace Video, Google Video, and Yahoo! Video

Later that month, YouTube announced two new advertising concepts— participatory video ads and brand channels. These new strategies complemented

YouTube's other offerings, which included banner ads, promotions, and sponsorships. (We'll review brand channels in Chapter 5.)

And on August 30, 2006, Lee Gomes of the *Wall Street Journal* did a scrape of YouTube and found there were 6.1 million videos. Based on how many videos had been uploaded to the site, the length of each, and how many times they had been watched, he did a little multiplication to find out the total time that people had spent watching YouTube since it had started. He said, "The figure is—drum roll, please—9,305 years!"

Eight months earlier, the online video market had been a wide-open field. It included 470 different online video sites, including video sharing sites like YouTube and MySpace Video as well as video search engines like Google Video and Yahoo! Video.

By August 2006, the ballgame was over. YouTube had won.

YouTube's strategy seemed to follow the advice of legendary baseball player Wee Willie Keeler: "Keep your eye clear, and hit 'em where they ain't." Although Keeler is one of the shortest players elected to the Baseball Hall of Fame, standing approximately 5′7″, his .385 career batting average after the 1898 season is the highest average in history at season's end for a player with more than 1,000 hits.

In other words, while video search engines were crawling the Web extracting what little metadata they could find for video content, YouTube was empowering millions of people to easily upload video clips and enrich the data by tagging, rating, and commenting. While video search engines were helping people find videos, YouTube was enabling people to discover and share video clips both on YouTube.com and across the Internet as embedded videos and links. While the video search engines seemed focused on beating old competitors, YouTube was focused on building a new community.

Oct. 2006: Google Acquires YouTube

On October 6, 2006, Prescott reported on her Hitwise Weblog, "Today's rumor that Google might be buying YouTube strikes me as highly unlikely, but deserves some analysis."

Although YouTube had a market share of visits four times greater than Google Video, Prescott observed, "Google is YouTube's second most important source of traffic other than MySpace. In September 2006, 10.7% of YouTube's upstream visits came from Google, while MySpace accounted for 16.2% of YouTube's upstream traffic."

Prescott also looked at the data from Google's perspective. She noted that Google had begun sending more traffic to YouTube than Google Video in late June.

Google Video's audience skewed more male and older than YouTube's. YouTube's average session time was double that of Google Video's, at 18 minutes, 33 seconds in the month of September versus 9 minutes, 9 seconds for Google Video. She observed, "YouTube is just plain sticky compared to Google Video."

Prescott concluded, "If there is any truth to this rumor, my feeling is that Google, with its great engineering team, could eventually build all the features of YouTube and make it even better for far less money than it would take to buy it, if indeed the going price is over $1 billion. However, YouTube has an amazingly large video library and seemingly loyal user base that is only six months old, which would be nearly impossible to replicate. That alone could be worth $1.6 billion, especially since Google is getting into the video ad space. Let's see what happens next week."

On October 9, 2006, Google Inc. announced that it had agreed to acquire YouTube for $1.65 billion in a stock-for-stock transaction.

In a press release, Eric Schmidt, chief executive officer of Google, said, "The YouTube team has built an exciting and powerful media platform that complements Google's mission to organize the world's information and make it universally accessible and useful."

Chad Hurley, CEO and cofounder of YouTube, added, "Our community has played a vital role in changing the way that people consume media, creating a new clip culture. By joining forces with Google, we can benefit from its global reach and technology leadership to deliver a more comprehensive entertainment experience for our users and to create new opportunities for our partners."

On a conference call and webcast to discuss the acquisition, Schmidt was asked why Google had acquired YouTube when it already had Google Video. Schmidt answered that Google Video was doing well but YouTube was a clear winner in the social networking side of video.

Yahoo! had also been in the bidding war for YouTube, until very close to the end. The other leading video search engine in the horse race recognized the benefit—or necessity—of having the leading video sharing site in its stable too.

On November 13, 2006, Google closed its acquisition of YouTube. In a press release, Eric Schmidt said, "We look forward to working with content creators and owners large and small to harness the power of the Internet to promote, distribute, and monetize their content." Chad Hurley added, "The community will remain the most important part of YouTube and we are staying on the same course we set out on nearly one year ago."

2007–2008: Middle Years

After Google officially bought YouTube, people wondered what would happen next. Google said that YouTube and Google Video would "continue to play to their respective strengths."

But YouTube's respective strength had been kicking sand in the face of Google Video's respective strength for more than a year.

Jan. 2007: Sibling Rivalry Halted

So, on January 25, 2007, Google provided a bit more detail. In a press release, the company said, "Starting today, YouTube video results will appear in the Google Video search index: when users click on YouTube thumbnails, they will be taken to YouTube.com to experience the videos."

Google added, "Ultimately, we envision most user-generated and premium video content being hosted on YouTube so that it can further enhance the YouTube experience. We also envision YouTube benefiting from future Google Video innovations—especially those involving video search, monetization and distribution."

Mar. 2007: First YouTube Awards Held

In March 2007, YouTube held the first YouTube Video Awards to recognize the best user-created videos of 2006 in seven categories: most adorable, best comedy, best commentary, most creative, most inspirational, musician of the year, and best series.

We'll take a closer look at two of the award winners in Chapter 4, but let's take a quick look now at three other winners of 2006 YouTube Video Awards and a fourth video that was nominated but lost. To create a new derivative work, I'll mash up my black-and-white descriptions of these videos with some of Virginia Heffernan's color commentary in the *New York Times* (March 27, 2007).

Most Adorable: "Kiwi!" (www.youtube.com/watch?v=sdUUx5FdySs) was uploaded to Madyeti47's channel on June 27, 2006, and has more than 27 million views today. The awards tell us a lot about the YouTube community, Virginia. "YouTube's winners also reveal the site's mystified attitude toward animation, in the form of the sweet but dull 'Kiwi!' cartoon, which takes the most adorable video prize."

Musician of the Year: "Say It's Possible" (www.youtube.com/watch?v=ARHyRI9_NB4) was uploaded to TerraNaomi's channel on June 16, 2006, and has more than 4.1 million views today. And how do you feel about that choice, Virginia? "That's a wonderful choice. The song has got a sustained ache to it, and the visual setup for the video—the singer at the guitar crowding the camera, before an unused keyboard—is painterly, in the tradition of the best YouTube bedroom guitar videos."

Best Commentary: "Hotness Prevails/Worst Video Ever" (www.youtube.com/watch?v=w-rcjaBWvx0) was uploaded to TheWineKone's channel on May 31, 2006, and has more than 3.2 million views today. Tell our readers what you really think about this guy and his commentary, Virginia. "The Wine Kone, a handsome guy with a steady gaze and a wheezy chortle, holds forth there on belly-button issues."

Also Nominated: "First Blog / Dorkiness Prevails" (www.youtube.com/watch?v=-goXKtd6cPo) was uploaded to lonelygirl15's channel on June 16, 2006, and has more than 3 million views today. In September 2006, it was revealed to be a hoax, Virginia. "The widespread animus toward 'lonelygirl15,' the hit online series that got its start on YouTube but then seemed to grow too big for its britches, also seems to be alive and well at the YouTube Awards, where it was nominated for several awards but won nothing."

May 2007: Universal Search Announced

At a Searchology event in May 2007, Google announced a universal search model that incorporated information from a variety of previously separate sources—including videos, news, images, maps, and websites—into a single set of results.

Marissa Mayer, vice president of search products and user experience at Google, said in a post on the Official Google Blog, "With universal search, we're attempting to break down the walls that traditionally separated our various search properties and integrate the vast amounts of information available into one simple set of search results."

At first, universal search results were subtle. But over time users discovered they didn't need to visit Google Video anymore to find a video. They could go to YouTube and run a search or execute a Google Web search and click on a link to a video.

Capiche?

June 2007: Local Versions Rolled Out

In June 2007, YouTube launched local versions in nine countries—including the UK. Canadian versions of YouTube in English and French were launched in November 2007.

Today, YouTube is localized in 25 countries across 43 languages. And 70 percent of YouTube traffic comes from outside the U.S.

July 2007: CNN/YouTube Debate (D) Held

In July 2007, the first CNN/YouTube debate was held live from Charleston, South Carolina. All eight Democratic presidential candidates on the You Choose '08 platform answered 38 questions users had submitted through videos on YouTube.

As Figure 1.5 illustrates, the Democratic debate included a question about global warming from Billiam the Snowman from Point Hope, Alaska (www.youtube.com/watch?v=-0BPnnvI47Q).

Most instant polls indicated that Barack Obama had decisively "won" the debate. But Deborah White of About.com wrote (July 24, 2007), "The break-out star of Monday's Jeopardy-style 'debate' between the Democratic presidential candidates was YouTube technology, because it allowed a newly authentic, direct connection between candidates and voters."

Figure 1.5 "CNN/YouTube Debate: Global Warming"

Aug. 2007: InVideo Ads Launched

In August 2007, YouTube offered select partners the ability to incorporate YouTube InVideo ads into their content. These are animated overlays that appear on the bottom 20 percent of a video.

If viewers were interested by what they saw there, clicking on the overlay launched an interactive video ad while the video they were watching was temporarily paused. If viewers chose not to click on the overlay, it would simply disappear.

Nov. 2007: CNN/YouTube Debate (R) Held

In November 2007, the CNN/YouTube Republican debate was held in St. Petersburg, Florida. All eight Republican presidential candidates on the You Choose '08 platform answered 34 questions users had submitted through videos on YouTube.

As Figure 1.6 illustrates, the Republican debate included a question about the vice president's power from a Dick Cheney cartoon (www.youtube.com/watch?v=rdVoL35SpWI).

After the Republican debate, there was some controversy about CNN's choice of questions. Despite the controversy, Blake D. Dvorak of RealClearPolitics wrote (Nov. 30, 2007), "As a political medium, the YouTube technology is useful for pretty much two things anyway: 1) Capturing candidates' more telling moments for endless replay to a universal audience; and 2) giving candidates the ability to speak directly to voters, without the hassle of buying airtime. Those are two very significant developments, and because of them, we can correctly say that politics has entered a 'YouTube Age.'"

Figure 1.6 "Cheney has a question for the Republican candidates"

Dec. 2007: Partner Program Expanded and Queen of England Launches Channel

In December 2007, YouTube invited YouTube users in the United States and Canada to join its expanded Partner Program. A month later, YouTube users in the UK were also invited to join the YouTube Partner Program.

This gave original content creators the chance to reap rewards from their work and receive the same promotional benefits given to YouTube's professional content partners.

In a YouTube Gram, the company said, "We hope this program will inspire our users to continue to create compelling, engaging and viral content for the YouTube community."

As Figure 1.7 illustrates, YouTube previewed its application process to a select group of users who had previously expressed interest in becoming partners—including Marina Orlova's HotForWords (www.youtube.com/hotforwords).

We'll examine the YouTube Partner Program in Chapter 5.

Later that month, the Queen of England launched The Royal Channel on YouTube (www.youtube.com/TheRoyalChannel), becoming the first monarch to establish a video presence this way.

Figure 1.7 HotForWords

Jan. 2008: YouTube for Mobile Debuts

In January 2008, YouTube announced the official debut of YouTube for Mobile (http://m.youtube.com), giving users of mobile phones access to tens of millions of videos. YouTube for Mobile was initially available in 17 countries, including Canada, the United Kingdom, and the United States, as well as in 11 languages, including English and French.

In a YouTube Gram, the company said, "Users will now have access to features regularly used on YouTube, including their YouTube accounts, Favorites, Videos, Channels as well as the ability to directly upload from mobile devices and share videos instantly. Users also will now have the ability to rate and comment on videos directly from their mobile phones."

Mar. 2008: Last YouTube Awards Held and YouTube Insight Released

In March 2008, the second and last YouTube Awards were held to recognize the best videos of 2007 in 12 categories: adorable, comedy, commentary, creative, eyewitness, inspirational, instructional, music, politics, series, short film, and sports.

We'll take a closer look at three of the award winners in Chapter 4. But why haven't the YouTube Awards been held again?

I asked Ricardo Reyes of YouTube that question via email in April 2009 and he replied, "Don't think we are doing it this year. With YouTube Live last quarter, and the YT symphony orchestra now, we're pretty booked."

Okay, that was true. But I believe there's another reason YouTube didn't hold its annual awards in 2009 or 2010.

As Elana Schor of guardian.co.uk observed (March 21, 2008), "Imagine an Oscars ceremony where the biggest stars go home empty-handed. That's what happened today at YouTube's second annual video awards, as Obama Girl, the "Don't Tase Me, Bro" student, and other stars of viral video got nominated but lost to unlikely newcomers."

Or, as Helen A.S. Popkin of MSNBC.com noted (March 24, 2008), "Chris Crocker isn't much fazed by his YouTube Awards shutout. The unofficial poster child for the video-sharing Web site never expected his infamous 'Leave Britney Alone!' post to win the 'Commentary' category for which it was nominated."

Why? Popkin explained, "The Chris haters seem to far outnumber his fans. Despite the million-plus views each new video draws, the majority of viewer comments he receives are fairly ugly."

So, I can understand why the YouTube Awards might have become the first casualty of a "culture war" that frequently simmers in American society and occasionally boils over in the YouTube community. They were expendable.

Later that month, YouTube released YouTube Insight, a free tool that enables anyone with a YouTube account to view detailed statistics about the videos they upload to the site.

"For example, uploaders can see how often their videos are viewed in different geographic regions, as well as how popular they are relative to all videos in that market over a given period of time," said Tracy Chan, YouTube's product manager, in a post on the Official Google Blog. "You can also delve deeper into the lifecycle of your videos, like how long it takes for a video to become popular, and what happens to video views as popularity peaks."

The tool also helps partners to better understand their audiences, enabling them to increase the number of monetizable views their videos get and, as a result, generate more revenue. We'll review YouTube Insight in Chapter 9.

June 2008: Video Annotations Announced

In June 2008, YouTube announced a new way to add interactive commentary to your videos—with video annotations. With this feature, you can add background information, create branching stories, or add links to any YouTube video, channel, or search results page—at any point in your video.

Uploaders have control over creating and editing an unlimited number of annotations on their videos. As you play your video, you can insert commentary by adding speech bubbles, notes, and highlight boxes anywhere you want. You can also use the menu to save a draft, delete commentary, edit start/stop times, or add links to your annotations.

Aug. 2008: Captions Added

In August 2008, YouTube added a new captioning feature which allows you to give viewers a deeper understanding of your video. Captions can help people who would not otherwise understand the audio track to follow along, especially those who speak other languages or who are deaf and hard of hearing.

One of the first to start using captions was BBC Worldwide, which provided captions in five different languages on "Top Gear - Richard Hammond toasts Nissan with a jet car - BBC," shown in Figure 1.8 with a caption in French (www.youtube.com/watch?v=XraeBDMm2PM).

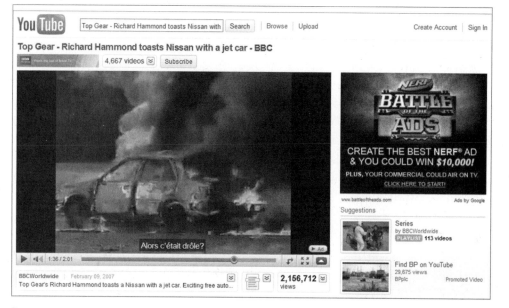

Figure 1.8 "Top Gear - Richard Hammond toasts Nissan with a jet car - BBC"

We'll dig deeper into annotations and captions in Chapter 3.

Sept. 2008: YouTube Becomes Second Largest Search Engine, after Google

On Sept. 20, 2008, I wrote in Search Engine Watch, "I've just had a chance to digest the latest data from comScore for August 2008 and its appears that YouTube has passed Yahoo—if you look at 'expanded' search queries instead of 'core' search queries."

According to comScore, a *core* search query is one that occurs on "the five major search engines." An *expanded* search query is one that occurs on "the top properties where search activity is observed." In addition to the five major search engines, this includes YouTube, Facebook, eBay, and other "expanded search entities."

Google had 7.4 billion core search queries and 7.6 billion expanded search queries in August to lead no matter how you define a *search query*. YouTube had 2.6 billion expanded search queries that month. And Yahoo! had 2.3 billion core search queries and 2.4 billion expanded search queries.

YouTube was now the second largest search engine. But YouTube doesn't crawl the Web trying to index videos posted on millions of websites. So the only way you can get your videos found in the second largest search engine is to upload them to YouTube.

Get it? Got it? Good.

Oct. 2008: eCommerce Platform Unveiled and Full-Length TV Shows Tested

In October 2008, YouTube unveiled its eCommerce platform by announcing that users could easily "click-to-buy" products related to the content they were watching from iTunes and Amazon.com.

A few days later, the YouTube Blog announced, "We are starting to test full-length programming on YouTube, beginning with some fan favorites requested by you."

"Apparently, YouTubers have been asking 'to be beamed up with Scotty, to devise a world-saving weapon using only gum and paperclips, and to get your grub on at The Peach Pit,'" I said in Search Engine Watch (Oct. 11, 2008), because YouTube was testing full-length episodes of *Star Trek*, *MacGyver*, and *Beverly Hills, 90210* through a deal with CBS.

The YouTube Blog added, "As we test this new format, we also want to ensure that our partners have more options when it comes to advertising on their full-length TV shows. You may see in-stream video ads (including pre-, mid- and post-rolls) embedded in some of these episodes; this advertising format will only appear on pre-mium content where you are most comfortable seeing such ads."

Nov. 2008: Promoted Videos Launched and YouTube Live Held

In November 2008, YouTube launched Sponsored Videos, which was later renamed Promoted Videos. The YouTube Blog added, "The popularity of YouTube has been out-standing—we have millions of viewers watching hundreds of millions of videos every day, and 13 hours of new video uploaded to the site every minute."

As Figure 1.9 illustrates, I interviewed YouTube's product manager Matthew Liu at SES New York 2009. He said Promoted Videos is like Google AdWords for YouTube.

And like AdWords, Promoted Videos is a self-serve advertising platform that allows you to promote your video to the audience you are interested in reaching on a cost-per-click basis. We'll analyze Promoted Videos in Chapter 3.

Figure 1.9 "YouTube Product Manager Matthew Liu on YouTube Insight and Promoted Videos"

Later that month, YouTube held YouTube Live. Part concert, part variety show, and part party, YouTube's first official user event was held in San Francisco at the Herbst Pavilion in Fort Mason Center. YouTube Live was also streamed online.

"For nearly three years the YouTube community has been defining pop culture and in the process has made the site both a place to find and be found," said Hurley in a press release. "YouTube at its core is a platform where everyone from the famous to the seemingly unknown shares a single stage and YouTube Live is a physical manifestation of this idea."

Dec. 2008: "YouTube Videos Pull in Real Money" and HD on YouTube Rolled Out

On December 10, 2008, Brian Stelter of the *New York Times* wrote an article titled "YouTube Videos Pull in Real Money." He said, "One year after YouTube, the online video powerhouse, invited members to become 'partners' and added advertising to their videos, the most successful users are earning six-figure incomes from the Web site. For some, like Michael Buckley, the self-taught host of a celebrity chatter show, filming funny videos is now a full-time job."

Buckley is the writer, producer and star of *What the Buck?!* (www.youtube.com/whatthebuckshow). *What the Buck?!* is one of the most popular entertainment shows on YouTube with over 1 million subscribers and more than 298 million views since the summer of 2006 (Figure 1.9).

Figure 1.10 *What the Buck?!*

Buckley quit his day job as an administrative assistant in September 2008 after his online profits greatly surpassed his salary. One of the original members of YouTube's Partner Program, he was earning over $100,000 a year from YouTube advertising.

Later that month, YouTube rolled out a HD player. Starting then, if you clicked the Watch In HD option below an HD player, the video would automatically play in widescreen.

2009–2010: Coming of Age

By 2009, YouTube was coming of age. Although it had begun as a personal video sharing service, it had quickly grown into the world's leading video community on the Internet.

Jan. 2009: House's, Senate's, President's and Pope's Channels Launched

On January 12, 2009, the United States Congress and YouTube announced the launch of official Congressional YouTube channels. Each member of the House and Senate could create their own YouTube channel that citizens could locate on a Google Maps interface on the House Hub (www.youtube.com/househub) and the Senate Hub (www.youtube.com/senatehub).

On January 20, 2009, the official White House channel on YouTube (www.youtube.com/whitehouse) was launched. We'll look at a case study of "the YouTube Presidency" in Chapter 10.

On January 23, the Official Google Blog and the YouTube Blogs both announced that the Vatican had launched a dedicated YouTube Blog (www.youtube.com/vatican).

Mar. 2009: Interest-Based Ads Tested, Disney Deal Signed

On March 11, 2009, Google launched a beta test of interest-based advertising on partner sites and on YouTube. Susan Wojcicki, Google's VP of product management, said on the Offical Google Blog, "These ads will associate categories of interest—say sports, gardening, cars, pets—with your browser, based on the types of sites you visit and the pages you view. We may then use those interest categories to show you more relevant text and display ads."

On March 30, 2009, Disney Media Networks and YouTube announced plans to launch multiple ad-supported channels featuring short-form content from ESPN (www.youtube.com/ESPN) and the Disney/ABC Television Group (www.youtube.com/ABC). Under the terms of the agreement, Disney Media Networks had the option to sell its own advertising inventory within the Disney/ABC and ESPN channels. Channels rolled out in mid-April for ESPN and early May for the Disney/ABC Television Group channels, which included ABC Entertainment, ABC News, ABC Family, and SOAPnet.

A month later, Disney announced that ABC would join NBC Universal and Fox as a partner in Hulu.

In an article in the *New York Times* (Aprril 30, 2009), Brad Stone and Stelter said, "The deal is a blow to YouTube, owned by Google and by far the largest video site on the Web. It also courted Disney but struck a deal to display only short clips from shows on ABC and ESPN. People familiar with the negotiations said talks between Disney and YouTube broke down over how a deal would be structured, with Disney insisting on owning a stake in any joint venture."

Apr. 2009: YouTube Symphony Orchestra Performs, Shows and Movies Launched

On April 15, 2009, over 90 musicians from around the world gathered in New York City for the historic YouTube Symphony Orchestra performance at Carnegie Hall. As Figure 1.11 illustrates, Tan Dun's composition Internet symphony "Eroica," as selected and mashed up from nearly 3,000 video submissions from around the globe, also had its world premiere on YouTube's home page.

On April 16, 2009, Shiva Rajaraman, product manager, and Sara Pollack, entertainment marketing manager, announced on the YouTube Blog a new destination for television shows and an improved destination for movies on YouTube. Partners like CBS, Crackle, Lionsgate, MGM, Starz, and many others made thousands of television episodes and hundreds of movies available to watch, comment on, favorite, and share.

On the same day, the Official Google TV Ads Blog announced the beta launch of Google TV Ads Online. Geoff Smith, product manager for Google TV Ads, said, "Today, YouTube launched a new destination for full-length shows and movies, and advertisers will be able to use Google TV Ads Online to reach the millions of people who come to YouTube to watch this content."

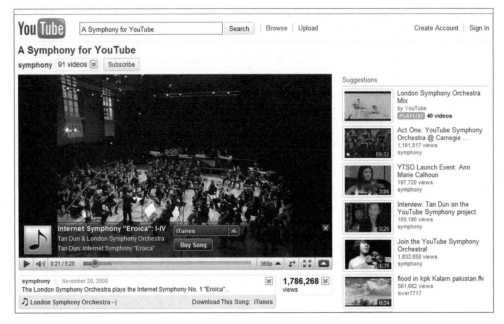

Figure 1.11 "A Symphony for YouTube"

May 2009: 20 Hours of Video Uploaded Every Minute

On May 20, 2009, Ryan Junee, product manager, reported on the YouTube Blog, "In mid-2007, six hours of video were uploaded to YouTube every minute. Then it grew to eight hours per minute, then 10, then 13. In January of this year, it became 15 hours of video uploaded every minute, the equivalent of Hollywood releasing over 86,000 new full-length movies into theaters each week. Now, 20 hours of video are uploaded to YouTube every minute, and it is a testament to the fact that you've made YouTube your online video home."

He added, "We couldn't have built this site without your commitment to sharing your thoughts, experiences, and creativity with each other. We have news clips and full-length shows and movies, music videos and how-to content, sports highlights and animation, short films, homegrown videos, and, yes, all the dogs on skateboards you can watch. There's an audience for every type of content on YouTube, and we hope that with all this video, you can find whatever it is you're interested in on the site."

June 2009: AutoShare Launched

On June 11, 2009, the YouTube Blog announced the launch of AutoShare. Brian Glick, product manager, said, "With a simple one-time log-in on our upload page, you can now have your YouTube account automatically update your Facebook friends, Twitter followers, and Google Reader shared items when you upload a video."

July 2009: 3D Launched

On July 22, 2009, the YouTube Blog announced 3D. Peter Bradshaw, software engineer, said, "The format is exploding in popularity, and already there are countless 3D videos on YouTube. We wanted to make it easier for you to watch and enjoy them in a variety of formats, since having a 3D experience usually requires special glasses or viewing techniques." We'll discuss 3D in Chapter 3.

Aug. 2009: Individual Video Partnerships Launched

On August 25, 2009, the YouTube Biz Blog announced the launch of individual video partnerships. Shenaz Zack, product manager, said, "Now, when you upload a video to YouTube that accumulates lots of views, we may invite you to monetize that video and start earning revenue from it." We'll talk about this topic in Chapter 5.

Oct. 2009: One Billion Views Per Day Announced

On October 9, 2009, Hurley said on the YouTube Blog, "Three years ago today, Steve and I stood out in front of our offices and jokingly crowned ourselves the burger kings of media. We'd just made headlines by joining with Google in our shared goal of organizing the world's information (in our case, video) and making it easily and quickly accessible to anyone, anywhere. Today, I'm proud to say that we have been serving well over a billion views a day on YouTube."

That day, I noted on Search Engine Watch, "According to comScore Video Metrix, 120.5 million Americans watched nearly *10 billion* videos on YouTube.com in August 2009.... According to comScore qSearch, Americans conducted *9.4 billion* searches on Google in August 2009. Yep, the numbers are right. There are more videos being watched on YouTube than there are searches being conducted on Google in the United States."

Nov. 2009: 1080p HD Launched

On November 12, 2009, the YouTube Blog announced support for watching 1080p HD videos in full resolution. Billy Biggs, software engineer, said, "YouTube's HD mode will add support for viewing videos in 720p or 1080p, depending on the resolution of the original source, up from our maximum output of 720p today."

Jan. 2010: Rentals Launched

On January 28, 2010, the YouTube Biz Blog announced YouTube Rentals. Through this new offering, content owners now could change videos from ad supported to rental. They could also set the price and rental duration. In short, they could test and customize their distribution to fit their audience's habits and their business' needs.

Feb. 2010: President Interviewed Live

On February 1, 2010, the YouTube Blog said its unique interview with President Obama at the White House would be live-streamed on CitizenTube (www.youtube .com/citizentube).

Steve Grove, head of news & politics, said, "For the past five days, since the president's State of the Union speech, people across the country have been submitting and voting on video and text questions in our Moderator platform on CitizenTube. Looking at your votes, we've scoured through the top tier of the over 11,000 questions—and we'll bring as many as we can to the president today."

Mar. 2010: 24 Hours of Video Uploaded Every Minute and Video Page Redesigned

On March 17, 2010, the YouTube Blog announced that 24 hours of video were uploaded to YouTube every minute. Hunter Walk, director of product management, said, "In just 60 quick ticks of the second hand, more than a full, action-packed day in Jack Bauer's life is now uploaded to YouTube."

On March 31, 2010, the YouTube Blog unveiled one of the largest redesigns in YouTube's history. Igor Kofman, software engineer, said, "We're simplifying the look and functionality of the video page. That's the page you see whenever a video plays, and this redesign is about going 'back to basics,' focusing attention on the reason why you came to YouTube in the first place— the video—and all the ways you engage with content and creators."

Apr. 2010: IPL Bowls Wicked Googly

On April 19, 2010, the YouTube Blog reported on the streaming of the Indian Premier League cricket season on YouTube. Amit Agrawal, strategic partner development manager, said, "We've been blown away by the response. We've seen views come in from countries around the globe, and the IPL channel on YouTube now has over 40 million views."

That was a wicked googly!

He added, "We've been particularly surprised by the number of cricket fans tuning in from the U.S. Total views from the U.S. for the IPL channel are second only to India. And fans in the U.S. are active, too: they're second only to those in India in terms of subscribing to the IPL channel and rating, commenting and favoriting videos."

May 2010: YouTube Turns Five!

On May 16, 2010, YouTube celebrated its fifth birthday. Although it was founded in February 2005, the first beta version of YouTube.com had been launched in May 2005.

The YouTube Blog also announced, "Our site has crossed another milestone: YouTube exceeds over two billion views a day. That's nearly double the prime-time audience of all three major U.S. television networks combined."

The company also launched the YouTube Five Year channel (www.youtube.com/user/FiveYear) to celebrate its birthday. And as Figure 1.12 illustrates, the YouTube team uploaded a quick overview of the history and highlights surrounding YouTube's first five years (www.youtube.com/watch?v=T1mho7SY-ic).

Figure 1.12 "YouTube Turns Five!"

YouTube has announced many new features and enhancements since turning five, but I have to draw the line between history and current events somewhere. Nevertheless, whether you are an aspiring videographer or a YouTube partner, a local retailer or an Ad Age 100 advertiser, the lesson that this short history of YouTube teaches is that things change.

What had started as a site for bedroom vloggers and viral videos has evolved into a global platform that supports HD and broadcasts entire sports seasons live to 200+ countries. YouTube brings feature films from Hollywood studios and independent filmmakers to far-flung audiences. Activists document social unrest seeking to transform societies, and leading civic and political figures stream interviews to the world.

Unfortunately, some marketers still think YouTube is a small video sharing site where any wanna-be director with a video camera and an Internet connection can upload their quirky and unusual amateur content for an audience of 18- to 24-year-olds to discover, watch, and share. Well, it was … five years ago.

But YouTube has come a long way since December 2006, when the cartoon in Figure 1.13 appeared in the *New Yorker*.

© Cartoonbank.com

Marshall

"God, this is going to be all over YouTube."

Figure 1.13 "God, this is going to be all over YouTube." (Cartoon by Marshall Hopkins in the *New Yorker*, December 25, 2006)

YouTube's early reputation explains why many marketers still need to debunk several myths before they can persuade their organizations to launch video marketing campaigns:

Perception #1: YouTube is limited to short-form user-generated content. Reality #1: You can find thousands of full-length feature films on YouTube, from cult classics like *Caddyshack*, *Scarface*, and *Taxi Driver* to blockbuster new releases like *Inception*, *The King's Speech*, and *Despicable Me*. You can also find thousands of full-length TV episodes on YouTube, from *Star Trek*, *MacGyver*, and *Beverly Hills, 90210* to *How I Met Your Mother*, *Nurse Jackie*, and *United States of Tara*. And YouTube has more than 20,000 partners, including Disney, Turner, and Channel 4.

Perception #2: YouTube videos are grainy and of poor quality. Reality #2: YouTube has more HD videos than any other video site. Ten percent of YouTube's videos are available in HD. Hundreds of thousands of HD videos are uploaded to the site every month, and tens of millions are viewed every day.

Perception #3: Advertisers are afraid of YouTube. Reality #3: YouTube is monetizing over 2 billion video views per week globally. As this was written, 94 of *Ad Age*'s Top 100 advertisers had run campaigns on YouTube and the Google Display Network. The number of advertisers using display ads on YouTube has increased tenfold in the last year.

Now that you've learned why YouTube took off, how it changed the online video landscape, and when it passed some memorable milestones, let's take a serious look at video marketing.

Map Out Your Video Marketing Strategy

The online video marketplace is very large, but it rarely acts like a mass market. And despite its slogan, "Broadcast Yourself," YouTube hardly ever works like a mass medium. So, in this chapter, you will learn to question your assumptions before you map out your video marketing strategy. You will also learn who discovers and shares new videos, what types of video they watch, and where they discover new videos as well as when they share new videos, why so few new videos go viral, and how YouTube and video marketing work. Finally, you will learn that it's okay to admit, "I still don't have all the answers, but I'm beginning to ask the right questions."

Chapter Contents:

Four *Ps* vs. Five *Ws* and an *H*

The online video marketplace is very large. How large is it?

According to comScore Media Metrix, almost 1.2 billion unique viewers worldwide watched more than 137.5 billion videos during June 2011:

- In the US, 178.4 million unique viewers watched 33.5 billion videos for an average of 16.8 hours per viewer.

- In Canada, 22.4 million unique viewers watched 5.9 billion videos that month for an average of 19.0 hours per viewer.

- In the UK, 32.8 million unique viewers watched 5.4 billion videos for an average of 18.3 hours per viewer.

But the online video marketplace rarely acts like a mass market. And despite its slogan, "Broadcast Yourself," YouTube hardly ever works like a mass medium.

So, what does the online video marketplace frequently act like and how does YouTube generally work (Figure 2.1)?

CARTOONBANK.COM

"I still don't have all the answers, but I'm beginning to ask the right questions."

Figure 2.1 "I still don't have all the answers, but I'm beginning to ask the right questions." (Cartoon by Lee Lorenz in *The New Yorker,* February 27, 1989.)

If YouTube were simply a new broadcast network, then video marketing would be simple. You could simply apply all the old mass marketing techniques that you learned in college to a new medium.

Mass marketing assumes a large number of individuals watch the same video on the same channel at the same time. This happens on special occasions. For example, the royal wedding of Britain's Prince William and Catherine Middleton was live-streamed 72 million times on the Royal Channel on YouTube to 188 countries around the world.

In his book *Diffusion of Innovations* (Free Press, 2003), Everett M. Rogers calls this model of communication "the hypodermic needle model." It presumes that the mass media has "direct, immediate, and powerful effects on a mass audience." Rogers could have been describing the impact of the final balcony kiss by the Duke and Duchess of Cambridge on romantics around the globe.

However, most video marketing uses what Rogers calls "the two-step flow model." In the first step, opinion leaders use a video sharing site to discover videos uploaded there. In step two, opinion leaders share videos they like with their followers. While the first step involves a transfer of *information*, the second involves the spread of interpersonal *influence* as well as information.

And it is worth noting that total streams on The Royal Channel (Figure 2.2) reached 101 million on April 29, 2011, as those who hadn't seen the Royal Wedding live took the opportunity to don their fascinators and catch up with the rebroadcasts later in the day.

Figure 2.2 The Royal Channel

Most of us didn't learn this stuff in college because most of us went to college before YouTube was launched and most of the marketing textbooks back then were focused on *mass* marketing.

That's why this book is about video marketing as well as YouTube. However, before we can tackle video marketing, you must (as Yoda would say) "unlearn what you have learned" about mass marketing.

My Father's Oldsmobile

My dad was the director of marketing for Oldsmobile. Coincidentally, he was the director of marketing in the 1980s when Oldsmobile launched the ad campaign that claimed, "This is not your father's Oldsmobile."

When my dad graduated from college in the 1950s, television was changing the media landscape of his generation. As a marketer in the mass media era, he learned the importance of focusing on product, price, place, and promotion. When I graduated from college in the 1970s, newspapers were setting the political agenda of my generation. As a journalist in the Watergate era, I learned the importance of asking who, what, where, when, why, and how.

In the 1980s, I moved from journalism into public relations, and my dad saw this as an opportunity to start a conversation between peers, since public relations was part of marketing.

One of the things we discussed was the difference in perspective between marketers and journalists. Marketers focus on the four *P*s of the marketing mix: product, price, place, and promotion. Journalists ask the five *W*s and an *H* for getting the full story about something: who, what, when, where, why, and how. Table 2.1 compares these two paradigms.

▶ **Table 2.1** Marketing and Journalism

Classic Marketing	Classic Journalism
?	Who
Product	What
Place	Where
?	When
Price	Why
Promotion	How

My father and I quickly recognized that marketers weren't focusing on two fundamental questions that journalists were asking: who and when. As we kicked this around, we both had some pretty powerful insights.

The reason classic marketing didn't focus on "Who" was that it was actually "mass marketing." It assumed that everyone was a prospect for products that were mass produced. That may have worked in 1909 when Henry Ford said, "Any customer can have a car painted any color that he wants so long as it is black." But it stopped working in 1924, when Alfred Sloan unveiled GM's famous market segment strategy of "a car for every purse and purpose."

My dad understood the power of market segmentation and recognized the importance of adding a fifth *P* to the marketing mix: the prospect.

"When" was another blind spot for mass marketing. My dad had started his career in the auto industry during the era of planned obsolescence. Each and every fall, a new line of cars was introduced—whether they featured cosmetic changes or fundamental improvements.

In contrast, I was starting a new career in the computer industry during an era when the price/performance of microprocessors was doubling every 18 months. I understood the power of Moore's Law and recognized the importance of adding a sixth *P* to the marketing mix: the pace of change.

Diffusion of Innovations

Our conversations helped prepare me for what came next: In 1989, I became the director of marketing for *PC Computing*. Coincidentally, the magazine's publisher back then was Michael Kolowich, our inside sales manager was Brian Cusack, and one of our inside sales representatives was Suzie Reider. Kolowich, who is now president of DigiNovations, is the subject of one of the case studies in Chapter 10. Cusack, who is now head of display, retail and Canada, at Google, wrote the foreward to the second edition of this book. And Reider, who is now director of display advertising for YouTube and the Google Display Network, wrote the foreword for the first edition of this book.

When I joined the magazine, we conducted some market research on how the readers of *PC Computing* informally influenced the purchase of innovative PC products and applications by their colleagues at work and friends in their neighborhood. We called our magazine's readers PC Champions.

When I presented our findings to an advertiser in Silicon Valley, she surprised me by asking, "Have you read *Diffusion of Innovations* by Everett Rogers?" I hadn't, so she lent me her copy of her marketing textbook for a graduate-level course at Stanford University. I was blown away.

Rogers segmented markets by combining who and when into *earlier adopters* and *later adopters* of innovations. As Figure 2.3 illustrates, diffusion forms an

S-shaped curve when you look at cumulative adoption and a bell-shaped curve if you look at adoption per time period.

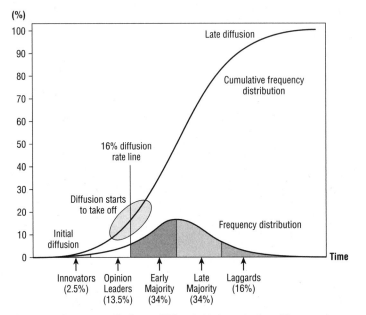

Figure 2.3 The S curve and bell curve. (Although this image is adapted from ones in *Diffusion of Innovations*, it captures many of the key findings in the book.)

I had seen markets segmented into the classic pyramid—with a few big customers at the top and lots of little customers at the bottom. But Rogers turned this point of view on its side. The most important customers weren't the biggest ones on the top of the pyramid; the most important customers were the early adopters on the left side of the S curve.

Even more important, his two-step flow model introduced a new dynamic into the process of deciding whether or not to adopt an innovation. Rogers showed that, in addition to the big brands communicating to the mass market through the mass media, the individual members of diffusion networks are also communicating with each other.

The most important people in these peer-to-peer conversations are opinion leaders. According to Rogers, "The diffusion curve is S-shaped because once opinion leaders adopt and begin telling others about an innovation, the number of adopters per unit of time takes off in an exponential curve."

And his two-step flow model implied that the mass media were neither as powerful nor as directly influential as had previously been thought. He said, "Mass communication channels are primarily knowledge creators, whereas interpersonal networks are more important in persuading individuals to adopt or reject."

Now, video marketing is far more complicated than just two steps. But the two-step flow model illuminates the two blind spots that cannot be seen while looking at either the rear-view or side mirrors of mass marketing: who and when.

So, let's apply the five *W*s and an *H* to the online video market to ensure that we are getting the full story about video marketing. Let's ask the following questions:

- **Who** discovers and shares new videos?
- **What** types of video do they watch?
- **Where** do they discover new videos?
- **When** do they share new videos?
- **Why** don't more new videos go viral?
- **How** does video marketing work?

It's a good idea to question your assumptions before you map out your video marketing strategy.

Who Discovers and Shares New Videos?

There's lots of data on how many people watch online video because most market research firms are still measuring video sharing sites the same way they've always measured mass media. If you mistakenly believe that all viewers are created equal, then whichever online video content property reaches the most unique viewers is ranked #1.

Using that yardstick, YouTube is the top online video content property in the US, Canada, and the UK.

- In the US, 149.3 million unique viewers watched 15.5 billion videos on YouTube .com in June 2011 for an average of 5.4 hours per viewer.
- In Canada, 20.6 million unique viewers watched 2.3 billion videos on YouTube that month for an average of 6.4 hours per viewer.
- In the UK, 27.2 million unique viewers watched 2.3 billion videos on YouTube that month for an average of 5.3 hours per viewer.

There's also data on the age and gender of YouTube's audience because advertisers want it for demographic targeting. As Table 2.2 indicates, Nielsen Netview stats for August 2010 showed the YouTube audience in the United States was more diverse than you may think.

But the size of an audience and its demographics only give us a two-dimensional (2D) view of YouTube.

If you look at a 2D map of Colorado, the state is a quadrangle with no natural borders. That's because its boundaries are defined solely by lines of latitude and longitude.

But if you look at a three-dimensional (3D) map of the Centennial State, you immediately see that eastern Colorado is flat and rolling land. But to the west of the Great Plains of Colorado are the Rocky Mountains. Notable peaks of the Colorado Front Range of the Rocky Mountains include Longs Peak, Mount Evans, and Pikes Peak.

► **Table 2.2** Demographics of YouTube's US Audience

Demo	Unique Visitors (MM)	Percent of Visitors (%)	Reach of Online Universe (%)
Total Audience	99.0	100%	51%
2–11	6.8	7%	39%
12–17	8.6	9%	61%
18–24	11.3	11%	62%
25–34	17.7	18%	57%
35–49	27.6	28%	53%
50–64	18.2	18%	43%
65+	8.8	9%	45%
Male	47.9	48%	52%
Female	51.1	52%	50%

Source: Nielsen Netview, August 2010, US only

So, what would a 3D map of YouTube show you?

If a video is uploaded to YouTube and opinion leaders discover it and then embed it in their blogs or share it with their followers via email, Facebook, Twitter, or Google's +1 button, then are all viewers created equal? Or, considering the role they played in discovering and sharing the video, are some of these viewers more notable than others?

That's the right question to ask. Unfortunately, there's much less data available on who discovers and shares new videos. In other words, most market research firms ignore the role of opinion leaders.

Pew Internet & American Life Project

The first market research I saw that looked at who discovers and shares new videos was conducted by the Pew Internet & American Life Project, one of seven projects that make up the Pew Research Center, a nonpartisan, nonprofit "fact tank" that provides information on the issues, attitudes, and trends shaping America and the world. The Project's findings were published in July 2007 in an online video report written by senior research specialist Mary Madden (Table 2.3).

► **Table 2.3** Online Video Gets Social: How Users Engage (Percentage of Video Viewers Who Do Each Activity)

Activity	Total	Men	Women	18–29	30–49	50–64
Receive video links	75%	75%	75%	76%	77%	71%
Send video links to others	57	59	54	67	55	45
Watch video with others	57	58	57	73	58	34
Rate video	13	15	10	23	11	4
Post comments about video	13	15	10	25	9	5
Upload video	13	16	9	20	12	5
Post video links online	10	12	9	22	7	2
Pay for video	7	8	6	10	7	3

Source: Pew Internet & American Life Project Tracking Survey, February 15–March 7, 2007

One of the key findings was this: "The desire to share a viewing experience with others has already been a powerful force in seeding the online video market. Fully 57% of online video viewers share links to the videos they find online with others. Young adults are the most 'contagious carriers' in the viral spread of online video. Two in three (67%) video viewers ages 18–29 send others links to videos they find online, compared with just half of video viewers ages 30 and older."

Now, 57 percent of online video viewers can't all be opinion leaders. If they were, then every Don Quixote would have only one Sancho Panza as a follower. So, sharing links to the videos they find online with others is a necessary but not sufficient condition of opinion leadership.

According to the Pareto principle, which is also known as the 80-20 rule or the 90-10 rule, no more than 10 to 20 percent of online video viewers should be opinion leaders. Rogers also observed that "the S-shaped diffusion curve 'takes off' at about 10 to 20% adoption, when interpersonal networks become activated so that a critical mass of adopters begins using an innovation."

So, we need to dig deeper into the Pew report to discover other social behavior that would be "just right" to identify opinion leaders.

Here it is: "Video viewers who actively exploit the participatory features of online video—such as rating content, posting feedback or uploading video—make up the motivated minority of the online video audience. Again, young adults are the most active participants in this realm." The findings from the Pew report are as follows:

Nineteen percent of video viewers had either rated an online video or posted comments after seeing a video online. Madden wrote, "One of the features popular on many video sites is the ability to rate or post feedback about the content on the site. For instance, during the now legendary run of Lonelygirl15 videos on YouTube, viewers used the comments field to debate the authenticity of the diary-style videos in which the young girl shared her thoughts and daily drama with the world." Unsurprisingly, those who engaged with online video by rating and commenting back in 2007 tended to be young; video viewers ages 18 to 29 were twice as likely as those ages 30 to 49 to have done so.

Thirteen percent of video viewers had uploaded a video file online for others to watch. Young adults also trumped older users back then in their experience with posting video content; 20 percent of viewers ages 18 to 29 had uploaded videos, compared with 12 percent of those 30 to 49 and roughly 5 percent of viewers age 50 and older who had posted video for others to watch.

Ten percent of video viewers shared links with others by posting them to a website or blog. Madden wrote, "Some who feel compelled to share the video content they find online prefer to do so in a more public way." Again, younger users had a greater tendency to share what they had found; although 22 percent of video viewers ages 18 to 29 had posted links to video online, just 7 percent of those ages 30 to 49 had done so. Madden added, "The flurry of link sharing by younger users has helped to shape the most-viewed, and top-rated lists on popular video sharing sites. Many young adults and teenagers, who are avid users of social networking sites and blogs, post videos to their personal pages and profiles, which then get linked to or reposted by many other users."

#OnionPulitzer Campaign

A lot of this kind of social behavior leaves fingerprints. You can see who has commented on a video, uploaded video responses, and embedded a video in their website or blog.

For example, some of the top trending videos in June 2011 were created in response to a satirical effort launched by Americans for Fairness in Awarding Journalism Prizes (AFAJP). The nonprofit watchdog group started an "astroturfing" campaign, an artificial grassroots movement, dedicated to getting the *Onion* a Pulitzer Prize.

As Figure 2.4 illustrates, AFAJP's video "Demand an #OnionPulitzer: A message from Americans For Fairness in Awarding Journalism Prizes" was uploaded on June 17, 2011.

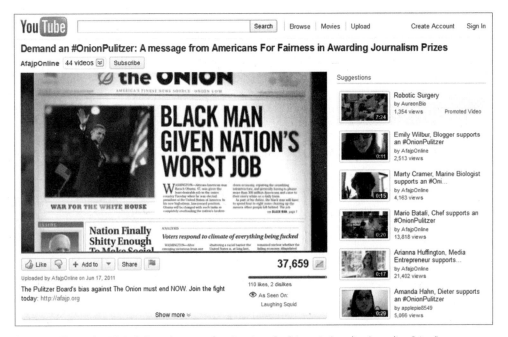

Figure 2.4 "Demand an #OnionPulitzer: A message from Americans For Fairness in Awarding Journalism Prizes"

As this was written, 15 comments had been posted underneath the video (http://youtu.be/v9nG5D3iFb8). This included "Thank you, AFAJP, for having the courage to stand up against the Pulitzer Board" by ifdogscouldwhistle as well as "I think it's disgusting that The Onion hasn't received a Pulitzer in its decades of outstanding, informative journalism" by prettylola89.

Laughing Squid (http://laughingsquid.com/) had also embedded the video in a post entitled "Grassroots Organization AFAJP Demands Pulitzer Prize for The Onion," as shown in Figure 2.5.

Figure 2.5 "Grassroots Organization AFAJP Demands Pulitzer Prize for The Onion"

If you click the "Show video statistics" icon under the video, you will see that "Demand an #OnionPulitzer: A message from Americans For Fairness in Awarding Journalism Prizes" has also been embedded in the AFAJP blog on Tumblr, the *Huffington Post*, the *Onion*, and half a dozen other blogs, websites, and Facebook pages. As this was written, embeds accounted for 26,365 out of the video's 36,687 total views.

Finally, more than 40 opinion leaders, including actor Tom Hanks, media entrepreneur Ariana Huffington, and Ira Glass, host of *This American Life*, filmed short clips in support of the *Onion* and against the Pulitzer board. The most viewed of these clips was "Tom Hanks, Actor supports an #OnionPulitzer" (Figure 2.6).

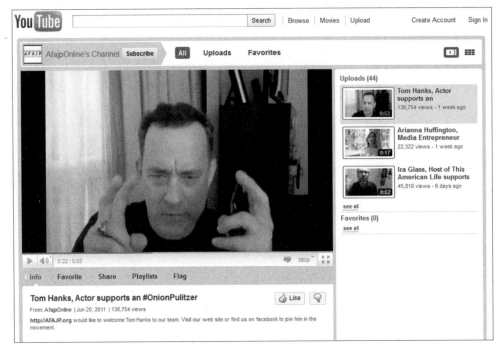

Figure 2.6 "Tom Hanks, Actor supports an #OnionPulitzer"

Click: What Millions of People Are Doing Online and Why It Matters

The next market research I saw that looked at who discovers and shares videos was conducted by Experian Hitwise.

As I was writing the first edition of this book, my firm started promoting an SES webcast with Bill Tancer, the general manager of global research at Hitwise and one of the keynote speakers at SES Chicago 2008. To encourage Q&A, we offered to give away 10 copies of Tancer's new book, *Click: What Millions of People Are Doing Online and Why It Matters* (Hyperion, September 2008) to participants who asked the best questions.

To prepare for that event, I read *Click* and had a sense of *déjà vu* as I read Chapter 10, which is entitled "Finding the Early Adopters." Tancer had also read *Diffusion of Innovations* by Rogers.

Click even included an expanded version of the chart I used in Chapter 1 (Figure 2.7) showing the market share of visits to YouTube, Yahoo! Video, and Google Video from July 23, 2005 to December 15, 2007. The data, naturally, came from Hitwise.

Tancer also observed, "Sometime between November 2005 and January 2006, the diffusion of YouTube use moved from Innovator to Early Adopter, and then crossed over to the Early Majority."

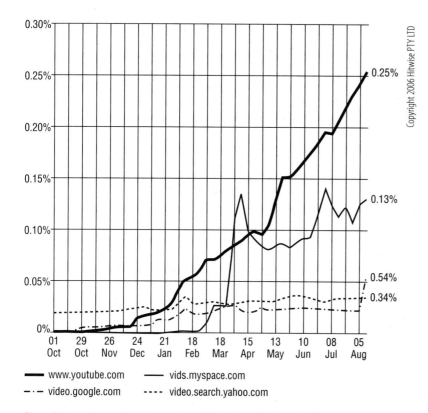

0.30%

0.25% — 0.25%

0.20%

0.15%

0.13%

0.10%

0.05% — 0.54%
0.34%

0%

01 Oct | 29 Oct | 26 Nov | 24 Dec | 21 Jan | 18 Feb | 18 Mar | 15 Apr | 13 May | 10 Jun | 08 Jul | 05 Aug

—— www.youtube.com   —— vids.myspace.com

— · — video.google.com   - - - - video.search.yahoo.com

Chart of the weekly all sites market share in 'all categories' based on visits.
Time periods represented with broken lines indicate insufficient data.
Generated on: 08/16/2006.

Figure 2.7 Market share of visits to YouTube, MySpace, Google Video, and Yahoo! Video

The only difference between Tancer's analysis and mine was that he used terms like *early adopter*, which Rogers explains in Chapter 7 of *Diffusion of Innovations*, while I use terms like *opinion leaders*, which Rogers explains in Chapter 8 of his book.

This may seem like a distinction without a difference, but they are as unlike each other as innovations and *interactive* innovations.

As Rogers says, "The interactive quality of new communication technologies creates interdependence among the adopters in a system. An interactive innovation is of little use to an adopting individual unless other individuals with whom the adopter wishes to communicate also adopt. Thus, a critical mass of individuals must adopt an interactive communication technology before it has much utility for the average individual in the system."

This difference also enables me to add some incremental value in this book, although Tancer and I are merely standing on different shoulders of the same giant.

Using another Hitwise tool, clickstream analysis, Tancer was also able to examine what sites Internet users were on just prior to visiting YouTube and where they went immediately afterward. This enabled him to understand how word of this new site spread and to describe the mechanism in *Click*.

In October 2005, 52 percent of the traffic to YouTube came from social networking sites like MySpace and Facebook. "Within just one month, the method by which users arrived at the YouTube site began to shift dramatically," wrote Tancer. Traffic from email services like Hotmail and Yahoo! Mail started contributing 17 percent of the traffic to YouTube, while traffic from social networking sites declined to just 30 percent. "On the YouTube site, once users viewed a video, they had the ability to send an email to friends that included a link back to the video that they had just viewed," Tancer observed.

I attribute this to opinion leaders sharing links to videos with their followers. The influence of these opinion leaders also explains why video sharing sites were eating the lunch of video search engines in this critical period.

Tancer found more clues about YouTube's meteoric rise hidden in the data. "Along with social networking and email traffic, visits from Google were showing up in YouTube's clickstream in January 2006."

For the four weeks ending January 28, 2006, 5 of the top 10 search terms that sent traffic to YouTube were "Lazy Sunday" (#4), "Narnia Rap" (#7), "SNL Lazy Sunday" (#8), "Chronicles of Narnia SNL" (#9), and "Saturday Night Live Lazy Sunday" (#10). The other 5 search terms were navigational—variations of "YouTube" and "YouTube.com."

In other words, opinion leaders were still buzzing about the skit by Chris Parnell and Andy Samberg on NBC's *Saturday Night Live*, which had aired the same week that YouTube debuted, and their followers were searching to find it.

As I pointed out in Chapter 1, LeeAnn Prescott of Hitwise had reached the same conclusion and posted similar data in her weblog back in December 2005 and January 2006. You can use Google Insights for Search (`www.google.com/insights/search/#`) to see this for yourself by typing "Lazy Sunday" or "Narnia Rap" into the search box.

Ad Age 100 advertisers and YouTube partners can use Hitwise data to identify opinion leaders and see what this segment is doing today. However, local retailers and aspiring videographers shouldn't be surprised that it costs about $20,000 a year to get access to Hitwise insights on how 10 million US Internet users interact with more than 1 million websites, across 160+ industries.

For less than $30, though, you can buy *Click* and find out that 39 percent of the early adopters of online video sharing in late 2005 and early 2006 were 18 to 24 years old, 57 percent earned less than $60,000 a year, and 25 percent lived in California. There were also significant percentages of segments that Claritas PRIZM (a set of geo-demographic clusters for the United States) calls the "Bohemian Mix," "Money and Brains," and "Young Digerati."

In *Click*, Tancer looked at what these segments were doing in early 2008 and found they were testing other online video sites beyond YouTube. I interviewed him following his keynote at SES Chicago 2008 (`http://youtu.be/2tnf9jSd5Bw`) about his latest findings (Figure 2.8). He said that the pattern had shifted again to sites that provided an editorial layer to surface video content that is specific to a particular viewpoint or interest.

Figure 2.8 "Bill Tancer on Search Patterns at SES Chicago 2008"

"It's as if these early adopters are telling us there's too much information out there and just relying on what's most popular on YouTube or just relying on search as a method to find what you are looking for may not work," Tancer said.

"This willingness to try new services demonstrates that this particular group of Internet users, while continuing to use mainstream services online, is always on the lookout for something better," he added.

It's also worth paying attention to another observation by Tancer: "YouTube's rise from the vast collection of unknown video sites didn't take years, or even months for that matter. The move from obscurity to ubiquity occurred in the span of just thirty-five days."

So, once you identify the opinion leaders in your segment of the online video market, you need to continue watching them like a hawk. If a video site can move from obscurity to ubiquity in 35 days, then you can't afford to be the last one to learn Elvis has left the building.

What Types of Video Content Do They Watch?

In addition to asking who discovers and shares new videos, you should also ask, "What types of video content do they watch?"

Several organizations have conducted surveys to identify the most popular types of online video content, including Advertising.com, Burst Media, Frank N. Magid Associates, Ipsos Insight, the Online Publishers Association, the Pew Internet & American Life Project, Piper Jaffray, and TNS. As Figure 2.9 illustrates, eMarketer looked at all this data and estimated in February 2008 that *news/current events* was the most popular genre of video, followed closely by *jokes/bloopers/funny clips (comedy)*.

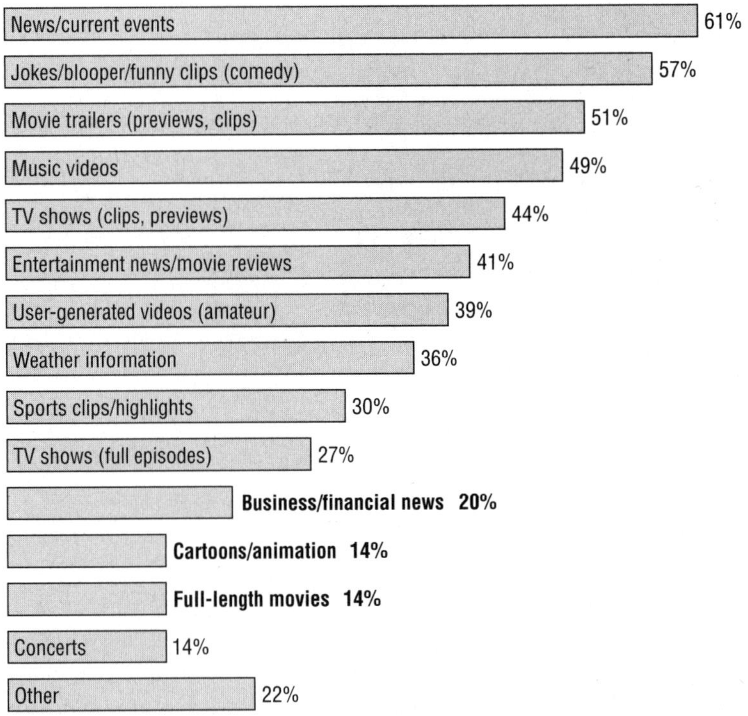

News/current events	61%
Jokes/blooper/funny clips (comedy)	57%
Movie trailers (previews, clips)	51%
Music videos	49%
TV shows (clips, previews)	44%
Entertainment news/movie reviews	41%
User-generated videos (amateur)	39%
Weather information	36%
Sports clips/highlights	30%
TV shows (full episodes)	27%
Business/financial news	20%
Cartoons/animation	14%
Full-length movies	14%
Concerts	14%
Other	22%

Figure 2.9 Types of online video content that US online video viewers watch monthly or more frequently (2007, % of viewers) (Source: eMarketer)

The Anatomy of Buzz Revisited: Real-life Lessons in Word-of-Mouth Marketing

As my firm started promoting SES Toronto 2009, I read the latest book by one of the keynote speakers. It was *The Anatomy of Buzz Revisited: Real-life Lessons in Word-of-Mouth Marketing* (Doubleday, 2009) by Emanuel Rosen.

It was *déjà vu all over again*. Rosen had also read *Diffusion of Innovations*. However, instead of using the term *opinion leaders*, Rosen calls these folks *hubs*. And he makes a distinction between social hubs—people who talk more because they know more people—and expert hubs—people who talk more because they know more about something.

In Chapter 15 of his book, Rosen observes, "People love to tell each other stories."

To demonstrate this, Rosen tells the story of Blake Mycoskie, who went to Argentina in 2006 to take some time off after losing in the reality travel show competition *The Amazing Race* by a slim margin.

While in Argentina, Mycoskie found lots of children had no shoes to protect their feet. Wanting to help, he created TOMS, a company that would match every pair of shoes purchased with a pair of new shoes given to a child in need, one for one. Later that year, Mycoskie returned to Argentina with a group of family, friends, and staff—and 10,000 pairs of shoes made possible by TOMS customers.

Rosen says, "They didn't just hand the shoes to kids—they actually put each pair on a child's feet. A short video of the shoe drop was posted on YouTube (a link is available at www.tomsshoes.com). Now the story starts to be more real. More authentic. It's not just a story, it's something that is happening."

As you watch the video in Figure 2.10, it's worth knowing that TOMS has far exceeded its initial expectations (http://youtu.be/aKhV9kpGM-k). As of September 2010, TOMS had given over 1 million pairs of new shoes to children in need around the world.

Figure 2.10 "TOMS – Giving new shoes to children in need – Song 'Coahuila' by Balmorhea"

At SES Toronto 2009, Rosen also showed Blendtec's "Will It Blend? – iPhone" and discussed the lessons learned from George Wright, who was Blendtec's vice president of marketing and sales at the time. Wright's Will It Blend? campaign is featured in Chapter 10 of this book.

Rosen said, "Watching a shiny new iPhone being dropped into a blender, where it is reduced to black powder, is something that lots of people will talk about."

He added, "Another reason it works is that the conversation hook (a guy blends unbelievable stuff) leads directly to the product benefit (this is one robust blender!)."

As you watch the video in Figure 2.11 (`http://youtu.be/R1qfZDC3iEc`), you will hear Rosen tell me after his keynote that more than 1,000 people had asked Wright to blend an iPhone. If that was the type of video viewers wanted to watch, then Wright was more than happy to create it.

Figure 2.11 "Emanuel Rosen on generating buzz in the online and offline communities"

The State of Online Video

On June 3, 2010, the Pew Internet & American Life Project published "The State of Online Video." Written by Kristen Purcell, the associate director for research, the report said there had been dramatic increases since 2007 in the number of American adults watching the following kinds of videos:

- Comedy or humorous videos, rising in viewership from 31 percent of adult Internet users in 2007 to 50 percent of adult Internet users in the 2010 survey

- Educational videos, rising in viewership from 22 percent to 38 percent of adult Internet users

- Movies or TV show videos, rising in viewership from 16 percent to 32 percent of adult Internet users

- Political videos, rising in viewership from 15 percent to 30 percent of adult Internet users

As Figure 2.12 illustrates, viewership of other types of online video had also risen in the same time frame.

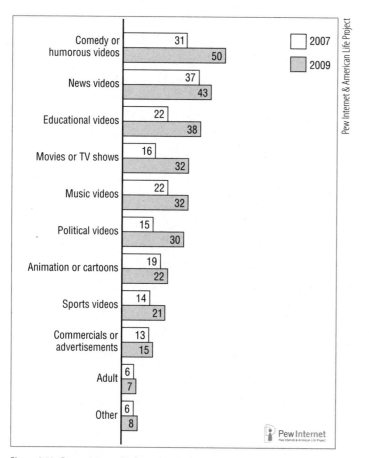

Figure 2.12 Entertaining and informational videos are both popular. (% of online adults who say they watch each type of video, by year)

Guy Kawasaki's *Enchantment*

While writing his best seller *Enchantment: The Art of Changing Hearts, Minds, and Action* (Portfolio/Penguin, 2011), Guy Kawasaki asked me to help him explain how to use YouTube to enchant people. He was kind enough to list me as a contributor, although I only contributed a rough draft for 4 of the 211 pages in his book. Kawasaki says, "The first thing Jarboe taught me is that video content that can enchant people must provide intrinsic value to your viewers." This value comes in four forms:

Inspiration "YouTube has brought to light thousands of inspiring stories of courage and bravery," says Kawasaki. For example, check out "Steve Jobs' 2005 Stanford Commencement Address" (http://youtu.be/UF8uR6Z6KLc). Drawing from some of the most pivotal points in his life, Jobs, the chief executive officer and cofounder of Apple Computer and of Pixar Animation Studios, urged graduates to pursue their dreams and see the opportunities in life's setbacks—including death itself—at the university's commencement on June 12, 2005.

Entertainment "Some videos are plain-and-simple guffawingly funny," says Kawasaki. For example, watch "United Breaks Guitars" (http://youtu.be/5YGc4zOqozo). In the spring of 2008, the rock band Sons of Maxwell was traveling to Nebraska for a one-week tour and United Airlines baggage handlers in Chicago were witnessed throwing Dave Carroll's Taylor guitar. He discovered later that the $3,500 guitar was severely damaged. United didn't deny the incident occurred, but for nine months the various people Carroll communicated with put the responsibility for dealing with the damage on everyone other than themselves and finally said they would do nothing to compensate him for his loss. So Carroll promised the last person to finally say no to compensation (Ms. Irlweg) that he would write and produce three songs about his experience with United Airlines and make videos for each to be viewed online by anyone in the world. This is the first of those songs.

Enlightenment "These are documentaries similar to what you'd see on PBS or the Discovery Channel," Kawasaki says. For example, view "Genocide: Worse than War | Full-length documentary | PBS" (http://youtu.be/w7cZuhqSzzc). Daniel Jonah Goldhagen's ground-breaking documentary premiered on PBS on April 14, 2010. It documents his travels, teachings, and interviews in nine countries around the world. In a film that is highly cinematic and evocative, Goldhagen speaks with victims, perpetrators, witnesses, politicians, diplomats, historians, humanitarian aid workers, and journalists, all with the purpose of explaining and understanding the critical features of genocide and how to finally stop it.

Education "Educational videos show you how to do things and use products," says Kawasaki. For example, take 2 minutes and 12 seconds to examine "How To Fold a T-shirt in 2 seconds" (http://youtu.be/An0mFZ3enhM). VideoJug presents a handy guide to cutting your folding time down to almost nothing!

Kawasaki says one way to remember these four types of video is recognizing that they form the acronym *IEEE*, which is funny in a nerd humor way. ("If you don't get it, don't worry," he adds.)

Kawasaki also makes another important point: "The goal of companies is often to create a 'viral video.' You know, the kind that millions of people watch in a few days—for example, the Old Spice guy videos. This is the kind of video every other company wishes it or its expensive agency created."

He concludes, "Don't make this your goal. Luck makes a video go viral, and 'get lucky' is not a good strategy. The right goal is to provide a steady supply of video that is inspiring, entertaining, enlightening, or educational and that, over time, enchants people."

Where and When Do They Discover New Videos?

This brings us to the next question: Where and when do opinion leaders discover new videos worth sharing with their followers?

There is lots of market research on where Internet users *watch* online video content and which video sites they visit.

For example, Nielsen reports that Americans streamed more than 15 billion videos during May 2011. Table 2.4 shows the top online video destinations by total streams in the United States that month.

▶ **Table 2.4** Top online video destinations by total streams (May 2011, US)

Video Brand	Total Streams (000)
YouTube	8,860,520
Hulu	852,173
VEVO	414,615
MSN/WindowsLive/Bing	266,712
Yahoo!	193,344
Dailymotion	150,340
Turner-SI Digital Network	149,102
AOL Media Network	148,727
Facebook	135,168
CBS Entertainment Websites	120,707

Source: Nielsen

In other words, 8.9 billion videos were streamed on YouTube via PCs/laptops from home and work locations during May 2011. But there is very little data on where viewers *discover* videos. One of the few studies that asked this question was conducted by TubeMogul research. It was published February 12, 2009, but it is no longer posted on the company's site. Fortunately, I saved the pie chart that showed the findings, which you can see in Figure 2.13.

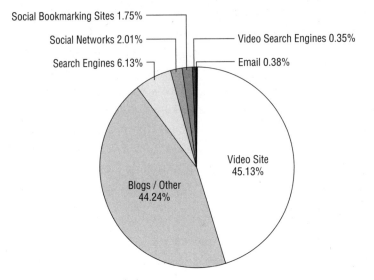

Figure 2.13 Video Discovery by Source

TubeMogul's research found that 45.13 percent of viewers discovered videos by going to a video site (i.e., going to YouTube and running a search or clicking around the featured or related videos). Another 44.24 percent of viewers discovered videos embedded on blogs and other sites. And 6.13 percent of viewers discovered videos with search engines. At that point, only 2.01 percent of viewers discovered videos on social networks.

Since almost as many viewers discover videos on blogs as on video sites, this makes most of the bloggers who embed videos opinion leaders. It also makes the new "As Seen On" links on YouTube's video pages a key way to identify many of the opinion leaders that helped specific videos "take off."

YouTube launched As Seen On pages on June 10, 2011. On the YouTube Blog, Kurt Wilms, product manager, and Nathan Hunt, software engineer, shared two messages.

To creators and partners, they said, "We've built dedicated pages that highlight your embedded videos. This means that there is now a place on YouTube to find videos mentioned on your favorite blogs and sites."

To bloggers and site owners, they added, "This is another way all that hard work you put into building your readership can pay off and generate even more traffic for your site. You might even get your site exposed to a whole new audience via people who encounter it for the first time on YouTube, so keep up the great work!"

Now that we've got a good idea of where opinion leaders discover new videos, let's look at when they discover them.

In April 2011, TubeMogul published a report on digital video advertising best practices. Among its findings, TubeMogul said, "A disproportionate share of online video viewing (42.3%) occurs during the eight-hour workday, making online video one of the best ways to reach people at work."

When and Where Do They Share New Videos?

This brings us to the next question: When and where do opinion leaders share new videos that they've discovered?

According to an Internet & American Life Project report published in July 2009, 19 percent of Internet users said they went to video sharing sites on a typical day.

However, few opinion leaders consistently find content that is compelling enough to share on a daily basis—although many share links with others at least a few times per month. Why are they so reluctant to share what they've discovered?

As Rogers noted in *Diffusion of Innovations*, "One role of the opinion leader in a social system is to help reduce uncertainty about an innovation for his or her followers. To fulfill this role, an opinion leader must demonstrate prudent judgment in decisions about adopting new ideas."

Pew also found that those who watched video "yesterday" reported more sharing compared with those who did not watch online video on the day prior to the survey.

This behavior is consistent with another observation by Rogers: "The interpersonal relationships between opinion leaders and their followers hang in a delicate balance. If an opinion leader becomes too innovative, or adopts a new idea too quickly, followers may begin to doubt his or her judgment."

This behavior is also consistent with the way people spread rumors. In the *Boston Sunday Globe* on October 12, 2008, Jesse Singal observed, "Aside from their use as a news grapevine, rumors serve a second purpose as well, researchers have found: People spread them to shore up their social networks, and boost their own importance within them." Researchers have also found that "people are rather specific about which rumors they share, and with whom."

So, does it take as much prudent judgment to share new videos as it does to share rumors? You be the judge. For example, if you had just discovered "T-Mobile Angry Birds Live" (http://youtu.be/jzIBZQkj6SY), shown in Figure 2.14, would you share it with your friends, contacts, or others?

The video shows how people use a simple smartphone to play a life-size version of the Angry Birds game—the single most successful mobile application of all time—complete with real shooting birds and exploding pigs! Sharing it via email, Facebook, Twitter, or Google's +1 button is shorthand for "this is pretty cool" or "you should check this out." But sharing a video also publicly gives it your stamp of approval.

"T-Mobile Angry Birds Live" was uploaded to YouTube on June 8, 2011, and within 10 days had become the most shared video in the Mashable Global Ads Chart. As Figure 2.15 illustrates, it had 433,038 shares as of June 26, 2011. This includes 404,563 Facebook shares, 27,814 tweets, and 661 blog posts.

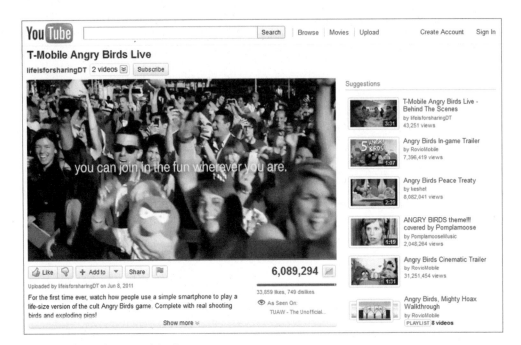

Figure 2.14 "T-Mobile Angry Birds Live"

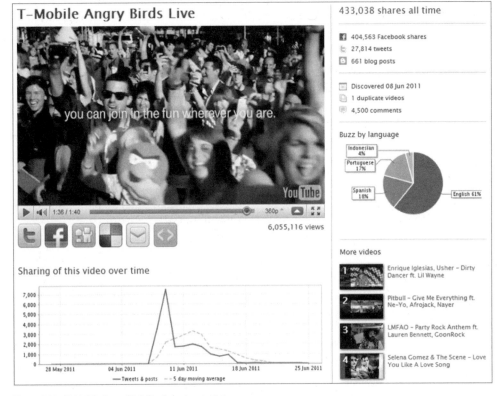

Figure 2.15 "T-Mobile Angry Birds Live" sharing statistics

However, you can see that sharing peaked quickly and then declined almost as quickly. This is why opinion leaders need to consistently find content that is compelling enough to share videos on a daily basis.

As Rogers observed, "Opinion leaders gain their perceived competency by serving as an avenue for the entrance of new ideas into their system." You won't maintain your opinion leadership very long if everyone else at work, home, or school has already seen the new video that you've just discovered.

Where They Share

Now that we've got a good idea of when opinion leaders share new videos that they've discovered, let's take a quick look at where they share them.

This brings us to a surprising finding in the Pew Research Center's July 2007 report: "Online video consumers are just as likely to have shared a video viewing experience in person as they are to have shared video online. The picture of the lone Internet user, buried in his or her computer, does not ring true with most who view online video."

Pew's 2007 report found that 57 percent of online video viewers had watched with other people, such as friends or family. Young adults were the most social online video viewers; 73 percent of video consumers ages 18 to 29 had watched with others.

Although the Pew Research Center has published several reports on video since then, it has never revisited this topic. However, the fact that videos are often shared in person was confirmed by Brian Stelter of the *New York Times*, who wrote an article on January 5, 2008, that observed, "In cubicles across the country, lunchtime has become the new prime time, as workers click aside their spreadsheets to watch videos on YouTube, news highlights on CNN.com, or other Web offerings."

Stelter added, "In some offices, workers coordinate their midday Web-watching schedules, the better to shout out punch lines to one another across rows of desks. Some people gravitate to sites where they can reliably find webcasts of a certain length—say, a 3-minute political wrap-up—to minimize both their mouse clicks and the sandwich crumbs that wind up in the keyboard."

So, go take a walk around your office at lunchtime. If you stumble across half a dozen people watching videos on YouTube, don't interrupt them. It's okay. They're probably opinion leaders. And it's prime time for sharing new content with their followers.

Then, watch closely to see if one member of the small group does the driving while others sit in the passenger seats. Does it appear that this opinion leader discovered some of these new videos yesterday and is only a day ahead of his peers?

Why Don't More New Videos Go Viral?

Now, there is at least some market research that asks the question, Why do some new videos go viral? But, there is no market research I know about that even begins to ask the question, Why don't more new videos go viral?

It seems that market researchers know that most of their paying clients want to hear about success stories. But this can give you a skewed view of the online video market. This tendency to overestimate the success rate of online videos is called the Lake Wobegon effect because it assumes that "all the women are strong, all the men are good looking, and all the children are above average."

This explains why so many new YouTubers are tempted to shoot first and ask questions later. But they aren't alone.

As this was written, YouTube was hosting about 299 million videos. And by the time you read this, there will be millions more.

As Figure 2.16 illustrates, the YouTube Blog announced on May 25, 2011, that more than 48 hours of video were uploaded to the site every minute.

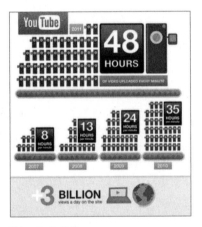

Figure 2.16 48 Hours

I teach a video marketing course in a couple of the Rutgers Mini-MBA programs, and many of the participants have trouble understanding what uploading 48 hours of video every minute means.

To help them to "grok" the significance of this data point, I tell them something my mom used to say: "That's more than you can shake a stick at." (Mom was a math teacher at East Lansing High School and one of the first female shop teachers in the state of Michigan.)

Then, I do the math. Let's say the typical YouTube video is 3 minutes long. So, 48 hours of video equals 960 3-minute videos. And if 960 videos are uploaded each minute, this means 9,676,800 new videos are uploaded to YouTube every week.

And that means aspiring YouTube stars have more competitors than New Jersey has inhabitants. With so many competing videos vying for attention, the odds that your video will "go viral" aren't good. Consider the statistics presented in Figure 2.17 for total views of YouTube videos: Only one out of every 250 videos uploaded to YouTube ever gets more than a million views.

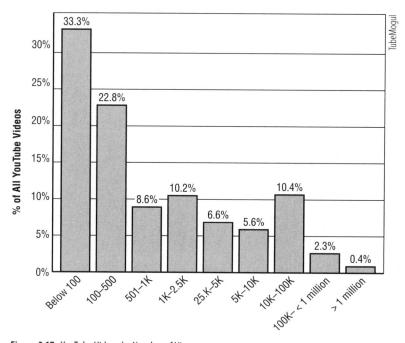

Figure 2.17 YouTube Videos by Number of Views

The stats in Figure 2.17 come from TubeMogul's May 2011 report "Digital Video Advertising Best Practices." The research took a random sample of YouTube videos to compare all-time views.

TubeMogul said, "Even getting featured on YouTube's homepage yields fewer views than it used to, despite the site's meteoric growth (or perhaps because of it). Videos in the 'Featured' or 'Spotlight' spots on YouTube's homepage average 86,100 views per day they are featured. That represents a 28.2 percent reduction compared to the same measure in 2008, when videos featured averaged 119,864 views per day."

TubeMogul added, "The result is that paid media is now necessary to get videos watched, even in viral video campaigns."

On April 19, 2010, James Zern, software engineer, wrote a post on the YouTube Blog about transcoding all the videos on the site into WebM. In paragraph four, he said, "So far we've already transcoded videos that make up 99 percent of views on the site or nearly 30 percent of all videos into WebM."

In other words, more than 70 percent of all videos on YouTube make up only 1 percent of the views on the site.

So, getting excited that you've just uploaded a new video to YouTube is funny—sorta, kinda like Navin R. Johnson (played by Steve Martin) getting excited that "The new phone book is here, the new phone book is here!" was funny in the 1979 movie *The Jerk*:

> Harry Hartounian: *"Boy, I wish I could get that excited about nothing."*
>
> Navin R. Johnson: *"Nothing? Are you kidding? Page 73—Johnson, Navin R.! I'm somebody now! Millions of people look at this book every day! This is the kind of spontaneous publicity—your name in print—that makes people. I'm in print! Things are going to start happening to me now."*

Seriously, let me share a story with you of an early failure in YouTube and video marketing that my long-time friend Michael Kolowich had the courage and integrity to share with readers of his Web Video Expert blog. It's the story of the Internet TV channel that Michael's firm, DigiNovations, created in January 2007 for the Mitt Romney for President campaign. Mitt TV is widely acknowledged to be the first comprehensive video channel for a presidential campaign.

However, on February 7, 2008, Romney suspended his campaign for the presidential nomination following the results of the 2008 Super Tuesday primaries—despite raising $110 million for his campaign ($45 million in personal loans and $65 million from individual donors). In other words, winning your party's nomination and getting elected president involves much more than just raising campaign contributions.

Lessons from Mitt TV

On February 10, 2008, Kolowich posted "Ten Lessons from Mitt TV." I encourage you to read the entire post on his Web Video Expert blog. But here's a sampling of lessons that you will want to know about and discuss with others:

YouTube is a two-edged sword. A lot of the 2008 presidential campaigns relied on YouTube channels generously "given" to them by the video site. And there's no question that a lot of independent traffic saw the clips based on YouTube searches. But if part of the idea was not just to inform but also to inspire people to act (give money, sign up, give us their email, etc.), then Kolowich thinks YouTube was weak at the "call to action" part. That was certainly true in 2007 and early 2008, although YouTube's "call to action" offerings got stronger in October 2008, when "click to buy" links were added to the watch pages of thousands of YouTube partner videos.

A YouTube channel is necessary but not sufficient. Because of #1, the Romney campaign decided to invest in its own very rich channel that eventually had more than 400 video clips on it, which were closely associated with its "calls to action" in the campaign. And, according to Kolowich, the most remarkable statistic of all is that more people watched the Romney campaign's clips on Mitt TV than on its YouTube channel. Other marketers have reported similar results.

A content-managed video platform is vital to success. Kolowich believed that a content-managed web video publishing system was vital to building something as sophisticated as Mitt TV. But he didn't realize at the time that the share of market of the video search engines that crawled this platform was getting smaller each and every month.

Seeds and feeds build viewership. Although the Romney campaign had its share of "I want my Mitt TV" people tuning in every day to see what was new, the key to building Mitt TV's audience (which got as high as 70,000+ viewings a day in the late stages of the campaign) was outreach—to bloggers, through press releases, through RSS feeds. The result was that there were more than 23,000 references to Mitt TV on Google and more than 2,800 sites linking to Mitt TV. However, the vast majority of videos that appeared in Google universal search results from May 2007 through November 2008 came from YouTube, not video search engines or individual websites.

Don't believe everything you read about clip length. The conventional wisdom is that video clips need to be under 2 minutes to have a prayer of getting watched. But looking over the viewing statistics, Kolowich saw that many of the most popular clips were complete speeches or events that were as long as 20 minutes or even more. It's also worth noting that YouTube raised the upload limit to 15 minutes for all users on July 29, 2010, and began allowing selected users with a history of complying with the YouTube Community Guidelines and its copyright rules to upload videos longer than 15 minutes on December 9, 2010.

Listen to the data. According to Kolowich, one of the advantages of having their own Internet TV channel was that they could get a tremendous amount of data about what worked and what didn't. Since YouTube Insight wasn't available until March 2008, Kolowich used Google Analytics to watch patterns of viewership and correlate it to different outreach efforts in 2007. He could see which clips were being viewed and for how long. And he could see where traffic was coming from. All this was useful in making Mitt TV a more effective channel.

So, why didn't more of Romney's new videos go viral?

For starters, Kolowich says the goal of Mitt TV wasn't to go viral. As he said, the objective was "to inspire people to act (give money, sign up, give us their email, etc.)." And Mitt TV reached this goal.

As Kolowich revealed in a post on April 23, 2008: "Without disclosing specific numbers, we found that when we could use web video to bring a viewer to the campaign website and call them to action, the payoff—in terms of contributions, volunteer sign-ups, referrals, event attendance, etc.—was orders of magnitude more than the cost of serving up the video. That's why we favored video on our own website over the many clips we posted on YouTube."

But the other reason so few of Romney's new videos went viral can be found in the previous paragraph: The campaign treated online video like it was just a new type of infomercial and it favored video on its own website over the clips it posted on YouTube.

Was this the right video marketing strategy back then? Would the Romney campaign have done any better if its goal had been to change people's presidential preference instead of prompting them to give money, sign up, and provide their email? Would the Romney campaign have done any better if it had favored YouTube over Mitt TV?

I still don't have all the answers, but I'm beginning to ask the right questions: If online video is better at informing, inspiring, and connecting than it is at direct response, then in addition to preaching to the choir on Mitt TV, shouldn't the Romney campaign have also spent more time reaching out to bring more people into the church? Should the Romney campaign have spent more effort reaching out to opinion leaders and trying to win the "invisible caucus" that was held on YouTube in 2007?

What's an invisible caucus? As Linda Feldmann of the *Christian Science Monitor* reported on February 26, 2007, there was a lot of media buzz about "what's come to be known as the 'invisible primary'—the early jockeying for money, top campaign staff, and high-profile endorsements that winnow the presidential field long before any caucuses or primaries are held."

On June 15, 2008, the Pew Internet Project reported 35 percent of Americans had watched online political videos—a figure that nearly tripled the reading Pew got in the 2004 presidential race. And Pew also found that supporters of Barack Obama outpaced supporters of both Hillary Clinton and John McCain in their usage of online video.

So, I'm calling the early jockeying for opinion leaders in YouTube's news and politics category an "invisible caucus." And it is worth asking, Did winning it help a former community organizer's presidential campaign "take off" while skipping it hurt a former CEO's chances of getting a critical mass of opinion leaders to share his videos with others?

Who knows? Maybe we'll learn more during the 2012 presidential campaign. Nevertheless, on April 23, 2008, Kolowich posted this to his blog:

> *Both the Romney and Obama campaigns understood the power of video not only to get the message out but also to attract, engage, and actuate supporters on the main campaign website…. It may be pure coincidence that the candidates' fundraising performance correlates with their sophistication on Internet video, but our experience suggests that sophisticated use of web video certainly has an impact on keeping an active, vibrant base of supporters who visit often and want to stay involved.*

How Do YouTube and Video Marketing Work?

That leaves just one more question to ask: How do YouTube and video marketing work? This is the question that eight of the nine remaining chapters in this book will tackle. (In the final chapter, we'll take a quick look at the future.)

To help set the agenda for the next eight chapters of this step-by-step guide, let me share a couple of stories and three models of communication.

As Robert McKee, a creative writing instructor and author of *Story: Substance, Structure, Style and the Principles of Screenwriting* (It Books, 1997) has observed, "Storytelling is the most powerful way to put ideas into the world today."

In 1939, Germany's frighteningly effective use of propaganda prompted US President Franklin Delano Roosevelt to create a group of "top men" to figure out how propaganda worked—just in case America went to war. One of these "top men" was Harold Lasswell.

Lasswell had received his bachelor of philosophy degree in 1922 and his Ph.D. in 1926 from the University of Chicago. He also studied at the Universities of London, Paris, Geneva, and Berlin during those years. In 1927, he wrote *Propaganda Technique in the World War.* He taught political science at the University of Chicago until 1938, when he went to Yale University to become a visiting lecturer at the Law School.

In 1939, Lasswell was named director of war communications research at the US Library of Congress. He quickly developed a "model of communication" that was just as quickly classified "top secret." Like a scene out of the movie *Raiders of the Lost Ark,* Lasswell discovered that propaganda—or what the Americans called the communication process—entailed five key elements.

As Figure 2.18 illustrates, Lasswell assembled these elements into a model and then turned the model into a simple question: Who says what in what channel to whom with what effect?

If you found the right answers to each of the five elements of the question, then you could create effective propaganda.

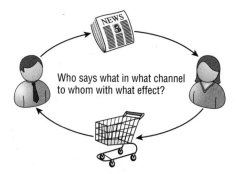

Who says what in what channel to whom with what effect?

Figure 2.18 Classic communication model

During World War II, US federal agencies used Lasswell's secret model to test a variety of propaganda techniques and to create some very powerful propaganda posters, films, and radio broadcasts. For example, it was discovered that "Help win the war" wasn't the most effective slogan to use for selling war bonds. It appealed to men, but not women. This led to the development of a more effective slogan: "Help win the war and bring the boys home."

Lasswell's model was declassified in 1948, and he published a paper on it. Both his model and his question, Who says what in which channel to whom with what effect?, have been included in Philip Kotler's textbook *Marketing Management*, which has been used by hundreds of thousands of college students from 1967 to the present.

Let's fast-forward to the early days of search.

In 1995, I was the director of corporate communications at Ziff-Davis when the company invested in a start-up named Yahoo! The company's name was an acronym for Yet Another Hierarchical Officious Oracle. But that was an improvement over the company's original name: David and Jerry's Guide to the World Wide Web.

After getting to know the cofounders and Chief Yahoos, Jerry Yang and David Filo, I began to realize that search engines reversed Lasswell's model.

In 1998, I gave a presentation to the Public Relations Society of America (PRSA) chapter in Portland, Oregon. The audience included both PRSA members and students from Portland State University (PSU) who were majoring in PR. The title of my presentation was "How has PR changed in the Internet Age?"

I explained Lasswell's model and then showed them a new one (Figure 2.19) that I had developed at Ziff-Davis, which reversed the model and asked: "Who seeks what in what channel from whom with what effect?"

Figure 2.19 Search reverses the classic model.

I explained, "The old view of marketing assumes communication is a one-way street. Advertising and PR professionals sent their brand messages to the media. The state side of the media runs the ad messages, because they've been paid for, while the church side of the media decides which if any PR messages to run, because they are free. Potential buyers receive both church's and state's messages and decide which ones they're interested in responding to."

I continued, "With search engines, this whole process is reversed. Many potential buyers are no longer waiting passively to receive messages—98 percent of which are of little interest to them anyway. Instead, they're using search engines to find the 2 percent that they're already interested in. If they find your site during that search, they're already predisposed to take action. It's revolutionary."

What impact did my presentation have on the audience? I got a round of polite applause and a couple of questions about alternative career choices from some of the PSU students. However, several PRSA veterans came up to me afterward and asked that I never, ever give that speech again. Their clients were happy and they didn't want me rocking the boat.

That brings us to the early days of online video.

By August 2006, I had uploaded my first video to YouTube (Figure 2.20) to promote "Hostage: The Jill Carroll story" for the *Christian Science Monitor*.

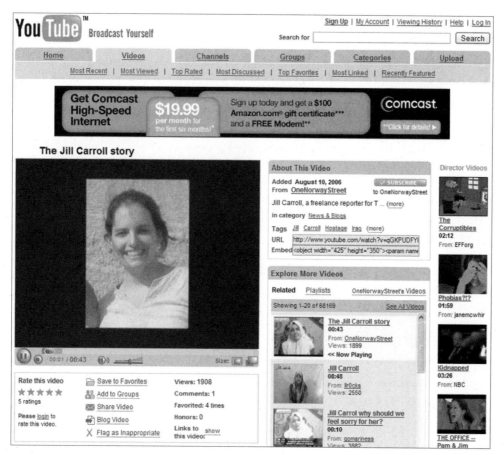

Figure 2.20 "The Jill Carroll story"

CNN, Yahoo! News, AOL News, *Huffington Post*, and Boing Boing used the video in their stories. Within the first 24 hours after the series went live, more than 450,000 unique visitors flooded CSMonitor.com, seven times its daily average in July.

Although video search engines fit into my model of communication, YouTube wasn't a video search engine. It was a video sharing site.

If YouTube were a search engine, it would be the second largest search engine after Google. According to comScore qSearch, more than 3.5 billion searches were conducted on YouTube during April 2011 in the United States. Another 764 million searches were conducted on YouTube that month in Canada. And 849 million searches were conducted on YouTube in the UK. Worldwide, 21.1 billion searches were conducted on YouTube during April 2011. More search activity was observed on a video sharing site that month than was observed on Yahoo! Search or Bing.

So I started developing a new model of communication.

And that's when I remembered what Rogers had written in *Diffusion of Innovations* about the two-step model of communication flows: "The first step, from media sources to opinion leaders, is mainly a transfer of *information*, whereas the second step, from opinion leaders to their followers, also involves the spread of interpersonal *influence*."

If search engines had reversed Lasswell's model, what had YouTube done to the two-step flow model? Figure 2.21 illustrates my new model of how YouTube and video marketing work.

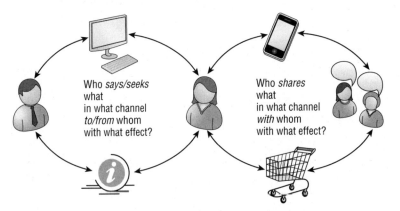

Figure 2.21 Video sharing changes the model again.

To left-brained people, my new model might look like the symbol for infinity. To right-brained people, it may appear like the butterfly's wings that flapped in Brazil and set off a tornado in Texas.

But, if you start in the center, here is how you would phrase the five key elements of the question on the left side of the model:

Who: Identify your top YouTube opinion leaders.

Seeks what: Produce original videos worth watching.

In what channel: Use YouTube, not Google Videos.

From whom: Optimize your video—particularly the headline, description, and tags.

With what effect: Obsess on Insights to determine where and how people are finding your videos.

As we've already seen with live streaming of the royal wedding, you can also "Broadcast Yourself" on special occasions using Lasswell's classic model, Who says what in what channel to whom with what effect?

You can also broadcast your video ad with a YouTube Homepage Roadblock, an option that costs some $375,000 and allows brands to own the homepage for 24 hours. The YouTube homepage averages more than 50 million impressions and over 18 million unique visitors per day in the United States, with some formats averaging above an 11 percent interaction rate.

But most marketers, advertisers, videographers, and partners will want to use the revised question, Who seeks what in what channel from whom with what effect?

Starting again in the center of my new model, here is how you would phrase the five key elements of the question on the right side of the model:

Who: Reach out to your YouTube opinion leaders.

Shares what: Create compelling content worth sharing.

In what channel: Use blogs, email, Facebook, Twitter, and Google's +1 button.

With whom: Get opinion leaders to reach 5 to 10 times more viewers.

With what effect: Add links and Call-to-Action overlays to drive traffic to off-YouTube web pages.

Since opinion leaders must continually look over their shoulders and consider where their followers are regarding new videos, this part of the new communications model is also a two-way street.

For example, if most of an opinion leader's followers have already seen Eepy Bird's "The Coke Zero & Mentos Rocket Car" (`http://youtu.be/i-hXcRtbj1Y`), then sharing it undercuts the opinion leader's "leadership."

On the other hand, if most of an opinion leader's followers aren't into JayFunk's "finger tutting," then sharing Samsung Mobile France's "Unleash Your Fingers" (`http://youtu.be/zyMfpJh3h4A`) also undercuts the opinion leader's "leadership."

These are a lot of elements to master, but the bulk of this book will help you map out your video marketing strategy. I thought about covering the left side of the model before covering the right side. But many of the elements on both sides need to be addressed in parallel.

Besides, a butterfly doesn't flap one wing at a time.

So, I'll alternate between the discovery process and the sharing loop. Unless you've got the exception that proves the rule, that's how YouTube and video marketing work.

Month 1: Make Videos Worth Watching

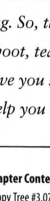

It's easy to make videos on YouTube. So some people shoot first and ask questions later. They tell others, "I figure we can blue-screen the kids in later." But it's hard to make videos worth watching. So, this chapter will help you get ready to shoot, teach you the basics of video production, give you some advanced video production tips, and help you evaluate your video advertising options.

Chapter Contents:

Happy Tree #3,079
Week 1: Get Ready to Shoot
Week 2: Learn Video Production Basics
Week 3: Get Advanced Video Production Tips
Week 4: Evaluate Video Advertising Options

Happy Tree #3,079

YouTube is designed to make producing videos as easy as possible.

But one of the videos on YouTubeHelp's channel makes it appear almost too easy. Go to http://youtu.be/Apadq9iPNxA and watch "How do I make a video?" As Figure 3.1 illustrates, "Painting with Pictures featuring Rob Boss" quickly covers the basics in just 2 minutes and 22 seconds.

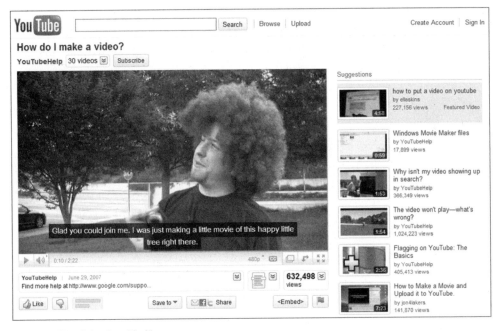

Figure 3.1 "How do I make a video?"

According to this spoof of Bob Ross, creator and host of *The Joy of Painting*, all you need to make a video is a device that can capture digital movies. This could be your cell phone, a digital camera, or a web cam. You will then copy the digital movies to your computer using a FireWire cable or USB mass storage device.

Next, you can either upload them as is or edit them with software such as Windows Movie Maker or iMovie to add titles and special effects. Or, you can use Adobe Premiere Pro or Apple's Final Cut Pro to edit and improve your videos.

Once you're happy with your final result, you'll need to save the video in a format that YouTube can accept. Unless you're a professional video producer, I recommend that you save your videos as QuickTime MOV, Windows AVI, or MPG files—these are the most common formats and they work well in YouTube.

The YouTube staffer in this spoof video, who calls himself "Rob Boss" says near the end, "I like to call this one, 'Happy Tree #3,079'. I really like it." Unfortunately, he does not cover all the tips and tricks for making better videos.

So, if you have told someone, "I figure we can blue-screen the kids in later," like the guy in Figure 3.2, then you will need more detailed information on special effects.

"I figure we can blue-screen the kids in later."

Figure 3.2 "I figure we can blue-screen the kids in later." (Cartoon by Alex Gregory in the *New Yorker*, January 31, 2000.)

This chapter is designed to help you out. It will even give you some tips about using the chroma-key technique, which is also referred to as blue-screen, green-screen, and color keying.

Week 1: Get Ready to Shoot

On March 24, 2011, Software Engineer Stanley Wang announced the beta launch of www.youtube.com/create. On this new page, anyone can use video creation sites GoAnimate, Xtranormal, or Stupeflix to make original videos and post them directly to YouTube—even if they don't have a video camera.

Wang said, "Creating animation can be pretty hard and often requires expensive software, but GoAnimate and Xtranormal Movie Maker let you create animated videos with just a text storyline. In minutes, you can make two bears discuss fiction-writing, or create your own cooking show parody."

He added, "Stupeflix lets you pull together your own images, clips and even maps into a dynamic video slideshow. You can tell a personal story or even make a jazzy promo for your craft company."

This means you can make an original creation in minutes—and it's free, although some of these sites also offer premium services that you can access directly from their sites.

However, many aspiring videographers are ready to take the next step. So let's start by answering some of the questions that they frequently ask:

Monday: What is the best camcorder?

Tuesday: What is the best video editing software?

Wednesday: What is the best video format for YouTube?

Thursday: How long should a YouTube video be?

Friday: How do I make a YouTube video worth watching?

Monday: What Is the Best Camcorder?

No one wants to buy a new camcorder in December only to discover that a better, cheaper model will be introduced in January at the International Consumer Electronics Show (CES). CES is the world's largest consumer technology trade show.

Because CES is such a key event for new camcorder launches, you might want to wait until the second week of January when it is held to find out what next year's best camcorder will be.

Or, if you can't wait until next January, try searching for "best camcorder" using Google, YouTube, or Bing to answer this question.

Or, read the latest camcorder reviews and buying guides:

CNET: `http://reviews.cnet.com/`

Consumer Reports: `www.consumerreports.org/`

PCMag.com: `www.pcmag.com/reviews`

Or, watch camcorder reviews on popular YouTube channels:

Gizmodo: `www.youtube.com/gizmodo`

LockerGnome: `www.youtube.com/lockergnome`

TigerDirect TV: `www.youtube.com/TigerDirectBlog`

And be forewarned: The camcorder category changes constantly. When the first edition of this book was published in 2009, the best camcorder was the $199 Flip UltraHD from Cisco (Figure 3.3).

Figure 3.3 Flip UltraHD camcorder

YouTubers loved the Flip because it worked: the first time, every time. When something happened worth shooting, you pressed the big red button on the back. You didn't have to mess with tapes or disks or menus or mode dials or flipping out a screen.

That's why the Flip became incredibly popular. Pure Digital Technologies sold 2 million Flips in the first six months. It became the best-selling camcorder on Amazon.com and remained there every month since.

Cisco Systems Inc. bought the company in 2009 for $590 million. As of April 2001, it represented 37 percent of all camcorders sold, and its market share was climbing.

Then, Cisco killed it. The whole division was shut down and 550 people were laid off.

So, what is the best camcorder now?

Check out some of the new pocket camcorders, which also make it easy to take and edit videos on the spur of the moment. You can plug many of them directly into your computer to easily upload video to YouTube.

In recent tests by *Consumer Reports*, both the JVC Picsio GC-FM2 and Kodak Playsport Zx3 got top ratings. At $180, the JVC Picsio GC-FM2 received very good marks for picture quality and ability to work in low light. At $135, the Kodak Playsport Zx3 has comparable picture quality but is less effective in low light.

At the high end, check out the Sony NEX-VG10 and the Panasonic HDC-SDT750. At $2,000, the Sony NEX-VG10 can use interchangeable SLR lenses. At $1,400, the Panasonic HDC-SDT750 has 3D capabilities and excellent HD quality.

And you may not need the best camcorder to start shooting your masterpiece. If you already have a digital camcorder that captures in Digital8, MiniDV, HDV, or any of the DVD formats, then you're ready to go. Your camcorder will need some kind of direct connection to your computer, either to the USB or FireWire port or by inserting the DVD you've recorded.

If you have an analog camcorder that uses VHS, VHS-C, SVHS-C, 8mm, or Hi8 tape, then you can still get your videos onto YouTube. It will require an extra step and some additional equipment, though, because these camcorders are not usually equipped with computer connections. You will also need to digitize the video with a converter box, which will convert the analog signal from the camcorder to a digital signal that the computer can understand. A good analog-to-digital video converter is Elgato's eyeTV hybrid; it's the size of a flash drive, costs $99, and works for both Macs and PCs.

Maybe buying the best web cam is an easier way to get started.

What's the best web cam? Check out the Logitech Webcam Pro 9000. You'll enjoy razor-sharp images—even in close-ups—thanks to Logitech's Carl Zeiss optics with premium autofocus. You'll also experience fluid, true-to-life widescreen video (720p) and snapshots at up to 8 megapixels.

Tuesday: What Is the Best Video Editing Software?

Most new computers come with basic video editing software installed, like Windows Movie Maker or Apple's iMovie. These programs allow you to not only edit the video, but add effects, titles, and music to make your video look and sound more interesting.

However, as Brad O'Farrell notes, "A lot of sounds and packaged special effects in iMovie and Movie Maker are so prevalent on YouTube that they're now clearly visible denotations of amateur content." He advises using plug-ins and original sound effects to avoid homogeneity.

If you want to be a bit more hands-on with your video, check out Adobe Premiere Pro or Apple's Final Cut Pro.

Adobe Premiere Pro is a real-time, timeline-based video editing software application. It is part of the Adobe Creative Suite, a suite of graphic design, video editing, and web development applications, although it can also be purchased separately. Even when purchased separately, it comes bundled with Adobe Encore and Adobe OnLocation. Premiere Pro supports many video editing cards and plug-ins for accelerated processing, additional file format support, and video/audio effects.

Final Cut Pro is a professional nonlinear editing software application developed by Apple Inc. The application is available only for Mac OS X version 10.4 or later and is a module of the Final Cut Studio product. The software logs and captures video onto an internal or external hard drive, where it can be edited and processed.

But, as Figure 3.4 illustrates, CyberLink PowerDirector 9 won the *PC Magazine* Editors' Choice award in this category on December 7, 2010. Therefore, it is what I would recommend today.

Figure 3.4 CyberLink PowerDirector 9

According to Michael Muchmore of PCMag.com, "The fastest consumer video editor around gets even faster with the latest release of PowerDirector 9, now available as a full 64-bit Windows app." He adds, "This is important for basic things like starting the program up and scrubbing through the timeline, and even more so when it comes to rendering a complex movie production with picture-in-picture and other effects."

So CyberLink PowerDirector 9 is the best video editing software (as of when this was written). But things change. So you may want to read more recent video editing software reviews:

CNET: http://reviews.cnet.com

PCMag.com: www.pcmag.com/reviews

Videomaker: http://www.videomaker.com/learn/product-reviews

Wednesday: What Is the Best Video Format for YouTube?

There is a wide range of **video codec formats, audio codec formats,** and **container formats** in use, and YouTube supports a very wide variety of them. Here's a list of some well-known formats that YouTube supports:

- WebM files (Vp8 video codec and Vorbis Audio codec)
- MPEG4, 3GPP, and MOV files (typically supporting H264, MPEG4 video codecs, and AAC audio codec)
- AVI (format output by many cameras, typically with an MJPEG video codec and PCM audio)
- MPEGPS (typically supporting MPEG2 video codec and MP2 audio)
- WMV
- FLV (Adobe, FLV1 video codec, MP3 audio)

But the best video format for YouTube is a moving target.

For example, YouTube originally offered videos at only one quality level, displayed at a resolution of 320×240 pixels using the H.263 Sorenson Spark codec with mono MP3 audio. In June 2007, YouTube added an option to watch videos in 3GP format on mobile phones. In March 2008, YouTube added a high-quality mode, which increased the resolution to 480×360 pixels. In November 2008, YouTube added 720p HD support. With this new feature, YouTube began a switchover to H.264/MPEG-4 AVC as its default video codec. In November 2008, the YouTube player was also changed from a 4:3 aspect ratio to a widescreen 16:9 aspect ratio. In November 2009, YouTube added 1080p HD support. In July 2010, YouTube announced that it had launched a range of videos in 4K format, which allows a resolution of up to 4096×3072 pixels. To give you some perspective on how big this is, the ideal screen size for a 4K video is 25 feet.

Table 3.1 is a summary of the audio and video specifications you need for the best results on YouTube (as of when this was written).

▶ **Table 3.1** Best video format for YouTube

Specification	Value
Video format	H.264, MPEG-4 preferred
Aspect ratio	16:9 aspect ratio recommended
Resolution	1080p, or full HD, recommended
Audio format	MP3 or AAC preferred
Frames per second	30
Maximum length	15 minutes (2–3 minutes recommended)
Maximum file size	2 GB

Since YouTube's file formats change fairly frequently, let me also offer some general tips:

- Always upload your video in the original format in the highest quality possible; YouTube will automatically convert it to the best quality available at the time.

- YouTube prefers deinterlaced files.

- If your file is using H.264 encoding, YouTube prefers files without PAFF/MBAFF encoding.

- Audio and video lengths should be the same and audio should start at the same time as the video.

To find the latest audio and video specifications you need for the best results on YouTube, check out Wikipedia's YouTube page. Its content on YouTube's video technology seems to be updated more frequently than the advice under "Best Formats for Uploading" in the YouTube Handbook.

Thursday: How Long Should a YouTube Video Be?

Long enough to reach a point.

The video shown in Figure 3.5, "NPR's Scott Simon: How to Tell a Story" (www.youtube.com/watch?v=tiX_WNdJu6w), which is a part of the YouTube Reporters' Center, gives similar advice.

Simon says, "A story ought to have a point. I don't mean a lesson or a moral or even a punchline, but a point—something that people can take away from it."

So, how long does it take to reach a point?

Generally, I recommend that a YouTube video should be about 2 to 3 minutes long, but it can be up to 15 minutes.

Andy Warhol said in 1968, "In the future, everyone will be world-famous for 15 minutes." Well, you can get "15 minutes of fame" on YouTube—if you need it.

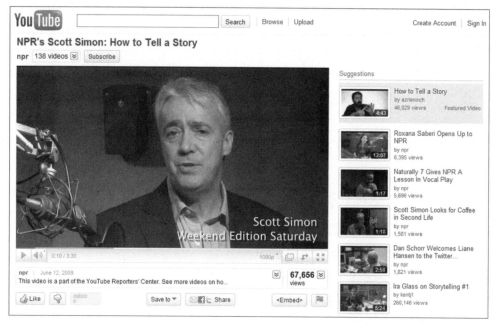

Figure 3.5 "NPR's Scott Simon: How to Tell a Story"

On July 29, 2010, Joshua Siegel, product manager of upload and video management, announced on the Official YouTube Blog, "We've increased the upload limit to 15 minutes." The upload limit for non-partners had been 10 minutes since March 26, 2006.

Why did YouTube change the limit?

According to Siegel, "Well, we've spent significant resources on creating and improving our state-of-the-art Content ID system and many other powerful tools for copyright owners. Now, all of the major U.S. movie studios, music labels and over 1,000 other global partners use Content ID to manage their content on YouTube. Because of the success of these ongoing technological efforts, we are able to increase the upload limit today."

So, what can you do with the new 15-minute limit that you couldn't do with the old 10-minute limit?

And how much of a typical online video is actually watched?

On December 1, 2008, TubeMogul research found that most videos steadily lose viewers once "play" is clicked, with an average 10.4 percent of viewers clicking away after 10 seconds and 53.6 percent leaving after 1 minute.

> **Note:** TubeMogul was able to conduct this viewer-engagement study because of its acquisition of Illumenix, a video metrics firm, in October 2008. Illumenix tracks how much of a video is actually watched, when a viewer clicks away, and what the most popular segments of a video are. TubeMogul renamed this Flash-based analytics service InPlay.

For a two-week period, TubeMogul measured viewed seconds for a sample of 188,055 videos, totaling 22,724,606 streams, on six top video sites. The study's findings were dramatic. As Figure 3.6 illustrates, most online video viewers watch mere seconds, rather than minutes, of a video.

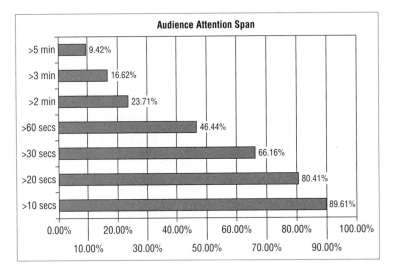

Figure 3.6 Audience attention span

On August 16, 2010, the comScore Video Metrix service reported that the duration of the average online content video was 4:48, while the average online video ad was 0:24.

Why are the TubeMogul and comScore data so different?

TubeMogul only studied short-form content—full television episodes being streamed on sites like Hulu were not included. And YouTube was also not included because TubeMogul's code was not in YouTube's player.

Fortunately, the folks at comScore shared some of the Video Metrix key measures with me. That enabled me to determine that the average video on Hulu is watched for 9:04 per viewer, while the average video on YouTube is watched for 2:38 per viewer.

That's why a YouTube video should be about 2 to 3 minutes long—although you can hold an audience's attention longer than average if your YouTube video is worth watching.

If you're scripting your video, you should keep in mind that the audience's patience is much shorter with online video than with other mediums. While you can usually get away with two or three minutes for your video to reach its "point," you also have to consider the crucial first few seconds. Movies and TV shows often begin with a gradual buildup, but with online video it's sometimes more effective to start with a blitz of confusion or intrigue.

You want to catch the viewer's attention quickly before you slow down the pace to build toward your ultimate "point" or else the majority of your potential audience will press the Backspace key. And if you're a YouTube partner, you'll get paid less if viewers don't watch until the 15 second mark when the banner ad pops up over your video.

Avoid things like title cards, long opening credits, and long establishing shots and try to open your video with snappy dialog, action, or special effects. Adding music to the very beginning of your video is another way to make the pacing seem faster and to hold the audience longer. Many of the most successful YouTube users, like WhatTheBuck?! and sxePhil, will start their videos with rapid-fire jokes before going into a brief catchy intro jingle and then finally starting the video proper at a more tra-ditional pace.

To see this for yourself, just go to the Viral Video Chart and look at the Mashable Global Ads Chart. As this was witten, the most shared ads of all time were: "Volkswagen Commercial: The Force," which is 1 minute, 2 seconds long, "Christmas Food Court Flash Mob, Hallelujah Chorus – Must See!," which is 4 minutes and 57 seconds long, and "Ken Block's Gymkhana THREE, Part 2; Ultimate Playground; l'Autodrome, France," which is 7 minutes and 42 seconds long.

But each one is long enough to reach a point.

Friday: How Do I Make a YouTube Video Worth Watching?

Using the best camcorder, best video editing software, and best video format for YouTube is important. But it is also important to tell a great story.

This is the key to making a YouTube video worth watching.

Of course, I'm not the only one who understands the importance of storytelling. Sony's Backstage 101 online learning center once had an article called "Tell a Story with Video." Unfortunately, Backstage 101 was permanently closed in April 2010.

According to Sony, "Before you shoot a single frame, you should understand exactly how you want your story to be told and what you want the audience to take away from it. No matter what kind of story you choose to tell, the best place to start isn't with a camera and microphone—it's with a pen and paper." Sony advised that you ask a few key questions:

Who is your audience? Is this video for a business audience, or is it for your fam-ily and friends?

What point of view will you take? Will you tell it from your own perspective or from that of one of your subjects, or will a third-person narrator do the talking?

Where does the story take place?

When do the key events that propel the story take place?

Why is this story worth telling?

How will you tell the story? How will your video connect emotionally with the audience?

Sony added, "There's also a language to storytelling. If you don't know how to speak it, you've watched enough movies and TV programs to understand it. Start wide to give the audience an idea of where you are. Cut to medium to learn more about your subject. Get tight to capture the emotion."

I miss Backstage 101. It had a lot of great content.

Week 2: Learn Video Production Basics

After getting answers to some of the questions that aspiring videographers frequently ask, you will want to learn the basics of video production.

You should start by going to YouTube's Video Toolbox at www.youtube.com/videotoolbox and watching the tips about camera techniques, lighting techniques, sound, and special effects. As Figure 3.7 illustrates, most of these tips and tricks are provided by *Videomaker* magazine.

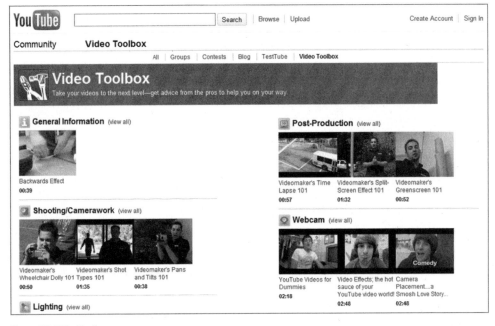

Figure 3.7 Video Toolbox

Published by York Publishing, *Videomaker* is the leading consumer magazine for video enthusiasts. If you go to the YouTube Handbook at www.youtube.com/t/yt_handbook_produce and compare it with the Video Toolbox, you will see that most of the videos are the same.

To take your videos to the next level, visit *Videomaker*'s channel at www.youtube.com/videomaker. Finally, to get more advice from the pros, go to www.videomaker.com/youtube.

If you sign up for *Videomaker*'s free e-newsletter, you'll also get a free tip sheet for videographers.

Here are some of the video production basics that you should learn:

Monday: Use storyboard software

Tuesday: Use classic camera techniques

Wednesday: Use a single lighting source

Thursday: Use natural sound

Friday: Use special effects

Monday: Use Storyboard Software

If you want to make videos worth watching, then a solid script and well-thought-out storyboard are basic ingredients.

In July 2010, Wynn Duncan, a freelance video producer and writer, wrote "Scriptwriting and Storyboarding Software Buyer's Guide" for *Videomaker*.

According to Duncan, there are two different types of scriptwriting software that you can choose from.

The first are stand-alone programs, such as Final Draft, Movie Magic, and Celtx. "These are self-contained with everything (supposedly) that you need to let your creativity take flight," he says.

The second type of scriptwriting software is actually a template for your word processor. "When you install it, your word processor then functions (at least in certain respects) as screenwriting software," he adds. Examples of this kind of product would include ScriptWright and Script Wizard.

Good scriptwriting software will have what's called an index card feature: the ability to create an initial outline, make notes about each point, and then rearrange to your heart's content. This feature can be found in programs such as Movie Magic.

If you get stuck, take a look at an "idea dictionary." Hollywood Screenplay has a tool called Storybase that provides hundreds of plot devices as well as story twists and turns to fuel your imagination. Another scriptwriting reference tool, The Writer's Software Companion, provides writing diagnostics, a dictionary of literary terms, story advice, and even a name dictionary.

A program's ease of use is important, but the way it handles revisions is even more important. "There's nothing worse than realizing you can't go back to an earlier script version when needed... and you don't remember what your changes were," says Duncan.

Final Draft allows you to clearly delineate between revisions as well as easily compare one with another so you can see how they differ. "Many scriptwriters both inside and outside of Hollywood make use of it," Duncan notes.

As Figure 3.8 illustrates, Final Draft has also reissued SCRIPT COPS, an award-winning web series by Scott Rice. The first video out of the gate is "SCRIPT COPS Episode #1: Drop the Script – Pilot episode." The hilarious parody warns screenwriters of the dangers involved when writing goes bad.

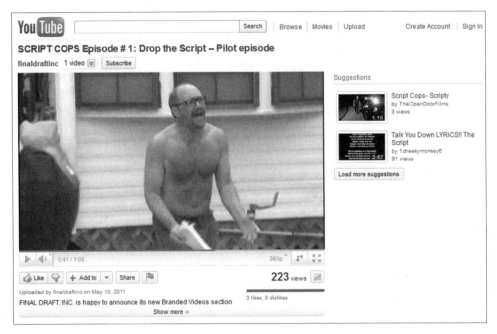

Figure 3.8 "SCRIPT COPS Episode #1: Drop the Script – Pilot episode"

Scripts contain the ideas, but storyboards contain the visuals.

"A storyboard is a vital tool for making sure the execution of the perfect script doesn't fall flat on its face," says Duncan. "It allows you to plan character movement and camera placement, as well as protects you from continuity errors and the unintended jumpcut," he adds.

A storyboard is especially important on a low-budget set. You don't have the luxury of extra time or money to fix a botched shot. Also, storyboarding will allow you to make maximum use of rented equipment. By glancing at your storyboard, you'll be able to easily identify which shots to use the jib or steadicam on and can then knock them out all at once.

A storyboard is also a great communication tool. When you verbally describe a shot to your crew, they must still create their own mental picture. When you show them the shot via a storyboard, they're able to see what you have envisioned. The storyboard empowers your crew to effectively bring about your visual ideas.

So what are your software options for storyboarding?

On the free side is Atomic Learning's Storyboard Pro, a very simple piece of free-ware that will accomplish the job without any bells or whistles.

If you want more features, but don't want to pay more, Celtx has storyboarding integrated into its software package.

For 3D previsualization (previz), look at Storyboard Lite and FrameForge 3D. Both offer 3D models and sets to use in your frames. FrameForge has an upgrade allowing you to visualize even stereoscopic 3D productions. Another new option on the market is Google's SketchUp. It's a bit pricey, but it has the ability to easily integrate with Google Earth so you can import satellite imagery.

Tuesday: Use Classic Camera Techniques

Next, read the YouTube Handbook tip "Nine Classic Camera Moves," which was written by Brian Schaller, a former TV news shooter, reporter, and producer who is now traveling worldwide working on a documentary. Or, you can read his full article at www.videomaker.com/article/10775.

According to Schaller, "Professional videographers usually follow this one rule of thumb: when it comes to camera movement, it must be motivated. 'Because it looks cool' is usually not a valid reason for using tricky camera moves." So, why would you use one of these nine classic camera techniques and how do you execute these shot types? Here are some short summaries of Brian's tips:

Pan This camera technique works great to show the distance between two objects or for a panoramic view from a mountaintop to the valley below. To execute this shot type, use a tripod to smoothly move the camera horizontally from left to right or from right to left.

Tilt This camera technique works best when it is used to show how tall something is or the top and bottom of a stationary object. To execute this shot type, tilt the camera up or down without raising or lowering its position.

Pedestal You use this camera technique to get the proper height for a shot. To execute this shot type, physically move the height of the camera up or down on a tripod.

Dolly You use this camera technique to follow an object smoothly. To execute this shot type, set the camera on tracks or wheels and move it toward or away from a subject.

Floating stabilizer You use this camera technique to follow an object through twists and turns or a person through hallways and doors as well as around rooms. To execute this shot type, strap the stabilizer device to the videographer and mount the camera on a series of metal joints controlled by gyroscopes. Brian adds, "You can also buy or make an inexpensive alternative that uses counterweights to get a similar effect."

Crane or boom This camera technique gives a bird's-eye view, as if the camera is swooping down from above. To execute this shot type, use the crane or boom for high, sweeping shots or to follow the action of your subject.

Handheld Many news crews and most documentaries use this camera technique because of the spontaneity of the action. To execute this shot type, rest the camera on your shoulder. Brian adds, "This balances the camera and keeps shaking to a minimum."

Zoom You use this camera technique to bring objects at a distance closer to the lens or to show size and perspective. To execute this shot type, press the lever on the camera to zoom in or out. Adds Brian, "Usually, the harder you press on the lever the quicker the zoom."

Rack focus This camera technique is used to switch from one actor's face to another during conversations or tense moments. It enables you to make a transition similar to an edit by constructing two distinct shots. To execute this shot type, focus on one object, like an actor's face, and then have everything behind him out of focus. Then adjust the focus so that his face becomes blurred and the actress behind him becomes clear.

As Figure 3.9 illustrates, Isaac's "Videomaker's Pans and Tilts 101" demonstrates the first two of the classic camera techniques that Schaller outlined. Isaac shows what a pan and a tilt are and how they can improve the quality of the shots in your videos.

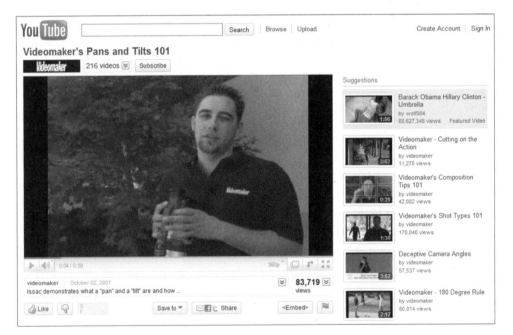

Figure 3.9 *"Videomaker's Pans and Tilts 101"*

Wednesday: Use a Single Lighting Source

If you need to learn lighting basics, watch "Videomaker's Lighting Techniques 101." As Figure 3.10 illustrates, Isaac gives some helpful hints for better lighting in your videos.

Figure 3.10 "Videomaker's Lighting Techniques 101"

This video accompanies another one of my favorite tips: "Illuminations: One-Light to Cover them All." It was written by Jim Stinson, author of *Video: Digital Communication & Production* (Goodheart-Willcox, 2008). You can read his full article at www.videomaker.com/article/11114.

Why work with only a single lighting source? According to Jim, there are three key reasons: "Poverty, portability, and power. You may not have the budget for a full light kit, or the need to do much interior lighting. You may be working out of your trusty Prius, with no room to store a bunch of lights and stands and cables, and no assistant to schlep all that stuff around. Or you may have to light a room with a single household circuit that may also have outlets in other rooms (Oh, how many times I've found this in older buildings). Plug in a second light and... BLOOEY!"

He says you can work with a single light either when the ambient light at a location is feeble or when you want to control the lighting perfectly. How you do this depends on your instrument of choice.

If you use a spotlight, Jim says you'll need something to bounce its light back from the other side of the subject. For head and shoulder shots, a standard reflector may work fine. However, it's often easier to work with a softlight—whether box or umbrella—because this light seems to wrap around the subject.

He adds that backgrounds may not be a problem if you have ambient light on location. However, when your lonely unit is the sole source, you have to light carefully.

With a spotlight, Jim suggests you reposition both light and reflector so that the bounce light hits the rear wall as well as the subject. With a softlight, about all you can do is move the subject closer to the wall, move the light farther from the subject, or a bit of both. "Be careful moving the subject closer, it may flatten the look of the shot," he advises.

Finally, if you have any choice in the matter, always use a light-colored background wall when working without ambient light. "That way, the bounce light will have a fighting chance of illuminating your subject," Jim concludes.

If and when you can, it's better to use three-point lighting. This can turn even a hotel meeting room into a studio. Three-point lighting uses three lights—the key, fill, and backlight.

- The key is your primary light. It is usually placed 45 degrees from your subject and aimed down. It provides the bulk of the illumination on your subject and may produce some strong shadows.

- The fill is 45-degrees from your subject on the opposite side and is broader and usually about two or three stops dimmer. The job of the fill is to keep the shadows from the key from being too strong.

- The backlight is aimed at your subject's head and shoulders from behind and above, also at about a 45-degree angle, and gives them a bit of a glow, which serves to give some separation between the subject and whatever's behind them. If you have a nice background, you can also aim the backlight at that. This works well if the background is textured—like draped fabric—and if you aim a light at it obliquely. This is common when interviews are conducted at a location chosen for the subject's convenience.

Thursday: Use Natural Sound

If you need to learn the basics of sound, watch "Videomaker's Better Sound for Online Video 101." As Figure 3.11 illustrates, Isaac's got a good tip for better sound, and that is to use an external microphone.

Then read the third of my favorite tips, "Sound Advice: Natural Sound to the Rescue." It was written by Hal Robertson, a contributing editor for *Videomaker* magazine as well as the cinematographer, editor, and entire crew for the independent digital feature *Breaking Ten*. You can read his full article at www.videomaker.com/ article/12249.

Hal asks, "Remember *MacGyver*? With his trusty Swiss Army knife, some bubble gum, and duct tape, he could fashion weapons, build flying machines, and repair almost anything—all this, just in time to thwart the bad guys and save the damsel in distress."

Figure 3.11 "Videomaker's Better Sound for Online Video 101"

He says, "You have a similar tool at your disposal—perfect for defeating the evils of audio editing. No, it's not gaffer's tape, it's Natural Sound or Nat Sot, for short. Natural sound is often misunderstood or, worse, ignored by many video editors, but it works great covering tough edits and creating a real sense of space."

Hal says it's easy to record natural sound from locations. Before the talent arrives (or after they leave), simply roll a minute or two of tape to capture the audio environment. As for microphones, you can use the same mics the talent will use, or use the stereo microphone in your camcorder.

He says you can capture your audio-only clips along with the other video material and remove the video to create your natural soundtrack. Although it's not difficult to do this in most editing software, he recommends using Adobe Audition, which has a feature called Open Audio from Video that simplifies the process. If the edited video goes longer than your recording, just loop it again and trim any excess. To create smooth transitions, apply a fade-in and fade-out to the ends of your audio segments.

Finally, Hal suggests that you always roll the tape before the interviews and create several seconds of material that would serve as audio Band-Aids. Before or after the shoot, have the talent clam up for a minute and keep the tape rolling. Using the same microphone in the same location is the best way.

He adds, "Whether you're shooting a movie, a training video or an infomercial, virtually every production will benefit with natural sound. It's a great mix element to reinforce the action onscreen and will cover you in difficult editing situations."

Friday: Use Special Effects

If you have told someone, "I figure we can blue-screen the kids in later," then the how-to video you're looking for is "Green Screen," aka "Videomaker's How to Use Green Screen Paper 101."

As Figure 3.12 illustrates, Issac explains how to create and use a green-screen effect using basic store-bought items and computer editing software in just 53 seconds.

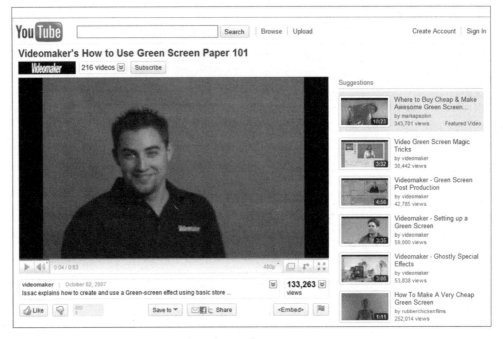

Figure 3.12 "Videomaker's How to Use Green Screen Paper 101"

For more tips on this topic, read "The Keys to Chromakey: How To Use A Green Screen" by Ed Driscoll at www.videomaker.com/article/13055/.

For example, Driscoll explains, "In the past, the main color for chromakeying was blue. Beginning in the late 1970s, there was a slow industry flip-over to green-colored screens for chroma. That's because of the detail in the green color channel that digital cameras retain."

He also recommends lighting the background as evenly as possible, with no hot spots. This makes postproduction work much easier.

In addition, Driscoll says, "It helps to stand the subject as far away from the backdrop as possible to separate the two. This helps to reduce spill from the lights illuminating the talent into the lighting on the green screen. It helps to blur the backdrop, which keeps wrinkling and other blemishes from affecting the key."

Week 3: Get Advanced Video Production Tips

After you've learned the basics of video production, you'll want to get some advanced video production tips.

YouTube is constantly rolling out new features that will help you make videos worth watching. Let's examine five of them:

Monday: Try the YouTube Video Editor

Tuesday: Learn how to upload

Wednesday: Use video annotations

Thursday: Add captions and subtitles

Friday: Create 3D content

Monday: Try the YouTube Video Editor

On June 16, 2010, YouTube introduced an online video editor. Without installing any software, it allows you to do the following:

Combine multiple videos you've uploaded to create a new longer video.

Trim the beginning and/or ending of your videos.

Add a soundtrack from YouTube's AudioSwap library of tens of thousands of songs.

Create new videos without worrying about file formats and publish them to YouTube with one click.

Rushabh Doshi, software engineer, said on the YouTube Blog, "The editor is ideal for merging single, short clips into a longer video. For example, you can transform clips from your vacation into a video travel diary set to music, or create a highlights reel from footage of your last basketball game."

He added, "It's also great for trimming a long video down to the moments you really care about. Say you've uploaded a wedding ceremony—beautiful event, but do you really need to see all the guests shuffle in? The video editor lets you easily remove unwanted footage so you can capture just the moment when they say 'I do.'"

As Figure 3.13 illustrates, powerposter rewboss created "Edit your videos online!" to give YouTubers a sense of how the YouTube Video Editor works:

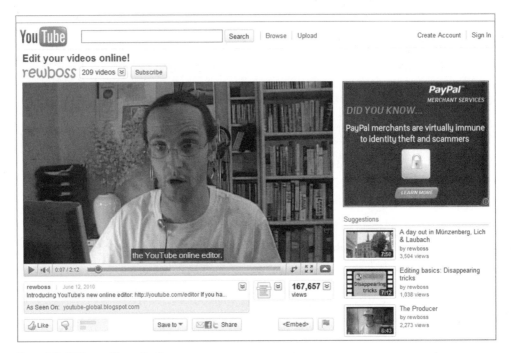

Figure 3.13 "Edit your videos online!"

To try it out, go to TestTube (www.youtube.com/testtube) and click Video Editor.

To add video clips in the Video Editor, select one to seven clips to make a new video, which will have a different URL and view count. Clicking the plus icon (+) will add a clip to the storyboard. You can also drag and drop a clip down to the storyboard.

To edit individual clips, select a clip in the Clip Editor by hovering your mouse pointer over it and clicking the scissors icon. You can shorten the clip by dragging the gray clip trimmer to the section of the video you'd like to trim. Then click the Save button to save the changes you've made.

To add an audio track, click the Audio tab in the Media Picker. Browse YouTube's AudioSwap library and click the plus icon to add an audio track to the storyboard. It's worth noting that the audio track on your video will be permanently replaced when you add a new soundtrack. If you change your video's soundtrack to one from the AudioSwap library, then the video won't be eligible for revenue sharing. In addition, ads may be displayed on the videos that contain soundtracks from the AudioSwap library.

To publish your new video, you just need to add the **new video's title** in the title field. Once you've done this, click **Publish.**

Tuesday: Learn How to Upload

Another popular article in YouTube's Help Center that I recommend you read is "How to Upload." It is accompanied by a video (Figure 3.14) called "How to Upload a Video to YouTube NEWEST VERSION" by Katie Stiles.

Figure 3.14 "How to Upload a Video to YouTube NEWEST VERSION"

Once you've finished editing your video, make sure it's less than 15 minutes long, smaller than 2 GB in size, and in an acceptable format. Then you're ready to upload it. According to YouTube's Help Center, here's how you do that:

1. Click the Upload button in the upper-right corner of any YouTube page.

2. Click the Browse button to browse for the video file you'd like to upload to YouTube. Select the file you want to upload.

3. Click the Upload Video button to start the uploading process.

4. As the video file is uploading, enter as much information about it as possible in the relevant fields, including title, description, category, and tags. You're not required to provide specific information, but the more information you include, the easier it is for users to find your video.

5. Click the Save Changes button to save the updates you've made to the video file.

You can upload up to 10 video files in a single uploading session. To upload multiple videos, follow these steps:

1. Click the Add Videos To Upload button.

2. Select the videos you want to upload.

3. Once you've added all the videos that you want to upload and confirmed that the total file size is less than 2 GB, click the Upload Videos button.

It can take 15 to 30 minutes for your video to upload to YouTube if Internet traffic is normal and you have a fast connection. But it can take up to an hour if you are uploading video during a busy conference at an old hotel.

In March 2009, YouTube released a new Flash uploader for all supported browsers. And it came with a long-awaited and much-requested feature: an upload progress bar that lets you know the status of your upload. YouTube's next step will be to provide the estimated video processing time for your upload so you know if you have time to get a cup of coffee.

In April 2009, YouTube added some new options for uploaders. You can now tweak the appearance of your video when played on YouTube or in an embedded player. Just insert some of the hint tags below into the tags field of your video:

yt:crop=16:9 This zooms in on the 16:9 area and removes windowboxing.

yt:stretch=16:9 This fixes anamorphic (widescreen) content by scaling it to 16:9.

yt:stretch=4:3 This fixes 720480 content that is the wrong aspect ratio by scaling it to 4:3.

yt:quality=high This sets the default to a high-quality stream, depending on availability.

If you receive an error message with your upload, you might want to make sure you're attempting to upload a file that's recognized by YouTube.

Remember, your video needs to meet YouTube's uploading requirements. If your video file doesn't meet these requirements, you will have to re-edit it on your computer and then upload the new file.

Wednesday: Use Video Annotations

On June 4, 2008, YouTube announced a new way to add interactive commentary to your videos—using video annotations. The video by Torley shown in Figure 3.15 explains how this feature enables you to add background information, create branching stories, or add links to any YouTube video, channel, or search results page—at any point in your video.

YouTubers have control over creating and editing an unlimited number of annotations on their videos. To start annotating, you need to upload videos to your account first. Then log in and view one of your videos. On the video page, click the blue Edit Annotations button to the right of the video.

Figure 3.15 "Add video annotations - YouTube Help Center"

In January 2009, YouTube made it easier to add annotations directly to your videos. Simply log in to YouTube, watch your video on the watch page, and then click it to start adding annotations. You can also change an annotation's color.

It's also easier for your annotations to link to a variety of different YouTube pages. You can link to another video, channel page, playlist, group, or search query. You can even link to a video response page or message window to prompt for feedback from your audience.

You can allow other YouTube users to add annotations to your video. Under the annotations window is a link only you can see (until you share it) that will lead anyone to your video's annotation editor. By sharing this link, you're allowing anyone to put annotations in your video. If you want to invalidate the link, click the red Disable & Reset Link button to the right of the text box containing the URL. You might consider putting new links in the description of your video to give viewers free rein to add annotations.

As you play your video, you can insert commentary by adding speech bubbles, notes, and highlight boxes anywhere you want. You can also use the menu on the left to save a draft, delete commentary, edit start/stop times, or add links to your annotations. Once you save the final version, click Publish to reveal your annotated video to other users.

If you want to see an example, watch the video by Roi Werner in Figure 3.16. Just go to www.youtube.com/watch?v=UxnopxbOdic.

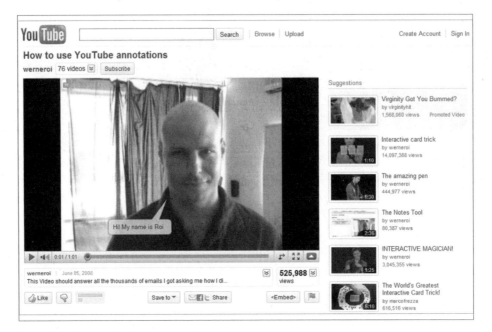

Figure 3.16 "How to use YouTube annotations"

To set the video page icon for your channel, log in to your account and navigate to the Branding Options page in the Edit Channel menu. In the Video Page Icon field, select the locally saved image that you would like to use for your video page icon and then click the Save Branding Options button at the bottom of the page to upload the image to YouTube. I recommend that you choose an image that is 10 KB or smaller.

If you are looking for some creative ways to use annotations, check out "Interactive shell game" on captdeaf's channel, "My 22nd Skydive" on hendrikm82's channel, and "Interactive card trick" on werneroi's channel.

Thursday: Add Captions and Subtitles

In August 2008, YouTube added a new captioning feature that allows you to give viewers a deeper understanding of your video (Figure 3.17). Captions and subtitles can help people who would not otherwise understand the audio track follow along, especially those who speak other languages or who are hearing impaired.

You can add captions to one of your videos by uploading a closed caption file using the Captions and Subtitles menu on the editing page. To add several captions to a video, simply upload multiple files.

If you want to include foreign subtitles in multiple languages, upload a separate file for each language. There are over 120 languages to choose from, and you can add any title you want for each caption.

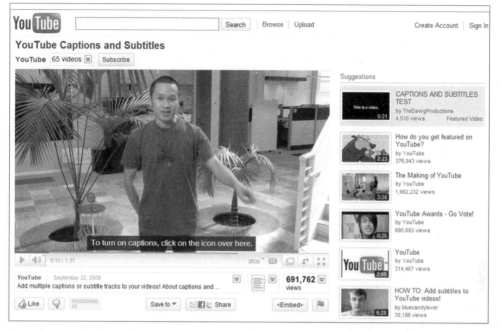

Figure 3.17 "YouTube Captions and Subtitles"

If a video includes captions, you can activate them by clicking the menu button located in the lower-right portion of the video player. Clicking this button will also allow viewers to choose which captions they want to see.

Some of YouTube's partners have already started using captions and subtitles to offer their users a better understanding of their videos—even with the audio turned off:

CNET "Crave: Do You Crave the iPhone 3G" (www.youtube.com/watch?v=ullmDNjb_ec) uses captions in this tech product review.

UC Berkeley "Opencast Project Open House at UC Berkeley" (www.youtube.com/watch?v= 4WJez1XjI88) uses captions in its footage.

Gonzodoga "BLASSREITER Episode 1" (www.youtube.com/watch?v=Iu3usSSQ_74) uses English subtitles in this Japanese animation.

What else should you know about captions? They can be searched for, so accurate captions will help people find your videos.

Friday: Create 3D Content

In July 2009, YouTube made it easier to create and watch 3D videos. Although, Peter Bradshaw, software engineer, said on the YouTube Blog, "This is a new feature and many of the kinks are still being worked out (for instance, 3D videos cannot be embedded)."

Here are some basics around shooting 3D videos (this isn't easy, so patience is key):

- Use two cameras arranged like a pair of eyes.

- Start both cameras recording simultaneously.

- In your video editing program, place the footage for the left and right eyes together in the frame side by side, with the right eye on the left and the left eye on the right.

- Upload your video. Edit your video's tags and add yt3d:enable=true. If video is widescreen, then add yt3d:aspect=16:9 too.

As Figure 3.18 illustrates, "YouTube in 3D" looks really weird if you don't have the right-colored glasses.

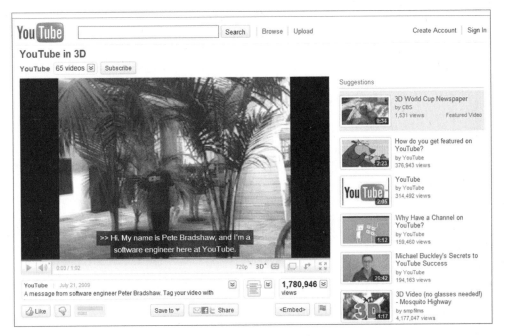

Figure 3.18 "YouTube in 3D"

Although the glasses from 3D cinema presentations will *not* work, there are various ways to watch 3D videos on YouTube:

- *Colored glasses.* Red/cyan glasses are the most common and are sometimes called red/green. Amber/blue glasses were distributed for the half-time commercials during Super Bowl XXXXIII. And green/magenta glasses came with some recent DVD releases (such as *Journey to the Center of the Earth* and *Coraline*).

- *Parallel and cross-eyed methods* involve relaxing your gaze or crossing your eyes until the two images merge (this technique isn't recommended for long viewing sessions since it may cause eye strain).

- *Mirror-split* involves using a mirror to view the two images. This method is a little more difficult to set up, but it has great results with no eye strain.

- If you don't have any glasses or a mirror, you can choose to watch a 3D video from one eye only.

Now, YouTube uploaders and partners have yet to use this feature to make a fascinating, funky 3D video that's worth watching. Who knows, maybe you will be the one who will make the equivalent of the 1953 3D thriller *House of Wax* or the Michael Jackson adventure *Captain EO*.

Keep in mind though, YouTube won't allow partners to monetize 3D videos— possibly because none of their ads are designed for 3D. So if you're a YouTube partner, making a 3D video is something you'd do "just for fun."

Week 4: Evaluate Video Advertising Options

In addition to getting ready to shoot, learning video production basics, and getting advanced video production tips, you should evaluate all the YouTube video advertising options.

Advertising on YouTube is about helping users, partners, and advertisers connect with each other through video. So, you have to make ads worth watching too.

For example, all advertisements must follow YouTube's Community Guidelines and advertising content policies. As you would expect, YouTube does not permit advertising for adult or pornographic content. In addition, advertising is not permitted for pay-to-click, pay-to-view, auto-surfing, automated ad clicking, and other guaranteed traffic programs. You can find more details at www.youtube.com/t/advertising_policies.

In addition, ads may not have fake hyperlinks, resemble dialog boxes, simulate fake interactivity, contain content of a sexual nature, initiate downloads, be intrusive, advertise competitive content, or have misleading content.

YouTube has tested lots of different kinds of ads over the past few years, and it is constantly working to develop the right ad format for the right content and environment. But different user experiences require YouTube to provide advertisers with lots of options. So it has created several products that work in different ways:

Promoted Videos program Reaches people who are *searching* YouTube for videos.

Partner watch ads Reaches people who are *watching* videos from YouTube's content partners.

Homepage Video Ads Reaches people who are *browsing* the YouTube homepage.

TrueView Video Ads Gives viewers control over which ads they want to see and only charges advertisers when a viewer has chosen to watch their ad.

Google Display Network Reaches more than 80 percent of global Internet users.

This week, we'll take a closer look at each of these options.

Monday: Explore Promoted Videos

Tuesday: Investigate YouTube Partner watch ads

Wednesday: Consider YouTube Homepage Ads

Thursday: Examine TrueView Video Ads

Friday: Look at Google Display Network

Monday: Explore Promoted Videos

First, let's explore YouTube Promoted Videos, an advertising program that enables all video creators—from the everyday user to a Fortune 500 advertiser—to reach people who are interested in their content, products, or services with relevant videos. You can use Promoted Videos to make sure your videos find a larger audience whether you're a startup band trying to break out with a new single, a film studio seeking to promote an exciting movie trailer, or even a first-time uploader trying to quickly build a following on the site.

With 24 hours of new video uploaded to YouTube every minute and millions of viewers watching hundreds of millions of videos every day, the popularity of YouTube can be a mixed blessing for marketers. Although it's easier to get your 15 minutes of fame these days, it's also harder for people to find your video in the first place, even if it's exactly what they're looking for.

But what if you could promote your video on YouTube and make it easier for people to find it? YouTube announced a way to do just that in November 2008 when it introduced Promoted Videos.

So how do Promoted Videos work?

Creating an ad is as simple as writing a few lines of text to accompany your video thumbnail. Your YouTube video is your creative, so there's no need to create an additional display unit.

Easy-to-use automated tools allow content owners to decide which YouTube search terms they'd like to target, place bids in an automated online auction, and set daily spending budgets.

Then, when people search for videos, YouTube displays relevant videos alongside the search results. These videos are clearly labeled as promoted videos and are priced on a cost-per-click basis.

Once you've driven potential customers to your video, make sure they know what to do next. By creating a free call-to-action overlay and linking back to your site, many of those viewers can become instant customers.

In addition to reporting on performance (impressions and click-through rate), integration with YouTube Insight enables greater understanding of how your Promoted Videos campaign impacts your video-level data.

As Figure 3.19 illustrates, you can learn more about this advertising option in the video entitled "YouTube Promoted Videos Overview" that features Matthew Liu, product manager at YouTube.

Figure 3.19 "YouTube Promoted Videos Overview"

As I mentioned in Chapter 1, Promoted Videos was initially called Sponsored Videos. It is a self-serve advertising platform that takes just a few minutes to set up, and you can set your budget at any level you wish.

Just as AdWords provides people with relevant, unobtrusive advertising, YouTube hopes that Promoted Videos will provide useful, engaging content, accessible to advertisers of all kinds. Visit https://ads.youtube.com to start your own Promoted Videos campaign.

Tuesday: Investigate YouTube Partner Watch Ads

Hundreds of millions of videos are streamed every day on YouTube, and the majority of these video views take place on watch pages.

On average, users spend more than 2:38 watching a video on partner watch pages. It is rare to get such a truly engaged audience on the Web.

While YouTube is selective about the content its partners can upload, the world's most popular online video community still has a huge variety of partners, with content to suit all users and most advertisers. The list is growing every day, but YouTube currently has more than 10,000 partners.

These partners range from large media companies such as Universal Music and Metro-Goldwyn-Mayer, through niche media properties such as Expert Village and Mondo Media, to members of the YouTube community like Fred or Smosh, who have created such consistently popular videos that they have been invited to join the YouTube Partner Program.

YouTube understands that some advertisers may be nervous about running advertising against unknown user-generated content.

So, your advertising will appear only against the videos of YouTube's tried-and-trusted content partners. Each partner goes through a thorough vetting and is regularly checked to ensure that they are uploading appropriate content.

YouTube offers multiple, complementary targeting options.

The simplest form of targeting is placement targeting, where you focus on the video genres you are interested in. This can be as granular as "golf videos" or as broad as "buzz videos" (all videos that are very popular at the moment). YouTube is introducing new targeting options all the time, so do check for updates.

You can also use demographic targeting (only advertise to users of a specific age, gender, or location) or interest-based advertising (target your advertising to users who are interested in golf, even if they are not watching a golf video); you can even target recent or frequent uploaders.

YouTube also offers a variety of advertising units.

InVideo overlays are noninvasive ad units that provide a great way of eliciting a user response while they are watching a video.

In the video "YouTube InVideo Ads" (Figure 3.20), Shiva Rajaraman, product manager, says a 480×70 flash overlay appears at the bottom of the player.

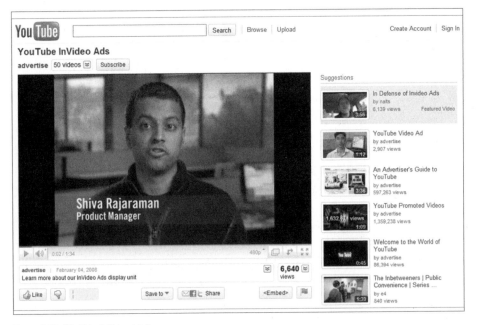

Figure 3.20 "YouTube InVideo Ads"

If users do not take action in 10 to 15 seconds, the ad will disperse. If a user is interested, clicking on the overlay temporarily pauses the video and the advertiser's video or flash creative will appear within the video player.

YouTube has found that less than 10 percent of users close the overlay, which has a click-through rate (CTR) 8 to 10 times the click-to-play rate of standard display ads.

Also included is a 300×250 companion banner ad that stays onscreen for the duration of the video. Although the companion display ad is optional, I highly recommend it. These elements are road-blocked for the same advertiser or campaign when presented together.

YouTube also enables advertisers that do not have any video or flash creative to run a 300×250 ad to the right of the video player. This can be a standard banner ad (image or Flash), a rich media ad, or a YouTube contest gadget ad. This is a great way of extending a broader display ad campaign to YouTube.

The *in-stream* (pre-, mid-, and post-rolls) ad format is for advertisers who want to re-create the TV advertising experience within online video, especially those wishing to repurpose existing TV advertising creative.

In addition, the in-stream ads can click through to an advertiser's website or brand channel. If bought through reservation, each in-stream ad also comes with a 300×60 companion ad unit that remains onscreen until a user gets to the next in-stream ad.

However, when YouTube first tested in-stream ads in 2007, it learned that abandonment rates (especially for pre-rolls) were as high as 70 percent and that users were far more likely to watch and engage with overlays. But over time YouTube found that different kinds of content provide different experiences for viewers and that in-stream ads work pretty well on certain videos, like clips from TV shows or full-length movies.

So, on November 11, 2009, YouTube started a small test of skippable pre-rolls, which allow users to choose whether or not they want to watch the ad that appears at the beginning of a video. If they skip the ad, they'll go straight to the video.

That day, "Skip, skip, skip to my video" was posted on the YouTube Biz Blog by Jamie Kerns, software engineer; Lane Shackleton, product specialist; and Dan Zigmond, technical lead.

They said, "Who would choose to watch an ad when they can skip it? Well, that's what we're trying to find out."

In YouTube's previous research, lots of users actually watched pre-rolls. Abandonment rates were affected by several factors, notably length and creative. When a pre-roll is only 15 seconds, YouTube saw completion rates as high as 85 percent.

Also, creative matters a lot: The quality and relevance of the ad itself seems to have 3× the influence on abandonment online as it does on TV. Viewers online tend to be much more active in making choices about what they watch.

As Figure 3.21 illustrates, "Kirk's friend, Gary Mitchell, is transformed into a god-like entity" in "Star Trek: - Where No Man Has Gone Before." Are viewers transformed when they see an in-stream ad for Fiber One yogurt?

Figure 3.21 "Star Trek: - Where No Man Has Gone Before"

The answer to this question depends on whether a specific pre-roll, mid-roll, or post-roll is endemic—or nonendemic—advertising. In other words, does high-fiber, low-calorie, strawberry yogurt help you live long and prosper?

When I watched the original *Star Trek* series from 1966 to 1969, all 80 episodes included TV commercials. But that was before TV remotes and TiVo helped eliminate "long, annoying commercials." Today, most viewers aren't willing to accept this kind of advertising experience when watching longer-form content on YouTube like TV shows and movies—unless it is endemic.

According to Kerns, Shackleton, and Zigmond, "Skippable pre-rolls have the potential to solve this problem and create a win-win-win for everyone on YouTube."

This format gives users more control over their experience. YouTube is working on a solution where advertisers pay only for ads that users actually watch and engage with. And skippable ads attempt to minimize abandonment rates, helping partners protect the audiences they've worked hard to build.

They add, "We've learned from Promoted Videos that advertisers are often willing to pay more money for an engaged opt-in view, as opposed to a forced view like an in-stream ad, so this also has the potential to increase CPMs," or cost per thousand views.

Wednesday: Consider YouTube Homepage Ads

Today, let's consider YouTube Homepage ads, which are an up-front way to connect with users when they visit the site.

In August 2006, YouTube unveiled brand channels and what was then called the Participatory Video Ad (PVA)—because it was designed to encourage dialogue between community and marketers.

YouTube's first brand channel partner was Warner Bros. Records, which created the Paris Hilton Channel for her debut album, *Paris*, which was released globally that day. The Paris Hilton Channel was sponsored by Fox Broadcasting Company's hit show *Prison Break*. (Hey, you can't make this stuff up.)

The pop singer created an original broadcast for the YouTube community, taking advantage of the new PVA offering on the YouTube homepage. Fox Broadcasting, working with digital communications agency Organic, Inc., also utilized the new PVA in conjunction with the Paris Hilton sponsorship to promote the fall season launch of *Prison Break*.

"Our vision is to build a new advertising platform that both the community and advertisers will embrace," said Chad Hurley, CEO and cofounder of YouTube, in a press release. "This new medium requires finding a balance between traditional online advertising and new creative approaches that engage consumers in an active way."

The PVA was a user-initiated video advertisement with all of the YouTube community features enabled. Consumers could rate, share, comment, embed, and "favorite" advertising content that they found interesting, informative, and entertaining. Rather than interrupt a consumer's experience, YouTube created a model that encouraged engagement and participation.

The YouTube community was very receptive to this new advertising experience and propelled PVA videos to the top of the Most Viewed, Most Discussed, and Top Favorite video rankings. Advertisers had the opportunity to participate and moderate discussions around their creative.

The Warner Music Group and YouTube parted ways in December 2008 because they couldn't reach acceptable business terms. And the PVA is now called the Homepage Video Ad.

And for big advertisers, the YouTube homepage is often seen as the holy grail. It's the highest-profile placement on YouTube, providing marketers with the ability to deliver a big impact and drive attention to content, trailers, or advertising.

On August 19, 2010, Mark Sabec, product marketing manager, said on the YouTube Blog, "To give you an idea of the scale we're talking about, the homepage has been delivering nearly 45 million impressions per day and 18 million unique visitors a day in the U.S.—that's the equivalent to the ratings of several top-rated prime-time television shows combined."

While impressions and unique visitors are never guaranteed, users who visit the homepage are actively looking for the next video to watch, so advertisers naturally want to be part of the action. And the Homepage Ad is a great way to create awareness and reach a wide audience with your marketing message.

Over time, best practices for the homepage ad have emerged:

Keep it short. Sixty seconds is a good yardstick. If the message is longer, the chances that users will tune out get higher.

Keep it engaging. Users will watch most or all of a video if it interests and engages them. So try to connect with your audience in a personal and targeted way.

Don't lecture, motivate. A couple of minutes of talking heads isn't very effective. Try to entertain, inform, and inspire instead of just trying to educate.

Deliver your messages early. Viewers are likely to tune out near the end of a video, so deliver your key message early.

Include a call to action. If your marketing objective is to increase visits to a destination, then give your audience a reason to go there. A call to action can be very effective if it's appropriate.

These tips are not only applicable to homepage ads, but are good tips for making a successful YouTube video in general.

As Figure 3.22 illustrates, YouTube also offers a masthead ad. As a full-width unit in the most prominent space on YouTube, a masthead ad offers rich media interactivity and DoubleClick metrics.

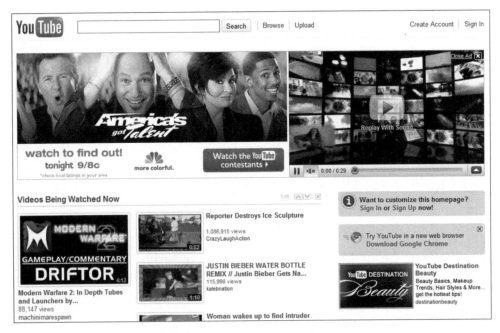

Figure 3.22 *America's Got Talent* masthead ad

The *America's Got Talent* masthead ad ran on August 11, 2010. The show was featuring 12 new acts chosen from 20,000 audition YouTube videos.

The YouTube candidates were culled to about 40 and then winnowed down to 11 by AGT producers and show judges Howie Mandel, Piers Morgan, and Sharon Osbourne. YouTube viewers then selected Jackie Evancho—a 10-year-old opera singer from Pittsburgh, Pennsylvania—to round out the competition.

Evancho moved on to the next round along with Maestro Alexander Bui, a 16-year-old pianist from Egg Harbor Township, New Jersey; Dan Sperry, a 25-year-old magician from Las Vegas, Nevada; and Kristina Young, a 22-year-old singer from Spearfish, South Dakota.

If you use a masthead ad, I strongly recommend that it (1) include video to capitalize on a video-hungry audience and (2) link to a watch page so the YouTube community features can create a cycle of virality. With full rich media interactivity enabled and custom DoubleClick metrics, this unit offers so much more than just video.

Thursday: Examine TrueView Video Ads

In the first edition of this book, I said, "It's too soon to know if the majority of advertising embedded in full-length TV shows will be endemic or nonendemic in-stream video ads (including pre-, mid-, and post-rolls). So, don't bet too heavily on the 'pre-roll,' the 15- to 30-second ad viewers commonly sit through before watching a video."

An advertiser may be targeting a specific demographic, but viewers decide if a pre-roll ad is endemic—it "belongs" to or "fits" with the video's content and community.

For example, in "Beverly Hills 90210 – Pilot Parts 1 and 2," twins Brandon and Brenda Walsh experience culture shock when they move from Minnesota to Beverly Hills. Do viewers experience culture shock when they see a pre-roll for Nature Valley Trail Mix before the video starts?

On December 2, 2010, YouTube announced a way to give viewers choice and control over which advertiser's message they want to see and when. And YouTube only charges advertisers when a viewer has chosen to watch their ad, not when an impression is served.

As Figure 3.23 illustrates, YouTube calls this new family of ad formats TrueView Video Ads.

In a post on the YouTube Blog that day, Senior Product Manager Phil Farhi said, "We think that giving viewers a choice of which ads they want to watch means it's even more likely that they'll be engaged with the ad, and that advertisers will get their messages across to the right person."

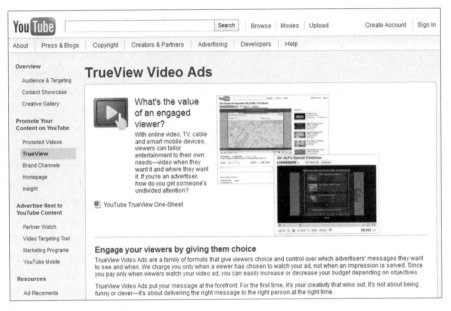

Figure 3.23 TrueView Video Ads

He added, "It works like this: when you see an ad start to play, look for a 5-second countdown button that will allow you to 'skip' it. If the ad doesn't seem relevant or engaging to you, skip it and continue to the video you wanted to watch."

In a related blog post on Inside AdWords, Gordon Zhu told advertisers, "We believe offering a cost-per-view video ad model is good for everyone: consumers choose ads that are more relevant to them; you more precisely find the audiences you want; and content creators continue to fund great content with an ad experience that is less intrusive."

He added, "Early results are encouraging with view-through rates of 20–70%. A view-through rate measures how many viewers have opted-in to watch your ad—a valuable signal which you can use in connecting the right message with the right audience at the right time."

Among the early advertisers who tested this ad format was GoPro, which makes and sells the HD HERO line of wearable, gear-mountable HD cameras. Lee Topar, director of online marketing for GoPro, told Zhu, "Thus far, we've seen about a 40% view-through rate—and since we only pay when potential customers actually watch a video, we have more control over our budget."

It's also worth noting that GoPro's business is growing 300 percent a year.

Friday: Look at Google Display Network

On June 18, 2010, Google introduced the Google Display Network, which enables advertisers to run video ads on websites and on television with Google TV as well as on YouTube.

In a post on InSide AdWords, Neal Mohan, vice president of product management, said, "In an effort to make our display media offerings clearer to advertisers like you and agencies, we're creating a new umbrella name for all these properties, the Google Display Network."

The Google Display Network now comprises all of the sites—apart from search sites—where you can buy ads through Google, including YouTube and Google properties such as Google Finance, Gmail, Google Maps, and Blogger as well as over one million AdSense and DoubleClick Ad Exchange partners.

This makes the Google Display Network the world's leading ad network, reaching more than 80 percent of global Internet users and serving more than six billion ad impressions each day across hundreds of thousands of websites, according to comScore Key Measures. Thousands of advertisers use Google AdWords to place ads on the Display Network.

"The Google Display Network offers all ad formats—text, image, rich media, and video ads—enabling you to unleash your creativity and engage potential customers across the Web," said Mohan.

"You can run ads on the Google Display Network the same way you always have. Either place bids through AdWords or make reservations on YouTube and Google Finance with the help of a Google account team," he concluded.

Before you do that, however, I recommend that you read *Pay-Per-Click Search Engine Marketing: An Hour a Day* (Sybex, 2010), shown in Figure 3.24. Written by David Szetela and Joseph Kerschbaum, the content is so useful I spent a whole Saturday reading it in my pajamas.

Chapter 7 of Szetela and Kerschbaum's book is about the Google Content Network, which has since been renamed the Google Display Network.

Figure 3.24 *Pay-Per-Click Search Engine Marketing: An Hour a Day*

According to Szetela and Kerschbau, advertising on the Google Display Network enables you to reach a huge number of Internet users. There are literally billions of ad impressions to be had on the Google Display Network every day, and click traffic typically comes at a deep discount when compared with search costs on a per-click basis.

"But tapping into this huge network requires specific best practices and techniques that are often counterintuitive to pay-per-click (PPC) advertisers who are accustomed to thinking in terms of ads displayed as the result of search engine searches," they add.

If advertising on the Google Display Network isn't always intuitive, then have any advertisers achieved success?

The Ad Council's "That's Not Cool" campaign used the Google Display Network and YouTube to reach 18 million teens and increase site traffic by 1,550 percent.

Infiniti launched a Google Display Network Blast and YouTube homepage masthead to drive traffic to a sponsored contest on CBSSports.com during March Madness 2010. The result: 80 million impressions and 154,000 signups.

And research showed that households exposed to the "Quaker Talk" campaign that launched on YouTube and the Google Display Network in the fourth quarter of 2009 purchased 9 percent more units of Quaker Instant Oatmeal and 8 percent less of Private Label.

So, yes, advertisers have achieved success with the Google Display Network. And you can too.

Now that we've covered getting ready to shoot, video production basics, video production tips, and video advertising options, let's tackle the next step in the process: creating content worth sharing.

Month 2: Create Content Worth Sharing

4

Yogi Berra said, "You can observe a lot just by watching." If you want to learn how to create content worth sharing, then what he said actually makes sense. In this chapter, you'll watch five YouTube Award winners, explore five popular YouTube videos, examine five of the most contagious viral ads of all time, and observe five of the top viral videos of 2010. After watching a lot of videos that have gone viral, you'll know how to create content worth sharing and what to tell others who believe, "Hoarding is just as human as sharing."

Chapter Contents:
Learn the Lesson of "The Last Lecture"
Week 1: Watch YouTube Award Winners
Week 2: Explore Popular YouTube Videos
Week 3: Examine Contagious Viral Ads
Week 4: Observe Top Viral Videos

Learn the Lesson of "The Last Lecture"

YouTube's slogan is "Broadcast Yourself." And millions of people are trying to broadcast themselves to the YouTube community, including amateur and professional and established filmmakers; aspiring and professional musicians; comedians; personal video creators such as cooking, beauty, health, and fitness experts; and professional content owners.

However, YouTube generally isn't a broadcast medium—with the exception of the YouTube Homepage Roadblock, which allows brands to own the homepage for 24 hours with a 100 percent takeover of "share of voice."

So, in addition to making videos worth watching, it is necessary to create content worth sharing.

Why? Not every new video worth watching contains content worth sharing with others. Some opinion leaders may consider a video inappropriate to share with their followers.

Watching a video is mainly a transfer of *information*, but sharing the content is primarily a use of *influence*. Let me give you an example to make this two-step process clear.

A couple of years ago, my wife, Nancy, read *The Last Lecture*, the *New York Times* best-selling book written by Randy Pausch, a professor at Carnegie Mellon University. The book was born out of a lecture Pausch gave in September 2007 entitled "Really Achieving Your Childhood Dreams."

After reading the book, which is 224 pages long, Nancy decided to buy copies to give as Christmas presents to all three of our kids. Although I hadn't read the book, I discovered "Randy Pausch Last Lecture: Achieving Your Childhood Dreams" (www.youtube.com/watch?v=ji5_MqicxSo) had been uploaded on December 20, 2007, to the CarnegieMellonU channel on YouTube.

Now, I'm not the only one who has discovered the video. As Figure 4.2 illustrates, "Randy Pausch Last Lecture: Achieving Your Childhood Dreams" had more than 12 million views on YouTube at the time I was writing this chapter.

Go to www.youtube.com/watch?v=ji5_MqicxSo, click the "Show video statistics" icon, and you'll see there are currently no honors for this video. But when this was written, the video had 28 honors:

- #71 – (Spotlight Videos) - Education - Germany
- #67 – (Spotlight Videos) - Education - Australia
- #65 – (Spotlight Videos) - Education - Canada
- #77 – (Spotlight Videos) - Education - United Kingdom
- #73 – (Spotlight Videos) - Education - Ireland
- #73 – (Spotlight Videos) - Education - India
- #66 – (Spotlight Videos) - Education - New Zealand

- #71 – (Spotlight Videos) - Education - Israel
- #71 – (Spotlight Videos) - Education
- #65 – (Spotlight Videos) - Education - South Africa
- #65 – (Spotlight Videos) - Education - Argentina
- #70 – (Spotlight Videos) - Education - Spain
- #90 – (Spotlight Videos) - Education - Mexico
- #72 – (Spotlight Videos) - Education - France
- #87 – (Spotlight Videos) - Education - Italy
- #99 – (Spotlight Videos) - Education - Japan
- #65 – (Spotlight Videos) - Education - South Korea
- #66 – (Spotlight Videos) - Education - Netherlands
- #73 – (Spotlight Videos) - Education - Poland
- #72 – (Spotlight Videos) - Education - Brazil
- #70 – (Spotlight Videos) - Education - Russia
- #81 – (Spotlight Videos) - Education - Hong Kong
- #83 – (Spotlight Videos) - Education - Taiwan
- #67 – (Spotlight Videos) - Education - Czech Republic
- #67 – (Spotlight Videos) - Education - Sweden
- #84 - Most Discussed (All Time) - Education
- #13 - Most Viewed (All Time) - Education
- #1 - Top Favorited (All Time) - Education

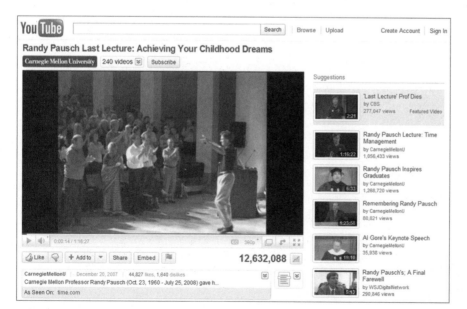

Figure 4.1 "Randy Pausch Last Lecture: Achieving Your Childhood Dreams"

And if you look closely, you'll also notice that the video is 1 hour, 16 minutes, and 27 seconds long. So my decision to watch it all the way to the end wasn't trivial. It's 29 times longer than the average YouTube video. But, I figured that I could click away at any time if the video turned out to be boring.

Pausch's moving presentation wasn't boring. His talk was modeled after an ongoing series of lectures where top academics were asked to think deeply about the question, What wisdom would you try to impart to the world if you knew it was your last chance?

A month before giving the lecture, Pausch had received a prognosis that the pancreatic cancer with which he had been diagnosed a year earlier was terminal. Before speaking, Pausch received a long standing ovation from a large crowd of over 400 colleagues and students. When he motioned them to sit down, saying, "Make me earn it," some in the audience shouted back, "You did!"

During the lecture Pausch was upbeat and humorous, shrugging off the pity often given to those diagnosed with a terminal illness. At one point, to prove his own vitality, Pausch dropped down and did push-ups on stage.

He offered insights on computer science and engineering education, multidisciplinary collaborations, and working in groups and interacting with other people. Pausch also offered his listeners inspirational life advice that can be applied to one's professional and personal life.

At the end of 1 hour, 16 minutes, and 27 seconds, I was in tears. On New Year's Day, I decided to share a link to the video with my wife and kids. Although there's no substitute for reading the book, the video content is compelling too. And even though they'd just received the book, I decided that once they had watched the video, no one would doubt my judgment.

According to the Viral Video Chart, which is powered by Unruly Media (http:// viralvideochart.unrulymedia.com/), "Randy Pausch Last Lecture: Achieving Your Childhood Dreams" has 32,885 Facebook shares, 1,232 tweets, and 6,519 blog posts. So the video has been shared at least 40,636 times by others who have also watched it.

So, first you decide you watch a video, and then you make a second decision about whether or not to share it with others.

Note: Brad O'Farrell, the technical editor of this book, adds this excellent advice: There are a lot of factors that go into whether or not you decide to share a video. One of the biggest factors is probably, Is this video something that the person I'm sending it to has never seen before? The Last Lecture video meets that qualification several times over. So many aspects of the video are unique and difficult to reproduce. The terminal illness angle, the sincerity, the energy of the crowd, the narrative, and the premise all contribute to make this video a rare gem. Your friends will likely never see a similar video. When crafting content that you want people to share, you should focus on making the video something "rare" that no one else but you can create. These kinds of videos are more likely to be shared than videos that are clearly just following the formula of other videos that have gone viral in the past.

To share or not to share, that is the question. And the answer will depend on whether opinion leaders think a video's content is worth sharing. That's what this chapter is about.

Week 1: Watch YouTube Award Winners

As I mentioned in Chapter 1, the YouTube Awards provided formal recognition to the best videos of the preceding year. The videos nominated were chosen by the YouTube staff, while the winners were selected by the YouTube community.

The winners of the 2006 YouTube Awards were announced in March 2007. There were awards in seven categories: Adorable, Comedy, Commentary, Creative, Inspirational, Musician of the Year, and Series. Each category comprised 10 videos that YouTubers ranked in order of preference.

One of the notable YouTubers who was nominated for several awards but won nothing was lonelygirl15, whose videos focused on the life of a teenage girl named Bree. However, the show did not initially reveal its fictional nature to the audience.

Lonelygirl15 (www.youtube.com/lonelygirl15) began in June 2006 and gained worldwide media attention in September 2006 when it was outed as a hoax by *Los Angeles Times* reporter Richard Rushfield.

As Figure 4.2 illustrates, "First Blog / Dorkiness Prevails" had more than 3.5 million views when this screen shot was taken.

Figure 4.2 "First Blog / Dorkiness Prevails"

Go to www.youtube.com/watch?v=-goXKtd6cPo to see the latest video statistics. At the time I was writing this chapter, the video statistics showed that it had mixed ratings: 4,844 likes and 3,665 dislikes. And the video had no honors.

For the 2007 YouTube Awards, five new categories were added: Eyewitness, Instructional, Short Film, Sports, and Politics. A general Music category replaced the Musician of the Year category from the previous year. In addition, the YouTube staff nominated only six videos in each category for which YouTubers could vote.

As I mentioned in Chapter 1, "Leave Britney Alone!" by vlogger Chris Crocker was nominated but didn't win.

Let's look at five videos that have not only been watched by millions of viewers, but also had content that a plurality of the YouTube community did vote for in March 2007 or March 2008. They were leading indicators of the social system's norms.

Monday: Observe "Free Hugs Campaign"

Tuesday: See "Here It Goes Again"

Wednesday: Check out "Potter Puppet Pals in 'The Mysterious Ticking Noise'"

Thursday: Look at "Battle at Kruger"

Friday: View "'Chocolate Rain' Original Song by Tay Zonday"

Monday: Observe "Free Hugs Campaign"

The 2006 YouTube Award winner in the Inspirational category was "Free Hugs Campaign - Official Page (music by Sick Puppies.net)" As Figure 4.3 illustrates, the video had more than 65 million views when this was written.

Figure 4.3 "Free Hugs Campaign - Official Page (music by Sick Puppies.net)"

At www.youtube.com/watch?v=vr3x_RRJdd4 you can see the latest video statistics. When I was writing this chapter, it had 158,953 likes and only 4,758 dislikes. The video also had 11 honors:

- #1 - Most Discussed (All Time) - Australia
- #1 - Most Discussed (All Time) - Entertainment - Australia
- #12 - Most Discussed (All Time) - Entertainment
- #2 - Most Viewed (All Time) - Australia
- #60 - Most Viewed (All Time)
- #1 - Most Viewed (All Time) - Entertainment - Australia
- #9 - Most Viewed (All Time) - Entertainment
- #2 - Top Favorited (All Time) - Australia
- #41 - Top Favorited (All Time)
- #1 - Top Favorited (All Time) - Entertainment - Australia
- #4 - Top Favorited (All Time) - Entertainment

According to the Viral Video Chart, the inspirational video has 146,270 Facebook shares, 4,520 tweets, and 9,417 blog posts. Why would so many opinion leaders share this content?

"In a society where we don't know the names of our neighbors, and disrespect for culture and community seems rife, one man . . . Juan Mann, in fact, will change the world; with signs," says Unruly Media.

Free Hugs is the real-life story of Mann, whose "controversial" mission was to offer hugs to strangers in public places. As the video's description says, "Sometimes, a hug is all that we need."

Mann's campaign started at the Pitt Street Mall in Sydney, Australia, in June 2004. The hugs were meant to be random acts of kindness—selfless acts performed just to make others feel better. "In this age of social-disconnection most all of us lack that simple human touch from another," he writes.

"As this simple gesture of kindness and hope spread across the city, police and officials ordered the Free Hugs Campaign BANNED," he adds. According to the authorities, Mann had not obtained public liability insurance worth $25 million for his actions.

After 10,000 people signed a petition, the authorities allowed the Free Hugs Campaign to continue without the insurance.

Shortly after starting his campaign, Mann befriended Shimon Moore, the lead singer for Sick Puppies. Over a two-month period in late 2004, Moore shot video footage of Mann and his fellow huggers.

In March 2005, Moore and his band moved to Los Angeles, and at first they didn't do anything with the footage. Meanwhile, Mann continued his Free Hugs Campaign throughout 2005 and 2006 by appearing at the Pitt Street Mall in Sydney most Thursday afternoons.

In mid 2006, Mann's grandmother died, and Moore made a music video using the footage he had shot in 2004 to send to Mann as a present, saying, "This is who you are." In September 2006, the video was uploaded to YouTube.

In October 2006, Mann was invited to appear on *The Oprah Winfrey Show* after the producer's doctor saw the Free Hugs video on YouTube. Mann made an appearance outside the studio that morning, offering free hugs to the crowd waiting to see the taping of that day's episode. The show's camera crews caught several people in the audience hugging Mann as the morning progressed.

Now, is that inspiring content that you'd share with others? Many YouTubers did. As Mann said in the video's description, "In the spirit of the Free Hugs Campaign please pass this video to a friend and HUG a stranger! After all, you CAN make a difference."

And is this an inspirational story that you'd have voted for in March 2007? Many YouTubers did.

As Mann added in the video's description, "The response to this video has been nothing short of overwhelming and touching. Hugs to every single one of you who messaged. There has been thousands of emails from all over the world from people seeking to participate in the Free Hugs Campaign and asking for permission. You don't need permission. This is the people's movement, this is *your* movement. With nothing but your bare hands you CAN make a difference."

What's the lesson learned from watching the Free Hugs Campaign? It is about emotion.

The effectiveness of emotion is difficult to quantify, but I've come to believe that video content that is nostalgic, inspirational, and even sentimental is well worth sharing. And emotion can be just as effective as any rational appeal, especially when "a hug is all that we need."

Tuesday: See "Here It Goes Again"

The 2006 YouTube Award winner in the Creative category was "OK Go - Here It Goes Again." Although Figure 4.4 indicates that the video had more than 5.3 million views, it had more than 46 million views in 2009 before being moved by EMI Music to VEVO.

Go to www.youtube.com/watch?v=dTAAsCNK7RA and you can see the current video statistics. When I wrote this, the video statistics showed it had 217,358 likes and only 8,374 dislikes. The video also had five honors:

- #75 - Most Discussed (All Time) - Music
- #84 - Most Viewed (All Time)
- #49 - Most Viewed (All Time) - Music
- #13 - Top Favorited (All Time)
- #6 - Top Favorited (All Time) - Music

Figure 4.4 "OK Go - Here It Goes Again"

According to the Viral Video Chart, "There's nothing like watching 4 full grown men execute a perfectly choreographed dance routine. Especially if the said dance routine incorporates treadmills, and the said men are geek-rock quadruplets OK-GO."

This helps explain why their award-winning video had 178,429 Facebook shares, 1,591 tweets, and 6,326 blog posts.

Originally from Chicago, the rock band OK Go now resides in Los Angeles. The band is composed of Damian Kulash, Tim Nordwind, Dan Konopka, and Andy Ross, who replaced Andy Duncan in 2005.

The music video of "Here It Goes Again" is an elaborate performance of the band dancing on treadmills in a single continuous take. Choreographed by Kulash's sister, Trish Sie, it took a total of 17 attempts to complete the video. Conceptually, the routine is a follow-up to their 2005 viral video, "A Million Ways," which was also a highly choreographed single-take music video.

The video debuted on YouTube on July 31, 2006. It premiered on VH1's Top 20 Countdown that same day. On August 23, 2006, Kulash appeared on the *Colbert Report* to talk about "Here It Goes Again." On August 31, 2006, OK Go performed the dance routine live at the 2006 MTV Video Music Awards.

In addition to winning the 2006 YouTube Award for most creative video, "Here It Goes Again" won the 2007 Grammy Award for Best Short Form Music Video.

Now, would you share their creative content with others? And why did so many YouTubers vote for "Here It Goes Again" in 2007?

On September 21, 2010, Salon's Matt Zoller Seitz asked, "Can OK Go save the movie musical?" after the band uploaded "OK Go - White Knuckles - Official Video" to YouTube.

Seitz observed that Kulash, Nordwind, Konokpka, and Ross aren't professional dancers and don't pretend to be. Seitz said, "They dance about as well as someone with a smidgen of rhythm might dance if he or she spent a couple of weeks rehearsing a routine with a professional choreographer and film crew—and that, paradoxically, is a big part of what makes these videos so beguiling."

According to Seitz, the band members "restore a sense of wonder to the musical number by letting the performers' humanity shine through and allowing them to do their thing with a minimum of filmmaking interference." In other words, "musical vignettes" with a parade of fleeting impressions were once fashionable but aren't worth sharing.

Wednesday: Check Out "Potter Puppet Pals: The Mysterious Ticking Noise"

The 2007 YouTube Award winner in the Comedy category was "Potter Puppet Pals: The Mysterious Ticking Noise." As Figure 4.5 illustrates, it had more than 94 million views.

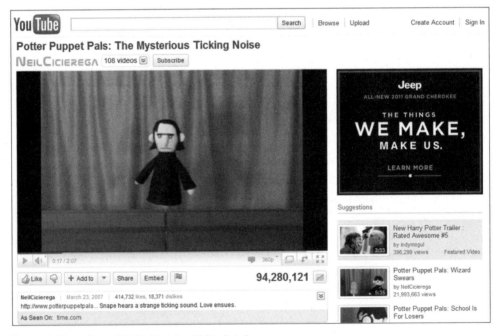

Figure 4.5 "Potter Puppet Pals: The Mysterious Ticking Noise"

Go to www.youtube.com/watch?v=Tx1XIm6q4r4 and you can see the current video statistics. When this was written, they showed it had 392,925 likes and only 17,847 dislikes. And it had eight honors:

- #44 - Most Discussed (All Time)
- #6 - Most Discussed (All Time) - Comedy
- #32 - Most Viewed (All Time)
- #5 - Most Viewed (All Time) - Comedy
- #5 - Top Favorited (All Time)
- #4 - Top Favorited (All Time) - Comedy
- #10 - Top Rated (All Time)
- #4 - Top Rated (All Time) - Comedy

According to the Viral Video Chart, "Puppet Potter Pals: The Mysterious Ticking Noise" has 199,061 Facebook shares, 6,547 tweets, and 3,104 blog posts.

"Potter Puppet Pals: The Mysterious Ticking Noise" was created by Neil Stephen Cicierega, an American comedian, filmmaker, and musician. He is also the creator of a genre of Flash animation known as animutation. And he lives near me, in Kingston, Massachusetts.

Cicierega's *Potter Puppet Pals* is a comedy series that is a parody of Harry Potter. It originated in 2003 as a pair of Flash animations on Newgrounds.com and later resurfaced in the form of a series of live-action puppet shows released in 2006 on YouTube and Potterpuppetpals.com.

"The Mysterious Ticking Noise," uploaded on March 23, 2007, won the 2007 YouTube Award with 33.6 percent of the votes in the Comedy category.

Cicierega has worked on videos with fellow Massachusetts Internet filmmakers and close friends Kevin James, Ryan Murphy, Max Pacheco, and J.L. Carrozza.

Several of Cicierega's short films have been featured on television shows such as G4's *Attack of the Show!*, The CW's *Online Nation*, and CBBC's *Chute!* In addition to *Potter Puppet Pals*, the director adds regular video content to the NeilCicierega channel on YouTube.

Although Cicierega is just 24 years old, he has been Internet-notable for a while. Back in 2000, when he was only 14, he formed the band Lemon Demon. The band's song/video "Ultimate Showdown of Ultimate Destiny" (in which several unrelated fictional characters fight) "went viral" on New Grounds in 2005.

A recurring theme in a lot of Cicierega's work is to play off of preexisting intellectual property and distort it in a way that is often disturbingly incompatible with the tone of source—for example, Mr. Rogers murdering people in "Ultimate Showdown of Ultimate Destiny" or Dumbledore being a sexual predator in *Potter Puppet Pals*. "Ultimate Showdown" and "Potter Puppets" are similar in that they became massively popular by incorporating content that the viewer was already invested in.

Unlike the creators of other videos from this week, Cicierega is someone who is very much aware of Internet memes and was actively pursuing mass Internet appeal via an established method of remixing pop culture rather than accidentally stumbling into it.

What other lesson can we learn from this award-winning video? Sound effects can make a video worth sharing. On the other hand, research has found that using background music is neither a positive nor a negative factor.

Thursday: Look at "Battle at Kruger"

This *National Geographic*-worthy footage was shot and uploaded to YouTube by a regular guy on safari with his family. The unbelievable confrontation between a herd of water buffalo, a pride of lions, and a couple of crocodiles—along with the surprise ending—has kept people on the edge of their seats since it was uploaded on May 3, 2007.

Clearly this viral video captured the world's attention. As Figure 4.6 illustrates, "Battle at Kruger" had more than 58 million views.

Figure 4.6 "Battle at Kruger"

Go to www.youtube.com/watch?v=LU8DDYz68kM and you can see the current video statistics. When I wrote this, they showed it had 136,524 likes and only 3,855 dislikes. And it had five honors:

- #2 - Most Discussed (All Time) - Pets & Animals
- #72 - Most Viewed (All Time)

- #1 - Most Viewed (All Time) - Pets & Animals
- #36 - Top Favorited (All Time)
- #3 - Top Favorited (All Time) - Pets & Animals

According to the Viral Video Chart, "Battle at Kruger" has 100,524 Facebook shares, 1,499 tweets, and 4,861 blog posts.

The amateur wildlife video was shot in September 2004 at a watering hole in Kruger National Park, South Africa, during a safari guided by Frank Watts. It was filmed by videographer David Budzinski and photographer Jason Schlosberg.

Taken from a vehicle on the opposite side of the watering hole with a digital camcorder, the video begins with the herd of buffalo approaching the water. The lions charge and disperse the herd, picking off a young buffalo and unintentionally knocking it into the water while attempting to make a kill. While the lions try to drag the buffalo out of the water, it is grabbed by a crocodile, which fights for it before giving up and leaving it to the lions. The lions sit down and prepare to eat but are quickly surrounded by the massively reorganized buffalo, who move in and begin charging and kicking at the lions. After a battle that sees one lion being tossed into the air by a buffalo, the baby buffalo—still alive, to the astonishment of the onlookers—escapes into the herd. The emboldened buffalo then proceed to chase the remaining lions away.

"Battle at Kruger" won the 2007 YouTube Award in the Eyewitness category. A *National Geographic* documentary on the video debuted on the National Geographic channel on May 11, 2008.

What other lesson can we learn from this award-winning video? Avoid visual banality. If you want visitors to pay attention to your video, show them something they have never seen before.

Friday: View "'Chocolate Rain' Original Song by Tay Zonday"

"'Chocolate Rain' Original Song by Tay Zonday" was the winner in the Music category in the 2007 YouTube Awards. It was also the underdog smash hit of the summer of 2007. The song, with its unconventional lyrics and delivery, struck a chord with the YouTube community and sparked imitations from everyday people and celebrities alike. Even Green Day's Tre Cool got in the mix!

It was clear that Zonday and his tune had pop culture abuzz when he appeared as a guest on both *Jimmy Kimmel Live* and VH1's *Best Week Ever*. Now Zonday's popping up in Internet commercials like the one for Dr. Pepper's new Cherry Chocolate beverage, and his breathe-away-from-the-mic move has become a meme of our time.

As Figure 4.7 illustrates, "'Chocolate Rain' Original Song by Tay Zonday" had more than 60 million views.

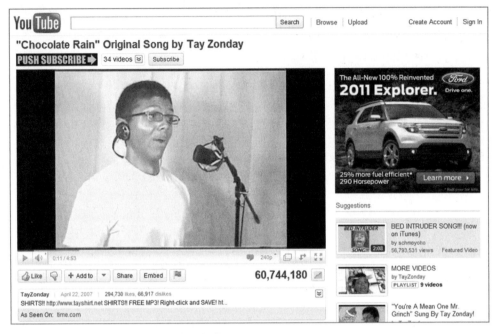

Figure 4.7 *"'Chocolate Rain' Original Song by Tay Zonday"*

Go to www.youtube.com/watch?v=EwTZ2xpQwpA and you will see the current video statistics. When this was written, they showed it had 284,129 likes and 64,807 dislikes. It also had six honors:

- #13 - Most Discussed (All Time)
- #6 - Most Discussed (All Time) - Music
- #68 - Most Viewed (All Time)
- #42 - Most Viewed (All Time) - Music
- #43 - Top Favorited (All Time)
- #20 - Top Favorited (All Time) - Music

According to the Viral Video Chart, "'Chocolate Rain' Original Song by Tay Zonday" has 47,434 Facebook shares, 1,729 tweets, and 2,484 blog posts.

Now, here's the backstory on "Chocolate Rain": Zonday's real name is Adam Nyerere Bahner. The video was originally posted on 4chan.org, an extremely popular, graphic, trend-setting message board. However, the discussion on 4chan was focused on mocking Tay rather than an earnest appreciation of his video. In fact, tons of parody videos were made in response, including ones by non-4chan users.

Although the video was posted on April 22, 2007, it didn't really go viral until July 26, 2007, when YouTube simultaneously featured all of the parody and response videos on its home page.

So, the opinion leaders who turned "Chocolate Rain" into a viral video were the 4chan community and a few members of the YouTube staff. Nevertheless, the history behind Zonday's "success" makes a fun backstory to tell as opinion leaders share his video with their followers.

There is another lesson to be learned here: Catchy songs are worth sharing. Even ones with cryptic lyrics like, "Zoom the camera out and see the lie." In fact, the piano riff and drum loop are hypnotic. Zonday has said, "I don't know what causes people to listen to my music. If I could speak it, there would be no reason to write songs."

Week 2: Explore Popular YouTube Videos

Now that you've watched some of the award-winning videos of 2006 and 2007, do you see a pattern? They fall into a variety of categories, including Inspirational, Creative, Comedy, Eyewitness, and Music. Although one is humorous in nature, four are not.

So what do the award-winning videos we've watched so far have in common? In addition to being among the most viewed, they are also among the most discussed and top favorited. I imagine that they are also ones that made their way into conversations both at work and at home because they tell unique stories. Each of these videos has a sense of authenticity and originality, which makes it worth sharing.

This is the key to creating content worth sharing.

Of course, I'm not the only one who understands the importance of storytelling. As Figure 4.8 illustrates, Sony's Backstage 101 online learning center once had an article entitled "Tell a Story with Video."

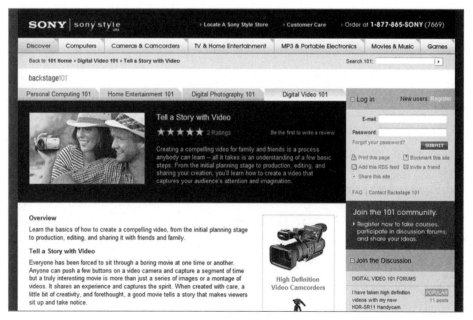

Figure 4.8 "Tell a Story with Video"

Unfortunately, Backstage 101 was permanently closed as of April 1, 2010. Fortunately, the first edition of this book captured some of Sony's advice.

For example, Sony advised, "Before you shoot a single frame, you should understand exactly how you want your story to be told and what you want the audience to take away from it. No matter what kind of story you choose to tell, the best place to start isn't with a camera and microphone—it's with a pen and paper."

Sony also advised that you ask a few key questions:

Who is your audience? Is this video for a business audience, or is it for your family and friends?

What point of view will you take? Will you tell it from your own perspective, from that of one of your subjects, or will a third-person narrator do the talking?

Where does the story take place?

When do the key events that propel the story take place?

Why is this story worth telling?

How will you tell the story? How will your video connect emotionally with the audience?

There's also a language to storytelling. If you don't know how to speak it, you've watched enough movies and TV programs to understand it. Start wide to give the audience an idea of where you are. Cut to medium to learn more about your subject. Get tight to capture the emotion.

With this in mind, let's explore some of the popular YouTube videos from 2008 and 2009 to discover their secrets. Like the award-winning videos you watched in week 1, some tell compelling stories and others have intriguing backstories.

The dramatic revelation of secrets from a backstory is a useful technique for developing a story. It was first recognized as a literary device by Aristotle.

Monday: Observe "Where the Hell is Matt? (2008)"

Tuesday: See "Fred Loses His Meds"

Wednesday: Check out "Susan Boyle - Britain's Got Talent"

Thursday: Look at "JK Wedding Entrance Dance"

Friday: View "David After Dentist"

Monday: Observe "Where the Hell is Matt? (2008)"

Matt Harding is best known as "Dancing Matt," the Internet celebrity who has danced his way around the world—three times.

Harding, who hates the "Dancing Matt" nickname, describes himself as "a 34-year-old deadbeat from Connecticut." He's actually a former video game designer and a friend of Brad O'Farrell, the technical editor of this book.

In February of 2003, he quit his job and used the money he'd saved to wander around Asia until the money ran out. He built a website at www.wherethehellismatt.com so he could keep his family and friends updated about where he was.

While in Hanoi, a travel buddy said to Harding, "Hey, why don't you stand over there and do that dance. I'll record it." His friend was referring to a particular dance that Matt does. According to Harding, it's the only dance he does. And he does it badly. Anyway, this turned out to be a very good idea.

Some opinion leaders found the video online and shared it with their followers, who then passed it along to others, et cetera, et cetera. Dancing Matt became quasi-famous and his video clips started appearing on several TV shows:

- *The Screen Savers* (March 17, 2005)
- MSNBC's *Countdown with Keith Olbermann* (August 18, 2005)
- *Inside Edition* (August 19, 2005)
- *The Ellen DeGeneres Show* (October 10, 2005)

The response to the first video brought Dancing Matt to the attention of the people at STRIDE, makers of the Ridiculously Long Lasting Gum. In 2006, they asked Harding if he'd be interested in taking another trip around the world to make a new video. He asked if they'd be paying for it. And they said yes. Harding thought this sounded like another very good idea.

With STRIDE as his sponsor, Harding took a six-month trip through 39 countries on all seven continents. The second video made Dancing Matt even more quasi-famous. In fact, he became *semi*-famous.

In 2007, Harding went back to Stride with a new idea. He realized that his bad dancing wasn't all that interesting, and other people were actually much better at bad dancing than he was. But, since he'd become semi-famous, his inbox was overflowing with emails from all over the globe. He wanted to travel around the world one more time and invite the people who'd written him to come out and dance with him.

The people at STRIDE thought that sounded like yet another very good idea, so they let him do it. And he did.

Harding released his third dancing video on June 20, 2008. The video is the product of 14 months of traveling in 42 countries.

As Figure 4.9 illustrates, "Where the Hell is Matt? (2008)" had more than 33.6 million views.

Figure 4.9 "Where the Hell is Matt? (2008)"

Go to www.youtube.com/watch?v=zlfKdbWwruY and you will see the current video statistics. When I wrote this, they showed it had 149,495 likes and only 2,907 dislikes. This video also had 15 honors:

- #100 - Spotlight Videos - Travel & Events - Germany
- #100 - Spotlight Videos - Travel & Events - Australia
- #96 - Spotlight Videos - Travel & Events - Canada
- #100 - Spotlight Videos - Travel & Events - Ireland
- #99 - Spotlight Videos - Travel & Events - New Zealand
- #96 - Spotlight Videos - Travel & Events - Israel
- #96 - Spotlight Videos - Travel & Events - South Africa
- #96 - Spotlight Videos - Travel & Events - Argentina
- #99 - Spotlight Videos - Travel & Events - South Korea
- #99 - Spotlight Videos - Travel & Events - Netherlands
- #99 - Spotlight Videos - Travel & Events - Brazil
- #4 - Most Discussed (All Time) - Travel & Events
- #1 - Most Viewed (All Time) - Travel & Events
- #42 - Top Favorited (All Time)
- #1 - Top Favorited (All Time) - Travel & Events

According to the Viral Video Chart, "Where the Hell is Matt (2008)" has 208,667 Facebook shares, 9,368 tweets, and 8,689 blog posts.

Harding's bad dancing has brought inspiration and joy to millions of people. One observer said, "It shows that no matter how different we are on the outside, inside we all just want to dance, laugh, and have fun." But all that bad dancing may not have sold much gum.

Amanda Watlington of Searching for Profit and I have been showing Harding's "Where the Hell is Matt" videos at Search Engine Strategies workshops since April 2007. And unless we point it out, no one notices the mention of STRIDE in the closing credits.

Is there a lesson to be learned here? There is, and it's "brand identification." Research has demonstrated that a shocking percentage of viewers remember a video but forget the name of its sponsor. And many marketers think it is crass to belabor the name of a sponsor.

So, for the benefit of those who are more interested in selling than entertaining, there is a nonintrusive way to register your brand name: Watermark your video content.

Since August 2008, Harding has been represented by Creative Artists Agency. And in November 2008, he was hired by Visa to star in its "Travel Happy" campaign.

In a press release, Visa said, "Visa's new travel-focused commercial recreates the dance made famous by internet celebrity Matt Harding in his self-made quirky video travel diaries. After tickling the funny bones of millions from the internet community for four years, Matt repeats his signature jig in China, Indonesia, Japan, Singapore, the USA and Vietnam—to celebrate how Visa has freed him from the hassle of exchanging cash for each country's local currency as he travels around the world."

It's worth noting that the Visa card and logo appear prominently in the travel-focused commercial.

Tuesday: See "Fred Loses His Meds"

You don't need to dance around the world to get opinion leaders to share your content with their followers.

You could create and portray a character like Fred Figglehorn, a lonely six-year-old who has a dysfunctional home life and anger management issues. That's exactly what Lucas Cruikshank, a teenager from Columbus, Nebraska, has done.

So, what does Cruikshank's fictional character do? Fred uses his mom's camera and starts posting videos to a YouTube channel.

Cruikshank's hyperactive videos of Fred's helium-voiced character quickly caught people's attention and helped make him the fastest-rising star in YouTube history. Cruikshank's second video, "Fred Loses His Meds," was his first to break a million views.

And as Figure 4.10 illustrates, "Fred Loses His Meds" had more than 31.1 million views when this screen shot was taken.

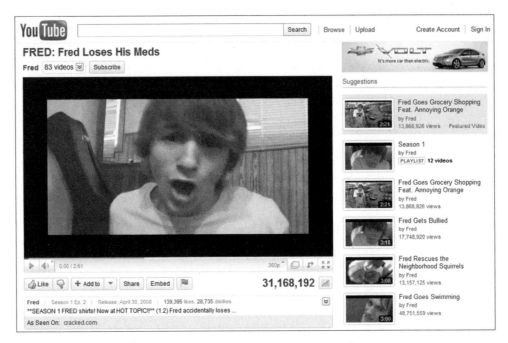

Figure 4.10 "Fred Loses His Meds"

Go to www.youtube.com/watch?v=m9MA0eW8yyw and you will see the current video statistics. When this was written, they showed it had 137,493 likes and 27,267 dislikes. And the video had one honor:

#51 - Most Discussed (All Time)

According to the Viral Video Chart, "Fred Loses His Meds" has 17,221 Facebook shares and 329 blog posts.

Cruikshank and his cousins, Jon and Katie Smet, initially set up the JKL Productions channel on YouTube in June 2006. Cruikshank uploaded his first Fred video in October 2006.

In April 2008, the videos that had already been filmed got added to the Fred channel, and in May 2008, the first official video, entitled "Fred on May Day," was released.

By April 2009, Fred's channel recorded its millionth subscriber, making it the first YouTube channel to do so. It hit two million subscribers on September 27, 2010.

As this was written, Fred's channel had more than 101 million channel views and over 641 million total upload views.

Cruikshank has made a few television appearances both as himself and as Fred. And in December 2009, he filmed *Fred: The Movie*, which aired on Nickelodeon on September 18, 2010.

Parents may wonder why anyone—even teenagers—would share Cruikshank's content with their friends, but Fred's channel has been described as "programming for kids by kids."

According to Cruikshank, the series is intended as a parody of people who "think that everyone is so interested in them." He believes that viewers either "automatically love Fred or automatically hate Fred, there is no in between."

The videos primarily consist of Fred speaking to the audience about what is happening in his life. He lives with his recovering drug-addicted and alcoholic mother, whose voice is often heard, and his grandmother. In the first three seasons, all characters other than Fred remained off screen, with the exception of animals.

Several times during the series, Fred mentioned that his father is on death row in the state penitentiary. The fictional six-year old hasn't met his father, who left Mrs. Figglehorn while she was still pregnant with Fred.

Fred has a crush on a girl in his kindergarten class named Judy. He describes Judy as "so mean... yet so attractive." In almost every episode, Fred sings a song he makes up.

The first season of Fred was sponsored by the Zipit Wireless Messenger, which had several cameo appearances in various videos posted to Fred's channel. Although the collaboration was originally kept low key, Fred now has a separate website promoting the device and has also starred in Zipit TV commercials on Nickelodeon.

Is there a lesson to be learned here? Yes, there is.

Know your audience. Fred's videos get millions of views because Cruikshank knows exactly what kids want to watch on YouTube and appeals to that in a very precise way. Think about the audience you're trying to attract and the kinds of things that audience likes. Incorporate those elements into your videos. It doesn't matter whether or not your video appeals to you or your peers. All that matters is that it reaches its intended audience.

Wednesday: Check Out "Susan Boyle - Britain's Got Talent"

The most watched YouTube video in 2009 was "Susan Boyle - Singer- Britain's Got Talent 2009." Uploaded on April 11 of that year, it and related videos had more than 120 million views as of December 16, 2009.

But this video is no longer available on YouTube due to a copyright claim by Alain Boublil Music Ltd. The clip was removed in August 2010 just as it reached 96 million views. However, other versions of the video can be still be found on a variety of online video sharing destinations.

As Figure 4.11 illustrates, one of these versions is "Susan Boyle - Britains Got Talent 2009 Episode 1 - Saturday 11th April | HD Quality." Uploaded to the UKAdvertChannel on YouTube, it had more than 55.9 million views as this was written.

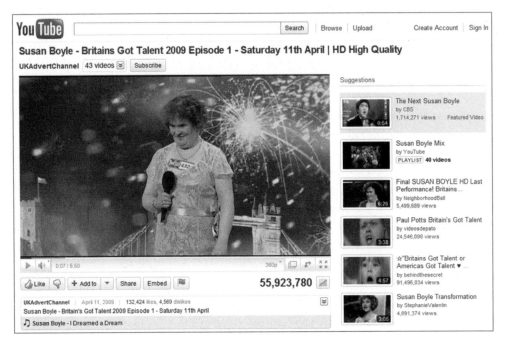

Figure 4.11 "Susan Boyle - Britains Got Talent 2009 Episode 1 - Saturday 11th April | HD Quality"

Go to www.youtube.com/watch?v=RxPZh4AnWyk and you will see the current video statistics. When I wrote this, they showed this version of the original video had 127,802 likes and 4,469 dislikes. And this stand-in had 10 honors:

- #8 - Most Discussed (All Time) - United Kingdom
- #1 - Most Discussed (All Time) - Entertainment - United Kingdom
- #8 - Most Discussed (All Time) - Entertainment
- #7 - Most Viewed (All Time) - United Kingdom
- #86 - Most Viewed (All Time)
- #2 - Most Viewed (All Time) - Entertainment - United Kingdom
- #15 - Most Viewed (All Time) - Entertainment
- #13 - Top Favorited (All Time) - United Kingdom
- #2 - Top Favorited (All Time) - Entertainment - United Kingdom
- #17 - Top Favorited (All Time) - Entertainment

According to the Viral Video Chart, "Susan Boyle - Britains Got Talent 2009 Episode 1 - Saturday 11th April | HD Quality" has 362,837 Facebook shares, 2,570 tweets, and 15,219 blog posts.

To get an idea of the video statistics that the original version must have had before being taken down, go to Visible Measures, which measures the total audience that has been exposed to community-driven video copies and derivative works. According to its 100 Million Views Club (www.visiblemeasures.com/hundred), "Susan Boyle: Britain's Got Talent" had a total audience of 347,670,927.

By now, Susan Magdalane Boyle's backstory is well known.

Born in Blackburn, Scotland, in 1961, Boyle was nicknamed "Susie Simple" at school. She never married and still lives in the family home, a council house, with her cat Pebbles. She has a reputation for modesty and propriety, admitting during her first appearance on *Britain's Got Talent* that she had "never been married, never been kissed."

But Boyle had sung in her church choir. After she won several local singing competitions, her mother urged her to enter *Britain's Got Talent* and take the risk of singing in front of an audience larger than her parish church. Boyle's performance on the show was the first time she had sung in public since her mother died.

On April 11, 2009, Boyle appeared on *Britain's Got Talent* and sang "I Dreamed a Dream" from *Les Misérables*. The contrast between her plain appearance and powerful voice stunned both the audience and the judges. Amanda Holden, one of the judges, commented on the initially cynical attitude of the audience, and called Boyle's subsequent performance the "biggest wake-up call ever."

The juxtaposition of the first impression of Boyle by the judges and audience with the standing ovation and judges' comments after her performance led to an international media and Internet response.

Boyle was one of 40 acts that went on to the semi-finals. On May 24, 2009, she performed "Memory" from the musical *Cats*. She received the highest number of public votes and went on to the final. Although the clear favorite, Boyle finished in second place in the final behind the dance troupe Diversity.

However, her first album, *I Dreamed a Dream*, became the biggest-selling album in the world for 2009. Released on November 23, 2009, it sold 9 million copies by the end of the year just six weeks later.

In September 2010, Guinness World Records officially recognized Boyle for the following achievements:

- Having the fastest -selling debut album by a female artist in the UK
- Having the most successful first week sales of a debut album in the UK
- Being the oldest person to reach number one with a debut album in the UK

YouTube and other social media were crucial to Boyle's rapid rise to fame. On the day following the performance, the YouTube video was the most popular article on Digg and made the front page of Reddit. Within three days, the most popular YouTube video of her audition had already garnered nearly 2.5 million views.

On April 15, four days after the performance, tweets about "Susan Boyle" spiked, according to TweetStats. On April 16, five days after the performance, mentions of "Susan Boyle" in blogs spiked, according to IceRocket's trend tool.

Within a week, Boyle's audition video had been viewed more than 66 million times, setting an online record. Within the same time, her biographical article on Wikipedia had attracted nearly half a million page views.

Within nine days, 165 duplicate videos of Boyle—from an earlier rendition of "Cry Me a River," her audition, the show, and interviews with her afterward—had a combined total of 103 million views on 20 different video sites.

In December 2009, YouTube named her audition the most watched video of the year with over 120 million views, more than three times higher than the second most popular video.

In addition, Boyle's first on-camera interview with her local newspaper was named as YouTube's Most Memorable Video of 2009. The video interview by Scottish journalist Richard Mooney of the *West Lothian Courier* went viral after being uploaded to YouTube on April 14, 2009.

Other mainstream media also played critical roles in turning Boyle into an overnight sensation. Within the week following her performance on *Britain's Got Talent*, Boyle was interviewed via satellite on CBS's *Early Show*, *Good Morning America*, NBC's *Today*, *The Oprah Winfrey Show*, and *Larry King Live*.

On April 17, Scott Collins and Janet Stobart of the *Los Angeles Times* wrote, "The case of this previously unknown amateur singer is a compelling study in how viral video can lather its subject into frothy international stardom within hours."

They added, "Indeed, a full range of emotion—first humor, then shock, followed by warm appreciation and perhaps a dollop of self-reproof for anyone who dares to judge others principally by their appearance—can be extracted from Boyle's seven-minute clip. And that is what makes her story perfect for the Internet, where short clips rule."

On April 19, Gillian Harris of the *Sunday Times* wrote, "Now the world knows Susan Boyle's name. The 48-year-old church volunteer's performance on *Britain's Got Talent* has propelled her from obscurity to global stardom. Boyle's powerful voice, which silenced the cynical judges and those in the audience who sneered because she wasn't groomed or glamorous, is expected to make her wealthy beyond her modest dreams."

Boyle told Harris, "I know what they were thinking but why should it matter as long as I can sing? It's not a beauty contest."

On April 20, 2009, Maria Puente of *USA Today* wrote, "After a week of unabashed hysteria about Scottish chanteuse Susan Boyle, it's time to pause and ask: What's that all about?"

Maybe it was the compelling content of the video: The 47-year-old Boyle, whom Puente calls "unglamorous, unfashionable, unknown," takes on a skeptical British audience and sneering panel of judges on *Britain's Got Talent*, including the unsparingly blunt Simon Cowell. "Then, in an instant, she turned jeers to cheers with her rendition of one of the weepier numbers from *Les Misérables*," wrote Puente.

Maybe it was Boyle's Cinderella backstory: "Youngest of nine, learning disabled and bullied as a child, caretaker for her dying mother, never been kissed, singer in the choir, possessor of big dreams," she wrote.

Maybe it was because people tend to root for the underdog. "Or maybe it's just a new reminder of an old truism: You can't judge a book by its cover," Puente concluded.

Although Boyle was not eligible for the 2010 Grammy Awards, the show's host Stephen Colbert paid tribute to her at the ceremony. On February 1, 2010, he told the assembled stars, "You may be the coolest people in the world, but this year your industry was saved by a 48-year-old Scottish cat lady in sensible shoes."

Ironically, Boyle's viral videos weren't able to help the three producers of *Britain's Got Talent*, FremantleMedia, Talkback Thames, and SYCOtv, or the program's distributor in Britain, ITV.

Despite the video getting 103 million views in its first nine days, Eliot Van Buskirk of Wired.com reported on April 20, 2009, that it was not being monetized.

On April 23, 2009, Dan Sabbagh of the *Times* did "a crude estimate" that indicated the parties involved had left about $1.87 million, or £1.3 million, on the table.

On May 24, 2009, Brian Stelter of the *New York Times* reported that videos of Boyle's performances in April had been viewed 220 million times at that point, but "her runaway Web success has made little money for the program's producers or distributors."

Although FremantleMedia Enterprises had hastily uploaded video clips of Boyle to YouTube in the wake of her performance, the show was produced jointly by two other companies and distributed in Britain by another, making it difficult to ascertain which of the four companies could claim the videos as its own.

Before the current season of the show had started on April 11, the parties had tried to cut a distribution deal with YouTube, but they couldn't agree on terms. Why? According to Stelter, "Major media companies have shown varying degrees of interest in these deals, in part because they are reticent to split much money with Google."

As Figure 4.12 illustrates, at least one of the producers believed "Hoarding is just as human as sharing." But, isn't it smarter to share buckets of money than to hoard absolutely no money at all?

"Hoarding is just as human as sharing."

Figure 4.12 "Hording is just as human as sharing." (Cartoon by Edward Frascino in the *New Yorker*, March 13, 1995)

There are three lessons to be learned here.

First, "Susan Boyle - Singer- Britains Got Talent 2009" told a story that was worth retelling to others. On April 14, 2009, Colette Douglas Home of the *Herald* in Scotland wrote, "Susan Boyle's story is a parable of our age."

Second, investigate the best routes to monetize your channel in conjunction with relevant partners *before* one of your videos goes viral unexpectedly. According to people with knowledge of the talks, YouTube was especially interested in a deal because it was essentially losing money by serving millions of video streams without recouping any of the costs. However, the other parties involved didn't realize how much money they would be leaving on the table before the money train had left the station.

Third, when you decide to monetize a video, be certain that you have the express permission from the person who created or produced all of the content within it. This includes, but is not limited to, the following content:

- Music (including lyrics, cover songs and background music)
- Performances (including concerts, events, and shows)
- Movie or TV footage or visuals
- Graphics and pictures (including photographs and artwork)
- Video game or software visuals

Alain Boublil is a librettist, best known for his collaborations with composer Claude-Michel Schönberg on *Les Misérables* and *Miss Saigon*.

Although Boublil told the Insider he was "bowled over" by Boyle's performance of his song "I Dreamed a Dream" on *Britain's Got Talent*, the video "Susan Boyle - Britain's Got Talent" is no longer available on YouTube due to a copyright claim by Alain Boublil Music Ltd.

Now, getting express permission from copyright holders takes work. And having a clip with 96 million views removed because it was finally being monetized without having that express permission is a miscarriage of justice. But that is what appears to have happened.

It reminds me of the famous quotation by Thomas Edison, "Opportunity is missed by most people because it is dressed in overalls and looks like work."

Thursday: Look at "JK Wedding Entrance Dance"

Based on the lessons learned yesterday, it's seems appropriate to look at the "JK Wedding Entrance Dance" today. Uploaded to YouTube on July 19, 2009, the video was viewed over 3.5 million times in its first 48 hours.

On July 30, 2009, YouTube's Chris LaRosa (technical account manager) and Ali Sandler (music partner manager) said on the Official Google Blog, "Jill Peterson and Kevin Heinz's wedding party transformed a familiar and predictable tradition into something spontaneous and just flat-out fun."

As Figure 4.13 illustrates, "JK Wedding Entrance Dance" had more than 59 million views when the screen shot was taken.

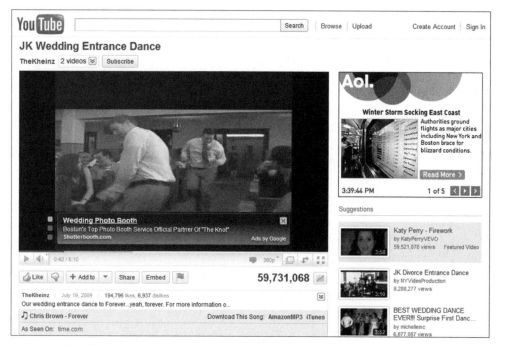

Figure 4.13 "JK Wedding Entrance Dance"

Go to www.youtube.com/watch?v=4-94JhLEiN0 and you will see the current video statistics. When this was written, they showed it had 193,854 likes and 6,919 dislikes. And the video had 10 honors:

- #69 - Spotlight Videos - Hong Kong
- #91 - Spotlight Videos - Taiwan
- #58 - Most Discussed (All Time)
- #4 - Most Discussed (All Time) - Entertainment
- #73 - Most Viewed (All Time)
- #12 - Most Viewed (All Time) - Entertainment
- #21 - Top Favorited (All Time)
- #2 - Top Favorited (All Time) - Entertainment
- #29 - Top Rated (All Time)
- #3 - Top Rated (All Time) - Entertainment

According to the Viral Video Chart, "JK Wedding Entrance Dance" has 440,565 Facebook shares, 11,714 tweets, and 8,827 blog posts.

The video, which was set to R&B star Chris Brown's hypnotic dance jam "Forever," became an overnight sensation, accumulating more than 10 million views on YouTube in less than a week. But as with all YouTube videos worth sharing, there's more to this story than simple view counts.

YouTube has sophisticated content management tools in place to help rights holders control their content in the world's most popular online video community. The rights holders for "Forever" used these tools to claim and monetize the song, as well as to start running Click-to-Buy links over the video, giving viewers the opportunity to purchase the music track on Amazon and iTunes. The song was even prominently featured on the TV show *The Office* in a direct reference to the "JK Wedding Entrance Dance" video, during the highly anticipated episode in which the characters Jim and Pam finally tied the knot.

As a result, the rights holders were able to capitalize on the massive wave of popularity generated by "JK Wedding Entrance Dance." In the first week, searches for "Chris Brown Forever" on YouTube skyrocketed, making it one of the most popular queries on the site.

This traffic was also very engaged. According to LaRosa and Sandler, the click-through rate (CTR) on the "JK Wedding Entrance Dance" video was two times the average of other click-to-buy overlays on the site. And this newfound interest in downloading "Forever" went beyond the viral video itself. "JK Wedding Entrance Dance" also appears to have influenced the official "Forever" music video, which saw its click-to-buy CTR increase by 2.5 times in the first week.

So, what does all of this mean? Despite compelling data and studies on consumer purchasing habits, many marketers and advertisers still question the promotional and bottom-line business value that video sites like YouTube provide artists.

But over a year after its release, Chris Brown's "Forever" rocketed up the charts again, reaching as high as #4 on the iTunes singles chart and #3 on Amazon's best-selling MP3 list in the week after "JK Wedding Entrance Dance" was uploaded.

What lesson can be learned here? If you are a rights holder, consider using YouTube's Audio ID and Video ID tools. Using YouTube's copyright tools is free and gives you control in a couple of ways:

- You can identify user-uploaded videos made up entirely *or* partially of your content.

- You can choose, in advance, what you want to happen when those videos are found, including make money from them, get stats on them, or block them from YouTube altogether.

Friday: View "David After Dentist"

The next popular YouTube video that we'll examine is "David After Dentist." Uploaded on January 30, 2009, it was the second most viewed video that year and created the catch phrase, "Is this real life?"

On March 18, 2010, Etan Horowitz of CNN wrote, "If you spend any time on the Internet, you've no doubt seen 'David After Dentist,' the YouTube video of a woozy 7-year-old boy in the back seat of a car, struggling to understand the effects of anesthesia."

As Figure 4.14 illustrates, "David After Dentist" had more than 76 million views when this screen shot was taken.

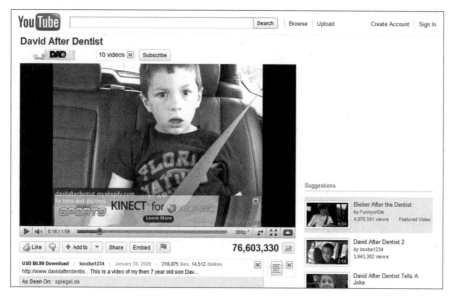

Figure 4.14 *"David After Dentist"*

Go to www.youtube.com/watch?v=txqiwrbYGrs and you will see the current video statistics. When I wrote this, they showed it had 217,015 likes and 14,359 dislikes. And the video had seven honors:

- #61 - Most Discussed (All Time) - Comedy

- #49 - Most Viewed (All Time)

- #8 - Most Viewed (All Time) - Comedy

- #8 - Top Favorited (All Time)

- #5 - Top Favorited (All Time) - Comedy

- #23 - Top Rated (All Time)

- #7 - Top Rated (All Time) - Comedy

According to the Viral Video Chart, "David After Dentist" has 326,934 Facebook shares, 10,790 tweets, and 6,737 blog posts.

Here's the backstory: In May 2008, David DeVore took his son David Jr. to a dental surgeon to have a procedure done to remove an extra tooth. The condition is called Hyperdontia. His wife, Tessie, also wanted to go. Unfortunately, she had a big meeting planned for the same day with executives coming from all over the country, so only the Davids went to the dentist. David Sr. had just bought a new flip video camera and decided he would use it, along with his cell phone camera, to record the day's events. After the procedure, the staff came out to get the father.

David Sr. says, "I noticed grins on their faces when I walked in. David (Jr.) was in rare form. I had to help him to the car, strapped him in his car seat and then proceeded to record him as I had planned. There was no coaching or editing. I just filmed what I was seeing and hearing. The deep questions David asks show his deep thinking that we have come to know as part of his personality."

David Sr. adds, "Once we got home and got some ice cream in him and a nap, David (Jr.) was fine and fully recovered. That night, I showed it to the family and we had a big laugh. David (Jr.) was rolling on the floor."

For the next several months, David Sr. shared the video with just family and friends. Then, he joined Facebook and started sharing it there. On January 31, 2009, he decided to post it on YouTube to make it easier to share.

David Sr. says, "Due to the limit YouTube has for the number of emails you can send the link to for private sharing, I chose to make it public thinking no one would think it would be as funny as we did. Shows you what I know!"

By the following Tuesday, the video had 3 million views. At first, the DeVore family didn't know what to think and were concerned that people might be making fun of their kid. David Sr. says, "Once we realized people thought it was cute and funny, we embraced the attention that came with it. We looked at it as a way for our family to have an experience we couldn't have had otherwise. What an experience is has been."

The DeVore family was soon invited to join the YouTube Partner Program. This gives YouTube the right to sell ads over and next to their popular videos, and in exchange, the DeVore family is given a share of the ad revenue. The DeVore family also sells T-shirts on their website at www.davidafterdentist.com that feature David's classic question, "Is this real life?"

According to *Time*, "And it's paying off: the DeVores have made nearly enough to cover David's (eventual) college education."

Again, there are two lessons to be learned here. First, slice-of-life videos can go viral. Who wouldn't share a video that features a kid who asks, "Why is this happening to me?" and "Is this gonna be forever?" Second, if YouTube invites you to include one of your more unforgettable videos in its Individual Video Program, just say yes. An extension of the YouTube Partner Program, the Individual Video Program recognizes the role that popular "one-off" videos play on YouTube. When you upload a video that accumulates lots of views, YouTube may invite you to monetize that video and start earning revenue from it.

To determine whether a particular video is eligible for monetization, YouTube looks at factors like the number of views, the video's virality, and compliance with the YouTube terms of service. If your video is eligible for monetization, you will receive an email and see an "Enable Revenue Sharing" message next to your video on the watch page as well as in other places in your account.

Once you've chosen to enable revenue sharing, YouTube will sell advertising against your video and pay you a revenue share into your Google AdSense account each month. If you don't have an AdSense account, you'll have the opportunity to create one.

Individual video partnerships are not eligible for many of the benefits of user partnerships, like enhanced channel features or the ability to monetize other videos in your account, so you might want to apply to be a member of the YouTube Partner Program.

In its first year, the Individual Video Program enabled hundreds of thousands of videos to earn money, enabled international users from 11 markets to earn revenue from their videos, and helped thousands of YouTube users to become official YouTube Partners.

"Is this real life?" Yes, this is real life.

Week 3: Examine Contagious Viral Ads

On September 19, 2008, Suzie Reider, the head of advertising at YouTube, gave a presentation entitled "Marketing with Video" at The Edge, a creative event thrown by the Boston AdClub.

Reider told the luncheon crowd about the lessons she had learned from her time with one of the world's largest social media communities. And from her point of view, YouTube is the combination of "both media and community."

One of the concepts that Reider shared was "Create ads that work as content." As an example, she showed "Amazing Ball girl catch," a Gatorade commercial directed by Baker Smith of Harvest Films.

As Figure 4.15 illustrates, this video had more than 2.7 million views when this screen shot was taken.

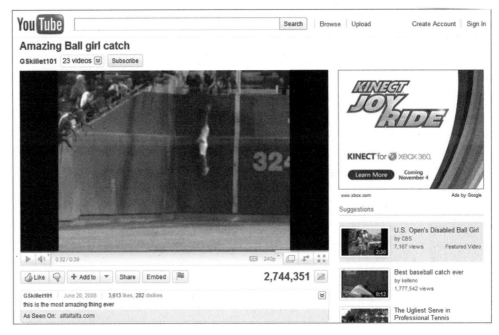

Figure 4.15 "Amazing Ball girl catch"

Go to www.youtube.com/watch?v=4SqJz0NgnnE and you will see the current video statistics. When this was written, they showed it had 3,588 likes and 279 dislikes.

According to the Viral Video Chart, "Amazing Ball girl catch" has 6,647 Facebook shares and 218 blog posts.

And hundreds of advertisers around the world are following Reider's advice. In fact, so many advertisers are creating viral ads that the Viral Video Chart lists the top 100 "most contagious" viral ads from the past 24 hours, 7 days, 30 days, 365 days, and all time.

The chart is a collaboration between Unruly Media and *Contagious Magazine*. It ranks viral videos and branded content worldwide based on the amount of times content has been shared on Facebook and Twitter and in the blogosphere.

Since there are so many ads that work as content, you might also want to check out YouTube's Show & Tell channel, which lists 28 viral hits. On December 21, 2010,

Chris Anderson, curator of TED, called these "examples of great creative" in his guest post entitled "What makes an ad worth spreading?" on the YouTube Blog.

Using both the Viral Video Chart and YouTube's Show & Tell channel to identify five "ads worth spreading," let's watch some of the most contagious viral ads of all time.

Monday: Watch "Evian Roller Babies international version"

Tuesday: Look at "Old Spice | The Man Your Man Could Smell Like"

Wednesday: Check out "The T-Mobile Dance"

Thursday: See "Inspired Bicycles - Danny MacAskill April 2009"

Friday: View "Ken Block Gymkhana Two the Infomercial"

Monday: Watch "Evian Roller Babies international version"

In November 2009, "Evian Roller Babies international version" was officially awarded a Guinness world record for "the most viewed online advertisement." As the video description says, "So small yet already incredible!"

Created by the advertising agency BETC Euro RSCG, the "rollerskating babies" video was part of its "Live Young" ad campaign for Evian water. As Figure 4.16 illustrates, "Evian Roller Babies international version" had more than 32.2 million views when this screen shot was taken.

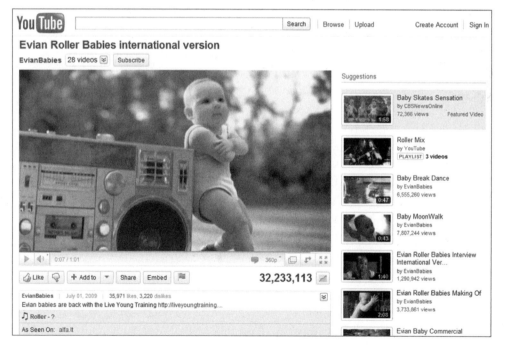

Figure 4.16 "Evian Roller Babies international version"

Go to `http://www.youtube.com/watch?v=XQcV11WpwGs` and you will see the current video statistics. When this was written, they showed it had 35,721 "Likes" and 3,204 "Dislikes." It also had 10 honors:

- #65 - Most Discussed (All Time) - France
- #9 - Most Discussed (All Time) - Entertainment - France
- #7 - Most Viewed (All Time) - France
- #37 - Most Viewed (All Time) - Entertainment
- #2 - Most Viewed (All Time) - Entertainment - France
- #6 - Top Favorited (All Time) - France
- #35 - Top Favorited (All Time) - Entertainment
- #2 - Top Favorited (All Time) - Entertainment - France
- #21 - Top Rated (All Time) - France
- #3 - Top Rated (All Time) - Entertainment - France

According to the Viral Video Chart, "Evian Roller Babies international version" has 576,162 Facebook shares, 8,261 tweets, and 6,040 blog posts.

The ad campaign was launched exclusively on YouTube in July 2009 with home-page ads in Canada, France, Germany, Japan, Russia, the UK, and the United States. It went on to become a smash hit and has proven the value of making big bets on YouTube.

On November 23, 2009, Gianni Pulli, industry leader, France, said on the YouTube Biz Blog, "We've learned from previous campaigns that paid views—like YouTube homepage ads or Promoted Videos—can drive organic views, and branding research conducted by Nielsen in France found that the advertising campaign was the key catalyst in building brand equity and sending the video viral."

He added, "Nielsen also found that 80% of those who saw the ad on YouTube in France and in the US considered discussing it, and 2/3 wanted to share it with friends."

Nina Boesch, senior interactive designer at And Partners in New York, says on YouTube's Show & Tell channel, "Babies doing grown up things is always freaky and funny...it's something I would share with friends."

It's worth noting that Unruly Media provided "video seeding" and social media monitoring for this spectacularly successful viral campaign.

To build buzz and whet appetites, Unruly Media launched two teaser videos two weeks before the official launch of the "Roller Babies" video. One was called "Baby Moonwalk" and the other "Baby Break Dance."

For "Roller Babies" itself, Unruly Media focused a significant amount of activity on Twitter, complementing the YouTube homepage takeovers that launched the clip in France, the United States, and other countries.

In a case study on its website, Unruly Media says it focused on the "Twitterati and Twitter-focused sites and apps such as Tweetmeme." Picked up and retweeted within seconds, "Roller Babies" benefited hugely from Twitter's ability to cross national boundaries and surface real-time trends, "leading to the fastest first million views we've ever seen," says Unruly Media.

To track the global spread of the campaign, Unruly Media fingerprinted the video file—taking a sample of its audiovisual DNA—and deployed web-tracking software to crawl 30 billion web pages looking for matches.

In the case study, Michael Aidan, global brand director of Evian, says, "The combination of seeding and posting the film worldwide on YouTube has helped us reach well beyond our expectations: the most viewed video ad on the web ever."

Is there any other lesson to learn from this viral ad? Here's an alternative wording: Yes, show the product in use—and, if possible, the end result of using it. You can be realistic. In a video for motor oil, show how the pistons look after 50,000 miles. You can also be fantastic. In this video, Evian showed the sensational effect that drinking bottled water can have on babies. In a video for motor oil, show how the pistons look after 50,000 miles.

Tuesday: Look at "Old Spice | The Man Your Man Could Smell Like"

On February 18, 2010, Christie D'Zurilla of the Ministry of Gossip blog in the *Los Angeles Times* wrote, "We looked at him. We looked away. We looked back at him. And dangit if we couldn't stop looking at him. Seriously, he's on a horse."

D'Zurilla was writing about Isaiah Mustafa, who is also known as "the guy who stars in that Old Spice commercial." Or, as the video description says, "We're not saying this body wash will make your man smell into a romantic millionaire jet fighter pilot, but we are insinuating it."

Eric Kallman and Craig Allen of Wieden + Kennedy were the creative rock stars behind the "Old Spice Guy" campaign. As Figure 4.17 illustrates, "Old Spice | The Man Your Man Could Smell Like" had more than 26.3 million views when this screen shot was taken.

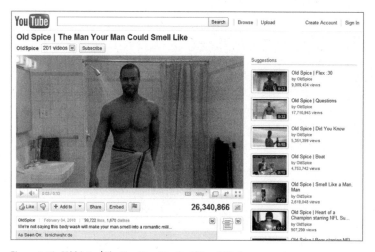

Figure 4.17 "Old Spice | The Man Your Man Could Smell Like"

Go to www.youtube.com/watch?v=owGykVbfgUE to see the current video statistics. When I wrote this, it had 98,456 likes and 1,638 dislikes. And the video had six honors:

- #40 - Spotlight Videos - Australia
- #76 - Spotlight Videos
- #87 - Most Discussed (All Time) - People & Blogs
- #17 - Most Viewed (All Time) - People & Blogs
- #3 - Top Favorited (All Time) - People & Blogs
- #6 - Top Rated (All Time) - People & Blogs

According to the Viral Video Chart, "Old Spice | The Man Your Man Could Smell Like" has 376,295 Facebook shares, 10,546 tweets, and 4,213 blog posts.

On October 6, 2010, Mark Sabec, product marketing manager, wrote on the YouTube Blog, "When you consider that the product in question is an everyday hygiene item, the buzz generated by their creative team is that much more impressive."

The Old Spice guy debuted on February 4, 2010, and helped the Old Spice channel on YouTube get more than 173 million views and over 205,000 subscribers.

It has also been parodied endlessly on the Web, TV, and radio. As Figure 4.18 illustrates, one of these parodies, "Sesame Street: Smell Like a Monster," had more than 6.2 million views.

On July 25, 2010, Noreen O'Leary and Todd Wasserman of *Brandweek* reported that sales of Old Spice Body Wash had increased 107 percent over the previous month according to the Nielsen Co.

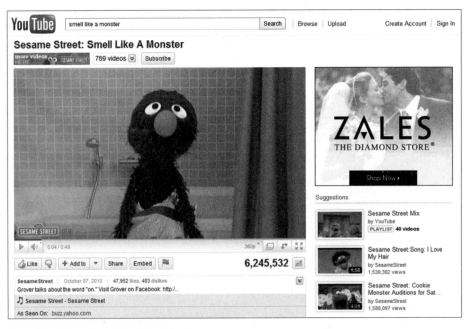

Figure 4.18 "Sesame Street: Smell Like a Monster"

But on August 26, 2010, Jack Neff of *Advertising Age* reported that the buy-one-get-one-free and other high-value coupons that Old Spice had distributed during the month could account for most of the brand's sales gains and all its market share gains.

Nevertheless, "Old Spice | The Man Your Man Could Smell Like" was the #5 most popular YouTube video in 2010 and the most memorable marketing campaign of the year. And as for the coupons, no one buys even one bottle of body wash to sit around in their bathroom cabinet. So, I think the 107 percent increase in sales is still a success story.

Is there a lesson to be learned here? Yes, there is.

It's about talking heads. This derogatory term was given to TV commercials that consist of a pitchman extolling the virtues of a product. Some people argue that talking heads aren't creative, but at least one monster uses them because they're above average in creating spoofs of ads worth spreading. I'm with the monster.

Wednesday: Check Out "The T-Mobile Dance"

On February 19, 2010, I taught a YouTube and Video Marketing workshop at SES London. Among the participants were a couple of marketing people from T-Mobile. Now, you'd think that they wouldn't need in-depth training because Saatchi & Saatchi had already created one of the most contagious viral ads of all time for T-Mobile.

Uploaded on January 16, 2009, the so-called "Ambient Advert" lets you watch the moment when Liverpool Street Station in London danced to create the iconic meme, Life's for Sharing. As Figure 4.19 illustrates, "The T-Mobile Dance" was and had more than 25.3 million views.

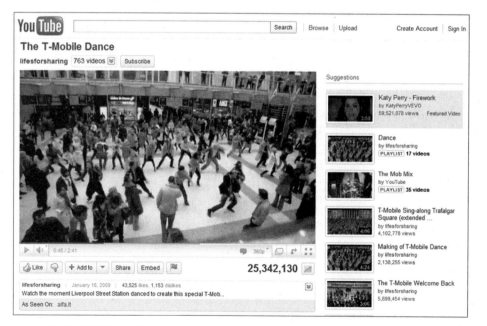

Figure 4.19 "The T-Mobile Dance"

Go to www.youtube.com/watch?v=VQ3d3KigPQM and you will see the current video statistics. As this was written, they showed it had 43,012 likes and 1,146 dislikes. It also had nine honors:

- #21 - Most Discussed (All Time) - Entertainment - United Kingdom
- #25 - Most Viewed (All Time) - United Kingdom
- #6 - Most Viewed (All Time) - Entertainment - United Kingdom
- #58 - Most Viewed (All Time) - Entertainment
- #17 - Top Favorited (All Time) - United Kingdom
- #4 - Top Favorited (All Time) - Entertainment - United Kingdom
- #21 - Top Favorited (All Time) - Entertainment
- #55 - Top Rated (All Time) - United Kingdom
- #8 - Top Rated (All Time) - Entertainment - United Kingdom

According to the Viral Video Chart, "The T-Mobile Dance" has 149,495 Facebook shares, 5,592 tweets, and 5,045 blog posts.

Here's the backstory according to a case study by MediaCom, which handled the media planning and buying for the campaign: "The nation was in the depths of winter and recession, making many people sensitive about corporate insincerity and dishonesty. In this climate, T-Mobile had to launch a new campaign, one that people could believe in and trust. One that would make people feel good about the brand. So we couldn't just tell people T-Mobile's new philosophy, we had to prove that, Life's for Sharing."

According to MediaCom, the creative solution to this problem was a technique as old as television: "We decided to create a live event so memorable that people just had to share it. At 11am on 15th January a single commuter started dancing. Moments later hundreds more joined in, including hundreds of genuine members of the public. Everybody there enjoyed a moment worth sharing."

What did the agency's creative execution accomplish? According to MediaCom, "The event was so memorable the public took their mobile phones out to share it with calls, texts, photos and videos. The dance became news in its own right, covered on national TV news, national press, radio phone-ins and bloggers."

From the agency's point of view, T-Mobile got £1.2 million worth of free media and press coverage. For example, the *Sun* newspaper in the UK described it as an "epidemic of joy."

From the client's point of view, you could deposit the results of its "Ambient Advert" in a bank. The MediaCom case study concludes, "In a recession, T-Mobile had a 52% increase in sales from last year."

So, why were T-Mobile's marketing people attending a YouTube and Video Marketing workshop a year later? They and their agencies were struggling to come up with another viral hit. T-Mobile had created a couple of other video campaigns that featured "Josh's Band" and "Night in TV ads." But these hadn't come close to getting the views of "The T-Mobile Dance."

Why? I think "Josh's Band" and "Night in TV ads" featured creative content designed to be watched, but "The T-Mobile Dance" featured content designed to be discovered, watched and shared.

Or, as Harry Flugelman (Joe Mantegna) says in ¡Three Amigos! (1986), "We strayed from the formula... and we paid the price."

In fact, if you look closely at the video statistics for "The T-Mobile Dance," you'll see that the YouTube search terms that generated the most views were the two-word term "flash mob" (more than 798,000 views when this was written), the one-word variation "flashmob" (over 387,000 views when this was written), and "dance" (more than 660,000 views when this was written).

A flash mob (or flashmob) is a large group of people who assemble suddenly in a public place without obvious leadership or prior planning, perform an unusual act for a brief time, and then disperse. These events are designed to be discovered, watched, and shared.

This provides an alternative backstory, which appears in a second case study by Unruly Media, called in to provide social media outreach services for the campaign.

Although "The T-Mobile Dance" was rushed out within 24 hours of the event, the creative for other paid media wasn't going to be available until the end of the following week because of production constraints. MediaCom asked Unruly Media to compensate for this potentially quiet period by making the video ubiquitous online.

Unruly Media quickly got the video out to flash mob fans, who had been carefully identified and qualified over the previous week. Hundreds of bloggers embedded the clip, which racked up 1 million views on YouTube over the first weekend. On Monday morning, Unruly Media took over popular video sharing applications within Facebook to make the video as easy as possible to rediscover and as frictionless as possible to forward on to friends and colleagues during the week-long hiatus before other online creative became available.

The clip spread like wildfire. For every person viewing the video, it was forwarded to an average of 3.6 other people, leading to 1.8 million forwards within Facebook alone. More than 50 T-Mobile Dance groups formed on Facebook, often to organize similar events at other UK rail stations.

If dance is socially infectious, what about a capella music?

On October 29, 2010, "The T-Mobile Welcome Back" was uploaded to YouTube. As the description of the flash mob video says, "Watch arriving passengers be given a welcome home to remember at Heathrow Terminal 5." The video also uses a super that explains, "No instruments were used in this film." So, how is it doing?

As Figure 4.20 illustrates, "The T-Mobile Welcome Back" received more than 5.8 million views in its first two months, quickly becoming the second most-viewed video on the T-Mobile Life's for Sharing channel.

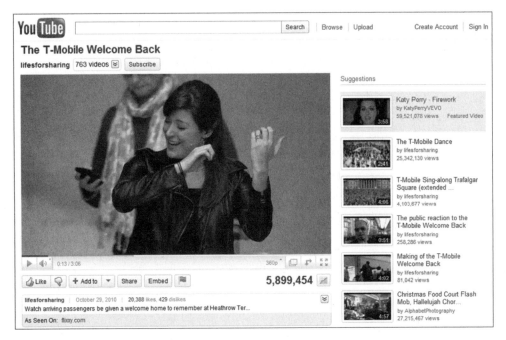

Figure 4.20 "The T-Mobile Welcome Back"

There are a couple of key lessons to be learned.

First, as Jacob Cohen, senior strategies - digital at Wolff Olins, says about "The T-Mobile Dance" on YouTube's Show & Tell's channel, "The crowd at the station really makes this video. Flash mobs have happened before but this one got the whole place going and makes you, as the viewer, really wish you were there and able to capture the moment. It just looks like great, sharable fun. Totally on brand."

Second, according to an aside in Unruly Media's case study, "Dance demonstrates a nuanced and sophisticated appreciation of the types of content that people want to share and the motivations driving them. Eschewing overused viral triggers such as sex, shock, and humour, Dance taps into people's propensity to feel touched, inspired and uplifted."

Thursday: See "Inspired Bicycles - Danny MacAskill April 2009"

Today, let's take a quick look at Danny MacAskill, a Scottish street trials pro rider for Inspired Bicycles Ltd.

On April 19, 2009, the then 23-year-old released a five-and-a-half-minute street trials video on YouTube set to "The Funeral" by Band of Horses.

Filmed by his flatmate, the video got a few hundred thousand views overnight. And as Figure 4.21 illustrates, "Inspired Bicycles - Danny MacAskill April 2009" now has more than 22 million views when this screen shot was taken.

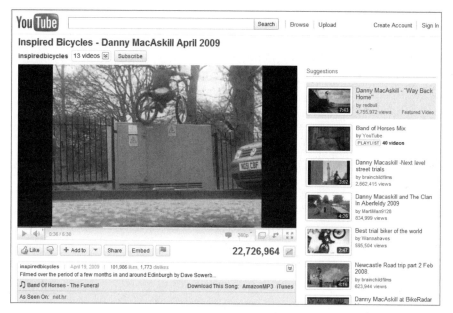

Figure 4.21 "Inspired Bicycles - Danny MacAskill April 2009"

Go to www.youtube.com/watch?v=Z19zFlPah-o and you will see the current video statistics. When I wrote this, it had 101,707 likes and 1,770 dislikes. And it had 13 honors:

- #49 - Most Discussed (All Time) - United Kingdom
- #3 - Most Discussed (All Time) - Sports - United Kingdom
- #8 - Most Discussed (All Time) - Sports
- #37 - Most Viewed (All Time) - United Kingdom
- #1 - Most Viewed (All Time) - Sports - United Kingdom
- #11 - Most Viewed (All Time) - Sports
- #5 - Top Favorited (All Time) - United Kingdom
- #72 - Top Favorited (All Time)
- #1 - Top Favorited (All Time) - Sports - United Kingdom
- #1 - Top Favorited (All Time) - Sports
- #9 - Top Rated (All Time) - United Kingdom
- #1 - Top Rated (All Time) - Sports - United Kingdom
- #1 - Top Rated (All Time) - Sports

According to the Viral Video Chart, "Inspired Bicycles - Danny MacAskill April 2009" has 223,537 Facebook shares, 6,781 tweets, and 3,930 blog posts.

The video description says, "Filmed over the period of a few months in and around Edinburgh by Dave Sowerby, this video of Inspired Bicycles team rider Danny MacAskill (more info at www.dannymacaskill.com) features probably the best collection of street/street trials riding ever seen. There's some huge riding, but also some of the most technically difficult and imaginative lines you will ever see."

On YouTube's Show & Tell channel, Kat Street, CCO of CP+B Europe, Sweden, says, "When ordinary people engage with the brand in an extraordinary way, the brand becomes extraordinary. This video inspires viewers to share the inspiration with other people."

Julia Rothman, founder/CD of Also Online in New York City, says, "This video blew my mind when I first saw it. I remember sending it out to everyone I knew. It seems homemade and authentic. It was as if some kid decided to show off what he can do, with his friend holding a video cam behind him."

And Marcos Kothlar, art director of AlmapBBDO in Sao Paulo, Brazil, says, "Truly inspiring work like this elevates brands to mythical status and people will share this like crazy."

Since the video went live, things happened quickly. MacAskill was featured in the *New York Times*, joined a Hollywood production as a stunt man, and appeared in a TV commercial for the new Volkswagen Golf Estate. He eventually gave up his job as a mechanic so he could ride full time and now lives in Edinburgh.

Sowerby shot another video, "Danny MacAskill - 'Way Back Home,'" which follows MacAskill on a journey from Edinburgh to his hometown Dunvegan, in the Isle of Skye. Produced by Red Bull, it had more than 4.7 million views when the screen shot in Figure 4.22 was taken.

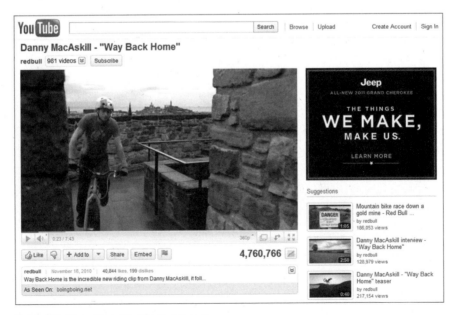

Figure 4.22 "Danny MacAskill - 'Way Back Home'"

Only one week later, a video MacAskill shot with his clothing partner Dig Deep in London hit the Web, dropping jaws all over the world once again.

What's the lesson from this example? Demonstrations that show how well your product performs are ads worth spreading. And demonstrations don't have to be dull.

Friday: View "Ken Block Gymkhana Two The Infomercial"

Today, let's watch "Ken Block Gymkhana Two The Infomercial." It was named one of *Ad Age*'s "Top 10 Viral Ads of All Time" and was #4 on *Ad Age*'s list of top viral videos of 2009.

As Figure 4.23 illustrates, this infomercial for DC Shoes by Mad Media had more than 21.2 million views when this screen shot was taken.

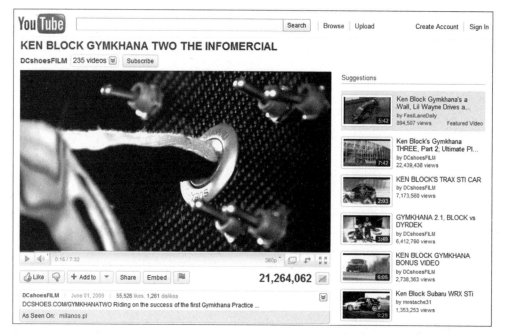

Figure 4.23 "Ken Block Gymkhana Two The Infomercial"

Go to www.youtube.com/watch?v=HQ7R_buZPSo and you will see the current video statistics. When this was written, it had 55,350 likes and 1,258 dislikes. It also had five honors:

- #66 - Spotlight Videos - Autos & Vehicles
- #19 - Most Discussed (All Time) - Autos & Vehicles
- #3 - Most Viewed (All Time) - Autos & Vehicles
- #1 - Top Favorited (All Time) - Autos & Vehicles
- #2 - Top Rated (All Time) - Autos & Vehicles

According to the Viral Video Chart, "Ken Block Gymkhana Two The Infomercial" has 223,252 Facebook shares, 2,900 tweets, and 1,602 blog posts.

The video description provides the backstory: "Riding on the success of the first Gymkhana Practice video that grabbed the attention of over 20 million viewers worldwide, the Gymkhana TWO video takes infomercials to the next level. Unlike other infomercials, this one sells the products with great action, cinematography, and a dramatic driving performance—and, no stereotypical cheesy infomercial pitchman!"

Produced to market Block's Rally TeamWorks Collection, the infomercial is filled with great driving stunts, surprises, explosions, and a guest appearance from DC team rider Rob Dyrdek. Filmed at the Port of Los Angeles, the infomercial also features nonstop motor sport eye candy as Block hits the all-new course in a custom-tuned, high-performance, and brand-new Subaru Impreza WRX STI.

On YouTube's Show & Tell channel, Benjamin Palmer, cofounder and CEO of The Barbarian Group in New York, asks, "How many ads have you seen, where when you heard that there was a sequel, you said out loud HELL YES and called a few folks over to watch it with you? How many times have you been excited that there was a sequel to an ad? The first Gymkhana video was 'mindblowingly rad.' The follow up has driving that is just as awesome, but it's now self-aware of both its internet-fame and its advertisingness, and works in some…product placement in a pretty naturally goofy sort of way."

Speaking of sequels, check out "Ken Block's Gymkhana Three, Part 2; Ultimate Playground; l'Autodrome, France." As Figure 4.24 illustrates, the video had more than 22.4 million views when this screen shot was taken.

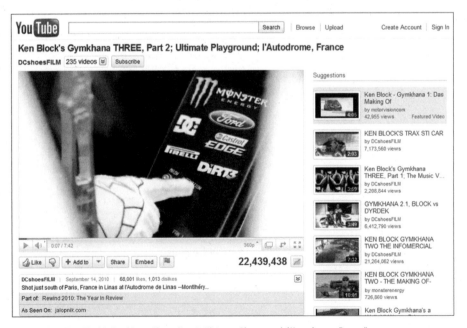

Figure 4.24 "Ken Block's Gymkhana Three, Part 2; Ultimate Playground; l'Autodrome, France"

And what's the lesson learned from these videos? It's about close-ups. It's a good thing to use close-ups when your product is the hero of your video ad.

Week 4: Observe Top Viral Videos

So, how do you create video content that's so compelling even prudent opinion leaders will decide its worth sharing with their followers?

First, as you've seen, it helps if your video tells a story. Although this story can be humorous in nature, it can also be serious. We've already uncovered the quirky and unusual, seen first-hand accounts of current events, and found videos about people's hobbies and interests. As the types of video content uploaded to YouTube continue to diversify, I expect to see videos from new artists and filmmakers as well as people's favorite TV moments go viral too.

Second, the most viewed viral videos are also among the most discussed, most liked, and top favorited. In other words, the stories they tell made their way into conversations because opinion leaders liked retelling them. These stories can be adorable, creative, funny, inspirational, or instructional. But they enable people to inform, educate, and entertain others at home, around the office, or across the globe.

Third, viral videos can come from original content creators large and small. As this was written, seven of the 10 most viewed videos of all time were music videos created by professionals and three were funny videos created by amateurs:

1. "Justin Bieber - Baby ft. Ludacris"—music video with **418,461,822 views**
2. "Lady Gaga - Bad Romance"—music video with **323,222,948 views**
3. "Shakira ft. Freshlyground - Waka Waka (This Time for Africa) (The Official 2010 FIFA World Cup Song)"—music video with 264,875,342 views
4. "Charlie bit my finger - again!"—funny video with **262,147,582 views**
5. "Eminem - Love The Way You Lie ft. Rihanna"—music video with **244,251,719 views**
6. "Miley Cyrus - Party In The U.S.A."—music video with **181,905,044 views**
7. "Eminem - Not Afraid"—music video with **173,183,012 views**
8. "Evolution of Dance - By Judson Laipply"—funny video with **159,639,278 views**
9. "Pitbull - I Know You Want Me (Calle Ocho) Official Video"—music video with **157,069,357 views; and**
10. "Hahaha"—funny video with **151,977,572 views.**

YouTube says it offers "a community for everyone." I think that YouTube actually offers almost 1,000 "communities," from broad topics (e.g., Hip-Hop) to narrow ones (e.g., BMW videos).

This increasing segmentation makes creating viral video content that much harder with each passing year. It reminds me of Ken Auletta's book *Three Blind Mice*, the story of how the TV networks lost their way in the 1980s as cable television started taking more than half of their audience.

The changes in viral video content from "Pokemon Theme Music Video," which was uploaded by Anthony Padilla and Ian Hecox of Smosh in November 2005, to "Smosh: Pokemon Theme Song Revenge," which was uploaded on November 26, 2010, may seem evolutionary, but considering all the other changes that have occurred in the space of just five years, they are revolutionary.

What should veteran marketers and new YouTubers do? You have two options.

First, you "could use a little churching up," as Curtis (Cab Calloway) advises Jake and Elwood in *The Blues Brothers* (1980). So, slide on down and take some action:

- Apply to the YouTube Creator Institute. Announced on March 10, 2011, the YouTube Creator Institute was established to help nurture content creators, existing YouTube partners, and the next generation of stellar YouTube talent with the skills they need to thrive online and offline. The inaugural programs began at the University of Southern California School of Cinematic Arts and the Columbia College Chicago Television Department. To apply online, go to www.youtube.com/creatorinstitute.

- Sign up for an online course like YouTube Marketing, which is offered by Market Motive. Part of the Social Media Marketing Certification course, it is $299 a month for the 90-day self-guided course or $3,500 for the 90-day faculty-led course.

- Register for in-class courses like Social Media Marketing or Digital Marketing, which are offered by the Rutgers Center for Management Development. Part of the Mini-MBA Program, a course costs $4,995.

Second, "You can observe a lot by watching," as Yogi Berra once said. This may sound like funny advice, but in a rapidly changing field like this one, it's a pretty good way to discover what works, what doesn't, and what's promising. And it's free.

However, knowing how to make a funny video doesn't mean you know how to make a music video. And we're all still learning how to make a viral video in other categories. So, let's watch some of the top viral videos and see what we can observe.

Monday: Watch "Justin Bieber - Baby ft. Ludacris"

Tuesday: Look at "Charlie bit my finger - again!"

Wednesday: Check out "Jeff Dunham - Achmed the Dead Terrorist"

Thursday: See shows from Next New Networks

Friday: View the meme, "Play him off, keyboard cat"

Monday: Watch "Justin Bieber - Baby ft. Ludacris"

Super-sensation Justin Bieber's song "Baby" was a chart-topper in 2010. The dream-date video (with a tip-of-the-hat to Michael Jackson) has also become the most viewed YouTube video of all time.

As Figure 4.25 illustrates, the music video had more than 420.3 million views when this screen shot was taken.

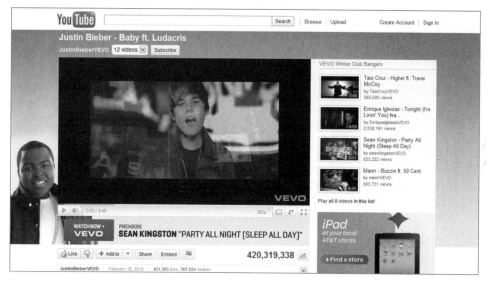

Figure 4.25 "Justin Bieber - Baby ft. Ludacris"

Go to www.youtube.com/watch?v=kffacxfA7G4 and you will see the current video statistics. When I wrote this, it had 429,873 likes and 762,700 dislikes. It also had eight honors:

- #1 - Spotlight Videos - Canada
- #27 - Spotlight Videos
- #1 - Most Discussed (All Time)
- #1 - Most Discussed (All Time) - Music
- #1 - Most Viewed (All Time)
- #1 - Most Viewed (All Time) - Music
- #7 - Top Rated (All Time)
- #4 - Top Rated (All Time) - Music

According to the Viral Video Chart, "Justin Bieber - Baby ft. Ludacris" has 2,189,833 Facebook shares, 41,542 tweets, and 5,966 blog posts.

What's Bieber's backstory? He was born March 1, 1994, in London, Ontario. Raised by his single mother, Pattie Mallette, he taught himself to play the piano, drums, guitar, and trumpet.

In 2007, Bieber sang Ne-Yo's "So Sick" for a local singing competition and placed second. Mallette posted a video of the performance on YouTube for their family and friends to see.

In 2008, the 13-year-old Canadian pop-R&B singer was discovered by Scooter Braun, who stumbled across Bieber's videos on YouTube by accident. Braun became Bieber's manager and arranged for him to meet with Usher in Atlanta. Bieber was soon signed to Raymond Braun Media Group (RBMG), a joint venture between Braun and Usher. Bieber was then signed to a recording contract with Island Records by Antonio Reid, who is known as L.A.

Bieber's debut single, "One Time," was released in July 2009 and reached #12 on the Canadian Hot 100 during its first week of release. It was followed in November 2009 by his debut album, *My World*, which went platinum in the United States, making him the first artist to have seven songs from a debut album chart on the *Billboard* Hot 100.

To promote the album, Bieber performed in several live shows, including mtvU's VMA 09 Tour, *The Today Show*, *Lopez Tonight*, *The Ellen DeGeneres Show*, and *Good Morning America*.

Bieber performed Stevie Wonder's "Someday at Christmas" for President Barack Obama and first lady Michelle Obama at the White House for *Christmas in Washington*, which was broadcast December 20, 2009, on TNT.

"Baby", which features Ludacris, was released in January 2010 and has become his biggest hit so far, charting at #5 in the United States and reaching the top 10 in seven other countries. In July 2010, his music video "Justin Bieber - Baby ft. Ludacris" surpassed "Lady Gaga - Bad Romance" to become the most viewed YouTube video ever.

On December 31, 2009, Jan Hoffman of the *New York Times* called Bieber "a creature of this era: a talented boy discovered first by fans on YouTube, then cannily marketed to them through a fresh influx of studiedly raw videos on the Web site."

Hoffman added, "Justin, his fans passionately believe, is homemade. Long before he released his EP, *My World*, in mid-November, the YouTube videos attracted millions of views."

Braun also recognized the appeal before flying Bieber to Atlanta. "I wanted to build him up more on YouTube first," he told Hoffman. "We supplied more content. I said: 'Justin, sing like there's no one in the room. But let's not use expensive cameras.' We'll give it to kids, let them do the work, so that they feel like it's theirs."

Bieber continues to upload videos to YouTube and has opened a Twitter account, from which he interacts with fans regularly. As this was written his Twitter account had more than 6.4 million followers.

Is there another lesson here?

Yes, watch comments, but not too closely.

Most videos enable users to leave comments, and these have attracted attention for the negative aspects of both their form and content. The comments to "Baby" are no exception.

On December 13, 2006, Lev Grossman of *Time* said, "Web 2.0 harnesses the stupidity of crowds as well as its wisdom. Some of the comments on YouTube make you weep for the future of humanity just for the spelling alone, never mind the obscenity and the naked hatred."

On November 3, 2009, the Technology Blog on Guardian.co.uk said YouTube's "dedicated army of commenters" had developed a language of their own. "Juvenile, aggressive, misspelled, sexist, homophobic, swinging from raging at the contents of a video to providing a pointlessly detailed description followed by a LOL, YouTube comments are a hotbed of infantile debate and unashamed ignorance—with the occasional burst of wit shining through."

On July 26, 2010, Rick Silvestrini, product marketing manager at YouTube, wrote on the YouTube Biz Blog, "Comments can provide valuable feedback and additional information about your videos and your audience. Viewers will tell you what they like and don't like about your videos. But you need to have a bit of a thick skin since there will always be haters and trolls; don't take them too seriously."

Tuesday: Look at "Charlie bit my finger - again!"

The most viewed video of all time in the Comedy category is "Charlie bit my finger - again!" As Figure 4.26 illustrates, the amateur video has more than 263 million views.

Figure 4.26 "Charlie bit my finger - again!"

Go to www.youtube.com/watch?v=_OBlgSz8sSM and you will see the current video statistics. When this was written, it had 539,230 likes and 64,639 dislikes. It also had 16 honors:

- #1 - Most Discussed (All Time) - United Kingdom
- #14 - Most Discussed (All Time)
- #1 - Most Discussed (All Time) - Comedy - United Kingdom
- #2 - Most Discussed (All Time) - Comedy
- #1 - Most Viewed (All Time) - United Kingdom
- #4 - Most Viewed (All Time)
- #1 - Most Viewed (All Time) - Comedy - United Kingdom
- #1 - Most Viewed (All Time) - Comedy
- #1 - Top Favorited (All Time) - United Kingdom
- #2 - Top Favorited (All Time)
- #1 - Top Favorited (All Time) - Comedy - United Kingdom
- #2 - Top Favorited (All Time) - Comedy
- #1 - Top Rated (All Time) - United Kingdom
- #4 - Top Rated (All Time)
- #1 - Top Rated (All Time) - Comedy - United Kingdom
- #2 - Top Rated (All Time) - Comedy

According to the Viral Video Chart, "Charlie bit my finger - again!" has 899,016 Facebook shares, 17,676 tweets, and 7,044 blog posts.

In the video description, Howard Davies-Carr, father of Charlie and his older brother, Harry, says, "Even had I thought of trying to get my boys to do this I probably couldn't have. Neither were coerced into any of this and neither were hurt (for very long anyway). This was just one of those moments when I had the video camera out because the boys were being fun and they provided something really very funny."

The Davies-Carr family lives in England. Howard uploaded the video onto YouTube so it could be watched by the boys' godfather, who was residing in the United States. Howard chose YouTube because the size of video file was so big that it couldn't be sent by email.

"Charlie bit my finger - again!" went viral and ranks #1 in *Time* magazine's list of YouTube's 50 greatest viral videos of all time.

What lesson can we learn from this amateur video?

Great content can come from anywhere. During 2010, more than 13 million hours of content was uploaded to YouTube by the greatest diversity of content creators imaginable.

And at last count, YouTube had around 15,000 content partners worldwide. These range from established media companies such as National Geographic to amateurs like Davies-Carr.

As a result of the success of their father's video, Harry and Charlie have gained stardom. And HDCYT's channel on YouTube says, "We do run adverts on this channel as we are YouTube partners. This generates money which is mainly going towards the boys' future or treats we would not normally have bought."

On November 1, 2009, Maurice Chittenden of the *Sunday Times* of London said, "Web experts believe the Davies-Carrs could be on their way to a £100,000 windfall, largely from adverts placed on screen around the video."

On June 18, 2010, Diana Ransom of the *Wall Street Journal* wrote, "Davies-Carr won't say exactly how much his family has earned from the video, but the added income made it more possible to afford a new house, he says."

Elixir Interactive CEO Fionn Downhill, who suggested that I include this viral video in the first edition of this book, recently asked, "Do you think Charlie knew what he was doing?"

Wednesday: Check Out "Jeff Dunham - Achmed the Dead Terrorist"

The most viewed video of all time in the Entertainment category is "Jeff Dunham - Achmed the Dead Terrorist." As Figure 4.27 illustrates, it had more than 125 million views when this screen shot was taken.

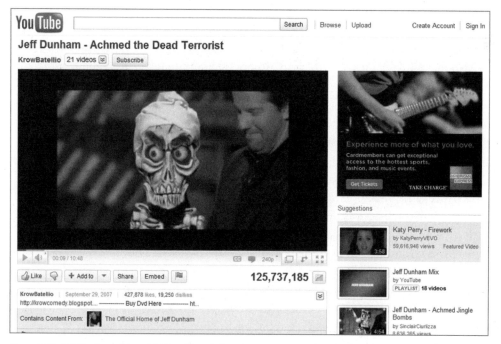

Figure 4.27 "Jeff Dunham - Achmed the Dead Terrorist"

Go to www.youtube.com/watch?v=1uwOL4rB-go and you will see the current video statistics. When I wrote this, it had 427,667 likes and 19,238 dislikes. It also had eight honors:

- #51 - Most Discussed (All Time)
- #3 - Most Discussed (All Time) - Entertainment
- #14 - Most Viewed (All Time)
- #1 - Most Viewed (All Time) - Entertainment
- #4 - Top Favorited (All Time)
- #1 - Top Favorited (All Time) - Entertainment
- #8 - Top Rated (All Time)
- #1 - Top Rated (All Time) - Entertainment

According to the Viral Video Chart, "Jeff Dunham - Achmed the Dead Terrorist" has 344,446 Facebook shares, 4,408 tweets, and 5,447 blog posts.

Dunham is an American ventriloquist and stand-up comedian. He has performed at comedy clubs across the United States since the late 1980s and has also appeared on numerous television shows, including *Late Show with David Letterman* and *The Tonight Show*. In January 2008, Dunham was voted the top comedian in Comedy Central's "Stand-Up Showdown."

Dunham's act includes seven puppets, known by his fans as the Suitcase Posse. Although each puppet has a backstory and Dunham brings them all to life, the one that's gone viral is Achmed.

The skeletal corpse of an incompetent suicide bomber, Achmed is used by Dunham to perform comedy based on the contemporary issue of terrorism. He is known for yelling, "Silence! I kill you!" to people in the audience who laugh at his customs.

The dead terrorist first appeared in *Spark of Insanity* and made an appearance in the *Very Special Christmas Special*, singing a song called "Jingle Bombs." The special's November 2008 premiere was the highest rated telecast in Comedy Central's history.

A TV commercial for a ringtone featuring Achmed was banned by the South African Advertising Standards Authority in 2008 after a complaint was filed by a citizen stating that the ad was offensive and portrayed all Muslims as terrorists. The ban angered Dunham, who issued a statement that read, "Achmed makes it clear in my act that he is not Muslim." In fact, the puppet jokes when asked about this that a label on him says, "Made in China."

In October 2008, Dunham told *Fox News*, "I've skewered whites, blacks, Hispanics, Christians, Jews, Muslims, gays, straights, rednecks, addicts, the elderly, and my wife. As a stand-up comic, it is my job to make the majority of people laugh, and I believe that comedy is the last true form of free speech."

There are three serious lessons to learn from this funny video.

First, characters are above average in their ability to change people's attitudes and opinions.

Second, there are advantages to being the only ventriloquist who uses a character named Achmed the Dead Terrorist.

On October 9, 2009, the comedian Bill Engvall told Jon Mooallem of the *New York Times* that the Achmed character was "a genius marketing move." Engvall framed the advantages of "Jeff Dunham - Achmed the Dead Terrorist" this way: "How many times a day is the word 'terrorist' Googled? But that (video) still pops up there near the top of the list." (It's usually in the top five organic results.)

Third, humor is hard. Very few stand-up comedians create funny videos that *are* funny. Unless you're one of the few, don't try.

Thursday: See Shows from Next New Networks

The most-watched video of 2010 was "Auto-Tune the News: Bed Intruder Song!!! (now on iTunes)."

In the strangest transformation of the year, the Gregory Brothers took the quirky television interview Antoine Dodson gave after his sister's attempted assault (itself a viral video) and turned it into a chart-topper.

As Figure 4.28 illustrates, this episode from the News Show had more than 56.7 million views when this screen shot was taken.

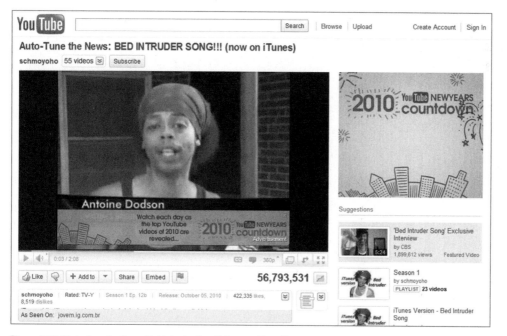

Figure 4.28 "Auto-Tune the News: Bed Intruder Song!!! (now on iTunes)"

Go to www.youtube.com/watch?v=hMtZfW2z9dw and you will see the current video statistics. When this was written, it had 420,487 likes and 8,446 dislikes. It also had five honors:

- #2 - Spotlight Videos - Australia
- #88 - Most Discussed (All Time)
- #95 - Most Viewed (All Time)
- #29 - Top Favorited (All Time)
- #9 - Top Rated (All Time)

According to the Viral Video Chart, "Auto-Tune the News: Bed Intruder Song!!! (now on iTunes)" has 698,865 Facebook shares, 20,443 tweets, and 1,652 blog posts.

The #2 most watched video of 2010 was "Key of Awesome: Tik Tok Kesha Parody: Glitter Puke - Key of Awe$ome #13."

The pop music parody loomed large in 2010 thanks to BarelyPolitical's take on Ke$ha's "Tik Tok" and the popularity of *Key of Awe$ome*, a weekly musical comedy show that's been seen over 100 million times.

As Figure 4.29 illustrates, this episode from the Celebrity & Entertainment Show had more than 55.4 million views when this screen shot was taken.

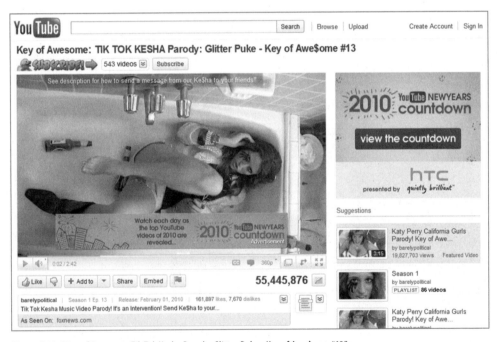

Figure 4.29 "Key of Awesome: Tik Tok Kesha Parody: Glitter Puke - Key of Awe$ome #13"

Go to www.youtube.com/watch?v=d7n8GqewJ2M and you will see the current video statistics. When I wrote this, it had 161,707 likes and 7,657 dislikes. It also had four honors:

- #3 - Spotlight Videos - Australia
- #97 - Most Viewed (All Time)
- #83 - Top Favorited (All Time)
- #51 - Top Rated (All Time)

According to the Viral Video Chart, "Key of Awesome: Tik Tok Kesha Parody: Glitter Puke - Key of Awe$ome #13" has 297,064 Facebook shares, 7,827 tweets, and 618 blog posts.

Key of Awesome was produced by Barely Political, which is also the home of Obama Girl. Barely Political is part of Next New Networks, which is a leading independent producer of online television networks.

The two shows were a big part of the success of Next New Networks, which got more than 1.2 billion video views in 2010. So, how did they do it?

On December 13, 2010, a post by Tim Shey on the Next New Networks Blog said there were three key drivers for the company's dramatic growth:

Betting on new talent for a new medium "We launched the Next New Creators program last December so that we could work with more of the top emerging creators in the space, and one year in, we've added over 65 Next New Creators series that already represent more than 50% of our monthly viewership," said Shey.

"Working with new talent required a new model, and without Next New Creators program, we wouldn't have gotten to work with the Gregory Brothers and had the #1 video on YouTube in 2010," he added.

Consistent programming, not just viral hits Shey said that "viral" video and "episodic" video don't need to be mutually exclusive. "In fact, the best episodic series often use a highly viewed, shared, and blogged video to bring in new fans and loyal viewers," he added.

Both the Gregory Brothers and the *Key of Awesome* regularly and consistently create new episodes to grow their fan base. The Gregory Brothers' schmoyoho channel on YouTube now has more than 715,000 subscribers, and BarelyPolitical's channel, home of *Key of Awesome*, just passed the one million subscriber mark. As a result, new episodes of each series regularly break the one million mark in views.

Optimizing for how audiences watch online Shey said, "For the past few years, some of the most important sources of audience in online video have been subscribers, search results, and related videos, and the most successful web series optimize to increase the impact of all three, focusing on great packaging in terms of branding, metadata, and thumbnails to stand out in search and related video results, and including calls to action within programming and packaging that drive viewers to subscribe on YouTube, social networks, or in email."

He added, "In 2010, we saw two other massive impacts on audience growth: effective cross-promotion of episodes, shows, and channels using tools like YouTube annotations, and increased viewership coming from sharing on networks like Facebook and Twitter."

On December 15, 2010, Claire Cain Miller and Brian Stelter of the *New York Times* reported, "YouTube, the video site owned by Google, is in talks to buy Next New Networks, a Web video production company, according to two people briefed on the discussions."

According to Miller and Stelter, "That production role is what YouTube is most interested in, said two people briefed on the discussions."

Now, who might those people be?

If Captain Renault (Claude Raines) in *Casablanca* (1942) ordered me to "round up the usual suspects," then I'd start with a bed intruder and a Kesha look-alike, who've got barely political motives.

There are a couple of lessons to learn from the success of these two shows and the latest news leak. First, shows that mash up news and spoof celebrities are above average in their ability to go viral. Second, if you are going to leak a story, leak it to the *New York Times*. According to Newsknife, it was the top news site of 2010 based on appearances of their stories in Google News.

Friday: View the Meme, "Play Him Off, Keyboard Cat"

Last but not least, let's examine the meme, "Play him off, Keyboard Cat." On May 25, 2009, Ben Parr of Mashable added Keyboard Cat as a bonus to his list of "Top 20 YouTube Video Memes of All Time."

What is a meme? According to Wikipedia, it "is a newly coined term for ideas or beliefs that are transmitted from one person, or group of people, to another. The name comes from an analogy: as *genes* transmit biological information, *memes* can be said to transmit idea and belief information."

What is the Keyboard Cat meme? As Parr explained, it is a viral video sensation "in which painful stunts and regrettable mistakes are followed by Fatso the cat playing the keyboard."

The video that Parr embedded in his post has been removed "because its content violated YouTube's terms of service." Copyright issues with Warner Music Group forced YouTube to disable the audio from the video.

But, as Figure 4.30 illustrates, another version is still on YouTube and "Charlie Schmidt's 'Keyboard Cat'! - Original!" had more than 11.6 million views when this screen shot was taken.

Figure 4.30 *"Charlie Schmidt's 'Keyboard Cat'! - Original!"*

Go to www.youtube.com/watch?v=J--aiyznGQ and you will see the current video statistics. When this was written, it had 61,095 likes and 3,150 dislikes. It also had one honor:

#85 - Top Favorited (All Time) - Comedy

According to the Viral Video Chart, "Charlie Schmidt's 'Keyboard Cat'! - Original!" has 82,191 Facebook shares, 2,153 tweets, and 1,072 blog posts.

Although this 54-second-long version does feature Fatso the cat playing the keyboard, this isn't preceded by any painful stunts and regrettable mistakes.

What's the backstory?

On May 15, 2009, Mark Milian of the *Los Angeles Times* wrote, "On its own, the Keyboard Cat video might elicit a smile and a chuckle. But when the adorable feline pounding its paws on a musical keyboard is preceded by an awkward, pain-inducing video of someone falling down an escalator or screaming at his parents, you have the latest Internet meme."

Schmidt filmed the original Keyboard Cat two decades ago but uploaded it to YouTube in June 2007, where it initially received a moderate number of views.

In February 2009, Brad O'Farrell, who was 22 years old at the time, saw the potential in Keyboard Cat and obtained Schmidt's permission to reuse the clip.

O'Farrell, who worked for My Damn Channel, appended an abbreviated version of Keyboard Cat to the end of a clip showing a person in a wheelchair tumbling down an escalator. That's when the meme really began to catch on.

The idea was to append Keyboard Cat to the end of a blooper video to "play" that person offstage after a mistake or gaffe, like getting the hook in the days of vaudeville. The meme became popular, Ashton Kutcher tweeted about it to more than 1 million followers, and more than 4,000 such videos have now been made.

"You can create a joke or a catchphrase, but you have very little control over whether or not it catches on," O'Farrell told Milian. "But I still did intentionally do a lot to try to get it to catch on."

For example, O'Farrell (who, as mentioned earlier, is technical editor of this book) emailed YouTube's editors at editor@youtube.com, who take suggestions from users and are always on the lookout for videos of interest, and his Keyboard Cat video landed on the site's home page,

"Keyboard Cat, it seems, could make anything seem funny. As more videos of injuries, domestic disputes, and, well, more injuries were getting the Keyboard Cat treatment, the juxtaposition appeared to mesh tragedy and comedy with Shakespearean-like elegance," Milian concluded.

On May 18, 2009, Keyboard Cat was further popularized during a "toss" from *The Daily Show with Jon Stewart* to *The Colbert Report* with Stephen Colbert. At the 2009 MTV Movie Awards, Andy Samberg's opening monologue suggested that award winners whose speech went on too long would be played off by Keyboard Cat. Kato Kaelin also spoofed Keyboard Cat in a segment of Tosh.0 entitled "Keyboard Kato."

As Figure 4.31 illustrates, Ellie Rountree of Rocketboom interviewed O'Farrell about the Keyboard Cat craze on May 15, 2009.

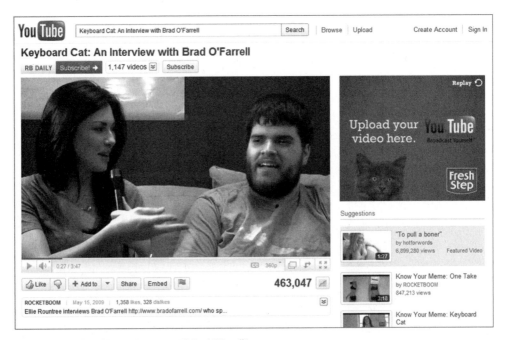

Figure 4.31 "Keyboard Cat: An Interview with Brad O'Farrell"

There are two lessons we can learn from the meme. First, "fail videos" and cat videos are both popular on YouTube. So, guess what happened when O'Farrell combined them in the "Play him off, Keyboard Cat" meme? Second, when Warner Music Group forced YouTube to disable the audio from the video, it won the copyright battle, but it may have lost the "remix culture" war.

On July 15, 2009, Caroline McCarthy of CNET News quoted one commenter on the muted YouTube video, who wrote, "I hate you, Warner Music Group. This video is hilarious and promotes a song that would otherwise never reach the ears of young people. What is wrong with you? When did the music industry go so wrong?"

Now that you've learned how to create content worth sharing, the next chapter will teach you how to customize your YouTube channel.

Month 3: Customize Your YouTube Channel

5

The most common way people find a new video is to go to YouTube and conduct a search, or they click one of the related videos. But people are just as likely to discover a new YouTube video embedded in a blog. This means YouTube should be the center, not the circumference, of your video marketing strategy. In this chapter, you will learn how to set up a basic YouTube channel, how to become a YouTube partner, how to create a YouTube brand channel, and how to stream live content on YouTube—although this may not stop some people from making comments like, "When I was a boy, I had to walk five miles through the snow to change the channel."

Center vs. Circumference

On December 5, 2005, three executives from video search engines spoke during the "Video Search" session moderated by Chris Sherman at the Search Engine Strategies (SES) conference in Chicago:

- Suranga Chandratillake, the cofounder and CTO of blinkx
- John Thrall, head of multimedia search engineering at Yahoo! Search
- Karen Howe, vice president of AOL Search and general manager of Singingfish

Although it was still "early days" for video search, the panelists agreed that the best strategy for marketers was to optimize the video content on their websites to make it easier for the video search engines to find it and make it available to searchers seeking such content.

This meant that making your website the center of your online video strategy appeared to be the smart thing to do back in the "early days"—before YouTube.

But Singingfish was defunct by February 2007. Yahoo! Search removed all user-generated content on March 15, 2011. And blinkx, which claims to be the "world's largest video search engine," gets less than 2 percent of the visits to video sites in the UK and less than 1 percent in the United States and Canada.

So, where should the center of your video marketing strategy be today?

The answer would be found in some TubeMogul research that was published on February 12, 2009, if it was still posted on TubeMogul's website. The research found that 45.1 percent of viewers discovered videos by going to a video site (i.e., going to YouTube and running a search or clicking around the featured or related videos), 44.2 percent of viewers discovered videos embedded on blogs, and only 6.1 percent of viewers discovered videos with search engines.

Drilling deeper, Experian Hitwise has found that YouTube gets 86.3 percent of visits to video sites in the United States, the same percentage in Canada, and 68.4 percent in the UK. A similar percentage of the videos discovered embedded on blogs are YouTube videos. And a similar percentage of the videos discovered with search engines are YouTube videos.

This data means that creating a YouTube channel should be the center of your video marketing strategy. We'll try to find the circumference of this circle—or perimeter of this area—in Chapter 6.

A channel is the page that is viewable by the general public and contains a user's profile information, videos, and favorites. But veteran marketers and new YouTubers will want to consider becoming a YouTube partner, creating and customizing a YouTube brand channel, as well as distributing videos beyond YouTube. We'll look at your options in these areas and I'll make some recommendations.

However, I can't promise that any of this will prevent some people from wishing we didn't have so many options or from making comments like the one in Figure 5.1, "When I was a boy, I had to walk five miles through the snow to change the channel."

"When I was a boy, I had to walk five miles through the snow to change the channel."

Figure 5.1 "When I was a boy, I had to walk five miles through the snow to change the channel." (Cartoon by Mick Stevens in the *New Yorker,* October 2, 2006.)

This is a new world, and some people haven't explored it yet. So we will also spend some time looking at the emerging best practices being used by a few of the best-known brands.

Week 1: Set Up a YouTube Channel

A YouTube channel page serves as a profile page for a veteran marketer or new YouTuber. On your channel page, other YouTube users can see your public videos, your favorite videos, and your bulletins and subscribers. Your channel page also displays several links that let other people connect with you (or your brand) by sending you a message, sharing your channel with friends, or adding comments to your channel.

For example, Figure 5.2 shows New York Habitat's channel at www.youtube.com/newyorkhabitat, which contains videos about things to do and places to go and tips about renting a furnished apartment in New York, Paris, London, and the south of France.

Figure 5.2 New York Habitat's channel

YouTube provides a lot of useful information for getting started in its Help Center. Let's go through the process of creating a YouTube channel step by step:

Monday: Create your YouTube account

Tuesday: Edit your channel's settings

Wednesday: Customize your themes and colors

Thursday: Select and move modules

Friday: Highlight videos and playlists

Monday: Create Your YouTube Account

The first step in setting up a channel is creating your YouTube account. Go to www.youtube.com/create_account and complete the form that appears in Figure 5.3.

The form asks you to specify the following information:

The E-mail Address field specifies the email address associated with your account. This address will not be displayed on your channel page, meaning people will not be able to see your email address. However, YouTube will use it to notify you of new subscribers, comments, or other events, depending on the email options that you set for your account. For example, if you allow it, people can find your account based on your email address.

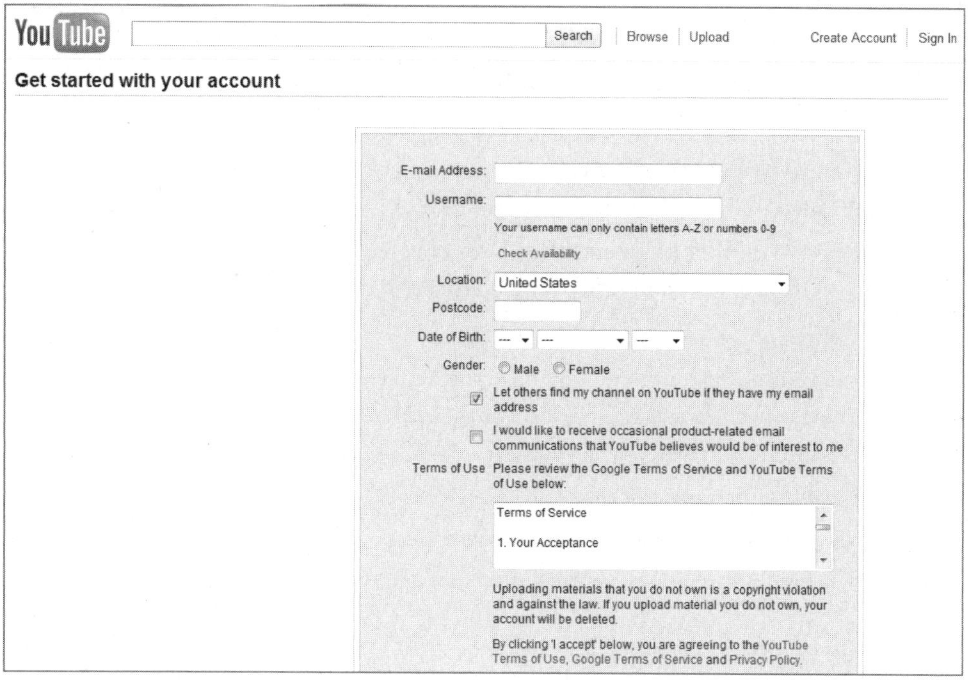

Figure 5.3 Get started with your account

The **Username** field specifies the permanent identification of your account in the YouTube community. Your username will be publicly displayed and will also appear in the URL for your channel page. Once you've created your account, you cannot change the username associated with it. Make sure the name you select represents your brand well. Usernames can be up to 20 characters long, and you may use only alphanumeric characters (*A–Z*, *a–z*, and *0–9*).

The **Location and Postcode** fields are both required. Enter the values that correspond to the location of your headquarters.

The **Date Of Birth** field lets YouTube calculate the age of a YouTube account's owner. YouTube does display this age on your channel page, so make sure you set a reasonable age. You must be over 13 to register. Although you can hide it by modifying your account settings, you cannot change it.

The **Gender** field specifies the gender associated with your account. Although this field is required to get demographic data for YouTube Insight, your YouTube channel doesn't display it.

The form then asks you to review the Google terms of service and YouTube terms of use. This is where you're told that uploading materials that you don't own is a copyright violation and against the law. If you upload material you don't own, your account will be deleted.

In the spring of 2010, YouTube launched a redesign of its channels. The updated channel design included the following features:

- **In-channel editing.** This allows you to edit your channel without leaving the channel page and see the results of your design change on your channel as you edit.

- **An interactive watch experience.** Visitors can browse through and watch multiple videos without leaving your channel.

- **Increased visibility for your videos.** You now have the ability to customize and rearrange how your uploads, playlists, and favorites are displayed on your channel.

All new accounts automatically have the new version of channels. If you want to see some great new channel designs, look at these examples:

- IceflowStudios at www.youtube.com/iceflowstudios

- ThadewGrum at www.youtube.com/ThadewGrum

- Vlogbrothers at www.youtube.com/Vlogbrothers

- The White House at www.youtube.com/whitehouse

Tuesday: Edit Your Channel's Settings

One of the areas in which you can make changes to your channel is its settings.

Sign in to YouTube and click My Channel. Below the search bar, you'll see a gray edit channel section. As Figure 5.4 illustrates, click the Settings button. Once you click the Settings button, the window will expand and you'll be able to make the edits to your channel from there.

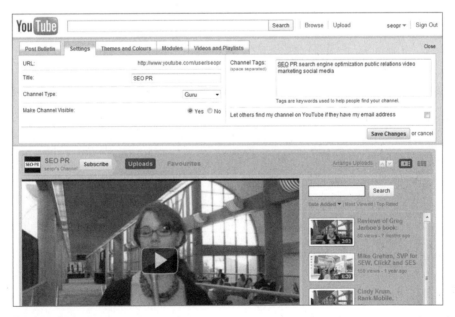

Figure 5.4 Settings

For example, you'll be able to view and edit the information associated with your channel, including your channel's title and tags to help users find your channel in a YouTube search. To update this information, just enter your edits and then click the Save Changes button in the lower-right corner of the window.

I strongly recommend conducting keyword research before editing your channel's title and tags. We'll cover this in Chapter 7.

You can also edit your account type. There are several types of YouTube accounts, including Comedians, Directors, Gurus, Musicians, Non-Profit, Politicians, Reporters, and YouTubers. They all share the basic YouTube features like uploading, commenting, sharing, and video responses. But each specialized account type also offers different customization options:

Comedians Allows custom logo, style, show date information, and CD purchase links on your profile page.

Directors This account type is perfect for people who take their videos seriously. If you own your own production studio or are just passionate about home videos, a Directors account can offer a lot of advantages. It allows customized performer info to be displayed on your profile page, describing yourself, your influences, and your style.

Gurus You might want to select this account type if you enjoy making videos that teach people a certain skill or explain how to do something. It allows custom logo, genre, and links on your profile page.

Musicians Allows custom logo, genre, tour date information, and CD purchase links on your profile page.

Non-profit A status obtained by 501(c)(3) nonprofit organizations accepted into YouTube's nonprofit program.

Politicians Only available to someone who is running for office or currently involved with the politics of government.

Reporters Allows you to describe your beat, your influences, and your favorite news sources.

In the past, people would change their account types to get higher rankings on the account-type lists. For example, there were more Directors than Gurus a couple of years ago. According to Brad O'Farrell, the technical editor of this book, this prompted the YouTube community to joke that Gurus were just people who were desperate to get to the top of a list, any list.

But YouTube eliminated the Channels tab, making these account-type lists much harder to find. And your channel now needs to have more than 35 million total upload views to become one of the top 100 Gurus. So, times change.

Wednesday: Customize Your Themes and Colors

You can also edit the background and color theme of your YouTube channel. To do this, click the Themes And Colors tab. As Figure 5.5 illustrates, the window will expand and you'll see certain **color theme options**.

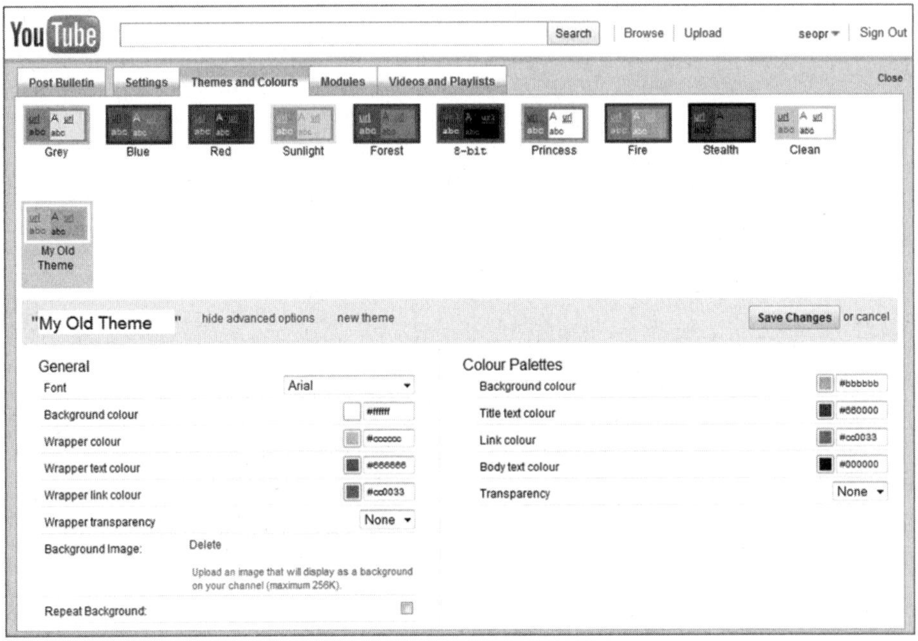

Figure 5.5 Themes And Colors

You can select one of the themes for your channel or create your own theme.

For example, to update your channel background, click one of the color themes. The background of your channel will change to show you a preview of how it will look if you select that theme.

If you like a theme and want to have it displayed on your channel, click the Save Changes button to update your channel. If you don't like the theme you're seeing in preview, simply click Cancel or click another theme to change the channel background.

If you want to customize your channel background and theme, click the Show Advanced Options link, which is located below the standard color themes. The window will expand and show you a variety of ways to create your own background theme.

Select different colors for the various aspects of your channel. Then, don't forget to click the Save Changes button in the lower-right corner of the window or all of the customization that you've just made won't be saved and applied.

To add an image as your channel's background, do this:

1. Click the Show Advanced Options link.

2. Click the Browse button and find an image from your computer that you'd like to use as your channel's background. Then select the image (maximum 256 KB).

3. The image will appear centered on your channel page. You'll be able to see a preview of this.

4. If you'd like to repeat the image across your channel's background, click and select the Repeat Background box.

5. Finally, click the Save Changes button to update your channel with these changes.

If you have trouble adding a new theme to your channel, it could be because you've reached the maximum number of customized themes. You can save only **10** themes for your channel at a given time. To create a new custom theme for your channel, just delete some of your themes. Once you've deleted a few themes, you'll be able to create a new custom theme for your channel again.

I recommend that you select a background image that mirrors the look and feel of your other online branding. For example, your background image can feature unique logos, images, and celebrities associated with your brand. Selecting the right background image provides a consistent and seamless branding experience for your brand enthusiasts.

Thursday: Select and Move Modules

To edit the modules that are displayed on your channel, click the Modules tab. As Figure 5.6 illustrates, the window will then expand to display various options.

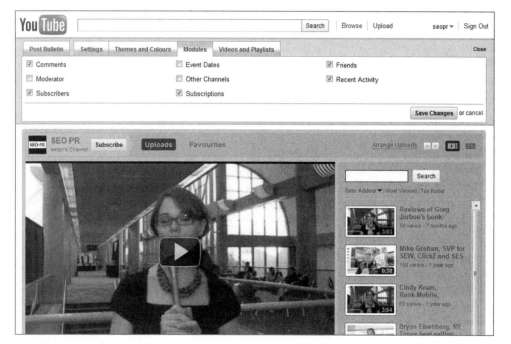

Figure 5.6 Modules

You have the option of displaying several modules on your channel, including these:

- Comments
- Friends
- Subscribers
- Subscriptions
- Recent Activity

If you'd like to show these modules on your channel, click and select the corresponding options. Then click the Save Changes button to update your channel.

Click and unselect the boxes (so that the boxes are blank) next to the module options you don't want to display on your channel page. Then click the Save Changes button to update your channel and hide those modules.

You can also change the order in which your modules appear on your channel:

1. Locate the module on your channel page.
2. In the right-hand corner of the module you'll see several white circular buttons with arrows on them.
3. Click on the buttons to move the module in question up, down, or across the channel page.

I recommend that you display several of these modules, especially Recent Activity. This module provides your channel viewers with a summary of the latest updates to your channel, making it appear more dynamic, fresh, and timely.

For example, if you recently added a new favorite to your channel, your channel's visitors can find it in the Recent Activity module as well as in the usual favorites box. And displaying recent activity—especially if you upload one to two new videos per week—encourages YouTubers to subscribe to your channel.

As this was written, nigahiga had just passed the three million subscribers mark; Fred, RayWilliamJohnson, ShaneDawsonTV, and smosh each had more than two million subscribers; and barely political, collegehumor, davedays, failblog, KassemG, kevjumba, MichellePhan, machinima, MysteryGuitarMan, realannoyingorange, ShaneDawsonTV2, sxephil, TheStation, and universalmusicgroup each had over one million subscribers.

It's worth noting that 14 of these 19 YouTube channels display the Recent Activity module.

Friday: Highlight Videos and Playlists

In addition, you can choose which videos are shown by default when users visit your channel.

You can choose from the following options to set what to display on the right-hand side of your channel page:

- All (playlists, uploads, and favorites)

- Just Uploads

- Just Playlists

- Just Favorites

- Playlist (a particular playlist)

On the left-hand side, you show your default video. Here you can choose from any of your uploads, favorites, or any video whatsoever, provided you have that video's URL.

To customize all of the above, click the Edit link in the upper-right corner of the video navigator box. You can then choose the featured video via the Featured Video drop-down menu, and you can customize the default right-hand-side browser using the Featured Content Set drop-down menu.

Now, if you're a visual learner, you might like to watch a couple of videos that summarize this week's lessons. To do that, start by going to www.youtube.com/watch?v=NykI2cJ9o80 and checking out "YouTube 101: Customizing Your Channel." As Figure 5.7 illustrates, it can be found on the official YouTube channel.

Figure 5.7 "YouTube 101: Customizing Your Channel"

You should also watch "YouTube Channels 2.0," which provides a brief overview of the new YouTube channel redesign. Just go to www.youtube.com/watch?v=cw-NILysH1w and check it out. As Figure 5.8 illustrates, it can also be found on the official YouTube channel.

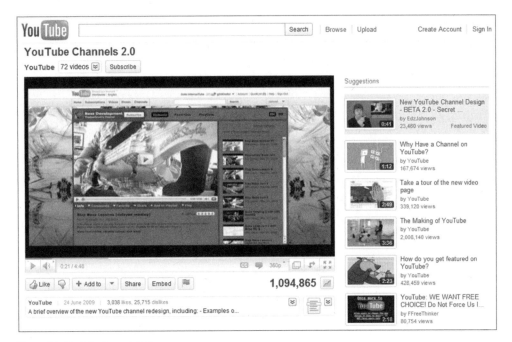

Figure 5.8 "YouTube Channels 2.0"

Why do I recommend that you watch both of these videos? To paraphrase Pfc. Mickey Zimmerman in the movie *Sgt. Bilko* (1996), "See, one is funny, but the other makes you think."

Week 2: Become a YouTube Partner

The next part of this step-by-step guide explains how to become a YouTube partner.

If you've got great videos and a growing audience, then take your channel to the next level through the YouTube Partner Program. It lets you generate revenue from your videos and access YouTube's specialized partner features and tools, including rentals and content management.

There are about 15,000 talented and entrepreneurial YouTube partners building the next generation of media companies in bedrooms, garages, and studios across the globe. They include established media companies like Sony Pictures and Universal Music Group; new media companies like Mondo Media, Machinima, and Next New Networks; and YouTube web hit-makers, users who have created extremely popular videos on YouTube.

Hundreds of these partners are making six figures a year, including Michael Buckley, the host/writer/producer of *What the Buck?!* As Figure 5.9 illustrates, *What the Buck?!* is one of the most popular entertainment shows on YouTube, with over one million subscribers and 263 million views since May 2007.

Figure 5.9 *What the Buck?!*

What'll we do this week?

Monday: Discover the benefits of partnering with YouTube

Tuesday: Verify that you meet the qualifications for partnership

Wednesday: Utilize your partner account tools

Thursday: Use partner channel best practices

Friday: Read some partner success stories

Monday: Discover the Benefits of Partnering with YouTube

It pays to be a YouTube partner. More than 483 million people worldwide are watching 2 billion videos a day on YouTube.

As a YouTube partner, you can share in the revenue generated when they watch your videos. You can also rent streaming videos directly to viewers. And with YouTube's content management tools, you can protect your copyrights while providing viewers with a high-quality branded experience.

Here are some of the benefits of partnering with YouTube:

Monetize your content The YouTube Partner Program gives you the ability to enable revenue sharing for all your existing videos and for any future uploads to your account. The Individual Video Partnership (IVP) program also gives you the opportunity to earn money from specific videos that you've uploaded. Because the IVP program is limited to specific individual videos, many of the other features associated with the YouTube Partner Program are not available to IVP members.

Rent your videos YouTube offers Rentals as part of the YouTube Partner Program, providing content owners with a pay-to-view model to generate revenue. YouTube Rentals is currently in beta and only available in the United States. It offers content partners flexibility and control over monetization, marketing, and distribution.

Customize your channel YouTube partners enjoy a number of perks, such as further channel customization, custom video thumbnails, and additional design and interactivity options.

Showcase your content Partners can upload long-form content with no length or file size limit and can present high-quality video inside a fully branded channel. All videos are streamed at the highest possible quality—up to a full 1080p HD if available—in a 16:9 aspect ratio player.

Protect your copyright YouTube's Content ID system offers you flexibility and control over your videos. You can choose to monetize, track, or block infringing content according to your policies with YouTube's fully automated tools. More than 1,000 partners use Content ID, including every major US network broadcaster, movie studio, and record label. Over a third of YouTube's total monetized views come from Content ID.

These are the benefits of partnering with YouTube. Are there any risks?

The YouTube Partnership Program is a nonexclusive agreement. In other words, YouTube doesn't restrict where you can upload and distribute your videos, so you can monetize them via YouTube and still use them elsewhere.

So, there are no risks.

Tuesday: Verify That You Meet the Qualifications for Partnership

To become a YouTube partner, you must meet these minimum requirements:

- You create original videos suitable for online streaming.
- You own or have express permission to use and monetize all audio and video content that you upload—no exceptions.
- You regularly upload videos that are viewed by thousands of YouTube users, or you publish popular or commercially successful videos in other ways, such as DVDs sold online.

In addition, YouTube uses AdSense to make revenue sharing payments to its partners, so you'll need to have an active AdSense account as well as a YouTube user account. Read the terms of use and other rules and regs to see if you are eligible. If you are, then fill out an application at www.youtube.com/partners, but keep in mind that not everyone who applies for the program will qualify.

Your application will be reviewed to determine whether you fit YouTube's eligibility criteria. This may take some time, so you need to be patient. To help ensure that your application is approved, make sure that you haven't violated YouTube's terms of service.

For example, don't use a photograph; any music; any movie or TV visuals; any artwork; or any play, theatrical work, or concert unless you have the express permission of the person who created or produced it.

According to YouTube, it's *not* okay to use someone else's material without permission, even in the following circumstances:

- You edit together or "mash up" other works.

- You alter any portion of the original material.

- You use only 30 seconds of a song or video clip.

- You found it on the Internet. This does *not* mean that it's in the public domain.

- You are performing a cover version of a song.

- You paid for it. This does *not* mean that you have permission to include it in your video.

- You give proper credits.

- Nobody sends you a copyright notice.

Now, I'm not a lawyer, but Lawrence Lessig, a professor of law at Stanford Law School, would describe the preceding list as intellectual property (IP) "extremism." Professor Lessig says the content industry has convinced industry in general that extremism in copyright regulation is good for business and economic growth.

He thinks that's false. In his book *Remix: Making Art and Commerce Thrive in the Hybrid Economy* (Penguin Group, 2008), Professor Lessig describes the creative and profitable future that culture and industry could realize if only we gave up IP extremism.

In 2008, I emailed Professor Lessig some questions and he emailed me his answers, which I posted on Search Engine Watch on October 20, 2008. Here is part of our Q&A:

Jarboe: *Who benefits from and who is harmed by IP extremism?*

Lessig: Benefits: Lawyers (certainly). The record companies (maybe). Harmed: Artists, businesses, consumers—and a generation of (criminalized) kids.

Jarboe: *Why is IP extremism bad for business and economic growth?*

Lessig: Practice moderation. When the lawyers in the room start insisting that the licenses you create must impose perfect control over everything you have, ask them to prove it. Ask them to demonstrate that the business return from that relationship of antagonism is higher than its cost. Don't give over your business's future to those who don't think like a business man or woman. Keep focused on the only undeniable truth: IP is an asset. Like any business asset, it should be deployed to maximize the value of the corporation.

Although I agree with Professor Lessig, you still can't violate YouTube's terms of use. To meet its criteria for partnership, you must own or have express permission to use and monetize all audio and video content that you upload.

However, on August 21, 2008, Bob Egelko of the *San Francisco Chronicle* wrote an article entitled "Woman can sue over YouTube clip de-posting." Here's what he said:

> *In a victory for small-time music copiers over the entertainment industry, a federal judge ruled Wednesday that copyright holders can't order one of their songs removed from the Web without first checking to see if the excerpt was so small and innocuous that it was legal. The ruling by U.S. District Judge Jeremy Fogel of San José was the first in the nation to require the owner of the rights to a creative work to consider whether an online copy was a "fair use"—a small or insignificant replication that couldn't have affected the market for the original—before ordering the Web host to take it down.*

And in July 2010, the United States Copyright Office granted an exemption for people remixing videos on YouTube, declaring it is not a violation of the fair use provisions of the Digital Millennium Copyright Act (DMCA) if they use excerpts from DVDs for the purpose of criticism or comment.

I hope this means it's okay to create YouTube remixes like "10 Things I Hate About Commandments" (shown in Figure 5.10).

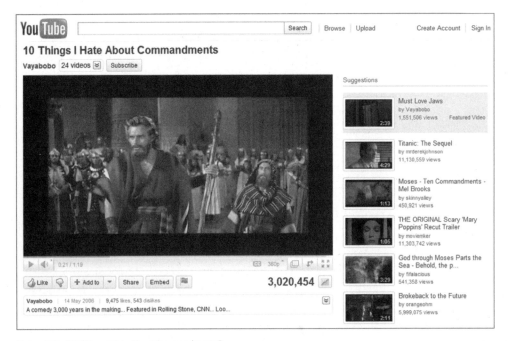

Figure 5.10 "10 Things I Hate About Commandments"

This comedy (http://youtu.be/u1kqqMXWEFs), which was "3,000 years in the making," had more than three million views when this screenshot was taken. It also had 9,455 likes and 542 dislikes as this was written.

According to the Viral Video Chart powered by Unruly Media, "10 Things I Hate About Commandments" had 9,208 Facebook shares and 426 blog posts when this screenshot was taken.

Remember, I'm not an attorney, and the information I present here is not legal advice. I'm presenting it for informational purposes only.

Wednesday: Utilize Your Partner Account Tools

YouTube provides a partner toolkit that you will want to utilize. We've already touched on several of these programs and tools:

AdSense ads The AdSense ads YouTube displays on your partner channel are determined automatically based on a number of contextual factors relating to your video, such as video category. For this reason, YouTube is not able to manually control all of the ads that appear on your video pages. Similarly, YouTube is not able to guarantee that specific ads will be displayed on your video pages.

YouTube rentals You can experiment with the different price points, availability windows, and rental durations to optimize the offering for a specific video. You can choose to make some content available via the ad-supported model or make some free for promotional purposes, for maximum control over your monetization, marketing, and distribution strategies.

Custom thumbnails YouTube partners have the ability to upload custom thumbnails for their videos. The best dimensions to use are 480×270 pixels. Thumbnails uploaded using the custom thumbnail image upload tool must follow YouTube's Community Guidelines and general criteria for revenue sharing. Thumbnails that are sexually suggestive, violent, or graphic may cause your video to be age-restricted. When a partner video is age-restricted, advertising will not be served against it and the video will not appear on YouTube's Most Viewed, Top Favorites, and other browse pages.

Video length limits When you become a partner, you no longer have a limit to the length of video you can upload. YouTube partners still have a file size limit of 20 GB per video uploaded through a web upload.

Content ID YouTube Content ID scans over 100 years' worth of video every day. YouTube's Audio ID and Video ID technologies let rights owners identify user-uploaded videos consisting entirely *or* partially of their content. Rights holders can choose, in advance, what they want to happen when those videos are found: (1) make money from them, (2) get stats on them, or (3) block them from YouTube altogether.

In addition to these programs and tools, YouTube has added a couple of new things to its partner toolkit:

YouTube for mobile In January 2011, YouTube exceeded 200 million views a day on mobile devices, a 3x increase in just 12 months. As the world goes mobile and more people watch videos on their smart phones, YouTube expects more partners will make more of their content available across more devices and take advantage of its new mobile advertising capabilities.

YouTube Leanback YouTube Leanback is a new way to watch YouTube videos on Google TV or any big screen. With simple controls and full-screen viewing, Leanback makes watching videos on YouTube as effortless as watching TV. As this was written, YouTube Leanback was not monetized, but YouTube's content partners can expect to be able to monetize their content on Leanback in 2011.

Live Streaming Live streaming enables partners to broadcast their content in real time to the YouTube community directly from the YouTube channel page. YouTube initiated its live-streaming program with a few of its large partners, including U2, the Indian Premier League, the White House, and E3. YouTube then opened up the platform to a wider array of partners, including Howcast, Next New Networks, Rocketboom, and Young Hollywood.

Thursday: Use Partner Channel Best Practices

YouTube has partnership deals with thousands of large content providers, including CBS, BBC, Universal Music Group, Sony Music Group, the NBA, and The Sundance Channel. YouTube also partners with made-for-YouTube content providers, such as Fred, FunnyorDie, Machinima, and MysteryGuitarMan.

These partners and the wide range of content they represent suggest a set of best practices for making the most effective use of your partner channel.

Create High Quality and Original Content

From annoying oranges to voracious vloggers, YouTube partners create original content that inspires, entertains, enlightens, and educates others across the globe. And they all focus on:

Quality Create original videos for which you own 100 percent of the copyrights and that comply with YouTube's Community Guidelines. Make videos that appeal to all kinds of audiences.

Freshness Try to upload one to two new videos per week. Be consistent with the day/time you upload new videos. Keep videos short and simple. I recommend under 5 minutes.

Engagement Use eye-catching titles. Engage your audience through shout-outs, comments, and subscriptions and by asking questions or soliciting ideas. Use Moderator on YouTube. Consider contests.

Utilize YouTube Features

From college friends making trick basketball shots into a career to a musician who's gone from bagging groceries to beatboxing around the world, YouTube partners also take advantage of the tools that YouTube provides them to make high quality videos and drive audiences to their channels. These include:

Branding Use the partner branding options available to you. Upload catchy and engaging banners and profile images.

Navigation Utilize the Featured Video option by featuring your latest video or one of your most popular. Put related videos in playlists.

Channel type Use the Performer Info box available for your channel type. For example, musicians can enter band details, album cover art, and event dates.

Search Use relevant and accurate titles, video descriptions, and tags. The discussion of optimizing video for YouTube in Chapter 7 will provide more details.

Increase Networking

From occasional collaborators like MysteryGuitarMan and FreddieW to the 25 individuals bodacious enough to be selected for the first ever Creator Camp, YouTube partners also network with each other and participate in the YouTube community. Many of them:

Connect Encourage comments. Post replies. Comment on other content. Create video responses. Encourage others to rate, subscribe to, and share your videos. Join forums and contests. You can learn more about connecting with your audience when we talk about engaging the online video community in Chapter 8.

Use Other Channel Links Use the Other Channel Links tool in Branding Options to list up to 16 destination channels. Link to your other channels/websites or to the channels/ websites of your business partners, industry colleagues, and friends.

Subscribe You can subscribe to your favorite channels. Enable the recent activity box. Display your favorite videos in the favorites box. And if you join an affiliate partner program, like the one BeautyChoice.com has in the beauty industry, then highlight affiliate content in the ratings box.

Cross-Promote Your Content

Finally, from original content creators to advertisers large and small, YouTube Partners cross-promote their content early and often. They know how to:

Promote You can promote your videos. Publicize your videos and your channel on the radio, TV, websites, forums, newsletters, and other social networking platforms. Call out your YouTube channel in as many places as you can.

Use badges Use YouTube application programming interfaces (APIs) to create YouTube badges for your website that display your YouTube presence and link to your YouTube channel.

Embed Allow embedding so others can distribute for you. Use the embed URL that comes with each video to embed your videos on your website. Send the links to blogs that may want to display your content.

Friday: Read Some Partner Success Stories

In May 2007, YouTube elevated some of its most popular users to partners. Until then, many marketers made a distinction between popular content created by amateurs and premium content created by professionals. YouTube wanted to start changing that perception so more advertisers would buy advertising on more channels than the ones created by established media companies. That was why it added several of the most popular and prolific original content creators from the YouTube community to its partnership program, including Lonelygirl15, LisaNova, renetto, HappySlip, smosh, and valsartdiary.

In December 2007, YouTube expanded the pilot of its Partner Program and added 100 new users, including tayzonday, hotforwords, apauledtv, and peteandbrian.

Viewers were watching "popular" video content, but some of the larger advertisers were limiting themselves to running advertising against only "premium" video content. So, YouTube gave each of these new partners a thorough vetting—and regularly checked to ensure that new partners were uploading appropriate content—in order to convince more advertisers to stop making a distinction without a difference.

Whether the content was produced by professionals or amateurs, it was all just video to viewers. Did it really matter if these talented and entrepreneurial YouTube partners were building the next generation of media companies in bedrooms, garages, or studios?

On December 10, 2008, Brian Stelter of the *New York Times* wrote an article entitled "YouTube Videos Pull in Real Money." He wrote, "One year after YouTube, the online video powerhouse, invited members to become 'partners' and added advertising to their videos, the most successful users are earning six-figure incomes from the Web site."

Stelter interviewed Cory Williams, who is known as smpfilms on YouTube. Williams said his big break came in September 2007, when he was 26 years old, with a music video parody called "The Mean Kitty Song." The video, which introduces his evil feline companion, had been viewed more than 43 million times as this was written.

With more than 483,000 subscribers to smpfilms's channel, Williams said he was earning $17,000 to $20,000 a month via YouTube. Half of the profits came from YouTube's advertisements, and the other half came from sponsorships and product placements within his videos, a model that he had borrowed from traditional media.

On February 23, 2009, Asjylyn Loder of the *St. Petersburg Times* wrote an article entitled "St. Petersburg man makes living sharing tinkering talents on Web." She wrote, "Kip Kedersha's fuzzy Havanese puppy paid for himself in 43 seconds, by shoving himself headfirst into a square hole while his owner chronicled his efforts in a video titled 'Round Dog vs. Square Hole.'"

The video has been viewed more than 502,000 times as this was written. More than 655,000 people subscribe to kipkay's channel. Loden added, "The channel is also how Kedersha makes a living. He earns thousands of dollars a month as part of YouTube's Partner Program, which places advertisements along the bottom of Kedersha's videos."

In early 2009, YouTube started posting partner success stories to its website. The first featured Demand Media, which had launched the ExpertVillage's channel in April 2006. Demand Media's channel was accepted into YouTube's Partner Program in 2007.

ExpertVillage's channel, shown in Figure 5.11, had more than 1.6 billion views as this was written, making it the #4 most viewed channel of all time, and more than 826,000 subscribers, making it the #29 most subscribed channel of all time.

Figure 5.11 Expert Village

Demand Media then launched other YouTube branded channels housing more than 150,000 videos, including eHow, Livestrong.com, Cracked.com, TypeF, Trails, and Golflink.

As this was written, Demand Media's channels had a total of 1.8 billion views and more than 1.1 million subscribers. "What originally began as a marketing-driven syndication effort has now turned into a seven figure revenue stream," Steven Kydd,

EVP of Demand Studios, Demand Media's content creation division, said in the YouTube partner success story.

We'll take a closer look at Demand Media in Chapter 6 and we'll look at some more success stories in later chapters.

Week 3: Create a YouTube Brand Channel

The next part of this step-by-step guide explains how to create a YouTube brand channel. Before tackling that, let's ask, "Why would anyone want or need to create a YouTube brand channel?"

As this was written, marketers needed to make advertising commitments on YouTube of $200,000 or more to build a brand channel. Since all pricing minimums are subject to change, you should verify the current contract requirements with a YouTube ad sales representative.

So, let's quickly review your options: (1) You can set up a user channel on YouTube for free, (2) you can become a YouTube partner and build a channel that can make money, or (3) you can create a brand channel if you spend $200,000 or more on YouTube ads.

Get it? Got it? Good.

So, why would anyone want or need to select option 3?

Let's start with an example of a marketer who wanted to create not one, but two YouTube brand channels.

Brad Haley, EVP marketing for Carl's Jr. and Hardee's, launched two new YouTube brand channels in June 2009 as part of a campaign that enlisted some of the most popular users on YouTube to make videos about the restaurant's new Portobello Mushroom Six Dollar Burger.

On June 1, 2009, Brian Morrissey of *Adweek* said, "Justine Ezarik might not be a household name, but the 25-year-old has a cable TV-size audience. The only difference: Ezarik's audience is on YouTube, Facebook and Twitter."

Ezarik not only has more than 996,000 subscribers to her iJustine's channel on YouTube, she also has more than 1.2 million followers on Twitter, and over 429,000 people like her Facebook page. As Morrissey observed, "These networks, in essence, comprise a new kind of media buy."

On June 4, Jesse Haines, YouTube's marketing manager, interviewed Haley for the YouTube Biz Blog. Here are a couple of the questions that they discussed:

Haines: Why did you decide to advertise on YouTube?

Haley: At Carl's Jr. and Hardee's, our advertising is targeted to 18–34-year-old males. We call them "young, hungry guys." And they are definitely on YouTube.

Haines: Tell us about this campaign.

Haley: This campaign has two goals—the first is to promote the introduction of Carl's Jr. Portobello Mushroom Six Dollar Burger. What better way to promote a new product than to have some of the hottest YouTube content creators show their millions of subscribers how they would eat the burger? The second goal is to gain traction with our new brand channels for both Carl's Jr. (www.youtube.com/CarlsJr) and Hardee's (www.youtube.com/Hardees). We launched them on the same day as the videos from the content creators to help drive traffic, subscribers, and interaction with the brands.

So, how did the campaign do?

The campaign echoed far and wide among Carl's Jr.'s target audience, resulting in nearly 10 million views for all of the videos. Figure 5.12 shows iJustine's video.

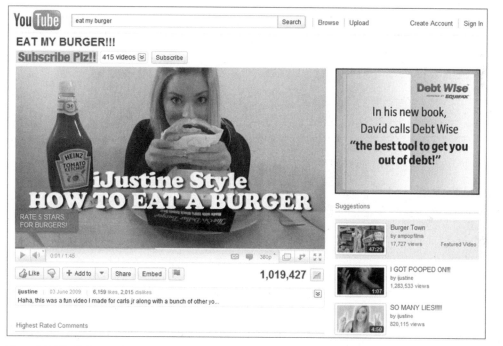

Figure 5.12 "Eat My Burger!!!"

Not only did the campaign create a dialogue and sense of community around a new product, but sales of the Portobello Mushroom Burger doubled from the period before the launch of the campaign on YouTube. The campaign also won an OMMA award that year in the Best in Show category.

Next, let's look at an example of a company that needed to create a YouTube brand channel in a hurry.

On April 20, 2010, the Deepwater Horizon exploded, killing 11 men working on the platform and injuring 17 others. The disaster caused an oil spill in the Gulf of Mexico that flowed for three months. It is the largest accidental marine oil spill in the history of the petroleum industry, and the impact of the spill still continues even after the well was capped.

The environmental disaster also became a PR disaster when BP's CEO Tony Hayward made some comments that underplayed the impact of the spill.

On May 14, 2010, Hayward told the *Guardian* that "the Gulf of Mexico is a very big ocean. The amount of volume of oil and dispersant we are putting into it is tiny in relation to the total water volume."

On May 18, Hayward told Sky News that "the environmental impact of this disaster is likely to have been very, very modest."

BP America launched a brand channel on YouTube on May 18, 2010 (Figure 5.13).

Figure 5.13 Gulf of Mexico response

In its Latest News module, the official YouTube channel for BP America said, "BP has created this YouTube channel to engage the public in an informative conversation and dialogue about our efforts associated with the oil spill in the Gulf of Mexico."

Now, spending $200,000 on YouTube advertising and creating a brand channel may sound pricey to some marketers.

But according to Google Zeitgeist 2010, "oil spill" was the most-searched-for news story of the year in the United States. And according to Google Insights for Search, there were a couple of top or rising searches for variations of "oil spill." One was "Gulf oil spill" and another was "BP oil spill."

That's why Jonathan Allen of Search Engine Watch estimated that BP was spending up to $1 million a month on an integrated search marketing campaign using Google AdWords and YouTube.

And Jake Tapper, Karen Travers, Sunlen Miller, and Matt Guttman of ABC News noted that BP had contracted for $50 million worth of television advertising to "manage their image during the course of this disaster."

So, the amount of money that BP put into YouTube was "tiny" in relation to the total amount it spent on advertising.

Now, after reading this example, I suspect that more than a few marketers are trying to reassure themselves that "it can't happen here."

But it can. Although crisis events are unpredictable, they are not unexpected. During the next five years, 83 percent of companies will face a crisis that will negatively impact their share price by 20 to 30 percent, according to Oxford-Metrica.

That's why it is important to learn how to create a YouTube brand channel. You may want or you may need to create one.

Here are the key steps:

Monday: Learn about the special features of brand channels

Tuesday: Set up a YouTube brand channel

Wednesday: Customize your brand channel

Thursday: Increase engagement on your brand channel

Friday: Take advantage of Google Analytics

Monday: Learn about the Special Features of Brand Channels

A YouTube brand channel offers a number of features that are not available on standard channels:

Video discovery Brands can keep users within the same branded space when using a channel. When a user arrives at a brand channel, the featured video plays automatically. When he then clicks another video, that video will also play within the brand channel. Marketers also have the option of featuring their other channels, playlists, vlogs, favorite videos, and much more.

Branding YouTube also enables the customization of brand channels through several modules, including channel banners, your background image, and a branding box.

Brand safety To ensure brand safety, marketers can moderate the comments as well as limit a channel's accessibility to users of a certain age or gender. Brands can also redirect users automatically to different brand channels, depending on their geographical locations.

But wait, there's more:

Gadgets These are small web applications—or rich media ads—that sit on a brand channel, offering deeper functionality for users. These often utilize YouTube's APIs to encourage video discovery and uploads, but they are not limited to that function.

Syndication Brand channels can live on any website, in addition to YouTube. Simply by copying one line of HTML, you can integrate the basic brand channel functionality into a website. The full gadget functionality can also be embedded easily into third-party sites and ad units.

Metrics Standard YouTube metrics are available through the brand channel itself or via the account dashboard: channel views, total uploaded video views, subscribers, friends, channel comments. Google Analytics can also be used for more in-depth tracking, reporting, and analysis. Third-party tracking can also be employed.

If the preceding list doesn't look like it's worth $200,000, then remember this: Marketers also get $200,000 worth of advertising on YouTube for their $200,000. And 94 of *AdAge*'s Top 100 advertisers have run campaigns on YouTube and the Google Display Network.

Brand channels allow these *AdAge* 100 advertisers to create a personalized interface, customizing the look and feel of their presence on YouTube. With a destination page on the site, brand channels give them the opportunity to create truly persistent relationships with their consumers.

Is this fair to local retailers? It's very hard to assure complete equality. As John F. Kennedy once said, "Life is unfair."

Tuesday: Set Up a YouTube Brand Channel

Today, I'll quickly cover setting up a YouTube brand channel account. I'll then provide a high-level overview of the process for designing your brand channel once you have signed up for an account.

Go to www.youtube.com/create_account and complete the form to begin creating a new account. The process is the same as setting up a user channel, so I won't repeat it here.

After creating your account, send your YouTube username to your salesperson and request to have your account converted to a brand channel.

You are now ready to begin uploading dummy video content and customizing your page. However, do not upload the videos that you want to appear on your channel page yet. Once you receive confirmation that your account has been converted to a brand channel, you can complete the additional customizations that are exclusively available to brand channels.

You can see a sample YouTube brand channel at www.youtube.com/user/brandedchanneldemo (Figure 5.14).

If you're one of the people designing and building the brand channel, then you will also want to read "Creating and Customizing a Brand Channel." It's hidden in plain sight with several other how-to guides in the Advertising section of YouTube. The URL is long:

www.youtube.com/pdf/YouTube_Brand_Channel_Redesign.pdf

Figure 5.14 Sample Brand Channel

It may be simpler to go to Google and search for the phrase "creating and customizing a brand channel."

If you are a marketing executive who has people designing and building the brand channel for you, you will still want to know about half a dozen of the modules that could be included on a channel page:

- The *channel banner*, which appears at the top of a brand channel page. It is available only for brand channels.

- The *video navigator*, which lets users locate and watch your uploaded videos, favorite videos, and playlists. The module also contains a video actions area, where users can view information about a video, read or add comments, and mark a video as a favorite. This module features a video player that can automatically play your channel's featured video when a user visits your channel page. On standard channel pages, users always need to click the video or play control to initiate the playback.

- The *channel ID module* helps YouTube users interact with a channel. This module appears on all channel pages. It displays the channel name as well as buttons for subscribing to the channel and for adding the channel owner as a friend. It also displays links to block a user or to send a message to the channel owner.

- The *channel information module* contains content that describes a channel and appears on all channel pages. The module has two components:
  - The *profile* section displays statistics for your channel, such as the number of times your channel has been viewed. It can also display some public information from your YouTube profile, such as your country and website.

- The *honors* section appears if your channel has achieved a notable ranking, such as being one of the most viewed channels or most subscribed-to channels. The section displays up to three honors and, if there are more than three rankings, also shows a link to view more rankings. YouTube automatically generates the content for this part of the module.

- The *side column image* is a graphic that can link to external websites or to YouTube video pages, playlists, or brand channels.

- The *video display ad* displays in the video navigator if someone is watching a monetized video that you have either marked as a favorite video or included in a playlist. You can disable the video display ad from appearing when your own uploaded videos are playing in the video player. However, if you want to ensure that this ad module does not display on your channel, avoid adding monetized videos owned by other YouTube partners to your playlists or favorite videos. You can determine that a video is monetized if YouTube displays an ad unit on that video's watch page.

The rest of the page real estate displays content modules that you can select for your channel.

For example, many brand channel owners place the optional *channel branding box* in a prominent location. This module, which is available only for brand channels, lets you feature promotional text and links related to your brand. The text can contain HTML markup, and the channel branding box section lists the HTML tags that you can use.

In addition, brand channel owners frequently use the Other Channel Links module to feature associated brand channels or other channels that might appeal to brand enthusiasts.

On the other hand, brand advertisers rarely use several additional modules that could be included on a channel page, such as a subscribers box, a friends box, and a comments box.

The day before your campaign begins, upload the videos that you want to be visible on your channel page. Only relatively new videos are eligible to be among the Most Viewed videos of the day. I also recommend that you remove any dummy videos that you uploaded while designing your channel.

Capiche?

Wednesday: Customize Your Brand Channel

If you're one of the people designing and building the brand channel, then you will want to read all 37 pages in YouTube's how-to guide about customizing your brand channel.

If you are a marketing executive who has people designing and building the brand channel for you, then you will still want to know about the key options for customizing your channel's content and appearance:

Selecting your profile icon   Your channel's profile icon is a square image that appears in several locations. I recommend that you upload an image of a product, logo, or spokesperson closely associated with your brand. Your original image should be at least 88 pixels square, though it can be larger than that as long as it is a square image. Since the image will display in the video navigator at the top of your channel page, I recommend that you verify that the image is recognizable when it is resized to be 36 pixels square.

Designing your channel   When you are logged in to your brand channel account, several channel editing options display between the YouTube page header and your actual channel content:

> **Choosing color schemes**   By default, your channel will use the Grey theme. However, to ensure that your channel truly reflects your brand identity, I recommend that you modify the colors by creating a custom theme.

> **Providing a background image**   I recommend that you select a background image that mirrors the look and feel of your other online branding. For example, your background image can feature unique logos, images, and celebrities associated with your brand. Brand channels have the option of uploading background images up to 1 MB. However, I recommend that you choose a background image that is 256 KB or smaller. Larger background images correlate to higher page latency, so if you upload a 1 MB image, users visiting your page will have to wait longer for your page to load.

Setting branding options   The channel banner is a 960×150-pixel image that appears at the top of your channel page. The option to upload a channel banner is only available to brand channels. I recommend that you choose an image that is 20 KB or smaller.

Thursday: Increase Engagement on Your Brand Channel

Today, let's look at how you can increase engagement on your brand channel.

YouTube currently has a selection of ready-made template gadgets that it calls "engagement products." These include a carousel, video wall, and video mosaic designed to improve discovery of videos as well as contests designed to elicit user uploads.

The *carousel module*, which is 875 pixels wide and 460 pixels high, appears at the top of your brand channel page just below the channel banner and can also be embedded on third-party websites. As Figure 5.15 illustrates, the Carousel typically replaces the Featured Video module on a brand channel page. It lets users scroll through a rotation of videos selected by the brand channel owner.

Figure 5.15 Carousel

The *video wall module* is a gadget that displays thumbnail images for a collection of YouTube videos on a grid. Users can scroll to see multiple pages of thumbnail images depending on the number of videos included in the video collection.

The video wall is available for inclusion on brand channel pages. It is 960 pixels wide and 465 pixels tall if it does not display a search field. If it does display a search field, then its height is 480 pixels. The video wall can appear either at the top of your brand channel page (just below the channel banner) or just below the video navigator module.

As Figure 5.16 illustrates, the video wall shows thumbnail images for 28 videos and does not display a search box. Alternate layouts showing 20 or 50 thumbnails are also available.

Figure 5.16 Video wall

The *YouTube video mosaic* is a Flash-based gadget that is available for display on qualifying brand channel pages. It provides a novel way to associate your brand or product with a collection of YouTube videos.

The video mosaic uses the thumbnail images for a collection of videos to create a mosaic. As Figure 5.17 illustrates, each mosaic tile shows a still frame from a video, and tiles are arranged to form a larger image, such as a logo, a still from a movie, or a photograph of a character or product. The code that constructs the mosaic matches the colors of video thumbnails to the colors of pixels in the larger target image. The code also matches shapes in the thumbnail images to similar shapes in the target image.

Figure 5.17 Video mosaic

Conducting *contests* is a core method of engaging YouTube community members and encouraging them to interact with your brand. Contests create unique opportunities to blend your own content with user-generated assets on your brand channel page.

Contests also encourage multiple levels of participation:

- Brand enthusiasts, motivated by loyalty and affinity for your product, create unique content that showcases your brand image.

- Budding video directors—encouraged by the visibility that your contest affords their videos and by the prizes for winning videos—channel their creative energies toward creating new videos that communicate your brand identity.

- YouTube community members are drawn to your brand channel, which becomes a source of interesting, new, and often professional-quality video content.

Information about your contest appears on your brand channel page, creating an integrated brand experience for YouTube users and allowing you to provide a single destination for your brand on YouTube. Brand channel pages that showcase contests still have access to all standard brand channel features, including custom graphics, a branding box, and automatic featured video playback.

However, an advertiser can spend $500,000 or more to create a YouTube contest on its brand channel, so make sure that you read all 55 pages of "Designing and Running a Contest" before creating one.

This PDF file is also hidden in plain sight with other brand channel how-to guides on designing a Carousel module, Video Wall, and Video Mosaic. To find it, go to Google and search for the phrase "designing and running a contest."

Friday: Take Advantage of Google Analytics

YouTube automatically collects the standard channel metrics:

- Number of channel page views, which is visible in the channel information module on your channel page and on your account dashboard
- Number of subscribers, which is visible in the channel information module and subscribers module on your channel page as well as on your account dashboard
- Number of friends, which is displayed in the friends module on your channel page and in your address book
- Number of channel comments, which is displayed in the comments module on your channel page

YouTube also collects the following statistics for each video uploaded to your channel:

- Views, which includes all views on the watch page as well as other views using YouTube's embedded player
- Number of comments
- Number of video responses
- Number of ratings
- Number of times the video was marked as a favorite video
- Average rating

These statistics are publicly visible on the watch page for each video, though counts may be delayed up to 24 hours. You can monitor this data in the following ways:

- Check the individual watch pages for your videos to collect the statistics.
- Write a script that uses the YouTube Data API to retrieve statistics for your videos.

Oh, and YouTube's Insight tool lets you analyze viewership data, based on registered users, for your videos. This includes the following data:

- Views for your videos over time, worldwide or by geographic region.

- Popularity of your videos over time relative to other YouTube videos. Popularity figures are available based on global or regional viewing trends.

- Gender and age demographics for your viewers

- Discovery sources, which identify the ways that other YouTube users find your videos. Discovery data is only available at the individual video level.

- Hot spots viewing information, which identifies viewing trends for each moment in a video. Hot spots information is also only available at the individual video level.

But, all YouTube channels—user, partner, and brand channels—get these metrics. And Chapter 9 covers YouTube Insight in more detail. So, there's nothing to see here; move along.

But Google Analytics is available on brand channels. And at this time, Google Analytics integration on YouTube is only available for brand channels.

Google Analytics enables YouTube brand channel owners to track and measure traffic to their channels. It provides a comprehensive view of how visitors access and interact with channels. Analytics reports provide data such as traffic referral patterns, repeat visitation, user demographics, and much, much more.

Google Analytics enables you to answer questions such as these:

- How do visitors find my brand channel?

- How loyal are my viewers: How often do they come back to my channel?

- How much time do people spend on my channel?

- Where are my users located and what languages do they speak?

Chapter 9 also covers Google Analytics in more detail. But I wanted you to know that brand channels let you take advantage of Google Analytics. As Vice President Joe Biden would say, "This is a big … deal."

Considering that brand channel owners are spending $200,000 or more on YouTube advertising, it's only fair that they get more and better metrics. Well, maybe it's not fair. But as Ronald Reagan once said, "I paid for this microphone!"

Week 4: Stream Live Content on YouTube

You can now stream live events on YouTube.

YouTube's first official live community celebration took place on November 22, 2008, at the Herbst Pavilion at the Fort Mason Center in San Francisco. Part concert, part variety show, and part party, the event brought to life many of the amazing videos and talent that YouTube viewers had already made popular.

Although YouTube users have been gathering informally for years, YouTube Live '08 was the first time the YouTube community leaped off the screen and onto a stage.

There were 30 special guests and performers at YouTube Live '08, including Will.i.am, Esmee Denters, Fred, Soulja Boy, and Tay Zonday. Since they were profiled in Chapter 5, let's profile five others: Katy Perry (the opening act), Joe Satriani and Funtwo, MythBusters, Bo Burnham, and Akon (the closing act).

As a sponsor for the event, Flip Video gave away a free Flip Video Mino to all of the audience members to record any part of YouTube Live. A station to upload videos to YouTube from the Mino was also provided, promoted, and sponsored by Flip.

The event was also streamed live on YouTube, enabling millions from around the globe to partake in the festivities (Figure 5.18).

Figure 5.18 YouTube Live

On April 8, 2011, YouTube closed the YouTube Live channel, effectively removing all the videos from the 2008 event. In its place, YouTube rolled out a brand-new YouTube Live browse page at www.youtube.com/live where users could find featured, live, and upcoming events happening on YouTube.

Under the redefined Live name, YouTube also started rolling out its live streaming beta platform, which allows certain YouTube partners with accounts in good standing to stream live content on YouTube.

The new platform had been tested in September 2010 by four YouTube partners: Howcast, Next New Networks, Rocketboom, and Young Hollywood. This platform integrated live streaming directly into YouTube channels. All a broadcaster needed was a webcam or external USB/FireWire camera. Included in the test was a live comments module that let users engage with the broadcaster and the broader YouTube community.

Based on the results of this initial test, YouTube decided to roll out the platform more broadly to its partners worldwide. This week, we'll take a closer look at this new way to engage the YouTube community.

Monday: Get started with live streaming

Tuesday: Broadcast an event using FMLE

Wednesday: Schedule an event

Thursday: Expect some bumps along the way

Friday: Bowl a wicked googly

Monday: Get Started with Live Streaming

YouTube is in the process of rolling out live stream broadcasting to YouTube partners. You can check to see whether the feature is enabled on your account by logging in and visiting your channel page. Look for a promotional message at the top. You can also look for the Live Streaming setting under Videos & Playlists.

If you find you have not been enabled, then YouTube welcomes your enthusiasm but kindly asks for your patience. There is no process for requesting live streaming for your account. All you can do is make sure that your account is in good standing and that you remain an active uploader who respects YouTube's Community Guidelines.

If your account is enabled for live streaming, you'll see a pop-up promotion when you log in and visit your channel page that looks like the one in Figure 5.19.

Figure 5.19 Live Streaming pop-up promotion

To stream live on YouTube, the first thing you need is a video encoder. This can be a piece of hardware or software that takes the video input from your camera and encodes it for distribution on the Web. Some examples of encoders are the NewTek Tricaster, Telestream Wirecast, and Elemental Live.

If you don't already have an encoder, you can download and install Flash Media Live Encoder (FMLE) from Adobe for free at the following location:

www.adobe.com/products/flashmediaserver/flashmediaencoder/

Tuesday: Broadcast an Event Using FMLE

To broadcast an event using FMLE, follow these step-by-step instructions:

1. Log in to your YouTube account and go to your channel page.

2. Click the promotion for live streaming and accept the terms of service.

   If you don't see a promotion, then you can turn live streaming on or off by clicking the Videos & Playlists tab and selecting or deselecting the Live Streaming checkbox.

3. Once the page refreshes, you will see a new Live tab at the top of your channel in the video navigator. Click it.

4. Click Start New Event.

5. Enter a title, description, tags, and category just as you would for any normal video upload.

6. Choose whether you want your live stream to be automatically archived.

7. For Source, select FMLE. This will give you an option to download an XML profile.

8. Click to download it to your local machine.

9. Run FMLE, select File > Open Profile, and choose the file you just downloaded. This will automatically configure FMLE to broadcast this event to YouTube.

10. In FMLE, validate your video and audio input sources, and then click Start.

11. Back on YouTube, click Preview Event.

12. Validate that your video and audio streams are coming through successfully, and then click Start Broadcast to let all viewers of your channel see your broadcast.

13. When your broadcast is complete, simply click Stop in FMLE. YouTube will automatically detect the end of the stream and stop broadcasting the event.

14. If you selected Archive Event Automatically, your live stream will automatically show up as a standard YouTube video on demand video.

15. When you want to stop the stream, just press Stop on your encoder and YouTube will automatically end the stream.

    I recommend using the following live stream settings:

- H.264 codec

- 700 Kbps bit rate

- 640×360 resolution

- 30 fps

- 64 k AAC mono audio

I also recommend using a hardware or software encoder on a dedicated machine with a fast dual-core CPU and plenty of RAM. In addition, make sure to broadcast over a hard-wired Internet connection with no less than 1.5 Mbps upstream bandwidth. And also make sure to test the product prior to going live to your audience.

Wednesday: Schedule an Event

YouTube lets you schedule live events ahead of time to promote them and drive awareness. When you schedule a live event, your subscribers will see a notification in their homepage feed. Visitors to your channel can also add the event to their calendars. The event may also show up on the YouTube.com live browse page.

To schedule an event, follow these steps:

1. Log in to your account and go to My Videos.

2. On the left side, click Live Events.

3. Click New Live Event.

4. Enter a title, description, tags, and category, just as you would for any normal upload.

5. Set a date, time, and time zone for the event.

6. Select the source of the event.

7. Click Save Changes. Your event is now scheduled and will appear in the Upcoming Events section of the live tab on your channel.

I encourage you to actively promote your upcoming live streams by scheduling them in advance and letting your users know about them through videos you upload, annotations, bulletins, and other social media services.

Thursday: Expect Some Bumps along the Way

To ensure a great live stream viewing experience, YouTube plans to roll its self-service live-streaming beta platform out incrementally to partners over the course of 2011.

But in a post on the YouTube Blog, Joshua Siegel, product manager, and Christopher Hamilton, product marketing manager, said, "Bear with us as we test this new platform as there may be some bumps along the way."

For example, you have to configure your encoder with a new RTMP URL and stream ID every time you broadcast to ensure the security of your account.

Your live stream could end abruptly if your encoder fails or your upstream network connection drops. I recommend that no one log out of the account you're using to stream during a broadcast.

Although embedding is not yet officially supported for live streams, you can embed the player once the stream is live by right-clicking on the player and selecting Copy Embed HTML. To embed a scheduled event, select the event from your channel, click the event title below the player, then use the Embed button on the watch page to copy the code. If you want the video to autoplay, you can add &autoplay=1 to the source embed code. However, the embed player does not yet work correctly in the scheduled event state. YouTube hopes to address this soon.

You can see how many viewers your stream has under your player while you broadcast. In addition, you can click the Stats tab to see a real-time viewer graph. However, YouTube is still working to incorporate additional live statistics into YouTube Insight after a broadcast.

As this was written, live events couldn't be archived to your channel. YouTube is still working on giving broadcasters this option.

Also, live stream views were separate from the standard video-on-demand view-count shown on the watch page.

In addition, you couldn't monetize your live streams. Once the product comes out of beta, YouTube plans to enable monetization features similar to standard VOD videos.

Although YouTube plans to publish an API for broadcasting and discovering events soon, it was not available as this was written.

Nevertheless, YouTube partners are live-streaming events *right now*. So, head over to www.youtube.com/live to check out some of the live streams taking place today, tomorrow, and over the next seven days.

Friday: Bowl a Wicked Googly

YouTube has already live-streamed a number of events, including a U2 concert, an Indian Premier League cricket season, a President Obama interview, and an E3 conference.

Let's look at the one that bowled "a wicked googly."

On March 12, 2010, Amit Agrawal, strategic partner development manager, announced on the YouTube Blog, "When the first ball of this year's Indian Premier League cricket season is bowled, fans across the planet will have a front row seat in the world's biggest online sports stadium."

The global YouTube community was able to tune in to the IPL's YouTube channel (www.youtube.com/ipl) for streaming and on-demand access to the start of what promised to be one of the most widely distributed sporting events in history. Fans could watch matches, highlight videos, player interviews, and much more, all on the IPL's YouTube channel.

The IPL was named by Forbes as the "hottest sports league in the world," and the IPL season was a 60-match, 43-day tournament that featured some of the best talent in cricket. Users could come to YouTube and keep up with the action anytime, anywhere, and connect with fans across the globe.

They could watch as the match happened, or if they missed a match, they could tune in later to see what happened. The entire season was streamed around the world on YouTube, except in the United States, where matches were time-delayed and made available 15 minutes after the match ended.

And for the fans who wanted to cheer or commiserate with others, there was a Twitter gadget on the channel page to enable them to be part of the conversation. Users could keep up with the discussion on Twitter with the hashtag #youtube_ipl. They could share, rate, and comment on videos throughout the channel or upload their own video responses to the action.

As Agrawal said, "We'll be watching the donkey drops, the five-fers, the flippers and floaters, the half-yorkers and slow sweeps—and cheering alongside you!"

On April 19, 2010, Agrawal posted an update to the YouTube Blog. He said, "We started streaming the Indian Premier League cricket season on YouTube with the hope that fans around the world would tune in to follow the action. With only five of 60 matches left in the tournament, we've been blown away by the response. We've seen views come in from countries around the globe, and the IPL channel on YouTube now has over 40 million views."

He added, "We've been particularly surprised by the number of cricket fans tuning in from the U.S. Total views from the U.S. for the IPL channel are second only to India. And fans in the U.S. are active, too: they're second only to those in India in terms of subscribing to the IPL channel and rating, commenting and favoriting videos."

With so much enthusiasm coming from the United States, YouTube made the semifinal and final matches available as they happened instead of keeping them time-delayed and unavailable until 15 minutes after the game had ended. At that point, fans in the United States could catch the action as it unfolded in real time as the four top-ranking teams progressed to the knockout stage of the semifinals.

On May 6, 2010, Agrawal posted a final update to the YouTube Blog. He said, "Season three of the Indian Premier League (IPL) ended last week when the Chennai Super Kings beat the Mumbai Indians in the final match."

He added, "Over the course of the season, the IPL channel racked up nearly 55 million views from 200 countries and territories around the globe, blowing away our expectations. But perhaps most surprising for us was the popularity of the IPL finals in the U.S., where the sport has a relatively small cult following: views from the U.S. of the IPL channel for the semifinals and finals actually exceeded views from India, where the sport is hugely popular."

Here are some additional stats that you might find interesting:

- On the day of the final match, the IPL channel got about four million views.

- The majority of users who viewed the final watched it in real time.

- The IPL channel became the #1 most subscribed channel in India of all time.

- The United States was second only to India in terms of total channel views for the entire season.

Agrawal concluded, "Before we launched the IPL channel on YouTube, we anticipated a total of around 10 million streams for the entire season. Your views beat our goals by over 5x."

As Jerry Seinfeld once said in an American Express commercial, "That was a wicked googly."

Month 4: Explore YouTube Alternatives

For almost 300 years, many explorers tried to discover the Northwest Passage, a commercial sea route around North America. And for the past five years, many marketers have tried to discover viable alternatives to YouTube. In this chapter, we will explore other video sites, survey video hosting services, look at online video platforms, and investigate video ad networks to discover if viable alternatives to YouTube exist. If one does, then you'll learn why the explorer who discovers it will say, "I name this place Terra Incognita."

Chapter Contents:
The Northwest Passage
Week 1: Explore Other Video Sites
Week 2: Survey Video Hosting Services
Week 3: Look at Online Video Platforms
Week 4: Investigate Video Ad Networks

The Northwest Passage

According to Google Insights for Search, web search interest in *YouTube alternatives* surged in 2006—right after Google announced its acquisition of YouTube for $1.65 billion in a stock-for-stock transaction. In other words, no one was searching for alternatives to YouTube until they suddenly needed to find a way around Google.

And web search interest in YouTube alternatives has continued into 2011, even as many of the leading alternatives to YouTube started throwing in the towel. What drives this ongoing search for ways around Google? Let me use a historical metaphor to suggest an answer.

After Christopher Columbus returned from his maiden voyage across the Atlantic Ocean, Pope Alexander VI created the line of demarcation in 1493 to divide new lands claimed by Portugal from those claimed by Spain. This left other European powers without a sea route to Asia via either the Cape of Good Hope or Cape Horn— unless their ships defied the pope and explored those waters anyway.

That's why England, France, and the Netherlands dispatched a number of explorers between 1497 and 1794 in an attempt to discover a commercial sea route north and west around North America. The Northwest Passage represented an alternate route to Asia.

The first recorded attempt to discover the Northwest Passage was made in 1497. Henry VII sent John Cabot on the voyage in search of a direct route to the Orient. The next of several British expeditions to find the passage was launched in 1576 by Martin Frobisher, who took three trips to what is now the Canadian Arctic.

The major rivers on the east coast were also explored in case they might lead to a transcontinental passage. Jacques Cartier's explorations of the Saint Lawrence River were initiated in hopes of finding a way through the continent.

In 1609, Henry Hudson sailed up what is now called the Hudson River in search of the passage. He later explored the Arctic and what is now called Hudson Bay.

Robert de La Salle built the sailing ship *Le Griffon* in his quest to find the Northwest Passage in the upper Great Lakes. *Le Griffon* disappeared in 1679 on the return leg of her maiden voyage.

A 1765 French globe like the one in Figure 6.1 depicted a fictional Northwest Passage connecting Hudson Bay with a mythical "Mer de l'Ouest" that occupied a vast part of the American west.

Although most Northwest Passage expeditions originated in Europe or on the east coast of North America and sought to traverse the passage in a westbound direction, some attempts were made to explore the west coast as well.

In 1776, the Admiralty in Great Britain dispatched Captain James Cook under orders driven by a 1775 act that promised a £20,000 prize for whoever discovered the passage. After journeying through the Pacific, Cook's west-east attempt failed to make any progress in sighting a Northwestern Passage.

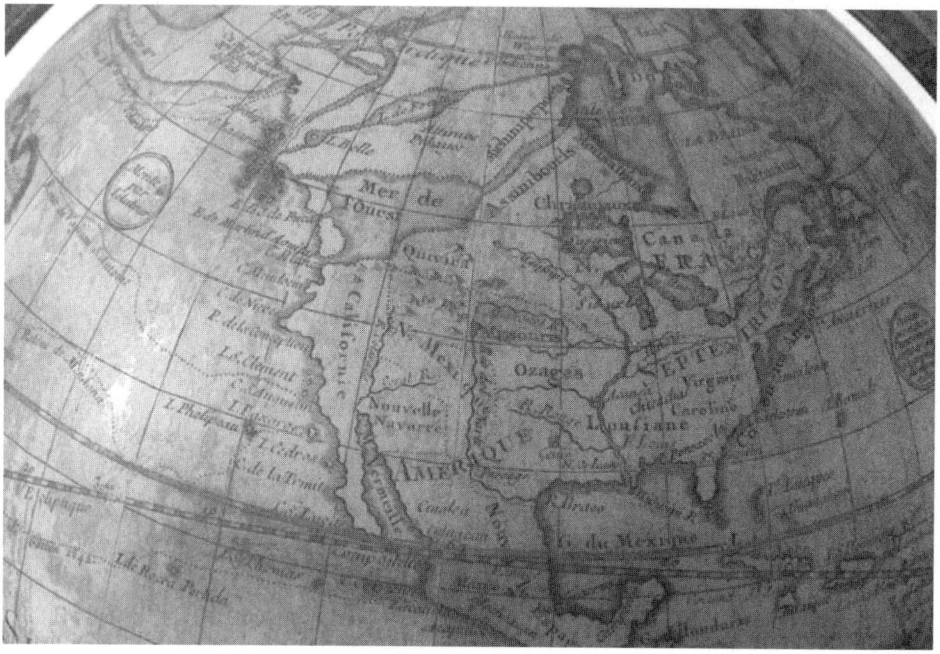

Figure 6.1 1765 French globe

From 1792 to 1794, an expedition led by George Vancouver, who had accompanied Cook, surveyed in detail all the passages from the northwest coast and confirmed that there was no such passage south of the Bering Strait. This conclusion was supported by the evidence of Alexander MacKenzie, who explored the Arctic and Pacific Oceans in 1793.

The search for YouTube alternatives shouldn't take as long to complete, but we may end up reaching a conclusion similar to the one that Vancouver and MacKenzie reached in this historical metaphor. Or, we may discover a way around Google that hasn't been explored by many marketers—yet.

Week 1: Explore Other Video Sites

In the first edition of this book, which was published in August 2009, I looked at a number of other online video sites. This included Yahoo! Video and Google Video. But we don't really need to explore these two video search engines anymore.

Yahoo! Video removed the functionality to upload video on December 15, 2010. And all user-generated content was removed by March 15, 2011. Google Video, which changed its name to Google Videos, no longer allowed users to upload videos beginning in 2009. And in April 2011, it asked users to migrate their Google videos to YouTube.

Both Yahoo! Video and Google Video started out in 2005 as video search engines that crawled the Web for video content. After YouTube sailed rings around them, both Yahoo! Video and Google Video allowed content to be uploaded and hosted on their own servers. But being more like YouTube didn't make much of a difference.

Now, both Yahoo! Video and Google Videos search YouTube, Dailymotion, Metacafe, and Hulu. And Google Videos also searches MSN, AOL, MTV, ESPN, and other video hosting sites.

So, where does that leave us?

If a viable alternative to YouTube does get found, then the explorer who discovers it can proudly say, "I name this place Terra Incognita," as Figure 6.2 illustrates.

"I name this place Terra Incognita."

Figure 6.2 "I name this place Terra Incognita." (Cartoon by Ed Fisher in the *New Yorker*, October 19, 1998.)

So, let's explore some of the other online video sites to see if we can find a potential YouTube alternative.

Monday: Watch bing Videos

Tuesday: Look at blinkx

Wednesday: Get into Dailymotion

Thursday: Check out Metacafe

Friday: Visit Todou and Youku

Monday: Watch Bing Videos

Bing Videos was officially released as Live Search Video in September 2007 and was rebranded as Bing Videos in June 2009.

As Figure 6.3 illustrates, Bing Videos helps users find TV shows, watch music videos, and see sports videos.

Figure 6.3 Bing Videos

Bing Videos indexes content from a number of video sites, including MSN, AOL, MTV, Hulu, ESPN, YouTube, Myspace, CBS, Dailymotion, and Metacafe. Bing Videos also has its own index of full-length television shows.

In Chapter 7, we'll discuss other ways that you can get the video content on your website into the Bing Videos index. And in Chapter 11, we'll talk about the possibility of Microsoft acquiring Hulu.

But here are some market share figures that you should consider here and now. According to Experian Hitwise, YouTube was the #1 most visited video site in May 2011, with almost 2.7 billion US visits. Hulu, which we'll cover later in this chapter, was #2 with 89.6 million US visits. And Bing Videos was #3 with 62.3 million US visits.

This means that YouTube got an 86.9 percent share of all visits to 78 video sites in the United States that month, Hulu got just 2.9 percent, and Bing Videos got only 2.0 percent. So unless something dramatic changes, Bing Videos is more of a supplement to YouTube than a viable alternative.

Tuesday: Look at blinkx

According to comScore Video Metrix, blinkx is one of the top 10 video properties in the United States and the UK ranked by content video views. And the company completed a successful IPO on the London Stock Exchange in May 2007. So, it is worth taking a quick look at the video search engine.

blinkx takes a holistic approach to video search: It uses every characteristic of the video to understand the content. For example, blinkx listens to the soundtrack using speech-to-text technology, looks at the images onscreen using advanced video analytics, and reads other information embedded into a file using media-analysis plug-ins.

As Figure 6.4 illustrates, blinkx has indexed more than 35 million hours of audio, video, viral, and TV content and made it fully searchable and available on demand.

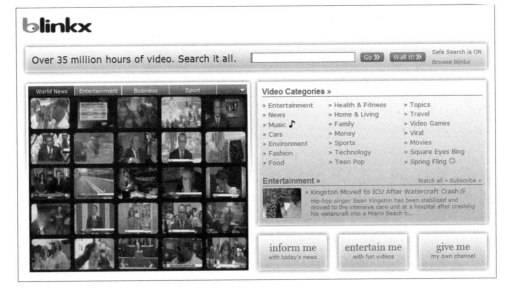

Figure 6.4 blinkx

In May 2011, the company announced its results for the year ended March 31, 2011. Here are some of the highlights:

- Revenue increased more than 96 percent over the previous fiscal year to $66.1 million.

- Video streams in the US and the UK grew by over 155 percent, according to comScore.

- Average Daily Video Search run rate increased to 44.5 million searches per day in the second half of the fiscal year.

- The acquisition of Burst Media, which was announced in April 2011 for $30 million, was completed in early May 2011.

According to Hitwise, blinkx ranked #6 in the UK in May with 13.1 million visits. By comparison, YouTube.com ranked #1 in the UK that month with 486.3 million visits.

So, the "world's largest video search engine" isn't a viable alternative to the "largest worldwide video sharing community." blinkx is a nice complement to YouTube; it's not a replacement.

We'll talk about how to submit your video content to blinkx in Chapter 7.

Wednesday: Get into Dailymotion

According to comScore Video Metrix, 16.4 million American, 3.5 million British, and 2.9 million Canadian Internet users watched online video content on Dailymotion in April 2011. And according to comScore, Dailymotion's network of sites attracts more than 93 million unique monthly visitors per month worldwide.

This makes Dailymotion, shown in Figure 6.5, one of the leading video sharing sites.

Figure 6.5 Dailymotion

Dailymotion includes content from users, independent content creators, and premium partners. It offers a group for original content creators called MotionMaker and another group called Official Content Partners, including record labels, film studios, news media, television channels, sports associations, and political parties. Both groups can do the following:

• Upload video files of unlimited length

• Upload HD quality videos

• Give their videos a chance to be featured

• Have an overlay added to their video thumbnails

Headquartered in Paris, Dailymotion is a French limited company. In January 2011, Orange, the key brand of France Telecom, entered into exclusive negotiations with Dailymotion with the plan to acquire a 49 percent stake in the online video site. Beginning in 2013, the plan allows Orange to increase its stake to 100 percent and also allows for the integration of new business partners.

In May 2011, Dailymotion ranked #6 in the United States with 24.7 million visits, #5 in the UK with 13.2 million visits, and #2 in Canada, according to Hitwise. The video sharing site's market share was 0.8 percent in the United States, 1.8 percent in the UK, and 1.8 percent in Canada.

New York Habitat, which sublets apartments in New York, Paris, London, and the south of France, has uploaded 43 videos to its Dailymotion channel and 79 videos to its YouTube channel. These videos provide tips on what you will want to know when renting a furnished apartment or an accommodation in these locations.

As this was written, New York Habitat's Dailymotion channel had 3,135 views and its YouTube channel had 171,965 total upload views. So, even for a business with a presence on both sides of the pond, Dailymotion is a supplement to YouTube, not an alternative.

Thursday: Check Out Metacafe

According to comScore, 14.7 million Internet users in the United States and 1.9 million in the UK watched online video content on Metacafe in April 2011. Also according to comScore, Metacafe attracts more than 40 million unique viewers each month worldwide, making it another one of the world's largest video sites.

As Figure 6.6 illustrates, Metacafe is an entertainment destination that showcases the best videos from the world of movies, video games, sports, music, and TV.

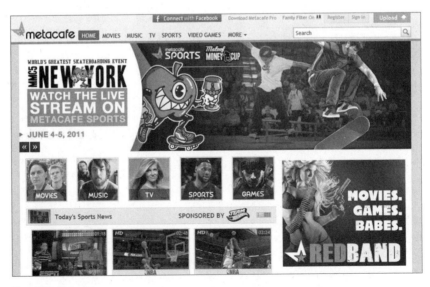

Figure 6.6 Metacafe

Headquartered in San Francisco, Metacafe specializes in short-form original content from new, emerging talents and established Hollywood heavyweights. The company is privately held, and investors include Accel Partners, Benchmark Capital, DAG Ventures, and Highland Capital Partners.

Metacafe differs from other video sites in three ways:

- Metacafe specializes in short-form video content. It doesn't have full-length television episodes or movies. The average video on the site is just over 90 seconds long.

- Metacafe only features videos that "amaze, inspire and make viewers laugh." This means that you won't find hard news stories, personal videos, or webcam chatter on the site.

- A community review panel of more than 80,000 volunteers takes a first look at each of the thousands of videos submitted to the site every day. And Metacafe's VideoRank system identifies and exposes the most popular videos by automatically gauging every interaction each viewer has with a video.

One of the things that marketers will want to watch for is the findings of Metacafe's annual sponsored study of online video consumption. In June 2010, the research, conducted by Frank N. Magid Associates as part of the Magid Media Futures 2010 study, found that half of all respondents watch online video weekly or more often, an increase from 43 percent in 2009.

To submit and rate videos, add comments, and join discussions, go to www.metacafe.com and click the Register link on the upper right of the home page.

According to Hitwise, Metacafe ranked #10 with 15.7 million US visits and #4 in Canada with x visits in May 2011. That gave it 0.5 percent of all visits to 78 video sites in the United States and 0.6 percent of all visits to 70 video sites in Canada that month.

So, add it to the list of other video sites to consider as complements to YouTube.

Friday: Visit Todou and Youku

Although YouTube is localized in 25 countries across 43 languages, the People's Republic of China has blocked access to the video sharing website.

This means the phrase "Here be dragons" should appear near the east coast of Asia to denote the dangerous or unexplored territories in this part of the world of video marketing. Nevertheless, there are some marketers and advertisers looking for YouTube alternatives who may want to visit this region despite the appearance of sea serpents in blank areas of the map.

They will discover that the two largest video hosting services based in the People's Republic of China are Tudou and Youku.

Tudou was founded in February 2005 by Gary Wang and Marc van der Chijs, and the Shanghai-based video hosting service went live in April of that year.

As Figure 6.7 illustrates, Tudou is focused on the Chinese audience. The company says it is one of the world's largest bandwidth users, sending more than 1 petabyte of video files per day.

Figure 6.7 Tudou

According to Chinese tracking service iResearch, Tudou has over 50 percent of the Chinese online video market. iResearch reported that Tudou's monthly unique visitors reached 170 million as of June 2010.

Youku was founded in March 2006 by Victor Koo, the former president of the Chinese Internet portal Sohu. A beta version of the site was launched in June 2006, and the website was formally launched in December 2006.

Youku, shown in Figure 6.8, initially emphasized user-generated content. However, the company has since shifted its focus to professionally produced videos licensed from over 1,500 content partners, including television stations, distributors, and film and TV production companies in China.

According to iResearch, Youku attracted approximately 203 million monthly unique visitors from homes and offices and 56 million monthly unique visitors from Internet cafes in September 2010. Youku had a 40 percent share of total user time spent viewing online videos among Chinese Internet users during the second quarter of 2010, according to iResearch. In January 2010, Youku and Tudou announced the creation of a video broadcasting exchange network, under which the two video hosting services will cross-license professionally produced video content.

Figure 6.8 Youku

So, YouTube alternatives do exist in the People's Republic of China. And if you plan to do any video marketing in the most populous country in the world, then you will need to use one or both of them.

Week 2: Survey Video Hosting Services

The first edition of this book looked at Myspace Video. Back in April 2009, YouTube. com ranked as the top US video property and Myspace.com ranked second, according to comScore Video Metrix.

That month, 107.1 million viewers watched 6.8 billion videos on YouTube. com—an average of 63.5 videos per viewer. And 49 million viewers watched 387 million videos on Myspace.com—an average of 7.9 videos per viewer.

Since then, the "social entertainment destination" has re-stylized its name to Myspace, or My_____, as shown in Figure 6.9, and redirected its subdomain from http://vids.Myspace.com to http://www.Myspace.com/videos.

Despite these changes, Myspace has continued to lose visitors and Myspace Video has continued to lose viewers. On June 29, 2011, News Corp sold Myspace to Specific Media for $35 million. Pop star Justin Timberlake also took a small stake in the deal.

There is an excellent analysis of Myspace's decline that marketers, advertisers, YouTubers, and YouTube partners will want to read.

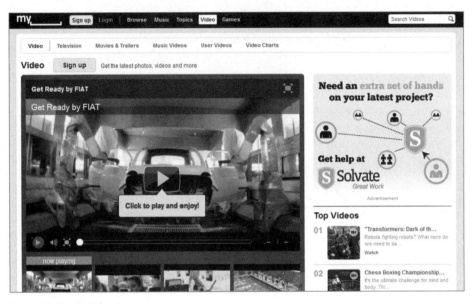

Figure 6.9 ■ Myspace Video

On April 7, 2011, Yinka Adegoke of Reuters wrote "Special Report: How News Corp got lost in Myspace." In the 4,000-word article, Adegoke says Myspace's decline "has become the latest example of what can happen when a traditional media company imposes its will—and business plan—on a start-up that has not yet reached its potential."

In July 2005, Rupert Murdoch's News Corporation acquired Myspace. And in August 2006, News Corporation's Fox Interactive Media signed a $900 million, three-year advertising deal with Google, making Google the exclusive search and keyword targeted advertising sales provider for Fox Interactive Media's network of web properties, including Myspace.

Although it was hailed as a major coup by News Corp as well as Wall Street, the deal started to be seen as a double-edged sword by Myspace executives. "The Google deal required a certain number of Myspace user visits on a regular basis for Google to pay Myspace its guaranteed $300 million a year for three years. That reduced flexibility as Myspace couldn't experiment with its own site without forfeiting revenue," wrote Adegoke.

A former Myspace executive close to advertising sales told Adegoke, "We were incentivized to keep page views very high and ended up having too many ads plus too many pages, making the site less easy to use than a site like Facebook."

According to Compete, Myspace dropped 56.4 percent from 75.5 million unique visitors in April 2009 to 32.9 million in April 2011. And according to comScore, unique viewers of online video at Fox Interactive Media, which includes Myspace, dropped 70.2 percent over that same period, from 58.8 million Americans to fewer than 17.5 million.

So, we don't really need to explore Myspace Videos anymore.

In addition to user-generated video sharing sites, there are a couple of other categories that support video sharing as an enhancement to their primary mission. This includes social networking services, photo hosting services, and video streaming sites.

This week, let's survey some of these video hosting services to see if we can find a serious YouTube alternative.

Monday: Investigate Facebook

Tuesday: Glance at Flickr

Wednesday: Look into Photobucket

Thursday: Watch Ustream

Friday: Scout Justin.tv

Monday: Investigate Facebook

According to Compete, Facebook had 142.7 million unique visitors in May 2011, up 65.2 percent from 86.4 million in May 2009.

And according to comScore, 46.7 million Americans watched 271.4 million videos on Facebook in April 2011, an average of 5.8 videos per viewer.

In Canada, 9.3 million unique viewers watched 72.9 million videos on Facebook that month, an average of 7.8 videos per viewer. In the UK, 8.5 million unique viewers watched 57.6 million videos on Facebook that month, an average of 6.8 videos per viewer.

This makes Facebook, shown in Figure 6.10, the leading social networking website where videos are viewed.

Figure 6.10 Facebook

Do I really need to tell you the backstory of Facebook? If you want the facts, you can read them on *Wikipedia*. If you'd prefer a good story, then watch *The Social Network* (2010). But what you really want to know is how to add your videos to Facebook. To upload a video to Facebook, just follow these steps:

1. Go to your Facebook home page.
2. Click the Photos filter on the left side of the page. (You may have to click More to reveal Photos.)
3. Click the Videos subfilter.
4. Select which type of video you want to make. You can choose File Upload to upload a video from your hard drive, Mobile Video to upload a video from your mobile device, or Record Video to record a video with your webcam. (You can upload a video if it is under 1,024 MB and under 20 minutes.)
5. Follow the onscreen directions for your particular upload type.
6. A successful video upload will generate a thumbnail of your video and store the video permanently in My Videos.

Of course, you can also upload a video to Facebook from YouTube or another video site. Here's how to share an external link on your Facebook Wall:

1. Go to your Facebook profile and click the Wall tab.
2. Click the icon to post a link in the Publisher box, which is located to the right of the video camera icon.
3. Type a link from the external site into the bar and click the Attach button.
4. After adding comments or making any necessary changes, click Share to post the external link to your Wall and share the video with your friends.

Although Facebook supports almost all video file types, the best format to upload is H.264 video with AAC audio in MOV or MP4 format. H.264 currently offers the best video compression available, and due to file size limitations, this format is the optimal choice for Facebook video.

To keep Facebook's encoder from rescaling your video, use a file with the larger edge of the video not exceeding 1,280 pixels. If your video is less than 1,280 pixels in size on the larger edge, try to keep your dimensions to multiples of 16 pixels for best compression.

Keep the frame rate of your video at or below 30 frames per second. And use stereo audio with a sample rate of 44,100 Hz.

Although only a fraction of the visitors to Facebook watch just a small number of videos on the social networking site each month, this could change in the future. However, many of the videos that are watched on Facebook may still be hosted on YouTube.

And before Facebook executives consider banning these videos, they might want to read "So, That's Why Myspace Blocked YouTube" by Carlo Longino of Techdirt.

On January 10, 2006, Longino wrote, "News Corp. raised the hackles of some Myspace users last month when the site blocked links to video-hosting site YouTube. It eventually capitulated, saying there had been 'a simple misunderstanding.'"

And according to Compete Referral Analytics, Facebook.com was the #2 referring site to YouTube.com, sending 193.3 million visits in May 2011. Google was the #1 referring site to YouTube.com, sending 201.6 million visits that month.

And YouTube.com was the #4 referring site to Facebook.com, sending 91.2 million visits in May 2011. Google was the #1 referring site to Facebook.com, sending almost 275 million visits that month.

So, it's hard to predict if Facebook will try to become a YouTube alternative, or if the leading social networking site and the leading video sharing site will continue to remain unlikely allies.

As Yogi Berra may have said, "It's tough to make predictions, especially about the future."

Tuesday: Glance at Flickr

Today, let's look at one of the image hosting services that have also become video hosting websites.

Flickr was launched in February 2004 by Ludicorp, a Vancouver-based company. Yahoo! acquired Ludicorp and Flickr in March 2005 for a reported $35 million.

As Figure 6.11 illustrates, Flickr still emphasizes its online photo management and sharing applications.

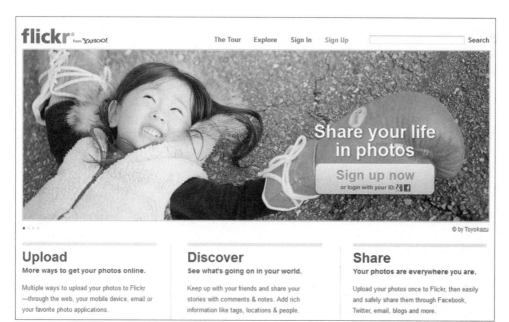

Figure 6.11 Flickr

However, in April 2008, Flickr began to allow paid subscribers to upload videos limited to 90 seconds in length and 150 MB in size.

In March 2009, Flickr added the ability to upload and view HD videos and began allowing free users to upload normal-resolution video. At the same time, the set limit for free accounts was lifted.

Flickr offers two types of accounts: Free and Pro. Free account users are allowed to upload 300 MB of images a month and two videos. Pro accounts allow users to upload an unlimited number of images and videos every month and receive unlimited bandwidth and storage.

According to Compete, Flickr got 22.8 million unique visitors in May 2011. This was down 7.7 percent from 24.7 million in May 2009.

So, once again, Flickr is an interesting addition, not a viable alternative, to YouTube.

Wednesday: Look into Photobucket

Another image hosting website that has added video hosting services is Photobucket. Founded in 2003 by Alex Welch and Darren Crystal, it was acquired by Fox Interactive Media in 2007.

In December 2009, Fox's parent company, News Corp, sold Photobucket to Ontela, a Seattle-based mobile imaging start-up. Ontela then renamed itself Photobucket.

You can't tell the players without a program.

As Figure 6.12 illustrates, Photobucket emphasizes that it is a place to store, create, and share videos as well as photos.

Figure 6.12 Photobucket

Photobucket offers 500 MB of free storage, which lets you host hours of video for free. You can get more space with a paid account. Uploaded videos must be no more than 5 minutes long, or 10 minutes long with a paid account. Go to http://register.photobucket.com to sign up for Photobucket. It's free.

According to Compete, Photobucket had 20.2 million unique visitors in May 2011. This was down 24.6 percent from 26.8 million in May 2009.

So, Photobucket won't replace YouTube, either. Although it's worth noting that on June 10, 2011, Photobucket signed a deal to host photos for Twitter's new native photo sharing service. Will a deal for videos "powered by Photobucket" follow? Stats from TubeMogul show that Twitter is quickly growing as a top referrer for online video traffic, outpacing Facebook. So stay tuned.

Thursday: Watch Ustream

According to comScore, 15.1 million Internet users in the United States and 1.7 million in the UK watched online video content on Ustream in April 2011.

Figure 6.13 shows the home page of Ustream, the leading live interactive broadcast platform.

Figure 6.13 Ustream

After meeting at West Point in 2007, Ustream's founders, John Ham and Brad Hunstable, joined with Gyula Feher to create a live streaming platform that would allow servicemen to communicate with their families and friends. The founders launched Ustream in March 2007, and the service has since found worldwide adoption.

Ustream has raised venture capital from SoftBank Group, DCM, Western Technology Investors, Band of Angels Fund, and Infinity Venture Partners.

Ustream enables anyone with an Internet connection and a camera to broadcast live a wide variety of content, including concerts, conferences, interactive games, movie premieres, personal milestones, political events, sporting events, and talk shows—around the clock.

For example, the Decorah Eagles became America's biggest reality-TV stars on Ustream. If you haven't yet heard, the Decorah Eagles are a family of bald eagles nesting in Decorah, Iowa.

The Raptor Resource Project, a nonprofit organization dedicated to restoring the Midwest's population of peregrine falcons, eagles, hawks, ospreys, and owls, established a Ustream channel that provided live, round-the-clock footage of a pair of bald eagles and their three eaglets.

The stream went live in February 2010, but the majority of traffic arrived after the pair's eggs began hatching on February 23, 2011. As this was written, the channel had more than 124.9 million views.

Ustream told TechCrunch that the Decorah Eagles stream has become the most-watched live stream in the company's five-year history, passing the 34 million views garnered by Ustream's Canal 5 news page, which covered the Chilean miner saga in September 2010.

YouTube's coverage of the royal wedding of Prince William and Kate Middleton generated 72 million total live streams, so Ustream believes its "eagle cam" is currently the most-watched live stream emanating from a single source, or provider.

Go to www.ustream.tv/login-signup to create your Ustream account. Then, just follow these steps:

1. Plug in your camera.

2. Log in and select Start Broadcasting.

3. Type the name of your show and click Create.

4. Allow the broadcast console to access your video camera or web camera.

5. Click Start Broadcast in the console and you are live.

According to Hitwise, Ustream ranked #8 with 18.3 million US visits in May 2011. That's 0.6 percent of all visits to 78 video sites that month.

So, is Ustream a viable alternative to YouTube?

No, the leading live interactive broadcast platform isn't a viable alternative to the largest worldwide video sharing community, but it is a viable alternative for live video streaming.

Why do you think YouTube announced the initial rollout of live streaming on April 8, 2011?

Friday: Scout Justin.tv

According to Compete, Justin.tv had 2.1 million unique visitors in May 2011, up 90.9 percent from 1.1 million in May 2009.

As Figure 6.14 illustrates, Justin.tv also gives you an easy way to create live video and let anyone in the world "watch what's happening" right now.

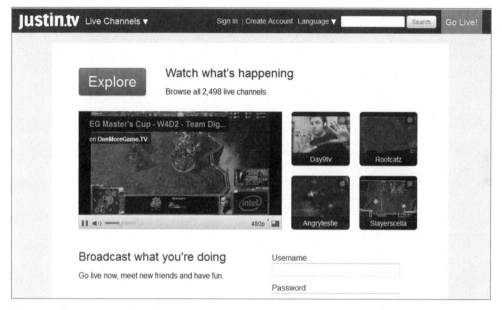

Figure 6.14 Justin.tv

Justin.tv was built from the ground up to support any audience, from 5 people to 50,000. One new live video starts each second, and users watch more than 300 million videos every month.

Headquartered in San Francisco, Justin.tv is funded by Alsop Louie Partners, Tim Draper, and Y Combinator.

To get started, go to www.justin.tv and create an account.

To broadcast, any kind of webcam will work, including ones built into laptops. You will also need a microphone for audio. Any microphone will do. There's no need to get a professional model. And many webcams have microphones built in. Finally, you'll need a computer with an Internet connection. DSL or cable is adequate for broadcast.

Then, go to Justin.tv. Click Go Live! Fill out a new account application. Click Allow to let Flash access your webcam and microphone. Finally, click the Start button and you will be broadcasting live on Justin.tv.

The company has also received a lot of favorable press coverage for its Android and iPhone apps, which enable users to broadcast live from a mobile phone at the click of a button.

According to Hitwise, Justin.tv ranked #7 with 18.3 million US visits in May 2011. That's 0.6 percent of all visits to 78 video sites in the United States that month.

So, keep an eye on this live video community too.

Week 3: Look at Online Video Platforms

In their search for YouTube alternatives, many bigger brands and larger organizations will want to look at online video platforms and enterprise video hosting providers.

And some won't let the facts get in the way of a good story.

What are the facts?

According to Experian Hitwise, YouTube had 86.9 percent of visits to 78 video sites in the United States, 93.3 percent of visits to 70 video sites in Canada, and 67.9 percent of visits to 89 video sites in the UK during May 2011.

And what is a good story?

As Figure 6.15 illustrates, it's the assumption that there's a route that top marketers can take to navigate around Google.

Figure 6.15 Assumed route of the Strait of Anian

Now, searching for a way to monetize the videos on your own website or blog without having to share revenue with YouTube is perfectly rational. But ignoring YouTube's dominant share of the online video market isn't.

What you will want is a blended strategy—although the right blend for your brand or organization will be unique.

Nevertheless, this week let's see if there is a rational way to navigate through this narrow passage.

Monday: Explore Brightcove

Tuesday: Scrutinize Ooyala

Wednesday: Examine Hulu

Thursday: Poke around VEVO

Friday: Inspect Demand Media

Monday: Explore Brightcove

Brightcove is a cloud content services company. It provides a family of products that are used to publish and distribute professional digital media. As Figure 6.16 illustrates, the company's products include Brightcove Video Cloud, one of the leading online video platforms, and Brightcove App Cloud, a new content app platform.

Figure 6.16 Brightcove

Based in Cambridge, Massachusetts, Brightcove was founded in 2004 by Jeremy Allaire, who now serves as CEO. In November 2009, Forrester Research named Brightcove as one of the top two US video platform vendors. On April 5, 2010, Camille Ricketts of VentureBeat reported that Brightcove had raised $12 million in fourth-round funding, nearing a total of $100 million, but was still barely breaking even with $50 million in projected annual revenue.

More than 3,000 customers in 50 countries use Brightcove's cloud content services. This includes networks and broadcasters, businesses and organizations, magazines, music labels, and newspapers as well as small and medium businesses.

Brightcove's video hosting and publishing solution provides a number of key features:

- YouTube sync—You can coordinate a blended distribution strategy by automatically synchronizing selected video content and related metadata in your Brightcove account with your YouTube channel.

- Content management—Brightcove sorts, manages, and organizes your entire media library.

- Mobile devices—Brightcove's software development kits, mobile-ready encoding, intelligent device detection, and player templates let you reach viewers on mobile devices. You can deliver video to devices like the iPhone, iPad, and iPod Touch with HTML5 smart players.

- Live streaming—You can broadcast live on the Web with multi-bitrate streaming and live DVR controls.

- Social media—You can encourage viral sharing with built-in social media tools for Facebook, WordPress, and Live Journal.

- Advertising and monetization—You can generate ad revenue and monetize your video content with overlays for persistent branding and in-player calls to action.

- Analytics—You can make better decisions and drive results with analytics and reports.

With Express editions starting at $99 per month, Brightcove is affordable for even smaller sites and starter projects. Contact Brightcove for pricing on the Professional and Enterprise editions, which are best for bigger brands and larger organizations.

Tuesday: Scrutinize Ooyala

In November 2009, Forrester Research also named Ooyala as one of the top two US video platform vendors.

Figure 6.17 shows the home page of Ooyala, a leader in online video management, publishing, analytics, and monetization.

Figure 6.17 Ooyala

Based in Mountain View, California, Ooyala was founded in 2007 by Bismarck Lepe, Sean Knapp, and Belsasar Lepe. Through September 2010, Ooyala had raised $42 million from Sage Venture Partners, Sierra Ventures, Rembrandt Ventures, CID Group (a Shanghai-based private equity fund), Hitochu, and Panasonic.

The founders selected Ooyala (pronounced *oo-YAH-lah*) after Knapp's girlfriend at the time suggested the word, which means *cradle* in the southern Indian language of Telugu. On their website, they say, "We like the name because it describes what we do: *give birth to new ideas and new innovations in online video.*"

Ooyala serves hundreds of global media companies and marketers, including Burton Snowboards, Caracol Broadcasting, Dell, ESPN, Fremantle Media, the Hearst Corporation, News International, the *New York Daily News*, the Recording Academy, Sephora, Telegraph Media Group, *TV Guide*, US Soccer, Vans, *Vice* magazine, Wenner Media, Whole Foods, Yahoo! Japan, and Yelp.

Ooyala's suite of technologies and services provide a number of capabilities, including delivering high-quality video to browsers, phones, tablets, and connected TVs via an easy-to-use interface, advertising and paywall options, and viewer analytics tools.

Wednesday: Examine Hulu

Of course, if your brands are as big as ABC, Fox, and NBC, and your organization is as large as Hulu's, then you might want to build an online video platform from scratch.

What might you be able to accomplish? Let's examine Hulu.

As Figure 6.18 illustrates, Hulu is an online video service that offers a selection of hit shows, web shows, clips, and movies.

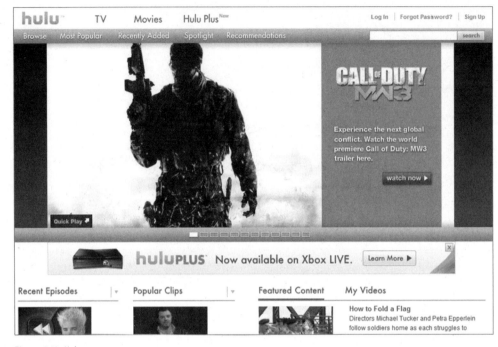

Figure 6.18 Hulu

Founded in March 2007, Hulu is operated independently by a dedicated management team headed by CEO Jason Kilar. Hulu is a joint venture of NBCUniversal, News Corporation, the Walt Disney Company, and Providence Equity Partners.

Hulu offers a large selection of videos from over 260 content companies, including ABC, A&E Networks, Comedy Central, Criterion, Digital Rights Group, Endemol, FOX, Lionsgate, MGM, MTV Networks, National Geographic, NBCUniversal, Paramount, Sony Pictures, TED, Warner Bros., and others.

Users can watch current primetime TV hits such as *30 Rock*, *The Colbert Report*, *The Daily Show*, *Glee*, *Jersey Shore*, *Modern Family*, *The Office*, and *The Simpsons*; classics like *Alfred Hitchcock Presents*, *The A-Team*, and *Buffy the Vampire Slayer*; full episodes and clips from *Saturday Night Live*; and original videos like *The Confession*, *The LXD*, and *twentysixmiles*.

Users can watch videos on Hulu.com or on many other sites. For example, Hulu videos are available on AOL, IMDb, MSN, *TV Guide*, and Yahoo! as well as blogs and other sites that embed the Hulu video player.

Hulu tells advertisers they can associate their brands with "premium" online video content. Currently, Hulu has more than 625 advertisers, including Allstate, Geico, Honda, Johnson & Johnson, McDonald's, Microsoft, Nestle, Nissan, Pepsi, Procter & Gamble, Purina, Sprint, State Farm, Target, Toyota, Verizon Wireless, Unilever, and Visa.

According to comScore, Americans viewed 3.8 billion video ads in April 2011, with Hulu generating the highest number of video ad impressions at more than 1.1 billion. Time spent watching video ads neared 1.7 billion minutes during the month, with Hulu delivering the highest duration of video ads at 470 million minutes.

Video ads reached 42 percent of the total US population an average of 30 times during the month. Hulu also delivered the highest frequency of video ads to its viewers with an average of 45 over the course of the month.

If there is a downside to this story, then it would have to be this: On June 21, 2011, an article in the *Wall Street Journal* by Jessica E. Vascellaro and Anupreeta Das reported that an "unsolicited offer" had caused Hulu to begin "weighing whether to sell itself."

Now, if you offer "premium" online video content, then the world is supposed to beat a path to your door. But according to Hitwise, Hulu ranked #2 with 89.6 million US visits in May 2011, which was only 2.9 percent of all visits to 78 video sites that month.

So maybe Hulu is making a distinction without a difference. Whether it's produced by amateurs or professionals, maybe it's all just online video content to viewers.

This explains why even Hulu hasn't been able to find a route around Google. In fact, Hulu has a YouTube channel, as Figure 6.19 illustrates. Go to www.youtube.com/huludotcom and check it out for yourself.

Figure 6.19 HuluDotCom

Thursday: Poke around VEVO

Of course, if your brands are as big as Universal Music Group (UMG), Sony Music Entertainment (SME), and EMI Music, and your organization is as large as VEVO's, then you might be able to get YouTube to build an online video platform for you.

What might you be able to accomplish? Let's poke around VEVO to see what we can discover.

According to comScore, VEVO was the #2 online video content property in the United States with 55.2 million unique visitors during April 2011. VEVO's viewership reached record levels that month, crossing the 300 million viewing sessions mark and averaging 1.7 hours per viewer.

VEVO was the #3 online video content property in Canada with 9.2 million unique visitors in April 2011. And VEVO was also the #3 online video content property in the UK with 9.2 million unique visitors that month.

VEVO, shown in Figure 6.20, is a premium online music video and entertainment platform.

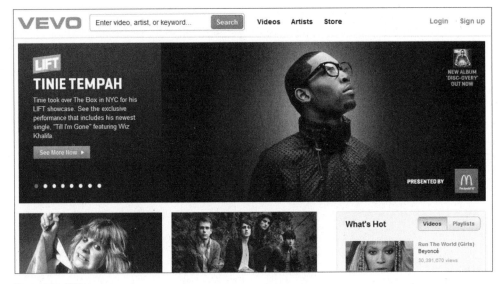

Figure 6.20 VEVO

In April 2009, UMG and YouTube announced that they were working together to launch VEVO. The two companies also announced they would share advertising revenue on YouTube and VEVO. In June 2009, SME joined the forces creating VEVO. In October 2009, VEVO received a strategic investment from Abu Dhabi Media Company (ADMC). And in December 2009, EMI licensed its content to the group without taking an ownership stake.

On December 8, 2009, VEVO was unveiled at an event at New York City's Skylight Studios, which featured a star-studded line-up that included Bono, Mariah Carey, Ciara, Ke$ha, John Mayer, Corinne Bailey Rae, Rihanna, Taylor Swift, Shania Twain, and many others. The evening ended with exclusive live performances by Lady Gaga and Adam Lambert. Guests were also treated to the world premieres of new videos by 50 Cent and Mariah Carey.

Powered by YouTube, VEVO became the most visited US web network in the Entertainment-Music category that month with 35.4 million unique visitors, according to comScore.

We get by with a little help from our friends. But if you are an aspiring musician, you will need a lot more than a little help from your friends.

At this time, VEVO receives all of its programming from its partners. If you are an independent artist, I suggest that you contact one of its distribution partners for information on having your videos distributed through VEVO.

The music industry is still dominated by four "major corporate labels": UMG, SME, EMI, and Warner Music Group (WMG). Greg Sandoval, who writes Media Maverick on CNET News, reported in October 2009 that WMG was discussing the possibility of joining VEVO, but WMG subsequently formed a rival alliance with MTV Networks.

So don't blame me if breaking into the music business is tough. It's been that way since the late nineteenth century, when the music industry was dominated by the publishers of sheet music.

The concept for VEVO has been described as being a Hulu for music videos, with the goal of attracting high-end advertisers. The site's other revenue sources include referral links to purchase viewed songs on Amazon MP3 and iTunes as well as a merchandise store. But VEVO has something that Hulu doesn't—VEVO's music videos are integrated into YouTube's music category. This means "Justin Bieber—Baby ft. Ludacris" is not only the most viewed video of all time on VEVO with 553.8 million views, it is also the most viewed video of all time on YouTube with 553.6 million views.

All the view counts you see on VEVO are the total plays a video receives across the VEVO platform, which includes VEVO.com, VEVO Mobile, and VEVO syndication partners, including YouTube. But it's not clear if all the view counts you see on YouTube include all of the total plays a video receives across the VEVO platform.

Here's another set of data points to ponder. According to Compete, YouTube. com had 123.4 million unique visitors in April 2011 and VEVO.com had 2.6 million. So, does Compete count only people who go directly to VEVO while comScore also counts people who come to VEVO from YouTube?

As Philip Henslowe says in the movie *Shakespeare in Love* (1998), "I don't know. It's a mystery."

Friday: Inspect Demand Media

If you are searching for a way to monetize the videos on your own website or blog without having to share revenue with YouTube, then inspect Demand Media. It uses a blended strategy that recognizes YouTube's dominant share of the online video market, but the company has also found a rational way to navigate through the narrow passage of YouTube alternatives.

According to comScore Media Metrix, Demand Media was the #12 largest online property in the United States with 69.7 million unique visitors in April 2011. And according to comScore, Demand Media had more than 122 million unique visitors worldwide in January 2011.

Figure 6.21 shows the home page of Demand Media, a leading content and social media company.

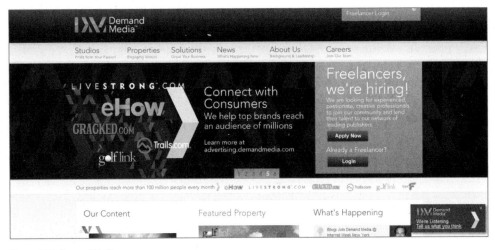

Figure 6.21 Demand Media

Demand Media's properties, which are supported by advertising, include eHow.com, LiveStrong.com, Cracked.com, Trails.com, and Golflink.com.

According to comScore, eHow.com had 92 million unique users worldwide in January 2011, while LiveStrong.com had 14.4 million, Cracked.com had 7 million, Trails.com had 2.3 million, and Golflink.com had 2.3 million.

Demand Media also has a number of YouTube channels, including Expert Village, eHow, LiveStrong, Cracked, Trails, Golflink, and TypeF. Demand Media has been a YouTube partner since 2007, and by January 2009, advertising had become "a seven figure revenue stream," according to Steven Kydd, EVP of Demand Studios, Demand Media's content creation division.

As this was written, Demand Media's channels on YouTube had more than 2.1 billion total upload views:

- Expert Village's channel had over 1.9 billion views.

- eHow's channel had 117.4 million views.

- LiveStrong's channel had 29.1 million views.

- Cracked's channel had 11.3 million views.

- Trails's channel had 2.4 million views.

- Golflink's channel had 4.7 million views.

Demand Media was created in 2006 by Shawn Colo, a principal with Spectrum Equity Investors, and Richard Rosenblatt, the former chairman of Myspace. In addition to being an online media company, Demand Media owns eNom, the second-largest domain registrar.

The company's initial public offering (IPO) was expected in December 2010, but it was delayed until January 2011 due to a Securities and Exchange Commission investigation into the company's novel accounting for "long-lived content."

On February 22, 2011, Demand Media reported its fiscal results for 2010. The company's Content and Media Revenue for fiscal 2010 was $152.9 million, up 42 percent compared to $107.7 million in 2009. In a press release, Demand Media's president and CFO, Charles Hilliard, said, "Ongoing revenue growth from high-quality, long-lived content published in prior years, compounded with new discretionary content investments, positions Demand Media for significant growth in 2011."

Demand Media says it uses "a rigorous process" for selecting the subject matter of its "long-lived content" that includes the use of automated algorithms along with several levels of editorial input. The company's objective is to determine what content consumers are seeking, if it is likely to be valuable to advertisers, and whether it can be produced cost-effectively. To produce content at scale, Demand Media uses an army of more than 13,000 freelance content creators.

Critics of this approach have called Demand Media a "content farm." What's that? According to Wikipedia, "the term *content farm* is used to describe a company that employs large numbers of often freelance writers to generate large amounts of textual content which is specifically designed to satisfy algorithms for maximal retrieval by automated search engines. Their main goal is to generate advertising revenue through attracting reader page views."

Who exactly is harmed by developing long-lived content to generate advertising revenue through attracting reader page views?

Mark Glaser, the host of *MediaShift* on PBS, convened a group in 2010 to discuss content farms—how they are changing journalism, bringing down pay rates for writers, and possibly polluting Google searches with poor quality content. Some panel members believed Demand Media was simply fulfilling a need, while others believed there were possibly dangerous repercussions from the proliferation of these low-cost articles across the Web.

If you ask me, today's critics of content farms are like the old critics of "yellow journalism." In the 1880s and 1890s, Joseph Pulitzer hired female reporters like Nelly Bly, cut the price of the *New York World* to a penny, and added bolder headlines, more prominent illustrations, sports pages, women's sections, personal advice columns, and comic strips. One comic strip featured a street urchin in a yellow shirt, and a hostile critic coined the term *yellow journalism* as a damning label for this kind of high-voltage content.

Today, virtually all newspapers have hired female reporters and adopted bold headlines, prominent illustrations, sports pages, women's sections, personal advice columns, and comic strips. And they'd be honored if one of their text reporters, photographers, videographers, graphic artists, producers, or journalists won a Pulitzer Prize.

So, yesterday's yellow journalism is today's award-winning journalism.

And according to Compete, eHow.com had 44.7 million unique visitors in May 2011, up 43.7 percent year over year. By comparison, NYTimes.com had 16.6 million unique visitors, down 12.3 percent year over year.

And according to Google Insights for Search, web search interest in *how to* has increased steadily from 2004 to the present, while web search interest in *news* has remained flat.

So, I expect many of today's critics of content farms will start developing their own long-lived content to generate advertising revenue through attracting reader page views. If they don't, they'll be yesterday's news.

Week 4: Investigate Video Ad Networks

In our search for viable alternatives to YouTube, there is one remaining category that still appears wide open: video ad networks.

According to comScore Video Metrix, Americans viewed 3.8 billion video ads in April 2011. The Tremor Media Video Network ranked highest among video ad networks with 603.2 million ad views, followed by Adap.tv with 601 million, the BrightRoll Video Network with 460 million, and the SpotXchange Video Ad Network with 258.4 million.

And according to comScore, the British viewed 238.4 million video ads in April 2011, with Adap.tv generating the highest number of video ad impressions at 59.8 million, followed by the SpotXchange Video Ad Network with 25.1 million, the BrightRoll Video Network with 23.3 million, and TubeMogul's PlayTime Video Ad Platform with 22.3 million.

Now, we won't need to investigate these video ad networks very deeply because each will be delighted to have a representative sail over to visit you. Nevertheless, you will want an overview that enables you to know if you can get around Google and when you are on thin ice.

So, this week, we will look at video ad networks:

Monday: Scan Tremor Media

Tuesday: Watch Adap.tv

Wednesday: Observe BrightRoll

Thursday: Look over SpotXchange

Friday: Consider TubeMogul PlayTime

Monday: Scan Tremor Media

According to comScore, the Tremor Media Video Network reached 59.3 million unique visitors in the United States during April 2011. And it reached 3.0 million unique visitors in Canada and 2.8 million in the UK that month.

Tremor Media, shown in Figure 6.22, is a digital video technology company that serves the complementary needs of the media community.

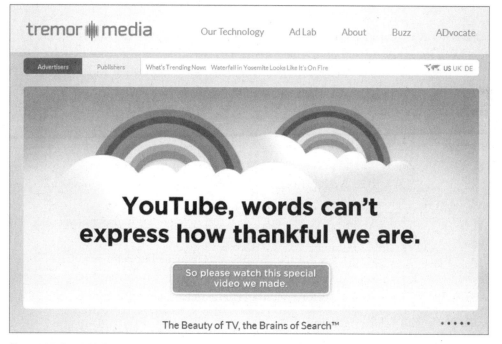

Figure 6.22 Tremor Media

Founded in 2005, Tremor Media provides in-stream video advertising solutions to Fortune 1000 brand advertisers and top-tier publishers and is widely regarded as the leading video company online. The privately held company is headquartered in New York City.

In April 2010, Tremor Media raised $40 million in a fourth round of funding. The latest round—which brings Tremor Media's total funding to nearly $80 million—was led by Draper Fisher Jurvetson Growth Fund. Tremor Media said existing backers, including Canaan Partners, Meritech Capital Partners, and SAP Ventures, also participated "significantly."

On November 8, 2010, Tremor Media acquired ScanScout, one of its smaller competitors. Michael Learmonth of *Advertising Age* wrote, "The Tremor deal is about creating the largest independent source of video ad inventory, in hopes it can better compete for the TV budgets moving online."

And on February 4, 2011, Tremor Media acquired Transpera, a leading mobile video advertising company. Leena Rao of TechCrunch wrote, "Tremor Media, which is one of the largest video ad networks on the web, is eyeing a share of the mobile video ad market. And now Tremor can offer its advertisers the ability to target consumers on a number of platforms within one campaign buy."

On May 23, 2011, Tremor Media announced the launch of Video Hub. Helen Leggatt of BizReport wrote, "It's an ad dashboard that not only lets marketers see where their videos are running, but also provides the ability to measure, track and report on the efficiency of online video campaigns for both real-time and past activity."

I'm sure a Tremor Media sales rep will be happy to tell you all about the company's SE2 technology and Ad Lab. Let me just add that science and art are fast friends at the company.

Tuesday: Watch Adap.tv

According to comScore, Adap.tv reached 54.2 million unique visitors in the United States during April 2011. And it reached 3.1 million unique visitors in Canada and 3.9 million in the UK that month.

As Figure 6.23 illustrates, Adap.tv builds technology that makes buying and selling video advertising simple and efficient.

Based in San Mateo, California, Adap.tv was launched in February 2010. The company closed a $20 million round of financing led by Bessemer Venture Partners on March 29, 2011. Existing investors Gemini Israel Funds, Redpoint Ventures, and Spark Capital also participated in the round.

Since its launch, more than 4,200 sites have adopted the Adap.tv Marketplace as a monetization solution, and hundreds of brand-name campaigns are running through it on a daily basis.

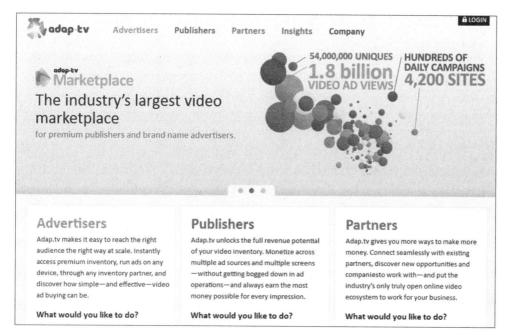

Figure 6.23 Adap.tv

Wednesday: Observe BrightRoll

According to comScore, the BrightRoll Video Network reached 66.4 million unique visitors in the United States during April 2011. And it reached 5.4 million unique visitors in the UK that month.

As Figure 6.24 illustrates, BrightRoll is a leading provider of digital video advertising services.

Figure 6.24 BrightRoll

BrightRoll was founded in 2006 by Tod Sacerdoti and Dru Nelson. The privately held, venture-backed company is headquartered in San Francisco.

When the BrightRoll sales rep visits you, ask for a copy of the company's third annual online video advertising report. The report includes new data showing that planned spending on online video is growing faster than all other online categories, with dollars being reallocated in large part from TV and display ad budgets.

Thursday: Look over SpotXchange

According to comScore, the SpotXchange Video Ad Network reached 30.7 million unique visitors in the United States during April 2011. And it reached 4.7 million unique visitors in Canada that month and 5.0 million in the UK.

SpotXchange, shown in Figure 6.25, is one of the largest global marketplaces of video ad inventory.

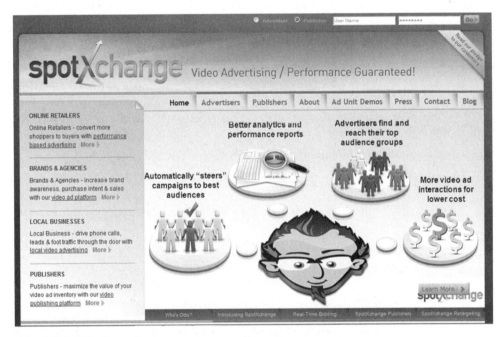

Figure 6.25 SpotXchange

SpotXchange was originally founded in 2005 as a division of the search engine marketing technologies and services company Booyah Networks. In March 2007, Booyah spun SpotXchange off into a separate company.

Headquartered in Denver, the company received a $12 million investment from H.I.G. Growth Partners in December 2010.

Ask the SpotXchange sales rep to tell you more.

Friday: Consider TubeMogul PlayTime

According to comScore, TubeMogul's PlayTime video advertising platform reached 27.9 million unique visitors in the United States during April 2011. And it reached 3.9 million unique visitors in the UK that month.

TubeMogul, shown in Figure 6.26, is a brand-focused video marketing company.

Figure 6.26 TubeMogul

Founded in 2006, TubeMogul is based in Emeryville, California. The company closed $10 million in Series B funding in October 2010. The Series B round was led by Foundation Capital. Existing investors Trinity Ventures and Knights Bridge Capital Partners also participated.

The company partners only with premium and transparent inventory sources. Advertisers pay only when someone chooses to watch their video, and they see exactly which sites their ads ran on, how their ads performed, and who watched them.

Beyond advertising, marketers can also use TubeMogul's OneLoad video distribution to seed their content on multiple sites as well as the company's InPlay video analytics to measure and compare the performance of their owned, paid, and earned video media.

And you will also want to check out TubeMogul Digital Video Research. For example, read the latest quarterly research report, "Brightcove & TubeMogul: Online Video and the Media Industry."

So, is there a Northwest Passage? Are there alternatives to YouTube that will provide you with a way around Google?

Well, there are some video sites worth exploring, video hosting services worth surveying, online video platforms worth looking at, and video ad networks worth investigating.

But YouTube remains the largest worldwide video sharing community by a very wide margin. You will want to adopt a blended strategy that includes YouTube and some alternatives, and find the right blend for your brand or organization.

Month 5: Optimize Video for YouTube

7

Americans conducted more than 3.8 billion search queries on YouTube during June 2011, but 48 hours of video is uploaded to YouTube every minute. So if you don't optimize your video for YouTube, you will probably be asked, "Have you tried searching under 'fruitless'?" In this chapter, you will learn how to research keywords, optimize video watch pages, optimize your brand channel, and optimize video for the Web.

What Is Video Optimization?

Marketers are often surprised to learn that YouTube is the world's second largest search engine, after Google. According to comScore qSearch, 22.6 billion searches were conducted on YouTube worldwide in June 2011. Americans conducted 3.8 billion search queries on YouTube that month, Canadians conducted 762 million, and the British conducted 880 million.

With 328 million videos already uploaded to YouTube and more than 960 new videos being uploaded every minute, you face a lot of competition. So if you don't optimize your video for YouTube, the odds that it will be discovered when someone conducts a search are very long.

And as Figure 4.1 illustrates, it also means you will probably be asked, "Have you tried searching under 'fruitless'?"

"Have you tried searching under 'fruitless'?"

Figure 7.1 "Have you tried searching under 'fruitless'?" (Cartoon by Danny Shanahan in *The New Yorker*, December 24, 2001.)

But let me make one thing perfectly clear: You need to optimize your video for YouTube and search engines like Google, but you don't need to optimize it for video search engines like Google Video.

Search engine optimizers are often surprised to learn that video search engine optimization (VSEO) has become as hopelessly outmoded as the buggy whip. Why? Because (1) YouTube does *not* crawl the Web for video content, and (2) the video search engines that still crawl the Web have a combined market share in the low single digits.

Now, Google indexes trillions of web pages, but the vast majority of videos that appear in Google universal search results are hosted on YouTube and other video sites. So optimizing videos on websites is as nonsensical and comical as "sewing buttons on eggs," as my mother used to say.

Now, I'm not trying to embarrass search engine optimizers who are still offering VSEO services. Instead, let me just observe diplomatically that they didn't get the memo: The horse race is over. YouTube won.

Uploaders are often surprised to learn that the Discovery tab in YouTube Insight will show them how many views came from YouTube search and how many came from Google search. And they are even more surprised that they can find out which keywords viewers used to find their video.

And even YouTube Partners aren't always sure how to increase the number of views their videos get from YouTube search, YouTube related video, and Google search.

So it may be helpful to define a few terms:

YouTube optimization is the use of various techniques to improve a video's ranking in YouTube search and YouTube related video in the hopes of attracting more views.

Video optimization is the use of various techniques to improve a video's ranking in Google, Bing, and other search engines in the hopes of attracting more views.

Video search engine optimization is the use of outmoded techniques to improve a video's ranking in Google Video, Yahoo! Video, and other video search engines, which have only a minor share of the online video market.

I should also explain that when I use the word *optimization* I am *not* talking about the best formats for uploading videos to YouTube. I talked about video format, aspect ratio, resolution, audio format, frames per second, maximum length, and maximum file size in Chapter 3, which was about making a *video worth watching*. High-quality video is important when people *watch* a video, but it won't help them *discover* it.

So when I talk about *YouTube* and *video optimization*, I'm talking about improving a video's ranking. This is important to help people *discover* a video.

So, this chapter will teach you how to research keywords, optimize video watch pages, optimize your brand channel, and optimize video for the Web.

Week 1: Research Keywords

Keywords—which are also called search terms—are the specific words or phrases that a searcher might type into a search field.

According to Jennifer Grappone and Gradiva Couzin, the authors of *Search Engine Optimization: An Hour a Day, Second Edition* (Sybex, 2008), "The keywords you choose *this week* will be the focus of your entire optimization process." I will take the same approach in this chapter.

Although some of the tools and techniques used to research keywords for video optimization are similar to the ones used for search engine optimization, others are different.

Why? There are several reasons. For starters, people searching for video content, as opposed to using a web search engine, are more likely to be looking for topics that entertain them and less likely to be doing research or looking for something to buy. So let's go through the process for finding video keywords step by step. Your tasks for this week are as follows:

Monday: Brainstorm keyword suggestions

Tuesday: Use YouTube's autocomplete feature

Wednesday: Try YouTube's Keyword Tool

Thursday: Examine other keyword tools

Friday: Analyze keyword effectiveness

Monday: Brainstorm Keyword Suggestions

The first step in keyword research is to get into the mind of your viewer. Think about the words people would type to find your video.

I find it useful to put keywords in buckets that I can use later when writing video titles, descriptions, and tags. As I brainstorm keywords, I think about Rudyard Kipling's poem in *Just So Stories*:

I keep six honest serving-men

(They taught me all I knew);

Their names are What and Why and When

And How and Where and Who.

For example, some of the most relevant keywords and keyword phrases will fall into the category *Who*. People often search for videos about celebrities, so some of the most popular keywords are their names. There is also a growing multitude of YouTube celebrities like Tay Zonday (Chocolate Rain), Lauren Caitlin Upton (Junior Miss South Carolina), and Judson Laipply (Evolution of Dance) whose names have become YouTube keywords. Even if you don't think the CEO of your company, the governor of your state, or the president of your university is a "celebrity," their names are likely to be keywords.

Many of the top YouTube search terms fall into the *What* category. People search for topics related to what entertains them, so choose your keywords accordingly: from song titles and movie titles to the objects in a video in YouTube categories like Autos & Vehicles and Pets & Animals.

As Table 7.1 illustrates, Compete found that most of the top 10 YouTube search terms in October 2008 fell into either the *Who* or *What* category.

▶ **Table 7.1** Top 10 YouTube search terms (October 2008)

Rank	Term	Category	% of All Searches
1	Lil Wayne	Music (Artist)	0.122%
2	Fred	Comedy	0.120%
3	Sex	Adult	0.082%
4	Beyonce	Music (Artist)	0.076%
5	Whatever You Like	Music (Song Title)	0.072%
6	Womanizer	Music (Artist)	0.072%
7	Chris Brown	Music (Artist)	0.067%
8	Porn	Adult	0.059%
9	Jonas Brothers	Music (Artist)	0.059%
10	Disturbia	Music (Song Title)	0.058%

Nevertheless, *When* can be a useful category on occasion. You'll find that certain days—New Year's Day, Martin Luther King Jr. Day (MLK Day), Groundhog Day, Valentine's Day, Presidents Day, St. Patrick's Day, Good Friday, Easter, April Fools' Day, Tax Day, Earth Day, Mother's Day, Memorial Day, Flag Day, Father's Day, Independence Day, Labor Day, Rosh Hashanah, Yom Kippur, Columbus Day, United Nations Day, Halloween, Election Day, Veterans Day, Thanksgiving, Black Friday, Cyber Monday, Hanukkah, Christmas, and Kwanzaa—are all part of search phrases.

Where is also useful, particularly in the Sports and Travel & Events categories. For example, conduct a YouTube search for "Where the Hell is Matt?" The 24 videos on MattHarding2718's YouTube channel have been uploaded since May 23, 2006, and star Matt, age 34, dancing on all seven continents with a cast of thousands. As this was written, the videos on MattHarding2718's channel had over 62 million upload views and his channel had over 61,000 subscribers. Do you think STRIDE, makers of the Ridiculously Long Lasting Gum, which sponsored Matt's dancing, is still dancing too? STRIDE's continued sponsorship of follow-up videos indicates that it is.

Why is an often overlooked category. But you'll find that adjectives like *funny* and *hilarious* are the root of YouTube search terms. So are *adorable* and *cute*, which are often used as adjectives when searching for such nouns as *animals*, *babies*, *kittens*, and *puppies*. Or think about trends in online video overall—like hot topics, political awareness, celebrity gossip, and popular videos—when choosing your keywords.

Finally, *How* is a category killer in online video, and how-to videos have gone mainstream. The most viewed YouTube channel in the Howto & Style category is Demand Media's ExpertVillage, which is known for its large selection of informative videos that provide answers to everyday questions. Its 138,786 videos had more than 1.4 billion total upload views as this was written, and the channel had over 732,000 subscribers.

Use these six honest serving-men as you brainstorm keywords.

Tuesday: Use YouTube's Autocomplete Feature

When researching keywords, many new YouTubers use the autocomplete suggestion drop-down menu on YouTube. Added in May 2008, this new feature was designed to help Tubers searching for videos.

As you type in your search terms, a menu will appear with suggested results to choose from to help you more quickly find the videos you're looking for.

As Figure 7.2 illustrates, as you type in "funny" you'll see funny video, funny pranks, funny cats, funny commercials, funny babies, funny stuff, funny animals, funny songs, funny dogs, and funny football. These suggestions might help you tap into the search intent of millions of YouTube searchers.

Figure 7.2 Query suggestions for "funny"

But be careful: Many of the query suggestions will be for the top YouTube search terms used by followers to find the most popular videos. These followers have already heard about a video from opinion leaders but aren't sure they know its exact title. In other words, the query suggestions option is less likely to be used by opinion leaders, who want to discover new videos before the rest of the world has beaten a well-worn path to their door.

For example, do you really want to optimize your video for the following query suggestions: "Justin Bieber" and/or "Lady Gaga"?

Well, you might if you are Michael Buckley and you've just uploaded a video to WHATTHEBUCKSHOW's channel entitled "Justin Bieber owns Lady Gaga!!!! YouTube NUMBER ONE! Brittany Does Britney on GLEE!"

Buckley uploaded his video on July 19, 2010, as Justin Bieber and Lady Gaga were battling it out to see which artist's channel would be the first to reach 1 billion views on YouTube.

But by October 11, 2010, Buckley's video didn't have a top ranking on YouTube if you searched for "Justin Bieber" or if you searched for "Lady Gaga."

But it did rank #3 if you searched for "Justin Bieber Lady Gaga" and it ranked #2 if you searched for "Lady Gaga Justin Bieber." And "Justin Bieber Lady Gaga" and "Lady Gaga Justin Bieber" had both become query suggestions by then.

So, take query suggestions with a grain of salt. There will be times when it is smart to use them, but there will also be times when it will be wiser to ignore the suggested results.

Wednesday: Try YouTube's Keyword Tool

You should also try YouTube's Keyword Tool. It was introduced in November 2008 along with Promoted Videos, but you *don't* have to be an advertiser to use it. You can access the Keyword Tool using the following URL:

    https://ads.youtube.com/keyword_tool

The Keyword Tool gives you three ways to build extensive, relevant keyword lists:

Descriptive words or phrases Enter a few descriptive words or phrases (e.g., "green tea").

YouTube video ID or URL Type in a YouTube video's ID or watch page URL (e.g., http://www.youtube.com/watch?v=3LbNI9u8vOA).

Demographic (beta) Choose the demographic you wish to target (e.g., male or female).

YouTube says, "We cannot guarantee that these keywords will improve your campaign performance." It's talking about advertising campaign performance. But I've also found that many of the suggested keywords don't appear to be relevant for organic YouTube optimization campaigns either.

For example, enter "green tea" and YouTube's Keyword Tool says the term has a monthly search volume of 21,800 using broad match. But as Figure 7.3 illustrates, the Keyword Tool also suggests that *hot rod* may be a relevant term.

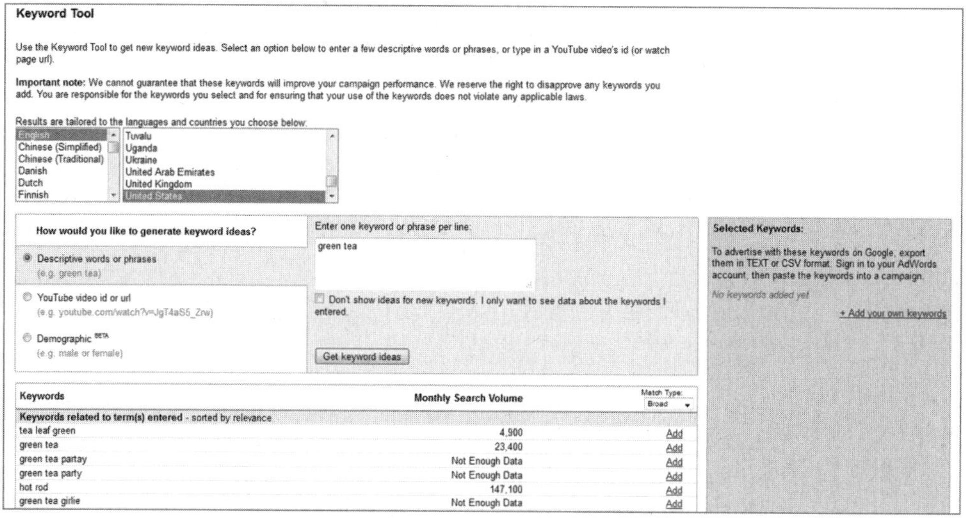

Figure 7.3 YouTube Keyword Tool

I can't explain it, but I have the funny feeling that the engineers and developers who created YouTube's Keyword Tool were playing the Six Degrees of Kevin Bacon game when they should have been working on their algorithm.

Enter the URL http://www.youtube.com/watch?v=3LbNI9u8vOA to find keywords related to the video "Harlem, New York City - Video Tour of West Harlem, Central Harlem & Apollo Theater" on NewYorkHabitat's Channel.

According to YouTube's Keyword Tool, "Harlem New York" is a relevant term. Yes, it is. But farther down the list, the Keyword Tool suggests that "Wikileaks" may also be relevant. No, it isn't.

So, marketers, advertisers, uploaders, and partners should try YouTube's Keyword Tool to get new keyword ideas, but before they use the words or phrases that it suggests, they should repeat three times, "Don't become a tool of your tools."

Thursday: Examine Other Keyword Tools

While you are trying YouTube's Keyword Tool, look up at the top of the page at the links to the Video Targeting Tool and Insight.

The *Video Targeting Tool* is tied to your AdWords account, so you have to be an advertiser to use it. The Video Targeting Tool is currently being beta tested, and it is available only in English. This means that the interface is likely to change and the number of videos exposed will fluctuate.

Introduced in December 2009, YouTube's Video Targeting Tool is modeled after similar Google planning tools and pretty much does what it says: It lets advertisers choose specific YouTube partner content they'd like to target.

Video targeting helps advertisers discover videos relevant to their campaign and their target audience. It suggests videos based on keywords (like "politics" or "fashion"), viewer demographics (like age and gender), interest-based categories, or some combination of the three. Or, if an advertiser has a specific video in mind, they can see if it's available to target.

As Figure 7.4 illustrates, there is probably an advertiser for every video, and vice versa—yes, even for rnickeymouse's video of a skateboarding dog.

The Insight link at the top of the YouTube Keyword Tool page takes you to a login page.

YouTube Insight can also help you with keyword research. Under the Discovery tab, you will be able to access the keywords that people are searching to find the videos that you've already uploaded. This information can help you come up with new keyword ideas for videos that you haven't uploaded yet.

Two other tools that you'll want to examine are YouTube Topics for Search and YouTube Insights for Audience. You'll find them in TestTube (www.youtube.com/testtube), YouTube's ideas incubator.

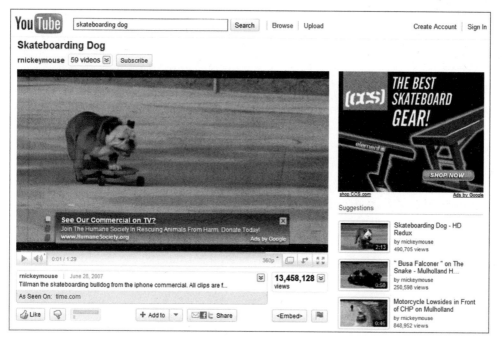

Figure 7.4 "Skateboarding Dog"

YouTube Topics for Search was introduced on November 10, 2010. Palash Nandy, software engineer, said on the YouTube Blog, "We know that sometimes people come to YouTube looking for a specific video, but at other times, they have only a rough idea of the kind of videos they want. We've been there too, and have been thinking for a while about this challenge of searching when you don't yet know exactly what you're looking for."

YouTube Topics on Search tries to identify topics on YouTube and associate videos with them. YouTube uses many different sources to find these topics, including frequently used uploader keywords, common search queries, playlist names, and even sources outside of YouTube such as Wikipedia articles.

YouTube Insights for Audience was also introduced in September 2009. And it can also be found in TestTube, where it is in open beta.

YouTube Insights for Audience is designed to help you explore audience behavior on YouTube. When using the tool, you'll start by defining the audience you care about, be it "people in Canada interested in physics," or "Women over 35 interested in travel."

After running your search, you'll see the video likes, video dislikes, and demographic breakdown of the audiences you've identified as well as YouTube search terms your audiences commonly use and examples of the videos they watch.

Using Insights for Audience can help you better understand how your customers interact with YouTube, and it might even lead to new discoveries about the overall mindset of your audience.

Friday: Analyze Keyword Effectiveness

Keyword research involves much more than generating a long list of potential search terms and then using keyword tools to discover which ones are the most popular. Generally, the most popular keywords are already being used by the most popular videos.

You also need to factor in competition when conducting your keyword analysis. Although there are no tools (yet) that help you do this for YouTube, there is an approach that was pioneered for web search that can be adapted for this purpose.

It's called the keyword effectiveness index (KEI) and it was created by Sumantra Roy, a respected search engine positioning specialist from 1stSearchRanking. KEI divides the number of times a keyword has appeared in searches performed by users by the number of competing web pages to identify which keywords are most effective for a campaign.

The commercial versions of both KeywordDiscovery.com and Wordtracker use KEI as part of their keyword analysis tools. As Wordtracker explains, "The higher the KEI, the more popular your keywords are, and the less competition they have. Which means you have a better chance of getting to the top."

The best use of KEI that I've seen comes from SEO Research Labs. Although its reports include the KEI analysis scores generated by Wordtracker, it uses this for comparison only because it is based on the total number of matches for a given search phrase, which overstates the competition your keywords face. As Table 7.2 illustrates, SEO Research Labs also shows you how many pages use your keywords in their title as well as the number of pages with the search term in both the title and incoming link text, which are more accurate measures of the level of competition for your keywords.

▶ **Table 7.2** KEI analysis report

Search Term	Count	Exact	In Title	Title+Anchor	KEI1	KEI2	KEI3
dedicated hosting	401	1,500,000	29,500	3,630	2.34120	31.26486	57.54134
dedicated server	452	1,980,000	38,600	7,010	1.95431	27.59823	35.54600

You can also create your own version of KEI by exporting data from YouTube's Keyword Tool into Microsoft Excel and then creating a new column that divides the monthly search volume (using Exact Match) by the number of results in a YouTube search.

This is a labor-intensive process. But, with 24 hours of new video being uploaded to the site every minute, you can't ignore competition when you research keywords.

Week 2: Optimize Video Watch Pages

Back in 2009, the YouTube Help Center explained how videos are ranked in the YouTube Search results:

> *After determining the content of the video using our spidering technology, YouTube combines sophisticated text-matching techniques to find videos that are both important and relevant to your search. Our technology examines dozens of aspects of the video's content (including number of hits and rating) to determine if it's a good match for your query.*

But, at some point in 2010, that page was removed. That was also about the time that YouTube added Upload Date to its list of ways to sort search results, joining Relevance (the default setting), View Count, and Rating. In addition, a New button started appearing next to videos that had been uploaded within the past week.

Even if they didn't say so explicitly, it was fairly obvious that YouTube's ranking algorithm had changed.

Fortunately, other tips have appeared in the YouTube Partner Help Center and on the YouTube Blog. In addition, several years of practical experience optimizing hundreds of videos for a variety of clients has helped me learn what works and what doesn't.

After you think about the words people would type to find your videos, you need to make sure your title, description, and tags actually include those words within them. This may appear obvious, but it comes as a surprise to many veteran marketers and new YouTubers who mistakenly think video optimization is just about the audio and video specifications they need for the best results on YouTube.

They are shocked—*shocked*— to find that they also need to change their title, description, and tags.

But, as Julie Kikla and Mahin Ibrahim, account managers, YouTube Partnerships, said September 21, 2010, in a post on the YouTube Blog, "Our algorithms are good, but they can only read, they can't watch your videos. So in order to properly classify your video and index it for search, we need your help."

According to Kikla and Ibrahim, "Titles, tags and rich descriptions (all categorized as metadata) will help your discoverability." A video's captions will also help.

Sophisticated text-matching techniques help find videos that are relevant to a search. To provide the most important results, YouTube's technology also examines other aspects of a video—including number of views and rating—to determine if it's a good match for a query.

Now, you don't control the number of hits (views) or rating your video gets. The YouTube community does. And, as Papa Bear, or Pops, said to Sonny Bear in "How do you get featured on YouTube?" (http://youtu.be/3eZTh94Fapg), you have a better chance of having your videos get more views and better ratings by "creating original work" and "becoming a fully vested member of the YouTube community."

So to optimize video for YouTube, you need to include your keywords in your title, description, and tags. Then, you also need to produce compelling content that the YouTube community will watch and share in order to increase the number of views and improve the rating of your videos.

Let's look at the five most likely factors:

Monday: Write an optimized title

Tuesday: Write an optimized description

Wednesday: Add optimized tags

Thursday: Get views the right way

Friday: Allow and ask for ratings

Monday: Write an Optimized Title

The most important text to optimize is the title of your video. Think of your title as a headline.

YouTube says that titles on video watch pages can be up to 120 characters (including spaces). However, I've found that the limit is 100 characters (including spaces). Since the average word is 5 characters long (plus a 6th character for the space), this means most titles are limited to about 16 words.

 Note: Before YouTube went wide-screen in November 2008, titles were limited to 60 characters. So things change.

And the typical search term is now about three words long. So it's now possible to optimize your title for up to five search terms. So, as the Knight Templar told Indiana Jones, "You must choose, but choose wisely."

As a former news editor of the *Beverly Times*, I learned to use Kipling's six honest serving-men to write front page headlines on deadline. I'd ask, "*Who* said *what?*" Or, "*What* happened to *whom?*" On occasion, I might ask, "*Why* did *who* say *what?*" Or, "*How* did *what* happen to *whom?*"

(Because the *Beverly Times* was a local daily newspaper, I rarely needed to ask, "*When* or *where* did a story occur?" The obvious answers were yesterday in Beverly.)

Feel free to ask Kipling's famous questions when writing the title of your video. And, if you've organized your keyword research into the six categories that Kipling once used, you'll discover that you can write optimized titles almost as quickly as unoptimized ones.

Let me share another tip for optimizing your title. I call this optimization technique "Russian nesting dolls." Russian nesting dolls, like the ones in Figure 7.5, are sets of dolls of decreasing sizes placed one inside the other. I look for popular keywords nested within longer search terms. For example, "nesting dolls" is a popular two-word term and "Russian nesting dolls" is a popular three-word phrase.

Figure 7.5 Russian nesting dolls

By using the longer three-word search phrase, my video will get found when someone is searching for "nesting dolls" or "Russian nesting dolls." However, if I used only the two-word term, then my video will get found only if someone searches for "nesting dolls." It won't get found when someone else searches for "Russian nesting dolls" because I hadn't included "Russian" in my title.

If you choose the longer phrase, then you have chosen wisely.

On a YouTube search results page, only the first 62 characters of the title will be displayed. So the first 10 words in your title will do double duty. They will help your video get a high ranking—and they will help the person who is searching select your video to watch.

If you want to include your brand name in the title, it should always go last. Your brand name faces less competition—or at least it *should* face less competition. So, put the terms that face more competition near the beginning of the phrase.

Tuesday: Write an Optimized Description

The next important text to optimize is the description of your video. It can be up to 5,000 characters long. That's about 833 words. YouTube encourages you to be as detailed as possible—short of offering an entire transcript: "The more information you include, the easier it is for users to find your video!"

Or, as Kikla and Ibrahim said in their post on the YouTube Blog, "The more words you include in your description, the higher your chances of being discovered by searchers, which means the larger your audience can grow, and the more potential revenue you can earn."

They added, "If you have a transcript available, make sure to upload it and turn on captions. This can help your discoverability as it will give us more data points to index your video."

But, only the first 140 characters of the description are displayed in YouTube Search results, so it's useful to include your search terms in the first 23 words of your description because they'll appear in bold.

Your description should include URLs to a relevant channel or playlist or to another website. Your links become clickable only if they are preceded by `http://`—so `www.yoursite.com` won't make the URL clickable but `http://www.yoursite.com` will.

Putting links into the first 140 characters of your description is the best way to drive traffic to a non-YouTube site. Offsite links aren't allowed *anywhere* but in the description, so use them.

Unfortunately, the limit on how much text gets displayed has led some people to mistakenly conclude that longer descriptions don't impact YouTube search result rankings. But they do, particularly for long-tail search phrases that are typically longer and more detailed than normal.

The bad habit of writing shorter descriptions is often reinforced by the logical fallacy that people watch a video; they don't read its description. This ignores the stubborn fact that people need to discover a video before they can watch it. And a longer description can often help them discover it.

David Ogilvy wrote about the importance of long copy in his classic book *Ogilvy on Advertising*. He said, "A blind pig can sometimes find truffles, but it helps to know that they are found in oak forests."

YouTube provides some advice on writing your video description. It says, "To best promote your video, you'll want its description to be both accurate and interesting." Here are a few tips to help you get started:

Make your description clear and specific. Your video should stand out from the crowd. Try to determine what content it contains that will help users find it and distinguish it from other videos. Using descriptive language in complete sentences is a good idea. In addition, many people will read the description while watching a video, especially if it starts slowly. If you use opening credits or a lengthy exposition, make sure your description tells as good a story as your video does. And if your video has a "surprise ending," don't spoil it by revealing "the butler did it" in your written description.

Give credit when appropriate. If people don't know the exact title or other keywords associated with your video, they might search the name of a participant or another website where it's featured. Be sure to include as much information as you feel comfortable including, but be careful to not include anything that shouldn't be publicly displayed. Also, if you use Creative Commons material or copyrighted material that you have permission to use, the lower half of the description is a good place to put all the attribution information. Then it's technically attached to the video, but it doesn't consume valuable screen real estate.

Categorize correctly. The category into which you place your video is part of its description as well. People are more likely to rate your video highly and watch it more frequently if it's placed in a relevant category. Now, some videos could go in one of several categories. And all categories are *not* created equal. Some categories are much more popular than others, but videos in popular categories often face more competition. A good way to check is to go to www.youtube.com/browse and examine the individual browse pages for relevant categories. Then select the category that seems "best." If that doesn't work, then you can always change the category of your video later by following these steps:

1. Go to the My Videos page.
2. Click the Edit Video Info button next to your video.
3. Choose the radio button for your new category within the Video Category section.
4. Click the Update Video Info button to save your video information.

Wednesday: Add Optimized Tags

The final text to be optimized is your tags. YouTube says you can use up to 120 characters in your tags. This means you can have as many as 20 tags.

Tags are the keywords that describe your videos. YouTube says, "Enter as many tags as you'd like into the Tags field." For example, a surfing video might be tagged with *surfing*, *water*, and *waves*. Users who enjoy watching surfing videos can then search for any of those terms and that video will show up in their search results.

YouTube provides this general information in its video toolbox about making your video easy to find:

> *When you upload your video, we require you to choose at least one category and enter at least one tag to describe the content in your video. Adding this information helps other YouTube members find your video, so if you want an audience, help them out! The more accurate the tags are on each video, the easier it is for everyone to find cool videos to watch.*

> *Make your tags as descriptive as you can—if you took a video of your friends at the beach, you might want to tag it like this:* party beach surfing. *Each tag is separated from the others by a space.*

Just as you can change your category, you can also change your tags.

Kikla and Ibrahim said in their YouTube Blog post, "Don't just include tags upon video upload. If you have a popular video that continues to get views over time, update your tags regularly to take advantage of new searches. Online search behavior is always changing, so your tags should change along with it."

Brad O'Farrell, the technical editor of this book, says you can see an excellent example of this at www.youtube.com/watch?v=JpBGRA6HHtY. It's shown in Figure 7.6.

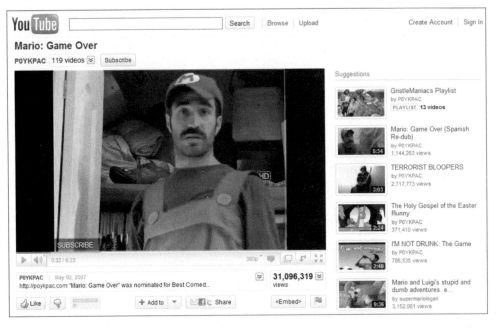

Figure 7.6 "Mario: Game Over"

"Mario: Game Over" from comedy group POYKPAC was nominated for Best Comedy Video of 2007 in the YouTube Awards. While views "peaked" that year, POYKPAC has continued to increase the views of their Super Mario sketch video (now up to 31 million views) by constantly updating it with newly relevant tags.

For example, POYKPAC added "Galaxy" when Mario Galaxy was released and "Super Smash Brothers Brawl" when it was released and got millions of views from people searching for gameplay footage. They even added tags that made it relevant to "Super Mario Rescues the Princess: Seth MacFarlane's Cavalcade" when it went viral in September 2008.

Thursday: Get Views the Right Way

As the "Mario: Game Over" example illustrates, making sure your keywords are actually included in your title, description, and tags helps the YouTube algorithm know that your video is relevant to a search. But don't go overboard.

In their post, Kikla and Ibrahim said, "Don't repeat words in your description or title, this will not help you. Rather use different words and variations that users might search on to find your video."

YouTube's technology also examines other aspects of a video's content to determine if it's important—including number of views. This has been the subject of a good deal of controversy over the viewing figures of some YouTube videos. There have been claims that automated systems—including robots, spiders, and offline readers—have been used to inflate the amount of views received. Use of any automated system that "sends more request messages to the YouTube servers in a given period of time than a human can reasonably produce in the same period" is forbidden by YouTube's terms of service.

For example, a YouTube video featuring the anime franchise Evangelion had a view count of around 98 million as of October 2008, but it has been barred from the YouTube charts due to automated viewing.

And "Avril Lavigne - Girlfriend" has also been accused of having an exaggerated number of views due to the use of a link with an auto-refresh mechanism posted by AvrilBandAids, a fansite devoted to Avril Lavigne. Clicking the link will automatically reload the YouTube video of "Girlfriend" every 15 seconds. Fans of Avril Lavigne are encouraged to "Keep this page open while you browse the internet, study for exams, or even sleep. For extra viewing power, open up two or more browser windows at this page!"

Finally, an unofficial video of the song "Music Is My Hot Hot Sex" by the Brazilian band Cansei De Ser Sexy briefly held the #1 slot for the all-time most viewed video, with around 114 million views in March 2008. However, it was temporarily removed from YouTube after allegations of automated viewing before being deleted by the uploader.

Italian writer Clarus Bartel, who had uploaded the video, denied attempting to boost its ranking, stating, "These gimmicks do not belong to me. I've got nothing to do with it."

A spokesperson for YouTube said, "We are developing safeguards to secure the statistics on YouTube. Although it is somewhat difficult to track how often this happens, it is not rampant. As soon as it comes to our attention that someone has rigged their numbers to gain placement on the top pages, we remove the video or channel from public view."

So, avoid using tricks to inflate the number of views your video gets. A good rule of thumb is whether you'd feel comfortable explaining what you've done to a reporter for the *New York Times*.

To get views the right way, don't forget the thumbnail! According to eye tracking studies conducted by Enquiro Research, the thumbnail images are the first things that attract a searcher's eyes. People look at the thumbnail and title before they click on a video, and it's beneficial if the two make sense together and create a compelling image/text combo.

However, "Users hate spam. Google hates spam," said Kikla and Ibrahim in their post. "Spammy tags and thumbnails may help increase views in the very short term, but our algorithm will catch on and punish you for spam. Long term, you want your users searching for videos to find what they are looking for and to associate your channel with accurate information," they added.

There are other tactics to get views the right way. For example, many people check out the most viewed videos for today, this week, and this month. As your video gets on these lists, it gets more views.

This means getting more views quickly is ultimately more beneficial than getting many views over a long period of time because your videos would also get bonus views from being on lists. So any promotional efforts—done through purchasing promotion from YouTube, getting a video featured by YouTube, or promoting it on your own channel—should be focused on getting a sharp spike at first rather than a steady stream.

There are other legitimate ways to easily boost your view count. Anyone can apply to be a partner at www.youtube.com/partners, and user partners get more promotional options than regular users. One of these is that the video featured on your channel page will "auto-play," meaning that when anyone visits your channel, it also counts as a view for your video. Not only is this not against the rules, you actually can't disable the auto-play feature.

Another thing that's different for user partners is that the most recent videos on their video watch pages are their own by default—whereas, for non-partner users, the "related videos" displayed on their watch pages are from non-partners by default. Watch "STELLA – Birthday," shown in Figure 7.7, at http://youtu.be/xdby-GkQ1g0 and you'll see more videos from: MyDamnChannel in the right column.

Two other techniques to drive traffic from one video to another—as opposed to just general promotion across your channel—are annotations and video responses. Annotations can be used to embed clickable text boxes within a video frame itself. If you have one video that is currently popular and another video that you want to promote, you can create annotations in the popular video that link to the other one.

In addition, if you post a popular video as a video response to an unpopular video, it'll slightly increase the unpopular video's views. However, this doesn't really work the other way around. In other words, posting your video as a response to a random popular video isn't helpful because the *many* videos that could be posted as responses to a popular video aren't as prominently linked to as the *one* video to which a popular video is posted as a response.

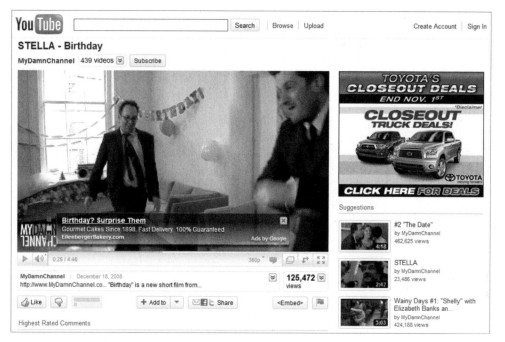

Figure 7.7 "STELLA - Birthday"

Friday: Allow and Ask for Ratings

One of the other aspects that YouTube's algorithm uses to determine if your video's content is important is its rating. The community is truly in control on YouTube, and they determine the rating of your video. But you need to enable them to do that by selecting "Yes, allow this video to be rated by others" in the Ratings section of your sharing options. This is the default option and you should leave it selected.

Now, you also have the option of selecting "No, don't allow this video to be rated." But you are then eliminating one of the signals that YouTube uses to determine if your video is a good match for a query. And if you *ever* disable ratings, your video can never be on the "top rated" lists.

If you want millions of people to discover, watch, and share your originally created videos, then you need to allow the YouTube community to rate them. And you don't need to be afraid that you'll be graded on a bell curve.

The YouTube Biz Blog revealed in September 2009 that the vast majority of videos had a five-star rating. This prompted YouTube to simplify its ratings on January 21, 2010, when the video page got a makeover. Now, YouTube uses binary ratings: I like this/I dislike this.

So, you should allow ratings. But should you ask for them too?

Michael Buckley of *What the Buck?!* frequently "breaks the fourth wall" and specifically *asks* his audience to give his video a good rating. And as Figure 7.8

illustrates, he also adds annotations that say, "Thank you for Thumbing Up This Video! Stay tuned for updates from Straight Buck! LOL".

Figure 7.8 "Cheryl Cole Turns ORANGE on X-Factor!!! - Aiden Grimshow, Mary Byrne, Matt Cardle Top 16"

The need to get good ratings to get high search result rankings also puts a premium on "making videos worth watching," which we examined in Chapter 3. And it puts a premium on "creating content worth sharing," which we tackled in Chapter 4.

Week 3: Optimize Your Brand Channel

With more than 3 billion videos viewed every day and over 48 hours of content uploaded every minute, it is easy for videos to get lost in the YouTube ecosystem. Brand channels make it easier for your fans to find all your videos—if you use the right title, info, tags, and category.

Access to this enhanced brand channel functionality is free to advertisers who meet a predetermined spending level, which was $200,000 as this was written. Since these promotional opportunities are included with brand channels, you should use them to "get views the right way," which makes your videos more discoverable.

So, let's look at these topics this week:

Monday: Name your channel thoughtfully

Tuesday: Add details to channel info

Wednesday: Use descriptive channel tags

Thursday: Choose the right channel type

Friday: Promote your videos the right way

Monday: Name Your Channel Thoughtfully

Consider naming your channel something more descriptive than your username.

For example, Ogilvy & Mather is one of the largest marketing communications companies in the world. The company has worked with several clients to launch brand channels on YouTube.

On February 10, 2010, Rob Davis, leader of Ogilvy's Interactive Video Practice, told the YouTube Biz Blog, "When we are working on a YouTube brand channel or campaign, we take a team approach that includes the client, YouTube, and Google as part of the working unit. Initial ideas may come from anyone on the team, but it's when we start ideating with YouTube that the big ideas gel."

One of those big ideas was announced on June 22, 2010, at a press conference at the Cannes Lions International Advertising Festival. It was a new YouTube brand channel founded and curated by Ogilvy & Mather that looks at inspiration.

As Figure 7.9 illustrates, the new brand channel is *not* named Ogilvy's Channel. Instead, it is named Create or Else.

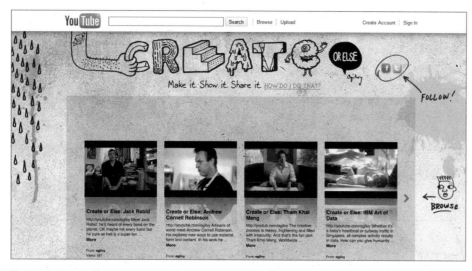

Figure 7.9 Create or Else

Tham Khai Meng, creative director and chairman of the Worldwide Creative Council of Ogilvy & Mather, said in a press release, "Create or Else is a destination to engage and encourage those around the world to become part of a community and conversation about what is inspiring. This supports our Pervasive Creativity initiative."

Rotating curators from around the world provide a changing line-up of video content that includes vignettes with inspirational subjects across all fields, from arts and science to industry and beyond. Lars Bastholm, chief digital creative officer for O&M North America and chief creative officer for O&M New York, was the first curator for Create or Else.

"If you're anything like most creative people, you're always looking for inspiration and unique expressions. If you're anything like me, you can easily spend untold hours scouring the wild west of the Internet in the vain hope of finding a glimmer of inspiration," said Bastholm. "Create or Else was created to give you a starting point for your journey."

The development of Create or Else was an evolution of Ogilvy's own online, integrated digital video practice. The company demonstrated that it can walk the walk as well as talk the talk. You can visit Create or Else at `www.youtube.com/ogilvy` and follow the conversation about inspiration at `www.twitter.com/create_or_else`.

And, because the company named its brand channel something more descriptive than its username, you can find Create or Else when you use the Channel's search option as well as Ogilvy when you conduct a YouTube search.

Tuesday: Add Details to Channel Info

Use the channel information module to your advantage by adding details such as city, state, category, and awards.

As Figure 7.10 illustrates, Lionsgate added these details to this prominent box of the brand channel for its feature film *KICK-ASS*.

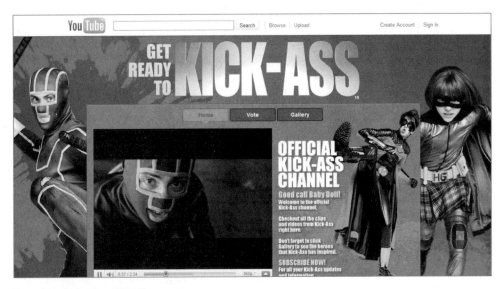

Figure 7.10 Get Ready to KICK-ASS

In addition to displaying statistics, such as the number of times KICK-ASS's channel has been viewed, the channel info box also displays some information from the studio's YouTube profile, such as country (United Kingdom) and website (`www.kickass-movie.co.uk/`).

Lionsgate also added the following information to KICK-ASS's channel info box to make it easier for users to find it:

About Me:

UK CINEMAS MARCH 26

A twisted, funny, high octane adventure, Matthew Vaughn brings KICK ASS to the big screen.

KICK ASS tells the story of average teenager Dave Lizewski (Aaron Johnson), who decides to take his obsession with comic books as inspiration to become a real-life superhero. As any good superhero would, he chooses a new name—Kick Ass—assembles a suit and mask to wear, and gets to work fighting crime. Theres only one problem Kick Ass has absolutely no superpowers.

His life is forever changed as he inspires a sub-culture of copy cats, meets up with a pair of crazed vigilantes—an eleven year old sword-wielding dynamo, Hit Girl (Chloë Moretz), and her father Big Daddy (Nicolas Cage)—and forges a friendship with another fledging superhero, Red Mist (Chris Mintz-Plasse). But thanks to the scheming of a local mob boss Frank DAmico (Mark Strong), that new alliance will be put to the test.

The honors section of a channel info box appears if a channel has achieved a notable ranking, such as being the #1 Most Subscribed (All Time) - Sponsors - United Kingdom. YouTube automatically generates the content for this part of the module.

Wednesday: Use Descriptive Channel Tags

Be as descriptive as possible. YouTube's search results depend on descriptive channel tags.

Figure 7.11 shows life around home's channel, which uses "life around home william moss healthy green living" as channel tags rather than "lifearoundhome."

Figure 7.11 Life Around Home

However, YouTube channel tags are based on single words rather than phrases. This has disadvantages.

For example, when users can freely choose tags—creating what is called a folksonomy—the resulting metadata can include homonyms (the same tags used with different meanings) and synonyms (multiple tags for the same concept), which may lead to inappropriate connections between items and inefficient searches for YouTube channels.

For example, the tag "orange" may refer to the fruit or the color, and items related to a version of Apple's operating system, Mac OS X, may be tagged "Leopard," "software," or a variety of other terms.

The creators of YouTube brand channels can also choose tags that are different inflections of words (such as singular and plural), which can contribute to navigation difficulties if the system does not include stemming of tags when searching.

Tags chosen informally and personally by the brand channel's creator are also open to tag spam, which is when people apply an excessive number of tags or unrelated tags to a YouTube channel or video in order to attract viewers. Fortunately, this abuse can be mitigated by limiting the number of tags that can be created.

So, if tags have so many disadvantages, then why do YouTube's search results depend on them?

In 2003, Delicious, the social bookmarking site, enabled its users to add tags to their bookmarks as a way to help find them later. Delicious also provided browsable aggregated views of the bookmarks of all users featuring a particular tag.

Flickr allowed its users to add tags to each of their pictures, constructing flexible and easy metadata that made the pictures highly searchable. The influence of Delicious and the success of Flickr popularized the concept, and YouTube also implemented tagging.

So, choose your channel tags wisely. Select descriptive, specific words that represent the video content of your brand channel fairly and accurately.

Thursday: Choose the Right Channel Type

Make sure to choose the right channel type (for example, YouTubers, Directors, Musicians, Comedians, Gurus, Reporters) so that users can find you. Also see the discussion of channel types in Chapter 5.

As Figure 7.12 illustrates, the most viewed channel in the Comedians category was Fred. As this was written, the channel's 76 videos had 603,365,506 views.

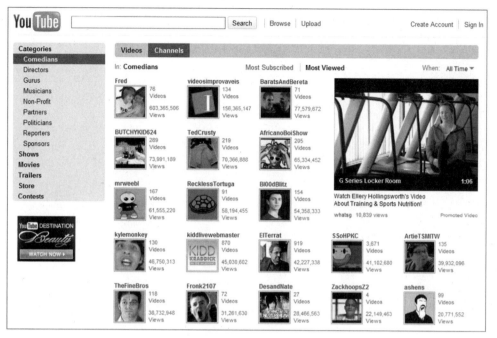

Figure 7.12 Fred

As Figure 7.13 illustrates, the most viewed channel in the Directors category was machinima. As this was written, the channel's 11,724 videos had 1,526,675,327 views.

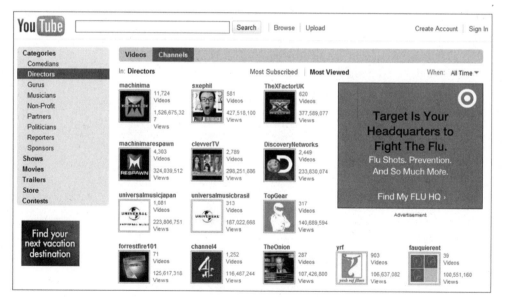

Figure 7.13 machinima

As Figure 7.14 illustrates, the most viewed channel in the Gurus category was hotforwords. As this was written, the channel's 584 videos had 365,147,082 views.

Figure 7.14 hotforwords

As Figure 7.15 illustrates, the most viewed channel in the Musicians category was EminemVEVO. As this was written, the channel's 33 videos had 579,019,545 views.

Figure 7.15 EminemVEVO

As Figure 7.16 illustrates, the most viewed channel in the Reporters category was diethealth. As this was written, the channel's 452 videos had 65,280,615 views.

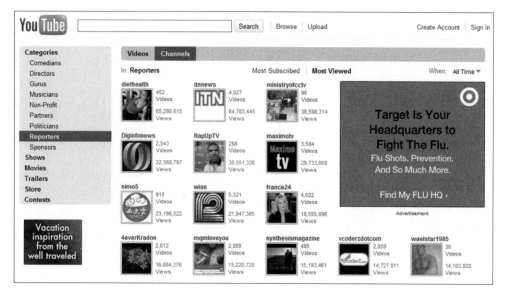

Figure 7.16 diethealth

You can easily change your account type by going to your account page, clicking Edit Channel (under More), and clicking the Change Channel Type link at the bottom of the page.

Friday: Promote Your Videos the Right Way

Creating a brand channel requires you to spend at least $200,000 on YouTube advertising. Although you can spend that on homepage, banner and pre-roll ads, I strongly recommend that you use most of this on Promoted Videos to "get views the right way." In a world where 24 hours of video are uploaded to YouTube every minute, Promoted Videos has become a critical way for creators to get their content in front of viewers across the Web.

In October 2009, Jonathan Goldman, software engineer, wrote in the YouTube Biz Blog, "We first launched Promoted Videos as a search advertising program on YouTube, allowing content creators to drive viewership of their videos by targeting the hundreds of millions of searches that happen on YouTube every day. But in the past year Promoted Videos has evolved into a much broader discovery vehicle, appearing on search, the YouTube homepage, video watch pages and recently across the AdSense network. We've also built better conversion opportunities via Call-to-Action overlays. As a result, Promoted Videos is now driving millions of video views per week, with clicks having increased 500% since January."

As Promoted Videos expanded and became easier to use, several small businesses started using YouTube's self-service tools to promote their products and drive engaged YouTube audiences to both their videos and their websites.

For example, Artbeads.com used Promoted Videos to teach its customers how to use its beads to create beautiful works of art. Steve Groenier, vice president of search marketing and customer service, also wanted to figure out a way to use his existing educational videos to drive sales and traffic to the company's website.

On February 2, 2010, Groenier told the YouTube Biz Blog, "The first thing that attracted us to advertise on YouTube was the ability to introduce a [Call-to-Action] overlay ad to our existing videos, which were already receiving thousands of views. The overlay ads helped...drive website visits and sales."

Videos like "Artbeads.com Handy Tip - How to Use Glue-In Bails and Caps," shown in Figure 7.17, help both bead veterans and those new to the craft learn how to use these products. When compared to an average Artbeads.com text ad, the videos were twice as effective at generating click-throughs.

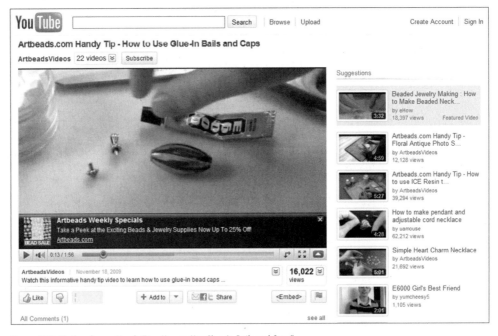

Figure 7.17 "Artbeads.com Handy Tip - How to Use Glue-In Bails and Caps"

Groenier soon discovered that Promoted Videos helped "get our videos listed at the top of the search results for relevant keyword phrases like 'how to make jewelry.'" After starting Promoted Videos, Steve saw referral traffic to Artbeads.com from YouTube increase by 150 percent.

So if you're looking for the next best way to promote your brand channel and attract customers to your website, maybe it's time to use Promoted Videos.

Week 4: Optimize Video for the Web

Now, I'm fairly confident that somebody in your organization will want to know if you can optimize video for the Web. You can. The upside of this approach is obvious: The YouTube community is *not* in control and doesn't determine which videos are popular. The downside is also obvious: Your videos will be found by only a small percentage of searches.

In other words, your organization faces the trade-offs that Genie faced in *Aladdin*, "Phenomenal cosmic powers! Itty-bitty living space!"

The good news is you have it both ways. You can optimize video for YouTube and optimize video for the Web at the same time. And video optimization best practices for YouTube and the Web generally don't conflict.

So here's what we'll do this week:

Monday: Research Google Video

Tuesday: Examine Bing Videos

Wednesday: Investigate blinkx

Thursday: Study Truveo

Friday: Explore VideoSurf

Monday: Research Google Video

Jennifer Grappone and Gradiva Couzin, the authors of *Search Engine Optimization: An Hour A Day*, offer some sound advice about optimizing video for the Web:

On-page text and links to the video First and foremost, make sure all the videos on your site are presented on individual URLs. Text surrounding the video file, and links pointing to it, give contextual help to search engines, so include keywords there.

Video filename Just like search-friendly URLs for HTML pages, video filenames should contain descriptive terms, separated by dashes.

Video file metadata Many video-production/encoding tools allow the input of metadata in the video file itself. This can include content-specific elements such as title, description, or even a text transcript, and it can also include technical information such as format/encoding quality. If you have control over these elements, be sure to include keywords.

Media RSS enclosures Of particular usefulness in SEO are the <title>, <description>, <keyword>, and <text> enclosures in your MRSS feed.

When the second edition of their book was published in April 2008, Jennifer and Gradiva had already spotted the importance of Google Video Sitemaps, which had only been introduced a few months earlier. They wrote, "With Video Sitemaps, Google is setting a new course—away from the Media RSS feed format that has been accepted for years. But we all know that when Google shows up at a party sporting a new fashion, the whole school will be wearing it the next day."

I agree.

The single best way to make Google aware of all your videos on your website is to create and maintain a Video Sitemap. Video Sitemaps provide Google with essential information about your videos, including the URLs for the pages where the videos can be found, the titles of the videos, keywords, thumbnail images, durations, and other information.

The Sitemap also allows you to define the period of time for which each video will be available. This is particularly useful for content that has explicit viewing windows so that Google can remove the content from its index when it expires.

Once your Sitemap is created, you can submit the URL of the Sitemap file in Google Webmaster Tools or through your robots.txt file.

Once Google has indexed a video, it may appear in its web search results in what Google calls a Video Onebox (a cluster of videos related to the queried topic) and in its video search engine, Google Videos. A video result is immediately recognizable by its thumbnail, duration, and a description.

You can get more information about creating a Video Sitemap at the following location:

www.google.com/support/webmasters/bin/answer.py? hl=en&answer=80472

A Video Sitemap uses the additional video-specific tags in Table 7.3. In its simplest form, a Video Sitemap can include a single tag to let Google know there is a video playable at a specific landing page URL. Optional fields let you specify other attributes of the video available on that page. The more information you provide in the Sitemap extension, the less Google will have to do to try to discover and extract that information. Google may use text available on your video's page rather than the text you supply in the Video Sitemap, if it differs.

▶ **Table 7.3** Video-specific tag definitions

Tag	Required?	Description
`<loc>`	Yes	This tag specifies the landing page (aka play page, referrer page) for the video. When a user clicks on a video result on a search results page, they will be sent to this landing page. This must be a unique URL, so don't host multiple videos on the same page.
`<video:video>`	Yes	
`<video:thumbnail_loc>`	Yes	A URL pointing to the URL for the video thumbnail image file. Google can accept most image sizes/types but recommends that your thumbs are at least 160x120 pixels in JPG, PNG, or GIF format.

Tag	Required?	Description
`<video:title>`	Yes	The title of the video is limited to 100 characters.
`<video:description>`	Yes	The description of the video. Descriptions longer than 2,048 characters will be truncated.
`<video:duration>`	Optional	The duration of the video in seconds. Value must be between 0 and 28800 (8 hours). Non-digit characters are disallowed. Strongly recommended.
`<video:expiration_date>`	Optional	The date after which the video will no longer be available, in W3C format. Acceptable values are complete date (YYYY-MM-DD) and complete date plus hours, minutes, seconds, and time zone (YYYY-MM-DDThh:mm:ss+TZD), such as, for example, 2007-07-16T19:20:30+08:00. Recommended when applicable, but don't supply this information if your video does not expire.

Tuesday: Examine Bing Videos

Today, we'll try to figure out what Microsoft is doing in the online video market. But it won't be easy.

Examine Bing Videos (www.bing.com/videos/browse). As Figure 7.18 illustrates, it is part of Microsoft's Bing search engine.

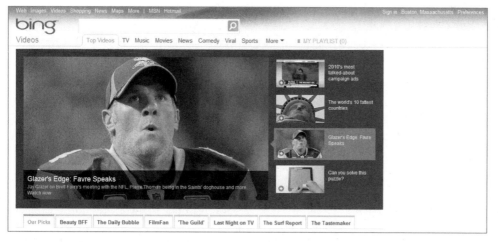

Figure 7.18 Bing Videos

Bing Videos enables users to search and view videos across various websites. It was officially released on September 26, 2007 as Live Search Video and rebranded as Bing Videos on June 3, 2009.

The Bing Videos home page allow users to browse for TV shows, music videos, the most-watched video content on the Web, and recent news and sports videos.

Bing Videos has the following features:

- *Smart Preview*, which enables users to preview a video by mousing over its thumbnail. This feature also allows users to instantly watch short previews of videos.

- *Filtering*, which filters results by the duration of videos.

- *Sorting*, which sorts results by either relevance or date.

- *View Selection*, which switches between a grid view and a list view.

- *Related People*, which occasionally suggests famous people who are related to queries.

Bing Videos is also integrated into Bing News.

So, how do you ensure that the video content on your website gets into the Bing Videos index?

On May 28, 2010, Rick DeJarnette posted this advice on the Bing Webmaster Center blog: "Well, if you have your video content embedded in your pages, you should look at implementing graceful degradation strategies for down-level users (which includes search bots). This plan includes associating the embedded video content with descriptive, keyword-rich, metadata that the bots can process."

Confused? As Winston Churchill said in a radio broadcast back in October 1939, "I cannot forecast to you the action of Russia. It is a riddle, wrapped in a mystery, inside an enigma; but perhaps there is a key. That key is Russian national interest."

Here the key is knowing that Bing is interested in getting video content into its index—but it is difficult and takes time for bots to crawl all of that video content automatically. So right now it seems that the best approach to ensure that the video content on your website gets into the Bing Videos index is to use Media RSS (aka MRSS).

Fundamentally, MRSS is a data feed that's like normal RSS feeds that define the title and description of content. However, MRSS offers custom tags associated specifically with media content metadata, such as video categories, copyright, ratings, season and episode numbers, and artists. By using keywords in the descriptions of your content, you can improve your video's rank in queries using those keywords.

And by using MRSS to submit your content to Bing, you can also improve the odds that your videos will be added to the Bing index more thoroughly and more quickly. It's worth noting, however, that video content does not get preferential ranking just because it comes from an MRSS feed. It's the keyword relevance of the metadata you supply in the MRSS feed that makes the difference.

Although you can use TubeMogul to feed your content to Bing, to truly optimize your video content's rank in the Bing index, I encourage you to create a Bing MRSS feed. Using a Bing MRSS feed will populate more of the critical metadata fields in the Bing index, which ultimately affects keyword relevance and the resulting rank of that content in the Bing search engine results pages (SERPs).

Unfortunately, Bing does *not* automatically pick up your MRSS feeds. You need to contact the Bing MRSS support team via email at bingfeed@microsoft.com to request consideration of your content feed. If the Bing media index team chooses to accept a feed to your content, they will work with you to set up a feed relationship so that the Bing crawler knows to look for your MRSS feed files.

If you want to read the entire Bing MRSS tag specifications, go to www.bing.com/toolbox/media/p/9602766.aspx to download a Word document. Or, if you want a helpful video content mRSS FAQ, go to www.bing.com/toolbox/media/p/9602765.aspx to download a PDF file.

Wednesday: Investigate Blinkx

You should also investigate blinkx. According to Compete, the video search engine had more than 4 million unique visitors as this was written, up 92 percent from the previous year.

Founded in 2004 by Suranga Chandratillake, the company has headquarters in San Francisco, California, and the UK. As Figure 7.19 illustrates, blinkx has an index of over 35 million hours of searchable video (almost 4,000 years) and more than 720 media partnerships, including national broadcasters, commercial media giants, and private video libraries.

Figure 7.19 blinkx

To help marketers maximize traffic to online video, blinkx offers a white paper on video search engine optimization. It covers the following topics:

- Cleaning and conversion of metadata

- Optimizing titles, description, and filenames

- Leveraging sitemaps

- Utilizing Media RSS

- Content management

- Where to submit

- What to avoid

Go to www.blinkx.com/whitepapers to download the video SEO white paper. It is a dozen pages long and provides very ecumenical advice.

For example, it covers first-generation video search solutions, like Singingfish, which depended entirely on metadata. It also outlines what you should do to optimize your content for second-generation video search engines that aim to understand and extract meaning from the video itself as well as spider textual metadata.

The blinkx SEO white paper also covers optimizing your title, description, and tags, which we've already covered, as well as optimizing other metadata, the filename, the sitemap, RSS and Media RSS, the format, in-format metadata, and content management, which are factors in video search engine rankings.

The good news is that none of these recommendations contradict what you need to do to optimize a video for YouTube. Video search engines just look at some things like metadata that YouTube ignores, while YouTube looks at some things like views that video search engines ignore.

For example, just because YouTube ignores the great metadata stored in your MOV file is no reason not to add it for video search engines. The blinkx SEO white paper recommends using tools like Sorenson Squeeze, Autodesk Cleaner, and CastFire to help you ensure that you maintain metadata between conversions and help you keep your metadata profile clean.

The blinkx SEO white paper also provides some guidelines to follow when optimizing your metadata:

- Make sure your tags are relevant to your content. This seems obvious, but it takes some thought as well as some keyword research to get into the minds of users.

- Use as many tags as you can. There is no penalty for using all of your available tag space.

- Spread your tags out among your clips. Adding more tags can help snag some long-tail terms.

- Use adjectives. Remember that lots of folks are browsing and they'll use adjectives to find what they are in the mood to view.

- Have some category descriptor tags.

- Match your title and description with your most important tags. SEO best practices apply here as well.

- Don't use stop words or waste tag space on noise words like *and* or *to*.

In other words, optimizing video for video search engines is similar to optimizing video for YouTube. You just optimize different things.

You can also go to `www.blinkx.com/rssupload` and use the form to submit your video to blinkx and request that someone contact you about including your content in the blinkx index. Blinkx accepts the Media RSS and RSS 2.0 specifications.

Thursday: Study Truveo

You will also want to study Truveo. According to Compete, the video search engine had more than 1.5 million unique visitors as this was written, up 96 percent from the previous year.

Founded in 2004, Truveo launched its first commercial video search service in 2005. It was acquired by AOL in January 2006 and currently operates as a wholly owned subsidiary of AOL, LLC.

Truveo, shown in Figure 7.20, is one of the largest video search engines on the Web. It currently powers video search for AOL Video, AOL Search, Brightcove, CBS Radio websites, Clevver, CSTV, Excite, Flock, Infospace, Kosmix, Microsoft websites, Pageflakes, PureVideo, Qwest, CNET's Search.com, Sportingo, *Sports Illustrated*, Widgetbox, YourMinis, and other sites worldwide, reaching an audience of over 75 million users a month.

Figure 7.20 Truveo

Truveo opened up its search engine to the online video community in 2006, and hundreds of content producers use its director accounts to make their video searchable by the millions of users across the Truveo network. The Truveo Director program is a free feature for site owners or content publishers. It uses a Media RSS feed to get your video content into Truveo's video search index in near real time. All you need to do is sign up for a director account, add a feed, wait for approval, and add more feeds.

To learn more about Truveo director accounts, send an email to info@truveo.com with the word "info" in the subject line.

In June 2009, Truveo announced a major update to its website that made it easier to find video on the Web. For example, its navigation lets users browse their searches by channel, category, show, popularity, and most followed on Twitter. Users can also easily filter results to find videos on their favorite websites and channels.

Friday: Explore VideoSurf

VideoSurf is a video search engine that claims it "has created a better way for people to search, discover, and watch online videos." And it backs up this claim with a radically different approach. As Figure 7.21 illustrates, VideoSurf's video search engine features full **TV episodes**, movie clips, the hottest new **music videos, funny videos,** celebrity **videos,** sports videos, **and breaking news clips.**

Figure 7.21 VideoSurf

Using a combination of computer vision and computation methods, VideoSurf has taught computers to "see" inside videos to find content in a fast, efficient, and scalable way. Basing its search on visual identification, rather than text only, VideoSurf's computer vision video search engine provides relevant results and enables users to find the specific scenes, people, or moments they want to see.

On June 2, 2009, Virginia Heffernan of the *New York Times* said, "VideoSurf helps users find videos of people online by spotting faces with uncanny accuracy."

With over 50 billion visual moments indexed from videos found across the Web, VideoSurf is rapidly growing. According to Compete, VideoSurf had close to 1.5 million unique visitors a month as this was written, almost 420 percent higher than the previous year.

VideoSurf was founded in 2006 by experts in search, computer vision, and fast computation technology. The company is based in San Mateo, California.

VideoSurf searches major video sites—including Hulu, CNN, TMZ, Metacafe, Fancast, Comedy Central, Dailymotion, and more—and it is adding new video sites.

Go to `www.videosurf.com/submitsite` to submit vidoes on your website or blog to the VideoSurf index. All you need to do is provide a valid VideoSurf Media RSS feed.

You can increase your content's exposure on this video search engine by implementing its "jump to moment" functionality in your flash video player. Adding this functionality takes just a few minutes and makes it much more likely that VideoSurf's users will watch your videos.

Month 6: Engage the YouTube Community

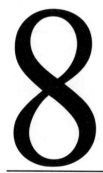

YouTube began as a video sharing site and has quickly grown into the largest worldwide video sharing community. In this chapter, you will learn how to become a fully vested member of the YouTube community. You'll also learn the secrets of YouTube success, find out how to build buzz beyond YouTube, and watch online video case studies. You'll meet the woman who said to Paul Revere as he galloped through her community, "Thanks, but what about those silver candlesticks I ordered?"

Chapter Contents:

Paul Revere's Ride

Although YouTube began as a video sharing site, it has quickly grown into the largest worldwide video sharing community.

According to Wikipedia, *community* has been traditionally defined as "a group of interacting people living in a common location." With the advent of the Internet, the concept has expanded because people can now gather virtually in an online community and share common interests.

The key to becoming an opinion leader in a community is to continually look over your shoulder and consider where the rest of the social system is regarding new ideas.

As I mentioned in Chapter 2, Everett Rogers, author of *Diffusion of Innovations*, noted, "The interpersonal relationships between opinion leaders and their followers hang in a delicate balance. If an opinion leader becomes too innovative, or adopts a new idea too quickly, followers may begin to doubt his or her judgment."

This delicate balance between opinion leaders and their followers explains the comic irony in Figure 8.1, where a woman says to Paul Revere as he gallops through her community, "Thanks, but what about those silver candlesticks I ordered?"

CARTOONBANK.COM

"Thanks, but what about those silver candlesticks I ordered?"

Figure 8.1 "Thanks, but what about those silver candlesticks I ordered?" (Cartoon by Peter Arno in *The New Yorker*, June 8, 1957.)

So, how do you become an individual who is able to informally influence other individuals' attitudes or overt behavior in a desired way with relative frequency? In other words, how do you become an opinion leader in the YouTube community or any other community?

As Harold Lasswell observed, the key is analyzing *who* says *what* in which *channel* to *whom* with what *effect*. Before we tackle how to engage the YouTube community, let's look at the how the interpersonal communication behavior of opinion leaders drives the diffusion process—and how it was able to create a critical mass of adopters long before the Internet was invented.

My favorite example of how this works is Paul Revere's ride. It demonstrates that opinion leaders and diffusion networks existed 230 years before YouTube was founded in 2005. That story also resonates for me, in part, because I live in Acton, Massachusetts, home of the Acton Minutemen (Figure 8.2). Actonians like to say, "The battle of Lexington was fought in Concord by the men of Acton."

Figure 8.2 Welcome to the home of the Acton Minutemen

And I recommend reading *Paul Revere's Ride* (Oxford University Press, 1994) by David Hackett Fischer, which tells a more compelling story than Henry Wadsworth Longfellow's famous poem tells. According to Fischer, Paul Revere was able to spread the alarm so effectively because he had played a key role earlier in the Boston Tea Party. He was also a member of several clubs in the Boston area, including the London

Enemies List, the North Caucus, and the Long Room Club. He networked socially at two taverns, Cromwell's Head and Bunch of Grapes. The other members of these clubs and people who gathered at taverns were the political leaders who ended up starting the American Revolutionary War in 1775.

It's also worth noting that Fischer's map of the Middlesex alarm is cited by Rogers to illustrate how opinion leaders and diffusion networks work. As Figure 8.3 illustrates, as many as 40 riders carried news of the British expedition throughout Middlesex County—a 750-square-mile area—from 11:00 p.m. on April 18 to 9:30 a.m. on April 19, 1775.

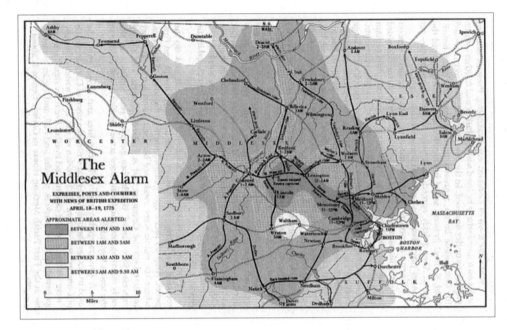

Figure 8.3 The Middlesex Alarm

Notice that the Waltham militia didn't join in the fighting, even though Lexington is next door. What happened?

Although Henry Wadsworth Longfellow made it sound like Revere was the only rider that night, there was another: William Dawes, Jr. Waltham, which was on Dawes's route, never received an effective alarm.

Rogers explained, "Revere knew exactly which doors to pound on during his ride on Brown Beauty that April night. As a result, he awakened key individuals, who then rallied their neighbors to take up arms against the British."

He added, "In comparison, Dawes did not know the territory as well as Revere. As he rode through rural Massachusetts on the night of April 18, he simply knocked on random doors. The occupants in most cases simply turned over and went back to sleep."

Table 8.1 outlines why the midnight ride of William Dawes failed to raise the alarm in Waltham. He didn't know the anti-British opinion leaders.

► **Table 8.1** Similarities and differences of alarm riders

Who	Paul Revere	William Dawes
Says what	"The regulars are out!"	"The regulars are out!"
In which channel	Word of mouth on a fast horse	Word of mouth on a fast horse
To whom	Opinion leaders	Random doors
With what effect	Rallied their neighbors to take up arms	Turned over and went back to sleep

It's also worth noting that neither Revere nor Dawes rode through Acton. On their ride from Lexington to Concord, they met Dr. Samuel Prescott at 1:00 p.m. When the three arrived near Hartwell's tavern in Lincoln, they were attacked by four British officers from a scouting party. Revere and Dawes were taken prisoner, but Prescott succeeded in escaping by jumping his horse over a wall. He was the only one of the three men to reach Concord and warn the town.

Prescott then proceeded farther west to warn Acton. He arrived at the Isaac Davis homestead between 2:00 and 3:00 a.m. to alarm the captain of the Acton Minutemen that "the regulars are out!"

In other words, Revere didn't broadcast his message to every Middlesex village and farm. The message that "the regulars are out" went viral from Revere to Prescott to Davis. And the midnight ride of William Dawes didn't have the same impact because he didn't know the opinion leaders in Waltham and they wouldn't have known him.

In this chapter, I'll show you what Revere did that you should do today, what Dawes did wrong that you shouldn't do, and why help from people like Prescott is unpredictable but not unexpected when you engage the community.

Week 1: Become a Member of the YouTube Community

The first thing you need to do to become a fully vested member of the YouTube community is follow the YouTube Community Guidelines. Here are some common-sense rules that will help you steer clear of trouble:

- Respect copyrights and don't violate YouTube's terms of use. Only upload videos that you made or that you are authorized to use. This means don't upload videos you didn't make and don't use content to which someone else owns the copyright in your videos, such as music tracks, snippets of copyrighted programs, or videos made by other users, without necessary authorizations.

- YouTube isn't for pornography or sexually explicit content. If your video is sexually explicit, even if it's a video of yourself, don't upload it to YouTube.

- Don't post videos showing animal abuse, drug abuse, underage drinking and smoking, or bomb making.

- Graphic or gratuitous violence isn't allowed. If your video shows someone being physically hurt, attacked, or humiliated, don't post it.

- YouTube isn't a shock site. Don't post gross-out videos of accidents, dead bodies, or similar things intended to shock or disgust.

- YouTube encourages free speech and defends everyone's right to express unpopular points of view. But YouTube doesn't permit hate speech.

- Things like predatory behavior, stalking, threats, harassment, intimidation, invading privacy, revealing other people's personal information, and inciting others to commit violent acts are taken very seriously. Anyone caught doing these things may be permanently banned from YouTube.

- Everyone hates spam. Don't create misleading descriptions, tags, titles, or thumbnails in order to increase views. It's not okay to post large amounts of untargeted, unwanted, or repetitive content, including comments and private messages.

Members of the YouTube community can flag a video if they believe it doesn't belong on the site. As Figure 8.4 illustrates, you can learn about flagging by watching a video that YouTube provides. The YouTube staff reviews flagged videos 24 hours a day, seven days a week to determine whether they violate YouTube Community Guidelines. If they do, the staff removes them.

Figure 8.4 "Flagging on YouTube: The Basics"

Monday: Comment on videos

Tuesday: Post video responses

Wednesday: Consider creating contests

Thursday: Create your own online discussion

Friday: Interact with the YouTube team

Monday: Comment on Videos

You can start the process of becoming a fully vested member of the YouTube community by commenting on your favorite videos.

To post a text comment for a video, start typing in the Comment on This Video field or click the Post a Text Comment link below the video player. Then, enter your comment and click the Post Comment button. Keep your comments respectful and relevant so they can be enjoyed by the full YouTube community.

Here are some tips on commenting on videos:

- Decide on the kind of image you want to convey. It's generally a good idea to be nice to people when making text comments to their videos, even if they are die-hard New York Yankees fans like Alec Baldwin and you pledge allegiance to Red Sox Nation as John Krasinski does. Although some of the text comments to the first four videos in New Era's 2011 "Rivalry" campaign (http://www.youtube.com/NewEraCapCompanyInc) include a little smack talk, we all have friends who root for terrible, despicable, how-in-the-hell-can-they-cheer-for-them teams. Just keep in mind that everything you're saying is public and archived.

- Think about whether you're talking to the content creator, the other commenters, or just yourself. If your comment is clearly addressed to the person who made the video ("Nice job on the effect at 1:20! How did you do that?"), then you're more likely to solicit a reply from the content creator, which could lead them to investigate your own channel and become a subscriber.

- Don't spam other people's video or channel comments with your videos. In the words of my technical editor, Brad O'Farrell, "It's lame and ineffective." Rather, you should participate in their discussions in an interesting way, which can encourage people to check out your own channel.

- On your *own* videos, it's nice to reply to as many comments as possible. Not only does it show you care, it will facilitate more discussion (people replying to your replies), which can raise your ranking on the most discussed list.

- Put offsite contact information in your profile. Sometimes discussions in the comments can lead to users clicking through to your profile to figure out how to get in touch with you, which can lead to a continued relationship. A lot of the YouTube community happens outside of YouTube itself. Be prepared to interact with the YouTube community through email, blogs, Facebook, Twitter, the Google+ project and other social media.

For example, if you post a text comment to "New Era Commercial - The Trash Talking Begins" (http://youtu.be/9e57d1q7ZA4) in Figure 8.5, it's much smarter to ask a question like, Is Alec Baldwin a Phillies fan now? There's no need for Boston Red Sox fans to be mean-spirited and scurrilous. That's the job of Gotham's tabloids.

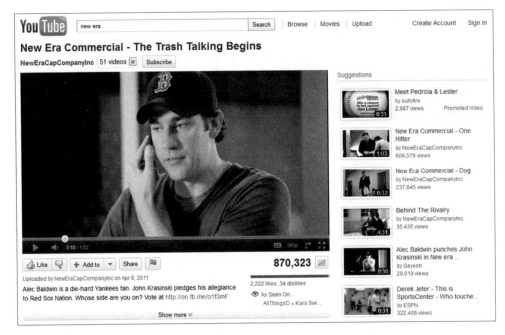

Figure 8.5 "New Era Commercial - The Trash Talking Begins"

Tuesday: Post Video Responses

The next step toward becoming a fully vested member of the YouTube community is to post responses to other videos.

If the owner of a video has allowed video responses, you can post one by clicking the Post A Video Response button, located under the video on its watch page. You will then be given two options for choosing your response video:

Choose a video The drop-down here allows you to respond with any video you've already posted. However, your video can be used as a response only once. If you've used a video as a response in the past and want to use it for a new response, it will no longer be listed as the earlier response.

Upload a video response This works pretty similarly to the normal upload process. Click the Upload A Video button to browse for the video file you'd like to upload. Select the file you want to upload and click **Open**. As the video file is uploading, enter as much information about your video as possible in the relevant fields —including Title, Description, Tags, and Category. You're not required to provide specific information, but the more information you include, the easier it is for users to find your video. Then click the **Save Changes** button to save the updates you've made to the video file.

Although text comments should be respectful and relevant, video responses can also be funny or interesting. Let me give you an example.

On August 30, 2007, Bryan Levi, a 21-year-old film and video student at Penn State who goes by the handle Levinator25 on YouTube, posted "Tiger Woods PGA Tour 08 Jesus Shot." As Figure 8.6 illustrates, Levi's Jesus Shot video showed a glitch in the world's #1 selling golf video game from EA Sports.

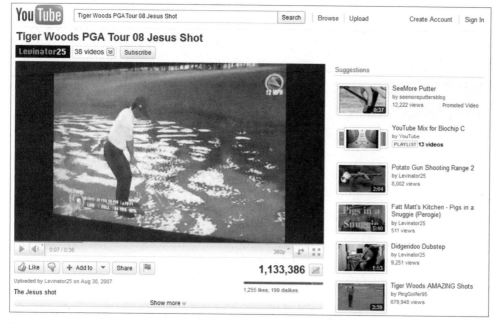

Figure 8.6 "Tiger Woods PGA Tour 08 Jesus Shot"

On August 19, 2008, Tiger Woods and EA Sports posted a video response to "Tiger Woods PGA Tour 08 Jesus Shot." They demonstrated that the "glitch" Levinator25 thought he found in the game was not a glitch at all. As Figure 8.7 illustrates, "It's not a glitch. He's just that good."

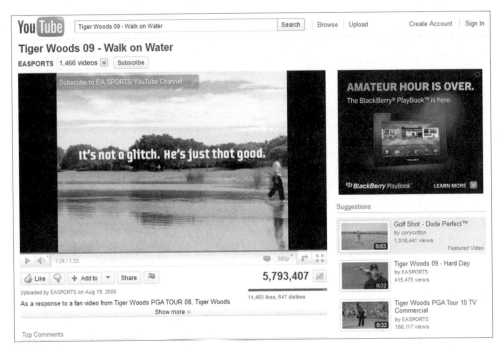

Figure 8.7 "Tiger Woods 09 - Walk on Water"

Both Levi and EA Sports president Peter Moore told David Sarno of the *Los Angeles Times* they thought the whole situation was very funny.

O'Farrell also says using video responses to your own videos is "one of the easiest-to-control ways to get traffic to flow from one video to the next" by creating a prominent link at the bottom of the popular video. For example, "Play him off, keyboard cat" was getting a huge surge in traffic from embedded players as this was written. So he made it a video response to "Jill," a new episode of Wainy Days. From May 15 to May 20, 2009, "Jill" got over 30,000 views.

Wednesday: Consider Creating Contests

Another way to become a fully vested member of the YouTube community is to create a contest. You can create your own, or a paid advertiser can spend $500,000 or more to create a YouTube contest on its brand channel page.

A contest is a competition in which users can submit videos and other users can vote on them. Nonofficial contests can be created by anyone in any number of ways.

If you're thinking of creating your own contest, I'd strongly recommend that you read the YouTube how-to guide "Designing and Running a Contest" at http:// bit.ly/f5gvwH. As this was written, it was more than 10,000 words long—and that's not counting three contest module wireframes.

In other words, contests aren't for the faint of heart. However, using contests is a core method of engaging YouTube community members and encouraging them to interact with your brand.

On April 18, 2007, Heinz spun the bottle and gave consumers a chance to create their own TV commercials celebrating their love affair with the thick, rich taste of America's favorite ketchup. Consumers could submit their 30-second TV commercials to TopThisTV.com, which was powered by YouTube.

How did the YouTube community respond? Members submitted more than 4,000 qualified contest entries, which got 5.2 million online views. This means consumers spent more than 43,000 hours watching submissions and even more time interacting with the brand.

Who was hungry for fame? Andrew Dodson of Wheelersburg, Ohio, won $57,000 and a well-earned place in the 130-year history of a bona fide cultural icon when his winning commercial titled "Heinz: The Kissable Ketchup" aired during *Primetime Emmy Awards* that September.

What was the business outcome? On June 1, 2007, Teresa F. Lindeman of the *Pittsburgh Post-Gazette* wrote an article entitled "Heinz's marketing blitz paying off." She quoted David Moran, president and chief executive officer of Heinz North America, who said, "We've already seen a pickup in the (ketchup) business."

How do we know the pickup was significant? Heinz announced Top This TV Challenge Take Two on December 14, 2007 (Figure 8.8).

Heinz received more than 2,000 qualified video entries for the sequel to its hugely successful Top This contest. The winner was Matt Cozza of Chicago.

Figure 8.8 Hungry For More?

A personal experience served as the inspiration for his entry, "Now We Can Eat," making him the winner of $57,000 and a 30-second spot on national TV.

In Cozza's winning video, a man and woman sit down in a restaurant and realize there's no Heinz ketchup on the table. The pair is dismayed as they look around for an extra bottle. Finally, a server swings by their table, dropping off a bottle of Heinz ketchup and the tagline "Now we can eat" flashes on the screen.

Thursday: Create Your Own Online Discussion

Although technology has changed dramatically since 1775, people's social behavior hasn't. So in the twenty-first century, create your own online discussion in an easy, democratic way, just as Revere did as a member of the London Enemies List, North Caucus, and Long Room Club.

You can do that by using Google Moderator on YouTube. Moderator is a social platform that allows you to ask your audience questions, solicit feedback, or brainstorm ideas on a topic. Then, you can let the community vote the best questions, suggestions, or ideas up to the top in real time.

As Figure 8.9 illustrates, YouTube has used Google Moderator as part of its World View interviews with President Barack Obama, Prime Minister David Cameron, and other world leaders.

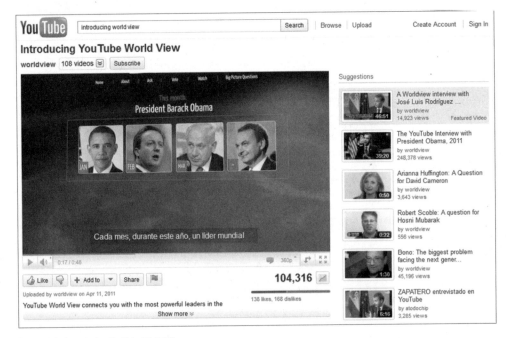

Figure 8.9 Introducing YouTube World View

To use Moderator, start by selecting the topic you want to focus on. Do you want to collect questions for an online interview, ideas for a topic you're thinking about, or feedback on a video you've created? Although any topic is fair game, be sure to clearly define what you're asking for, and be ready to respond to the top-voted submissions that come in. Once you've got a topic for your Moderator series, follow these steps:

1. Go to your channel page and click the Modules tab in the Edit Channel bar.

2. Then, click the check box next to Moderator to enable the Moderator module on your channel and click Save.

3. Next, find the Moderator module on your channel and click the Edit link in the top-right corner.

4. Finally, give your Moderator series a title and description. You can upload a YouTube video to help your audience understand exactly what your particular Moderator is about. You can have the video show up on the right side of your Moderator by adding the YouTube URL to the Video field in the admin panel.

After that, watch the submissions as they get voted up or down by your audience, and then respond to the top-voted submissions by posting a video on your channel. The platform operates in real time, and you can remove any content that you think is off-topic or your audience flags as inappropriate. You can also embed Moderator on your own website or blog.

Friday: Interact with the YouTube Team

Back in 1775, social networking in places like Cromwell's Head and Bunch of Grapes helped Revere to become a fully vested member of the Sons of Liberty. Today, there are places like the YouTube Blog and TestTube where you can become a fully vested member of the YouTube community.

You can't rub elbows with Samuel Adams, John Hancock, or Dr. Joseph Warren anymore. However, by commenting on the posts in the YouTube Blog, you can interact with the following members of the YouTube team:

•   Kevin Allocca, YouTube Trends Manager

•   Andrew Bangs, Sports Manager

•   Sarah Bardeen, Music Community Manager

•   Tom Bridgwater, Software Engineer

•   Becky Chappell, Product Marketing

•   Alon Chen, Israel Product Marketing Manager

•   Bing Chen, YouTube Creator Initiatives and Product Marketing

•   Bene Cipolla, Editorial Director, Howcast

•   Ivan Cobenk, Editor-in-Chief, Bacon Quarterly

- Jeremy Doig, Director, Google Video Technology
- Jeff Ferguson, YouTube HR
- Steve Grove, YouTube News & Politics
- Christopher Hamilton, Product Marketing Manager
- Tai Hasegawa, Product Marketing Manager
- Margaret Healy, Strategic Partner Manager
- Sam Kvaalen, Software Engineer
- Austin Lau, Partner Program Specialist
- Paul Leo, *Party Builders* Series Producer, Howcast
- Darlene Liebman, *Party Builders* Series Producer, Howcast
- Sara Mormino, Head of YouTube Online Content Partnerships EMEA
- Michael Ortali, YouTube Web Developer
- Tom Pickett, Director of Global Content Operations and YouTube Next
- Ramya Raghavan, News and Politics Manager
- Mark Sabec, Product Marketing Manager
- Ed Sanders, Group Marketing Manager
- Andrew Schulte, Associate Product Marketing Manager
- Joshua Siegel, Product Manager
- Ernesto Soriano III, YouTube Australia
- Supriya Sharma, Product Marketing Manager
- Heather Wall, New Business Development
- Stanley Wang, Software Engineer
- Nate Weinstein, Entertainment Marketing Manager
- Shenaz Zack, Product Manager

Why would you want to interact with these members of the extended YouTube team? Well, some of them play a role in selecting spotlight videos. Although YouTube's members rate videos they like, the YouTube team plucks out some interesting and timely content from the community and partners to showcase on the Categories page. Spotlight videos are not advertisements and are not based on any commercial relationship.

However, the more important question is why would these members of the YouTube team want to interact with you? Who wants to engage in a conversation with "nattering nabobs of negativism" or "self-seeking sycophants of servility"?

So, instead of becoming a troll or a sockpuppet, I recommend you be yourself and share input and feedback that communicate your experience, talent, and expertise. That's why the YouTube Blog was created in the first place.

Another way to interact with the YouTube team is to participate when YouTube NextUp asks, "Are you the next big thing on YouTube?" or you're invited to "ask Gaga a question!"

For example, Hunter Walk, YouTube's director of product management, posted an item to the YouTube Blog on March 3, 2009, asking members of the YouTube community to "Adopt a Feature." SteveDutzy responded by making a video (http://youtu.be/mMqzqZ80S4Y) that let the rest of the community in on a fun (if perverse) game he plays with Insight (Figure 8.10).

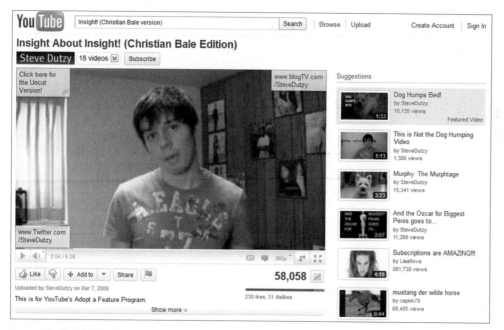

Figure 8.10 "Insight About Insight! (Christian Bale Edition)"

Petercoffin broadcast a video (http://youtu.be/0i51agcWsyY) from space to explain how Insight can contribute to inspiration, monetization, and, um, you'll see (Figure 8.11).

Two weeks later, Walk mentioned—and linked to—both of these videos in the YouTube Community Help Forums. SteveDutzy and Petercoffin gave the Insight feature some TLC by making videos explaining how it works. And their mixture of straightforward instruction and comedy is "something that never looks bad on your permanent record," as Greg Marmalard said in *Animal House* (1978).

If you are able to interact with the YouTube team on a technical level, then go to TestTube, their ideas incubator. That is where YouTube engineers and developers test out recipes and concoctions that aren't quite fully baked and invite you to tell them how they're coming along. As this was written, the mixtures they were working on included YouTube Leanback + YouTube Remote Android App, Comment Search, Insights for Audience, Caption Editor, HTML5 Video, YouTube Music Discovery, Feather, and 3D Video Creator.

Figure 8.11 "Insight... IN SPACE!"

O'Farrell adds, "The best way to interact with the YouTube team is to volunteer for anything you can, report any bug you can, send a video to the editors anytime you find something good and unseen. The best way to get in touch with the staff is through the editor@youtube.com email address. They will appreciate the help, and it will put you on their radar. But don't treat the YouTube staff as a means to an end; just try to be genuinely helpful. If you can't do this, it's best to just not bother them."

Week 2: Learn the Secrets of YouTube Success

Just as Revere networked socially at two taverns, Cromwell's Head and Bunch of Grapes, you can network socially at the YouTube Blog at http://youtube-global .blogspot.com/ and YouTube's official YouTube channel at www.youtube.com/YouTube.

But instead of befriending political revolutionaries, like Samuel Adams, John Hancock, and Dr. Joseph Warren, you can befriend YouTube revolutionaries, like Michael Buckley, Chris Pirillo, and Zack Scott. And instead of learning the secrets of the Boston Tea Party and getting tips for alarm riders, you can learn the secrets of YouTube success and get tips for partners.

The times have changed—and so has the technology. But 236 years later, social networking still involves opinion leaders and their followers. That's why it's worth listening to five of the opinion leaders on YouTube and following their video marketing advice. Then, we'll be ready to carry their messages to our communities.

So this is what we'll do this week:

Monday: Watch Michael Buckley of *What the Buck?!*

Tuesday: Follow Betty of Betty's Kitchen

Wednesday: Review Zack Scott of Zack Scott's channel

Thursday: Listen to Linus of Linus Tech Tips

Friday: Catch Chris Pirillo of Lockergnome

Monday: Watch Michael Buckley of *What the Buck?!*

In May 2009, Curtis Lee, product marketing manager on the YouTube team, asked readers of the YouTube Blog if they wanted Michael Buckley, writer, producer, and star of entertainment news show *What the Buck?!*, to share the secrets of his success.

More than 100 readers submitted 84 questions and cast 1,623 votes to determine the top 10 queries :

1. How did you get noticed on YouTube?
2. Best day/time to upload?
3. What would you advise against?
4. Keywords/tags?
5. How to build an audience?
6. Best tags?
7. YouTube partnership?
8. Equipment to make videos?
9. Top tips for YouTube?
10. Insight?

In June 2009, Buckley explained how he managed to make a six-figure salary through YouTube. You can find "Michael Buckley's Secrets to YouTube Success" (Figure 8.12) on YouTube's official YouTube channel or at http://youtu.be/YZsMgrxGaMA.

Although the video is 26 minutes and 42 seconds long, you will want to watch the whole thing. For example, Buckley's answer to question 9 includes his top 10 tips:

1. Be patient building an audience—it takes time.
2. Engage with other users.
3. Don't try to please the masses.
4. Have mentors and role models.
5. Be kind and respectful.
6. Don't call people "fans."

7. Remember: It's just a video-sharing website—keep things in perspective.

8. Do not let praise go to your head or mean comments go to your heart.

9. Don't be afraid to change your format.

10. Have fun!

Figure 8.12 "Michael Buckley's Secrets to YouTube Success"

Tuesday: Follow Betty of Betty's Kitchen

In September 2010, Julie Kikla and Mahin Ibrahim, account managers, YouTube partnerships, announced a series of posts on the YouTube Blog on how to increase discoverability and viewership for all YouTubers and increase revenue for partners.

The first segment of this educational series was posted on September 23, 2010, and featured a video of Betty of Betty's Kitchen (http://youtu.be/ZElz5HlnsmM).

Betty joined the partner program in 2009 and makes cooking videos with simple recipes ranging from cheddar jack whipped potatoes to healthy and natural granola bars, which all have one thing in common: They're incredibly delicious.

As Figure 8.13 illustrates, Betty told the YouTube community how she used metadata to increase her discoverability, chose her tags wisely, and came up with the perfect title.

Figure 8.13 "Using Metadata in YouTube Videos"

Betty's advice reinforces recommendations that we covered in Chapter 7: The first and most important step to increasing awareness of your videos is metadata.

YouTube is the world's second largest search engine with 22.6 billion searches worldwide conducted on the site in June 2011, according to comScore qSearch. But, you need to help people find your videos or they'll get lost in the mix. YouTube's algorithms are good, but they can't watch your videos. They can only read your metadata. So in order to properly classify your video and index it for search, YouTube needs your help.

Here's what this means:

- Optimize your titles, tags, and descriptions, which are all categorized as metadata by YouTube. This will help your discoverability and, if you're a partner, increase your ad revenue. As mentioned in Chapter 7, descriptions can include up to 5,000 characters and tags can be 120 characters. Push both of these limits for each of your videos.

- Include more words in your description, which increases the chances of being discovered by searchers, which means your audience can grow larger, which increases the potential revenue you can earn.

- Update your tags regularly to take advantage of new searches, even if you have a popular video that continues to get views over time. Online search behavior is always changing, so your tags should change along with it. Use YouTube's Keyword Tool to update your tags. It will give you good suggestions for related queries.

- Make sure to upload a transcript, if one is available, and turn on captions. This can help your discoverability since it gives YouTube more data points to index your video.

However, it also means this:

- Don't use spammy tags or thumbnails. YouTube's algorithm will catch you fairly quickly and punish you for using spam. Besides, you want to help users searching for videos find what they are looking for and associate your channel with accurate information.

- Avoid repeating words in your title or description. It won't help you. Instead, use synonyms or related phrases that users might search on to find your video.

Wednesday: Review Zack Scott of Zack Scott's Channel

On October 7, 2010, the "tips for partners" series featured Zack Scott (www.youtube .com/zackscot), who does a great job creating playlists on his channel and also using annotations to call out interesting things in his videos or to ask for subscribers and comments.

Scott joined the partner program in 2008 and his channel features amazing facts, funny cats, giant spiders, and "comedy." He caught YouTube's eye with popular videos such as "Another Giant Garage Spider" (http://youtu.be/crvI1SOPavA) and "Kitten Still Loves Puppy" (http://youtu.be/pTstzR4gwAw).

As Figure 8.14 illustrates, Scott told the YouTube community how he uses playlists to group his wide array of videos and shed some light on his best tips for annotations in "Annotations and Playlists" (http://youtu.be/Zsx52NhrOWY).

If users like one of your videos, they may want to see more, but they might not know where to go or what to do next. So, make it easy for them to watch more of your videos without having to hunt around for them.

In the description of his video, Scott gives the following advice:

- DO use annotations to encourage your viewers to take actions such as commenting, rating, or subscribing.

- DO use annotations to provide your viewers options as to what to watch or do as your video comes to an end.

- DO NOT use annotations to trick or spam your viewers.

- DO NOT overuse annotations.

- DO use playlists to organize your videos by similar content.

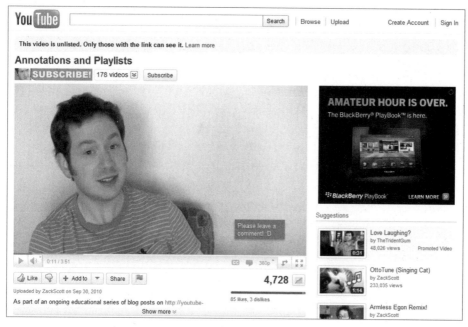

Figure 8.14 "Annotations and Playlists"

Although we covered annotations in Chapter 3, here are some additional tips on how to use annotations and playlists to direct viewers to your other videos:

- At the end of your video, you can instruct the viewer to click the Videos button next to the Subscribe button and check out your other videos. If they click it, it'll activate an auto-play feature that will automatically play all of your videos in succession. If your videos are engaging, the viewer might watch more than one or two.

- You can use annotations as call-outs to direct viewers to take a specific action. You can use them to link your videos together or to create a menu that enables users to watch more of your videos without having to move to another tab.

- Annotations let you interact with your viewers on another level. You can tell viewers what to watch next, let them "choose their own ending," ask them to subscribe, or encourage them to post a comment at the end of your video.

However, there are also some things to avoid:

- Although annotations are a great way to link your videos and create a call to action, don't go crazy. You can add as many annotations as you like, but a good rule of thumb is to limit yourself to three to five annotations per video.

- And avoid being spammy. For example, if a user expects to be taken to a related video, then don't take them to an unrelated video. Don't bait and switch your viewers.

Thursday: Listen to Linus of Linus Tech Tips

On October 14, 2010, the "tips for partners" series featured Linus of Linus Tech Tips (www.youtube.com/linustechtips). He told the YouTube community how he found his niche—unboxing tech products—and how he had used YouTube Insight to track the online viewership trends of his videos.

In their post, Kikla and Ibrahim said, "It took some time and multiple attempts before Linus found his niche as a 'Professional Unboxer.' When Linus started his channel, he began to use YouTube Insight to figure out which of his videos were the most popular. He realized he'd found his specialty when he got thousands of views on his unboxing of the Radeon 5770 Direct X11 video card, which to this day remains one of his most viewed videos."

In 2009, Linus joined the partner program. He has specialized in unboxing and reviewing products. His most viewed video is "Rampage III Extreme 24GB RAM Core i7 980X SUCCESS!! Linus Tech Tips" (http://youtu.be/_CIsUdwEOwQ). He also sells "awesome swag," including a line of T-shirts for unboxing enthusiasts.

As Figure 8.15 illustrates, Linus shared some great tips on using YouTube Insight in a video entitled, "YouTube Partner Blog Video Using Insight to Optimize Your Channel Linus Tech Tips," which you can find at http://youtu.be/M-R1SVU4L1o.

Figure 8.15 "YouTube Partner Blog Video Using Insight to Optimized Your Channel Linus Tech Tips"

It's important to find a niche with your videos. To accomplish this, it's equally important to analyze the data in YouTube Insight to determine how viewers are finding your content. We'll cover that in Chapter 9.

When you first start out, experiment with different approaches and topics until you find one that connects with your viewers. It could be vlogging, beauty tutorials, a character sketch, or wherever your passion takes you. YouTube gets over 3 billion views a day, so tap into the world's largest focus group.

Once you find your niche, pay attention to YouTube Insight. It will give you actionable data to tweak your videos and keep your audience coming back.

Here are some suggestions:

- Review the Views & Popularity charts to check out your most viewed videos and how you stack up to other videos. Or, if you have a brand channel, use Google Analytics to understand who watches your videos. The better you understand your audience and what it likes, the better you'll be able to produce new content, engage your audience, and build your brand.

- Find out how people are discovering your content. Is it through YouTube search or related videos? Is it from embedded players on blogs or an external website? To find out, click Discovery, and under Links Followed To This Video, you'll see your top referrals. You can also click YouTube Search to find keywords that viewers queried to find to your video, and then you can add these as tags to your video to increase your ranking in the search results.

- Use Hot Spots to see if your video is hot or not. If you see a full red thermometer in the top red corner of your Hot Spot report, you're above average. If your video hovers on or below the Average line on the graph, then you aren't holding your viewers' attention. To keep your audience engaged, consider adding annotations at the spots where viewers are leaving.

- It's important to keep a video upload schedule, and I encourage you to upload videos consistently. Many successful partners have used this technique to maintain a weekly schedule that their subscribers will remember.

We'll cover YouTube Insight in more detail in the next chapter, but it's worth noting that it is one of the secrets of YouTube success.

Friday: Catch Chris Pirillo of Locker Gnome

On October 21, 2010, the YouTube Blog's "tips for partners" series wrapped up with advice from Chris Pirillo, the founder of Locker Gnome (http://www.youtube.com/lockergnome). Pirillo revealed how he'd created a hit channel, increased subscriptions, and interacted with his audience using social media.

Pirillo, who joined the partner program in 2007, maintains a network of blogs, web forums, mailing lists, and online communities. A "technology enthusiast and self-proclaimed geek," he streams video of his office live and has a large community of dedicated supporters that watch his frequently recorded videos on various tech-based and non-tech-based topics. And on occasion, he also will give viewers some Halloween pet costume ideas.

As Figure 8.16 illustrates, Pirillo shared some great tips on how to build your brand and audience in a video entitled, "YouTube Tips," which you can find at http://youtu.be/418Zkr5T1wQ.

Figure 8.16 "YouTube Tips"

In the description of his video, Pirillo gave the following recommendations:

- Don't let people go without letting them know where you are!
- Lead with a link in your video description!
- Bring people elsewhere!
- Embed your videos elsewhere!
- Support your most prolific supporters!

Now, it might help to think of YouTube as your big, extended family or lots of friends who share common interests and want to help you be successful. So help them help you. Use Facebook, Twitter, Google +1, and other social media to engage your audience, tell them about your different YouTube channels and social media outlets, and let them know how to contact you.

In addition to using YouTube Insight to see what specific sites are your top referrals, you can use a tool like Yahoo! Site Explorer (`http://siteexplorer.search.yahoo.com/`) to see the inlinks to your channel from all the web pages indexed by Yahoo! Search.

You can customize your interaction with your audience based on your top referrals. If your top referrals are Facebook or Twitter, then make sure to let your audience know via those mediums when your next video is live. If your top referrals are from YouTube subscribers, then post a bulletin to your subscribers letting them know you'd love for them to share your video with one new person.

Here are some more recommendations:

- Use AutoShare to automatically share your YouTube activity feed to Facebook, Twitter, and Google Reader.

- Reach out to relevant and influential bloggers. A huge amount of view counts come from embedded playbacks, so ask opinion leaders to embed your videos.

- Ask viewers to become subscribers. Ask them on your channel, in your videos, or through annotations. And then ask subscribers to share your videos on their blogs and social media.

- Ask for feedback—but you need to have a thick skin. Make a video asking your viewers what they liked or didn't like so far or what types of videos they'd like to see from you in the future.

- Look at your comments, see what your viewers are saying, and respond when appropriate. Using Insight, you can also see the words most commonly used in the comments on your videos.

- Use Promoted Videos to get more views of your videos and drive traffic with call-to-action overlays.

- Add a YouTube button to your website so your visitors are aware of your channel and can easily access it.

- Network with other YouTubers and collaborate with them to create something amazing. Two minds are really better than one.

We'll cover how to engage with your audience in more detail next week.

Week 3: Build Buzz Beyond YouTube

This week, you'll find out why you should build buzz beyond YouTube.

The reasons are as straightforward as the routes of the British Expedition and the Patriot Messengers on April 18 and 19, 1775. As Figure 8.17 illustrates, these routes were relatively straightforward, at least for colonial New England.

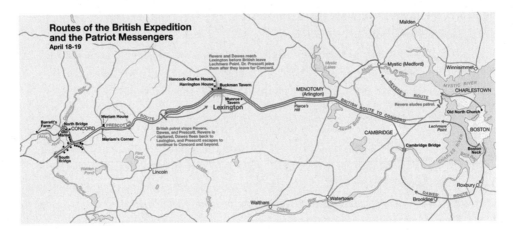

Figure 8.17 Routes of the British Expedition and the Patriot Messengers (Source: nps.gov)

You should add YouTube to your site and share videos because you want to be more like Revere and less like Dawes. In his book *The Tipping Point: How Little Things Can Make a Big Difference* (Back Bay Books, 2002), Malcolm Gladwell compares the two alarm riders.

Revere was able to galvanize the colonial minutemen so effectively in part because he was what Gladwell calls a "Connector." Revere was "the man with the biggest Rolodex in colonial Boston." He knew just about everybody, particularly the revolutionary leaders in each of the towns that he rode through.

In contrast, Gladwell calls Dawes an "ordinary man." He wasn't a "maven" who gathered extensive information about the British, he didn't know what was going on, and he didn't know exactly whom to tell.

This analogy also explains why you need to network socially beyond the larger community like Boston (or YouTube) and into the smaller villages like Waltham (or Vimeo). If you're ever called upon to knock on doors (or promote videos) in the middle of the night (or on short notice), you want to rally your neighbors (or potential viewers) to take action; you don't want them to simply turn over and go back to sleep.

So, you should embed your YouTube videos or channels on your websites or blogs. You should also use AutoShare to automatically share your YouTube activity feed to Facebook, Twitter, and Google Reader.

Aspiring videographers can use TubeMogul OneLoad or Media RSS (MRSS) to syndicate or distribute their videos to other video and social networking sites. News publishers can share their videos on Google News.

Finally, you should send links to bloggers who may want to embed your videos in their blogs. All of these activities can build buzz beyond YouTube and significantly increase the chances of viewers discovering your videos.

So here's what you learn to do this week:

Monday: Embed YouTube videos or channels

Tuesday: Share your YouTube updates through AutoShare

Wednesday: Distribute videos to top video and social networking sites

Thursday: Share news videos on Google News

Friday: Send links to video bloggers

Monday: Embed YouTube Videos or Channels

You can add YouTube videos to other web pages and blogs by embedding the video.
Follow these steps to embed a video into another website or blog:

1. Copy the code in the field marked Embed located to the right of the video.

2. Paste the code in the provided field of the website in which you'd like to embed
the video. The video will then appear on that page.

You may also customize your own embeddable player by clicking the embed
code. When you do this, the space below the embed code will expand and reveal your
customization options. You can choose the following for your embedded player:

- The color and size.

- Whether or not to include related videos.

- Whether or not to display the player border.

SonoSite, a specialist in bedside and point-of-care ultrasound, started embedding videos from its YouTube channel on the company's website in January 2011
(Figure 8.18). This increased the total upload views on www.youtube.com/sonosite from
an average of 2,619 a month to an average of 21,591 a month.

You can also embed YouTube channels on external websites that you own. Each
YouTube channel has an embedding code listed on the channel page. To embed the
channel onto your website, just copy the embedding code from the channel and then
paste it onto your website.

Visitors to your web page are able to view the channel that you embedded and
play the channel's videos without leaving your website. The embedded channel also
allows your site's viewers to navigate to the actual YouTube channel or subscribe to the
channel directly from your site.

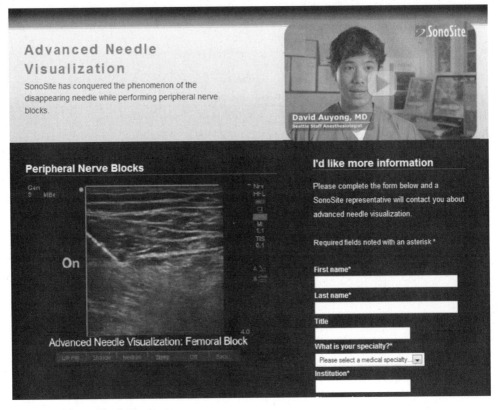

Figure 8.18 Advanced Needle Visualization

Tuesday: Share Your YouTube Updates through AutoShare

In 2009, YouTube introduced AutoShare, which allows you to automatically share your YouTube activity feed to Facebook, Twitter, and Google Reader. When you opt into AutoShare, it will send an update to your friends on Facebook, a tweet on Twitter, and notification in Google Reader when you perform certain actions.

For example, if you'd like share your YouTube uploads to Facebook, then just follow these steps:

1. Sign into your account.

2. Click the Account link located in the top-right corner of your screen.

3. Click the Sharing option located in the left navigation column.

4. Next, select AutoShare Options, which shows you the sites to which you can autoshare your YouTube activity. Your options include Facebook, Twitter, and Google Reader.

5. Click the Facebook option. You'll see a window asking you to connect with Facebook. It will ask you to enter your Facebook account info, then click the

Connect button. Once you enter the requested information, your YouTube account will be connected to your Facebook account.

6. Click the Save Changes button. You've now successfully set up AutoShare and will be able to let your Facebook friends know about your recent YouTube activity.

It takes about 1 minute and 35 seconds to get started and activate AutoShare for Twitter. Just go to http://youtu.be/_nGsF0YR7NU and watch the helpful video by DvdOwens in Figure 8.19.

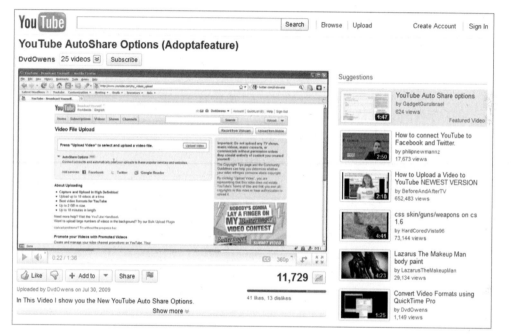

Figure 8.19 YouTube AutoShare Options (Adoptafeature)

Once you've set up AutoShare, your YouTube activity feed will be shared with Facebook, Twitter, and/or Google Reader. However, uploads will be posted to the sites that you've selected after the videos have finished processing. This might take a little time.

And you'll need to have a linked Google-YouTube account to use AutoShare. If you have a Gmail account, you already have a Google account. If you don't have a Gmail account, then conduct a search for the phrase "linking my YouTube account to a Google Account". A Google support page with a 64-character URL (http://www.google.com/support/youtube/bin/answer.py?answer=69964) should rank #1 in the results.

It's also worth noting that AutoShare is connected to your activity feed, which is connected to the Recent Activity box. This underscores why you should display the Recent Activity module on your channel page.

Wednesday: Distribute Videos to Top Video and Social Networking Sites

Even though YouTube accounts for more than six out of seven US visits to online video sites, it's still worth distributing your videos to other top video and social networking sites.

There are two ways to do this: Use TubeMogul OneLoad, a video distribution service, or use Media RSS, an RSS extension used for syndicating multimedia files in RSS feeds.

TubeMogul supports distribution to more than two dozen different video hosting sites. As Table 8.1 shows, OneLoad partner sites include iTunes, Dailymotion, and Metacafe.

▶ **Table 8.1** OneLoad partner sites

Site	Distribution	Analytics	Inplay Analytics
"Any Site" via Destinations	Yes	Yes	Yes
Dailymotion	Yes	Yes	Yes
Facebook	Yes	No	No
Flickr	Yes	No	No
iTunes	Yes	No	No
Linkedin	Yes	No	No
Metacafe	Yes	Yes	Yes
Myspace	Yes	Yes	No
Photobucket	Yes	No	No
Twitter	Yes	No	No
Veoh	Yes	Yes	No
Vimeo Plus	Yes	Yes	No
YouTube	Yes	Yes	No

Source: www.tubemogul.com/solutions/oneload/sites

TubeMogul offers four different tiers for its OneLoad video distribution service. For example, its Business tier provides users with commercial content of up to 200 video deployments per month.

One video distributed to five sites counts as 5 video deployments, so 20 videos distributed to 10 sites counts as 200 video deployments. The Business tier costs $50 per month with a one-year commitment or $100 per month without a one-year commitment.

OneLoad distribution is accompanied by TubeMogul's powerful analytics showing you who, what, and where videos are being viewed. We'll take a closer look at TubeMogul's InPlay analytics in Chapter 9.

The second way to distribute your videos is to Media RSS (aka MRSS). This is how a video content collection site can work with Bing to get its content indexed

Fundamentally, MRSS is a data feed not unlike normal RSS feeds. However, MRSS offers custom tags associated specifically with media content metadata, and that extra information about each item of content can make a big difference in the way content is ranked in the Bing index.

Getting more specific information about video content enables Bing to have greater confidence in associating its relevance to the keywords you use in your descriptions, and thus it can improve your content's rank in queries using those keywords. And by using MRSS to submit your video content to Bing, you get a higher assurance that your content collection may be added to the Bing index more thoroughly and more quickly.

It's worth noting, however, that video content does not get preferential ranking because it came from an MRSS feed. It's the keyword relevance derived from the metadata you supply in the MRSS feed that makes the difference.

As this was written, Bing does not automatically pick up your MRSS feeds. You need to contact the Bing MRSS support team at `bingfeed@microsoft.com` to request consideration of your content feed.

Thursday: Share News Videos on Google News

If you are a news publisher, then you should know that Google News and YouTube have teamed up to help you build a bigger audience for your video content.

In June 2009, Olivia Ma, YouTube news manager, invited any professional news outlet that was already one of the more than 25,000 sources in Google News to also become an official YouTube partner. This makes it easier to share news videos on both YouTube and Google News.

If you are not already included in Google News, search for the phrase "suggest news content for Google News" to find the long, complex URL where you can submit your site for review.

Here are some of the benefits for news publishers who join the YouTube Partner Program:

Featured placement YouTube news partners receive featured placement of their videos on the YouTube news page, `www.youtube.com/news`. In addition, if you allow your videos to be embedded, they'll appear on Google News, which means additional exposure.

Lower costs and greater revenue YouTube offers free hosting for all of your video content and allows you to embed your videos anywhere on the Web for free. And as a YouTube partner, you're also eligible to participate in the site's revenue-sharing program for advertising.

Viewership analysis You can learn more about the people viewing and interacting with your videos with YouTube's Insight tool. The demographic and geographic information it provides can also help you focus your marketing efforts.

Wider audience YouTube and Google News have millions of visitors searching for the latest news and information every day. You can raise awareness of your brand and reach new audiences by making your video content available on these sites. As a YouTube partner, you can maintain your brand's look and feel with your own customized YouTube channel, and you can also drive traffic back to your own website.

Community At its core, YouTube is a social environment that includes thousands of micro-communities. You can build one around your content by encouraging people to interact through comments and video responses. You can take advantage of YouTube as a social platform.

Apply to the YouTube Partner Program, if you haven't already. Don't forget to include the website of your news organization in the Company Web Site field on your application form—this is a critical step to getting your application approved. If you don't already have a YouTube account, make sure to use an email address with the same domain as your website when you register.

Once your application has been reviewed, you'll receive an email confirming whether you have been included in the YouTube Partner Program. If you're included, you'll have the option of participating in revenue sharing and customizing your brand channel.

The Google News team will do a separate review and follow-up about including your videos in Google News. And this process can take months.

For a detailed explanation of how to submit your video content to Google News, search for the phrase "submitting video and other multimedia content." The Google News (Publisher) Help article at www.google.com/support/news_pub/bin/answer .py?answer=93985 should rank #1 in the results.

Friday: Send Links to Video Bloggers

According to Technorati's 2010 edition of *State of the Blogosphere*, 90 percent of bloggers are using some form of multimedia on their blogs. Although photos are the most popular form of multimedia, half of the bloggers surveyed said they use video on their blog.

This means a public relations specialist, social media expert, community manager, or you should reach out to bloggers who might want to embed your videos in their blogs.

Whoever handles this key assignment should use blogger outreach best practices. Here are the most important ones:

- Reach out to bloggers because you have some "remarkable" video content that might be of interest to them and you respect their influence.

- Spend time reading the blogs that you plan to contact and don't pretend to have read a blog if you haven't.

- Before you email bloggers, check out their About and Contact pages to see if they prefer to be reached a specific way, and adhere to those requests.

- In your outreach email, explain why you think they might be interested in your video content.

- Always be transparent and clearly disclose who you are and for whom you work. Explain how blogger outreach and their blog in particular fits into your campaign strategy.

- Try to give bloggers a range of opportunities to work together around a campaign so they can create the best experience possible for their audience. When it comes to knowing their audience, remember they're the experts.

- Bloggers are free to write about a video or information you give them in any way they see fit. (Yes, they can even say they hate it.)

- Understand that when a blogger agrees to write about a video, it may not happen overnight. They usually have their own scheduling of blog posts to deal with and might take a "I'll post it when I post it" attitude toward you. If you bug them too much, they may not post it at all!

- If bloggers are initially interested in your video but don't respond to one of your follow-up emails, don't follow up a second time. Leave them alone.

- If you reach out to bloggers with a video, don't offer to provide monetary compensation because many believe that it's unethical to "buy" favorable publicity and you don't want to appear as if you use illicit practices.

- If bloggers have advertising opportunities on their blogs, then you can consider purchasing ads as a way to reach their readers. Understand, however, that paying for advertising doesn't mean that they'll post something about your video or, if they do, that they'll say something favorable.

- Don't be afraid to contact as many of blogs as possible. If you have the time and resources to do so, you might as well; other bloggers won't see it as a slight unless you promised exclusivity. The more places your video gets posted, the better its odds of being filtered up to the mainstream.

If blogger outreach has high risks, it also has high rewards. According to Compete, HuffingtonPost.com got more than 21.2 million unique visitors in June 2011. And in many industries, blogs are the new trade press.

So, when building buzz beyond YouTube, make sure you include reaching out to influential bloggers.

Week 4: Watch Online Video Case Studies

Finally, you can discover how to engage the YouTube community by watching online video case studies.

Although YouTube's slogan, "Broadcast Yourself," makes it sound like a television network, YouTube calls itself "the largest worldwide video-sharing community."

The mass media model sees an audience as a large number of isolated individuals. The social media model sees "community" as a communication network of interconnected individuals who are linked by patterned flows of information. Although there are unplanned aspects of the communication process in both models, the key to understanding how communication flows through these interpersonal networks, according to Rogers, is analyzing "who relays messages to whom."

Perhaps the best example of this can be seen when Revere and Dawes relayed their message to Prescott at 1:00 a.m. on April 19, 1775.

Dr. Warren in Boston had dispatched Revere and Dawes as alarm riders to warn Hancock and Adams in Lexington that the British army was coming to arrest them and then march on Concord to seize the patriots' store of arms.

But Prescott was on the road at that hour after an evening with his fiancée, Lydia Mulliken. He joined Revere and Dawes on their ride from Lexington to Concord. And the key is that Prescott joined them as an unplanned alarm rider.

When the three had arrived near Hartwell's tavern in the lower bounds of Lincoln, they were attacked by four British officers of a scouting party. Revere and Dawes were taken prisoner. The reins of his horse's bridle cut, but Prescott succeeded in making his escape by jumping his horse over a wall. Taking a circuitous route through Lincoln, he pushed on with the utmost speed to Concord. He was the only one of the three men to reach Concord and warn the town.

Prescott then proceeded further west to warn Acton. Although his midnight ride to this community was unpredictable, it was not unexpected. There is strong circumstantial evidence that he was an express courier for the Sons of Liberty and Committees of Correspondence and that he was an important liaison between the Concord Defense Committee and John Hancock and other leaders of the patriots.

Prescott reached Captain Davis in time to muster the Acton Minutemen, march to Concord, and engage the British army at the "rude bridge that arched the flood" (Figure 8.20). In Acton, Prescott's ride is reenacted on Patriots Day eve.

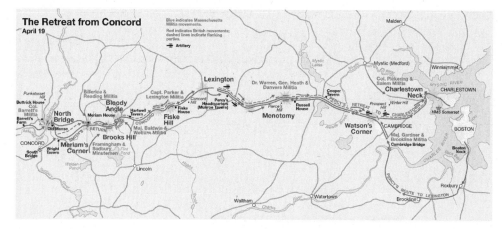

Figure 8.20 The Retreat from Concord (Source: nps.gov)

Monday: See Greg Jarboe of SEO-PR discuss YouTube case study

Tuesday: Observe Michael Fisher of Coldwell Banker talk about successful viral marketing campaigns

Wednesday: Look at Terrence Kelleman of Dynomighty Design share his video marketing case study

Thursday: Check out Jordan Blum of BeautyChoice.com reveal his product placement secrets

Friday: Watch Jeffrey Harmon and Abe Niederhauser of Orabrush tell their YouTube success story

Monday: See Greg Jarboe of SEO-PR Discuss YouTube Case Study

In the first edition of this book, I recommended using email marketing best practices to notify your friends and colleagues—or people you've interacted with—when you have posted new videos specifically of interest to them.

Now, email isn't the latest and greatest social media marketing tool or channel. But it still works. Or at least it can work if you use the best practices described by Seth Godin in his classic book *Permission Marketing: Turning Strangers into Friends and Friends into Customers* (Simon & Schuster, 1999).

To demonstrate how effective email can be, I shared the backstory of one of the most viewed videos on SESConferenceExpo's channel. It's entitled "Matt Cutts, Google, discusses mobile search at SES San Jose 2008." It was uploaded on November 18, 2008, and has more than 4,500 views as this was written.

But the views of the video spiked on December 3, 2008 – more than two weeks after it was uploaded. And the sources of almost 75 percent of the total views came from the embedded player. And close to 49 percent came from just one blog—

Matt Cutts: Gadgets, Google, and SEO. As Figure 8.21 illustrates, that's our video embedded in a post on his blog.

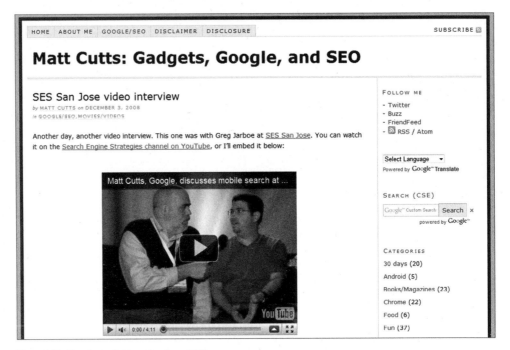

Figure 8.21 Matt Cutts: Gadgets, Google, and SEO

In his post, Cutts writes, "Another day, another video interview. This one was with Greg Jarboe at SES San Jose. You can watch it on the Search Engine Strategies channel on YouTube, or I'll embed it below."

I also shared this YouTube case study at SES London 2009 during a session entitled "Online Video Update—The Next Wave." Afterward, Liana "Li" Evans, who is now the cofounder and CEO of LiBeck Integrated Marketing, asked me to tell the story behind the story.

As Figure 8.22 illustrates, the video interview is entitled "Greg Jarboe of SEO-PR discusses YouTube case study at SES London 2009" (http://youtu.be/iiBkobaP2w8). It was uploaded on February 24, 2009, and is only a minute and 34 seconds long.

The video case study is that short because there wasn't that much to tell. Around Thanksgiving, we sent Cutts an email saying, "Hey, Matt, your video interview has just been posted."

Figure 8.22 "Greg Jarboe of SEO-PR discusses YouTube case study at SES London 2009"

Tuesday: Observe Michael Fisher of Coldwell Banker Talk about Successful Viral Marketing Campaigns

Less than a week before the first edition of this book was published in August 2009, I had a chat with Michael Fisher, the senior vice president of marketing at Coldwell Banker Real Estate LLC, during the Social Media & Video Strategies Forum held in conjunction with SES San Jose 2009.

We talked about the Coldwell Banker's On Location channel on YouTube (www .youtube.com/coldwellbanker), which offers consumers a new way to search for and interact with real estate information and listings. The channel, shown in Figure 8.23, had been created in May 2009.

On Location was the first branded YouTube channel to use dynamic IP lookup, which automatically serves up local results when visitors first hit the site. To create On Location, Coldwell Banker Real Estate closely collaborated with both YouTube and Google to develop what is arguably one of the most comprehensive and immersive brand channels on YouTube.

Figure 8.23 Coldwell Banker On Location

And I was kicking myself for not mentioning this YouTube channel in the first edition of this book, which I had finished writing in May 2009. It was like visiting Concord in April 1775 and missing a chance to see the Old North Bridge.

Two areas of strategic focus set Coldwell Banker On Location apart from other real estate websites. First, it showcased the power of video to bring real estate more vividly to life—offering behind-the-scenes looks at towns and neighborhoods, smart tips and timely news on real estate topics, and video listings of homes for sale. Second, content posted to On Location had a strong emphasis on local information and insights, so consumers can dig deeper into the areas of the country that interest them most.

Supporting this highly localized perspective was one of the more unique aspects of Coldwell Banker On Location, the ability to search for videos through a special map feature that has been developed specifically for the site. The map "widget" was a prominent feature at the top of the On Location site and the main starting point for consumers searching for a home, a specific area of the country, or more information on a real estate topic.

Visitors to the site were automatically shown video search results from their own area/zip code. Then by clicking the link Browse By Map, consumers could enter the city/state or zip code of their choosing, which pulled up all videos posted to On Location associated with that area. These video results were displayed as icons on the map.

Each search returned a wide range of video results, including video listings, spotlights on that local community, and Coldwell Banker sales associate/representative profiles. Consumers could click through to view specific videos as well as connect back to the main Coldwell Banker website to learn more about a specific property for sale.

I interviewed Fischer after the session at the Social Media & Video Strategies Forum about some of the Coldwell Banker Real Estate agents who add their individual personalities to the YouTube video experience (Figure 8.24).

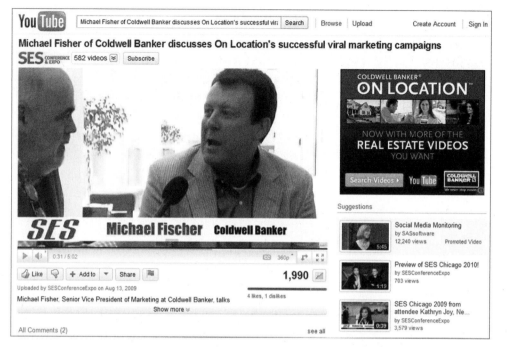

Figure 8.24 "Michael Fisher of Coldwell Banker discusses On Location's successful viral marketing campaigns"

On November 8, 2010, Coldwell Banker On Location surpassed 2 million channel views. A press release on the milestone said the brand's YouTube channel had grown steadily since its launch but had seen its fastest growth between April 2010 and October 2010, when the On Location channel received more than 1 million views.

Significantly, mobile use was up. Since April 2010, the number of people who had viewed the site from a mobile device had doubled. Although property listings make up the majority of the On Location content, Coldwell Banker disclosed that community videos attracted the highest number of comments, with visitors chiming in with input on their hometown or current city.

On April 11, 2011, Coldwell Banker On Location surpassed 2.5 million channel views. In a post on the Coldwell Banker Blue Matter blog, David Marine in marketing said, "A recent infographic put together by Postling, which was featured on Mashable, made us reflect on what we have done and what we are doing in the future when it comes to video."

He added, "The infographic had an impressive statistic when it comes to how real estate customers view the importance of video. The study showed that 73 percent of homeowners are more likely to list with a Realtor offering to do a video, yet only 12 percent of the Realtor population is doing video."

Wednesday: Look at Terrence Kelleman of Dynomighty Design Share His Video Marketing Case Study

On February 2, 2010, Lane Shackleton, product specialist, posted "Advertisers you wouldn't expect to find on YouTube" on the YouTube Biz Blog. Among the marketing minds at small businesses who were using Promoted Videos was Terrence Kelleman, founder of Dynomighty Design.

Kelleman used to work a day job in IT before he decided to try his hand at jewelry making and creating whimsical gift ideas. His first YouTube video, "The Bandoleer by DYNOMIGHTY, Be Mighty! DYNOMIGHTY," demonstrated the uses of a bracelet made entirely out of super-strong magnets. As Figure 8.25 illustrates, it had more than 3.9 million views when this was written.

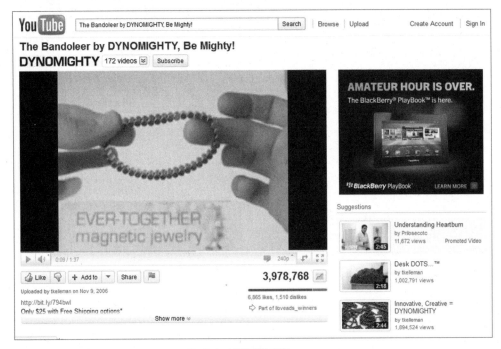

Figure 8.25 "The Bandoleer by DYNOMIGHTY, Be Mighty! DYNOMIGHTY"

After his initial video success, Terrence continued creating videos to showcase his products and engage the YouTube community. Videos are "an easier format to convey your message to people," Kelleman told Shackleton. "It has more of a residual effect."

The videos that Dynomighty has promoted on YouTube have helped the company grow throughout the country and expand its product line to include everything from magnetic bracelets to paper wallets. More than 50 percent of the referring traffic to Dynomighty's website (www.dynomighty.com) comes from YouTube.

At SES New York 2010, Kelleman was one of the speakers on the keynote panel "Video: The Next Digital Marketing Frontier."

As Figure 8.26 illustrates, I interviewed Kelleman after the panel, and you can look at "Dynomighty YouTube video marketing case study" at http://youtu.be/gRzQ1MAhstA.

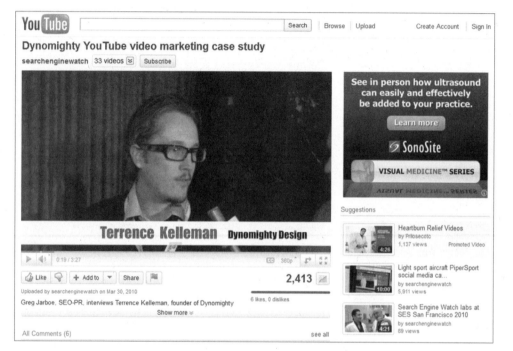

Figure 8.26 "Dynomighty YouTube video marketing case study"

Kelleman said that his first YouTube video not only got millions of views, it also generated $130,000 in sales in three months. The experience literally changed his small business overnight.

Since then, his fun quirky and viral videos have become a major marketing strategy for all new products and have also help shaped the perception of Dynomighty as a creative independent brand.

Thursday: Check Out Jordan Blum of BeautyChoice.com Reveal His Product Placement Secrets

If you haven't heard of BeautyChoice.com, it is a three-year-old Internet pure-play retailer that sells over 11,000 name-brand items for the hair, skin, and body as well as more than 5,000 name-brand fragrances.

As a new company in a highly competitive category, it was difficult for BeautyChoice.com to get Web traffic. The website did not feature the articles, customer reviews, blogs, or professional beauty tips that better financed health and beauty sites offered. The retailer experimented with Google AdWords and banner ads, but these channels did not drive as much traffic as BeautyChoice.com wanted. The retailer knew it needed an innovative way to bring shoppers to its site.

Jordan Blum, the president of BeautyChoice.com, helped build the new company's pioneering LaunchPad marketing platform that seamlessly places products in highly popular beauty- and fashion-related online videos watched by millions of engaged users worldwide. These videos are produced by BeautyStars who are credible and proven influencers. Collectively, their videos have been viewed more than 800 million times and they had over 4 million followers on Twitter, YouTube, and Facebook.

BeautyChoice.com initially considered producing its own videos, with the goal that they would be compelling enough to go viral. But then the retailer discovered a young woman on YouTube who had more than 100,000 views of her makeup tutorial.

The company then found several other people with almost as many views who were just making their beauty tips videos for fun. BeautyChoice.com decided to see whether these amateurs—most of whom were 18 and 19 years old—would be interested in trying some of the products on its site and giving an honest review that could be shared with the retailer's customers.

According to Blum, they were ecstatic. So BeautyChoice began sending them products to review with very few instructions. The young women either got a flat fee, a flat fee plus a commission, or just the product.

In 2009, a BeautyStar named Michelle Phan created a video on how to create a makeup and hair-style look modeled after the pop singer Lady Gaga in her music video "Poker Face." As Figure 8.27 illustrates, Phan's how-to video "Lady GaGa Poker Face Tutorial" (http://youtu.be/YFMaLuI1uxc) had more than 27 million views when this screen shot was taken.

BeautyChoice.com supplied Phan with the wig and some gloves for the video. In the video description, a link went directly to the wig and the pair of gloves at BeautyChoice.com. Although the wig is no longer available, the retailer sold a lot of the gloves just before Halloween in 2009.

In 2010, BeautyChoice.com had about 20 young women on contract who uploaded a number of videos a month. They were asked to insert a link into the comment box on their YouTube video page that goes to the product page at BeautyChoice.com so that consumers can buy the featured product.

BeautyChoice.com reports that around 43 percent of its site traffic comes from YouTube. The conversion rates for no-name product promotions it has run have been as high as 15 percent. By comparison, the highest rate BeautyChoice.com ever achieved with Google AdWords was about 6 percent.

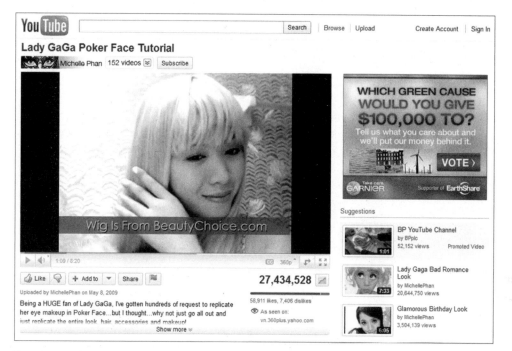

Figure 8.27 "Lady GaGa Poker Face Tutorial"

The products that realize the highest conversion rates are those that show before-and-after results. And while eye cream used by an 18-year-old isn't going to jump off the screen in a before-and-after demonstration, showing someone how to transform pin-straight hair into wavy hair is visually demonstrable.

At the Affiliate Marketing Forum, which was held in conjunction with SES New York 2010, I interviewed Blum, who had spoken at a session entitled "Affiliate Marketing and Social Media."

Shown in Figure 8.28, the video interview "Product placement on steroids with Jordan Blum, Beautychoice.com at SES New York 2010" (`http://youtu.be/jfoGhcPaFpw`) reveals how the company's pioneering LaunchPad marketing platform generated "millions of dollars in transactions in less than a year."

YouTube videos proved to be more cost effective than paid search for driving traffic to BeautyChoice.com. In addition, YouTube videos also produced higher-quality leads. A prospect who had just watched an 8-minute, 20-second-long video showed a higher level of interest in its products.

BeautyChoice.com also recognized that it could jump-start its business by working with YouTube video makers who already had a large following rather than trying to create compelling videos in-house that had no guarantee of going viral.

Figure 8.28 "Product placement on steroids with Jordan Blum, Beautychoice.com at SES New York 2010"

The amateur quality of the beauty tips videos also worked to BeautyChoice. com's advantage. Blum told eMarketer that a "girl next door" with a conventional camcorder showing how she can transform herself in her own bathroom was more believable than a professional model shooting a makeover video with perfect lighting in a state-of-the-art production studio.

Friday: Watch Jeffrey Harmon and Abe Niederhauser of Orabrush Tell Their YouTube Success Story

One of the other small businesses mentioned in the post "Advertisers you wouldn't expect to find on YouTube" was Orabrush, which markets a tongue cleaner that helps cure bad breath.

According to "The Story of Orabrush" on the company's website, Dr. Bob Wagstaff, the 76-year-old inventor of the Orabrush, spent eight years trying to bring Orabrush to market.

Wagstaff had spent over $40,000 on an infomercial, but it only generated about 100 orders. He approached Walmart, Walgreens, CVS, and many other retailers, but no one was interested in stocking his tongue cleaner. He approached Oral-B and Colgate to see if they wanted to buy his patent, but they weren't interested.

As a last-ditch effort, Wagstaff went to the Marriott School of Management at Brigham Young University (BYU) in 2009 and asked a market research class to see if they could come up with new ways to market the product online. A group of students in the class presented their findings and said, "92 percent of the people who would actually like to try Orabrush will not buy Orabrush on the Internet. We suggest you drop the idea of marketing Orabrush on the Internet."

Jeffrey Harmon, a student who was also a member of the class, raised his hand and asked, "That means 8 percent probably will buy Orabrush. That is millions of people. Why don't you focus on them?"

After the class, Wagstaff offered Harmon his old motorcycle—which, at 76, he didn't ride anymore—in return for help in marketing Orabrush online. Harmon was thrilled—he was riding a bicycle at the time—and started working on Orabrush in the mornings and at nights before and after his full-time job.

Harmon recruited Austin Craig, a guy on the team he managed at his full-time job. Craig had just graduated with a degree in broadcast journalism from BYU and was working as an intern. The other members of the team would provoke Craig into little rants about politics or other issues that he was passionate about. While Craig was ranting one day, another coworker leaned over and told Harmon, "I would pay money to watch Austin rant like this. It is the best part of my day."

That's when the idea for a YouTube video was born. Harmon asked Craig, "How much would I have to pay you to be in a video for me where you rant about bad breath?" Craig replied, "A hundred bucks."

Harmon took his idea to his friend, Joel Ackerman, a talented local script writer, and asked if he could do some magic on this YouTube idea. As a favor for a friend, Ackerman quickly whipped out a clever script featuring a rant on "halitophobia."

Wagstaff, Harmon, Craig, and Harmon's old roommate Devin Graham, a film major, shot the first Orabrush movie in a pool club. Wagstaff held the mic while Craig acted, and Harmon did his best to direct his first video ever.

Shown in Figure 8.29, "Bad Breath Test - How to Tell When Your Breath Stinks" (http://youtu.be/nFeb6YBftHE) was a huge success, garnering more than 15 million views as this was written, and bringing Orabrush to the attention of major distributors and retailers.

As Harmon, who is now chief marketing officer at Orabrush, explained on the YouTube Biz Blog, "As an experiment, we decided to create an 'infomercial' for YouTube. We had made a couple of videos that we could see were showing signs of going viral, so we decided to give them a jump-start with Promoted Videos."

Promoted Videos quickly helped Orabrush's fun and quirky videos get off the ground, and they soon saw video views and sales soar. "Promoted Videos has worked better than any other ad platform we have used online," Harmon added.

Of the video's first 7.8 million views on YouTube, 6 million came from Promoted Videos. The Orabrush campaign was also successful in large part because the infomercials were less like ads and more like popular YouTube videos that users searched for and wanted to watch.

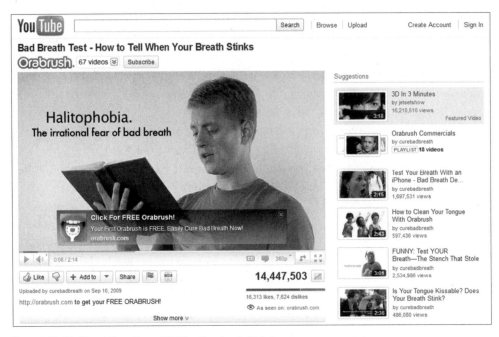

Figure 8.29 "Bad Breath Test - How to Tell When Your Breath Stinks"

At SES San Francisco 2010, Baljeet Singh, senior product manager of YouTube and the Google Content Network, told the Orabrush story during the Video Lab.

On September 26, 2010, Claire Cain Miller of the New York Times, wrote an article entitled, "To Fix Bad Breath, a Gadget Seen on YouTube." It updated the Orabrush story—and provided a powerful punch line: Funny YouTube videos had helped the small business make a million dollars in one year.

When I was asked to moderate the "Social Media Solutions on a Budget" session at SES New York 2011, I asked the organizers to invite Harmon to be one of the panelists.

I interviewed Harmon and Abe Niederhauser, the Marketing Manager at Orabrush, to get the latest update on the Orabrush story (Figure 8.30). In "The Orabrush You-Tube story: How to build your brand using video" (http://youtu.be/L5D8CFtdH2Q), they revealed that curebadbreath's channel, the official YouTube channel of Orabrush (www.youtube.com/orabrush), had more than 35 million views and the company had now sold more than one million tongue cleaners.

Just as there were a lot of riders carrying the news to every Middlesex village and farm on April 18, 1775, there were a lot of opinion leaders who shared "Bad Breath Test - How to Tell When Your Breath Stinks" with their followers.

This includes more than 5,800 members of the YouTube community who posted text comments, over 18,000 who liked the video, and 20 who uploaded video responses. And it includes the Bruce Clay blog, which embedded the video, according to the As Seen On YouTube page.

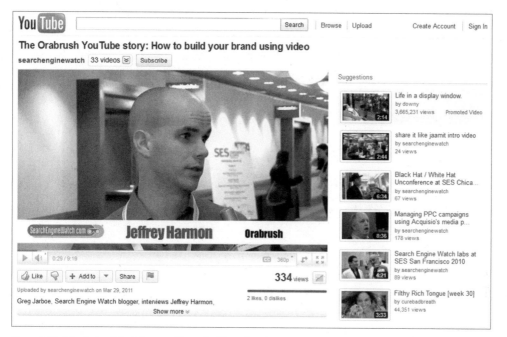

Figure 8.30 "The Orabrush YouTube story: How to build your brand using video"

It includes more than 150,000 subscribers to curebadbreath's channel and over 10,000 YouTubers who posted channel comments.

In addition, there was an outer circle of opinion leaders who told and retold the Orabrush story. This includes reporters at the *New York Times*, MediaPost, Reuters, Boing Boing, Brandchannel, *Advertising Age*, the *Wall Street Journal*, *Deseret News*, KSL-TV5 Salt Lake City, and *Nightline* on ABC News.

So, engaging the YouTube community requires you to build buzz outside of a small circle of friends. The most effective way to do this is to reach the opinion leaders who influence other people's awareness, attitude, and behavior in social networks.

Month 7: Trust but Verify YouTube Insight

Galileo once wrote, "Count what is countable, measure what is measurable. What is not measurable, make measurable." This is still challenging advice 400 years later. In this chapter, we will look at what is countable by YouTube Insight and what is measurable by TubeMogul InPlay, and Google Analytics. We'll also look at other tools that make measurable what is not measurable by these tools. But we will need to continue explaining, "The chart, of course, is nonrepresentational," until currently available metrics get more robust.

Chapter Contents:

The Map Room
Week 1: Trust YouTube Insight
Week 2: Verify with TubeMogul
Week 3: Verify with Google Analytics
Week 4: Master Web Analytics 2.0

The Map Room

Galileo's advice was also controversial back when the prevailing view of the cosmos was geocentric (the earth is the center of the universe), not heliocentric (the sun is the center of the solar system). In fact, Galileo's ability to make measurable Copernicus's heliocentric hypothesis, which was not measurable before telescopic observation, got Galileo in trouble with the Roman Inquisition in 1615.

Another historic figure who understood how difficult it is to make measurable what is not measurable was Winston Churchill. At the beginning of World War II, Churchill was appointed First Lord of the Admiralty and a member of the War Cabinet. He inherited a navy that counted only capital ships and measured only victories over other fleets—pretty much the same as it had since the Battle of Jutland in 1916.

But Churchill understood that victory depended on getting a higher percentage of Allied convoys through German U-boats and surface raiders. So, after becoming prime minister in 1940, he coined the term "Battle of the Atlantic" to get the War Cabinet, Royal Air Force, and Royal Navy to focus more attention on this strategic threat.

Churchill had a large map of the Atlantic Ocean hung on the southern wall in the Map Room down the hall from his War Cabinet Rooms. It was used to plot the position of convoys and the movements of individual warships—and the thousands of pinholes left by markers still mark the principal convoy routes, which can still be seen from the other end of the room today.

The Map Room remained open day and night, and the chief task of the officers manning this room was to collate and summarize all relevant information on the progress of the war and present it on maps, which would be constantly updated. In other words, Churchill required the map keepers to make the Battle of the Atlantic as measurable as possible—even if it was not as easily measurable as the army's position on land.

This, in turn, kept the pressure on the chiefs of staff to develop new weapons, tactics, and countermeasures, which eventually drove the German surface raiders from the ocean by the middle of 1941 and decisively defeated the U-boats in a series of convoy battles between March and May of 1943.

As Churchill wrote afterward, "The only thing that ever frightened me during the war was the U-boat peril.... It did not take the form of flaring battles and glittering achievements, it manifested itself through statistics, diagrams, and curves unknown to the nation, incomprehensible to the public."

Veteran marketers and new YouTubers are fighting similar battles today. Whether your YouTube video has 100 or 500,000 views, you will want to know the answers to these questions: Who is watching the videos in this channel? How popular are my videos relative to those of other uploaders? How are people finding the videos in this channel? How many times have viewers shared, rated, favorited, or commented on this video?

The battles to answer these questions are part of a larger war to develop a successful web analytics strategy. If you want to learn web analytics the right way, I strongly recommend that you read *Web Analytics 2.0: The Art of Online Accountability and Science of Customer Centricity* by Avinash Kaushik (Sybex, 2009). His thought-provoking analysis of the challenges and opportunities facing today's web analytics questions conventional wisdom and debunks popular myths.

If you like Kaushik's book, you'll love his blog, Occam's Razor. He also has a day job: Kaushik is the analytics evangelist for Google. And on the swing shift, he's the cofounder and chief education officer for Market Motive, where I'm also on the faculty. Like Galileo and Churchill, Kaushik is one of my heroes, and I try to apply his thought-provoking recommendations to video marketing.

So, in this chapter, we'll look at what is countable by YouTube Insight, what is measurable by TubeMogul and Google Analytics, and what is not measurable by these tools...yet. As Figure 9.1 illustrates, veteran marketers and new YouTubers need to explain to colleagues and clients, "The chart, of course, is nonrepresentational," until currently available metrics get more robust.

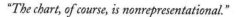

"The chart, of course, is nonrepresentational."

Figure 9.1 "The chart, of course, is nonrepresentational." (Cartoon by Leo Cullum in *The New Yorker*, September 20, 2004.)

Week 1: Trust YouTube Insight

On March 26, 2008, Tracy Chan, product manager at YouTube, posted this item to the Official Google Blog: "I remember the first time a video I posted to YouTube cracked 100 views. I wasn't so much surprised as curious: Who were these people? How did they find this video? Where did they come from?"

Chan then announced YouTube's first step toward answering these questions by introducing YouTube Insight, a free analytics and reporting tool that enables anyone with a YouTube account to view detailed statistics about the audience for the videos that they upload to the site.

For example, uploaders can see how often their videos are viewed in different geographic regions as well as how popular they are relative to all videos in that market over a given period of time. Users, partners, and advertisers can also delve deeper into the life cycle of their videos, like finding out what pages viewers were on before they navigated to a video, how long it takes for a video to become popular, and what happens to video views as popularity peaks.

Insight also gives video creators an inside look into the viewing trends of their audience on YouTube. This information can help video creators increase views and get better ratings. Partners can evaluate metrics to understand and better serve their audiences as well as increase ad revenue. And advertisers can study their metrics and successes to tailor their marketing—both on and off the video sharing site—in order to reach the right viewers. As a result, Insight turns YouTube into one of the world's largest focus groups.

How can this help you? Well, let's say you learn that new videos that play off your previous content become popular more quickly, your videos are most popular on Wednesdays and Thursdays, and you have a huge following in Canada. Using these metrics, there are some things you can do to increase your videos' view counts and improve the popularity of your channel:

- Create compelling new content that appeals to your target audience.
- Post these videos on days these viewers are on the site.
- Post your next video in French as well as English.

Brad O'Farrell, the technical editor of this book, finds that Insight doesn't report much variation from video to video. He says, "Most of the time Insight just tells me that videos are extremely popular in areas that are more populated and that their views spiked up when they were featured. I'm hoping they'll eventually add a weighted Insight feature."

Brad notices that video views dip down near the end of the week, spike up on Sunday, then remain steady until about Thursday at MyDamnChannel's channel (www.youtube.com/MyDamnChannel), which features "original originality by comedians, filmmakers, musicians, and photoshoppers."

I notice that video views dip down near the weekend, spike up on Monday, then remain steady until about Thursday at SESConferenceExpo's channel (www.youtube.com/SESConferenceExpo), which features a global conference and training series focused on search engine optimization and search engine marketing.

So, your mileage may vary, but I agree with Brad that YouTube needs to continue adding features and functionality to Insight. In April 2009, YouTube added a link that allows you to export your Insight data into CSV files. CSV files are open-format files that organize data so it can be moved and analyzed using spreadsheet software such as Microsoft Excel and Google Docs.

As Figure 9.2 illustrates, Chan also uploaded a video in 2008 that provides a basic understanding of the YouTube Insight tool.

Figure 9.2 "YouTube Insight Overview"

Some of the features were made available fairly quickly—like the specific breakdown of how viewers discovered the video. Other features were rolled out over the next three years. Let's take a closer look at some of the more important ones.

Monday: Count your video views

Tuesday: Discover how people find your videos

Wednesday: Take demographic data with a grain of salt

Thursday: Observe your most engaging videos

Friday: Figure out a video's hot spots

Monday: Count Your Video Views

To see YouTube Insight for your own videos, simply sign into your YouTube account, then click My Videos, and click the Insight link to check out this analytics and reporting tool.

As Figure 9.3 illustrates, the default is set to display a summary page that shows how many views your videos were getting in the past two weeks, your top 10 videos for that period, the demographics of the people watching the videos in your channel, and how popular your videos are relative to those of other uploaders.

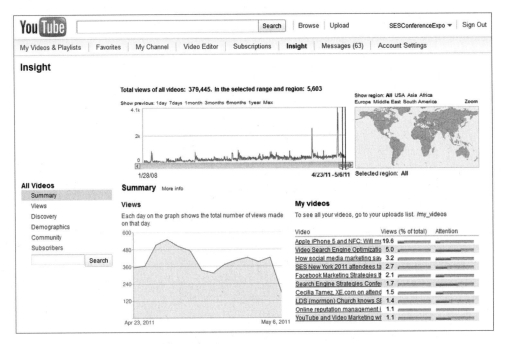

Figure 9.3 The summary page for YouTube Insight

If you click the Views link, you'll see video views charted on an interactive timeline and map, allowing you to drill down into different geographic regions and see the viewing activity in those regions over selected time periods.

The *Views graph* captures the viewing trend of all videos or a specific video in a specific geographic region over a certain period of time. Adjust the slider bar on the top graph to change the date range. You can also click 1 day, 7 days, 1 month, 3 months, 6 months, 1 year, or max to see how viewing for all videos or a particular video has trended over a period of time.

The *Views map* captures the geographic distribution of views for the time period defined by the slider on the graph. Click on a particular country to see how viewing for a particular video has trended over a period of time for that country, or click on the name of a region under Show Region above the top map to view a larger regional map. The graph shows data over time for the geographic region defined by the map. If you change various settings on the graph (e.g., pulling the slider bar to a different time frame), the colors on the map will change to reflect the new time period, selected on the graph. Conversely, if you select a country (e.g., USA) or a new map (e.g., Europe), the graph will update to reflect the viewing trends in that geographic market.

The default graph shows views, which is the number of times viewers watched a video or all of your videos. The aggregate data includes views from YouTube.com, the embedded player, and mobile YouTube applications. If you tick the Show Unique Users box, you will see the number of viewers who watched your video or videos. It's worth noting that unique user metrics are displayed as aggregated data. As with all Insight statistics, no personally identifiable information is collected or shared.

Using the drop-down menu, you can also view a graph that uses a "popularity index" of 0 to 100, which measures how many other videos in the chosen region are getting more or less views than your video. For example, if your video is indexed at 67 on the graph, this means that only 33 percent of all videos have been viewed more than your video in the selected region and time range.

As Figure 9.4 illustrates, the popularity map shows the relative popularity of a particular video within the different states of the United States. The scale is relative, so the states where the video is most popular will be dark green and the one in which it is least popular will be lighter green.

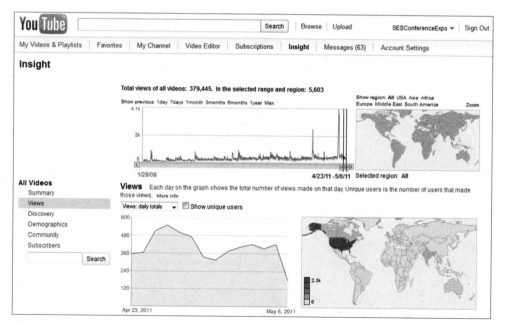

Figure 9.4 Views in YouTube Insight

Tuesday: Discover How People Find Your Videos

The Insight Discovery link shows you how viewers got to your video. There are many ways people find videos: They search for them on YouTube, click "Related videos" thumbnails, or follow links from social networking websites like Twitter or Facebook.

As Figure 9.5 illustrates, the graph at the top of the page shows you how those traffic sources evolve over time, which can help you build an understanding of a typical traffic cycle in a lifetime of a video. The table at the bottom of the page shows you the total number of referrals from each different source.

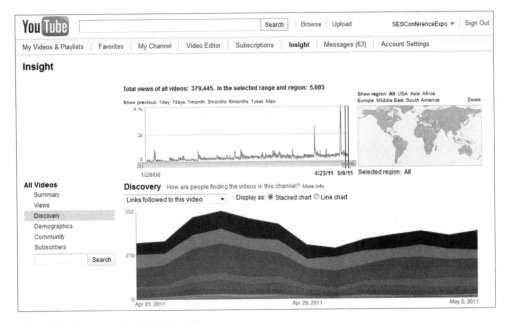

Figure 9.5 The Discovery tab in YouTube Insight

The Discovery drop-down menu allows you to break out your video's traffic information in two different ways:

Links followed to this video Where did people click from to get to your video? Did they follow a link from another website to your video? Or did they come from the "Related videos" thumbnail on another YouTube page? Or did they find your video using YouTube search?

Location of player when viewed On what page or device did people watch your video? Most views occur in the normal context of the YouTube video page, but people can also see your video on your channel page, or on another user's channel page, if it was featured in a playlist there. This view also indicates views that happen on a mobile YouTube application like the one for iPhone or in an embedded player when someone posts your video on their blog.

It's worth noting that every video view is classified into exactly one of the categories in the "Links followed to this video" report and into exactly one of the categories in the "Location of player when viewed" report.

There are more than a dozen categories of "Links followed to this video." Here are some of the most significant ones:

YouTube-related video shows you which related YouTube videos are driving views to your video. You can click each title to see the particular video that sent the views.

YouTube-search shows you where people have clicked through to your video from YouTube search results. In the detailed view, you can see the keywords people used to find your video and the number of click-throughs from each.

No link referrer (embedded player) means someone has embedded your video on their site and people watched it embedded within that page. In the detailed view, you can drill down to see which sites have brought the most embedded views and the number of views from each.

No link referrer (mobile devices) means people are watching your video on mobile phones and tablets.

Google search shows you which terms viewers searched for on Google to find your video.

External website shows you which websites are driving views to your video. In the detailed view, you can drill down to see which websites have brought the most views to your video.

YouTube featured video shows you the number of click-throughs from your thumbnail if your video has been featured by YouTube.

YouTube advertising means views from paid ad campaigns coming from your Promoted Videos or YouTube video ads.

When you look at Discovery reports, focus either on the largest sources of traffic or on new emerging trends rather than small, episodic occurrences of traffic. If you get most of your views from related videos and search but don't get many from embedded players, consider using blogger outreach as many successful YouTube channels do, and use Discovery reports to track effects of that effort.

And when it comes to trends, think of mobile traffic, which is steadily increasing for most video uploaders. On January 12, 2011, the YouTube Blog announced, "YouTube now exceeds 200 million views a day on mobile, a 3x increase in 2010." Consider how you should tailor your content or content promotion based on these findings.

Wednesday: Take Demographic Data with a Grain of Salt

On May 15, 2008, demographics became available in YouTube Insight. In a post to the Official Google Blog, Nick Jakobi, product manager at YouTube, announced the addition of some new features to Insight. One was a new demographics link that displays view count information broken down by age group (such as ages 18 to 24), gender, or a combination of the two to help you get a better understanding of the makeup of your YouTube audience. He added, "We show you general information about your viewers in anonymous and aggregate form, based on the birth date and gender information that users share with us when they create YouTube accounts. This means that individual users can't be personally identified."

In addition, some of the demographic data might represent the gender and age of the individual setting up a YouTube account for an organization instead of all the other people who might also be using it.

Plus, some people lie about their age. You need to be at least 13 years old to have an account; a younger kid might pretend to be older just to become a subscriber of Fred.

I was born September 2, 1949, and have learned that it's not just the young who lie about their age; Jack Benny celebrated his 39th birthday 41 times. So, an older user might pretend to be Benny's age when signing up on YouTube.

Fortunately, *Nielsen Netview* independently confirmed in August 2010 that YouTube's audience in the United States mirrors the demographics of the online population: 48 percent of YouTube visitors are male, 52 percent are female. As for age:

- 16 percent are 2–17
- 11 percent are 18–24
- 18 percent are 25–34
- 28 percent are 35–49
- 18 percent are 50–64
- 9 percent are over the age of 65

As Figure 9.6 illustrates, the default of the Demographics tab is to display age ranges for both genders and genders for all age groups. However, if you click male or female, you will see the age ranges of male or female visitors.

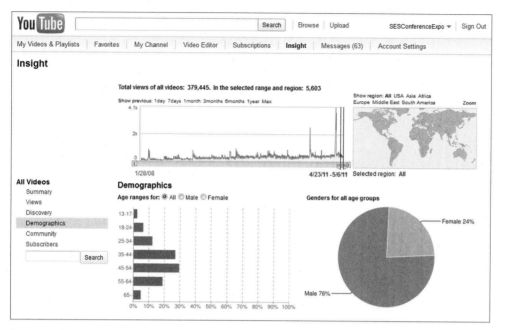

Figure 9.6 The Demographics tab in YouTube Insight

Thursday: Observe Your Most Engaging Videos

The Community report shows you how many times users have engaged with your videos by rating them, commenting on them, or favoriting them. You can see total number of events per day in a given time period and region. You can also see the countries where users have engaged with your content the most.

As Figure 9.7 illustrates, the drop-down menu enables you to see more detailed reports on each type of engagement: ratings, favorites, comments. To see how many people have liked and disliked a given video, choose **Ratings** in the drop-down menu and then the **Likes And Dislikes** option next to the drop-down menu.

Subscriptions are becoming the primary measure of engagement on YouTube. Subscribed viewers are more engaged with content and watch your videos on a regular basis.

Insight Subscribers shows you how many people have subscribed and how many people have unsubscribed from your channel each day in the chosen region. This report can help you spot countries where you are building a particularly strong audience.

You can also track the effectiveness of your marketing efforts aimed at increasing your number of subscribers. Just check if your new effort has caused significant uptake in daily subscriptions.

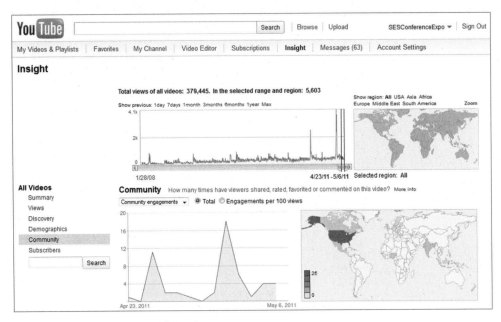

Figure 9.7 The Community tab in YouTube Insight

For any given day, the chart shows how many times people subscribed and unsubscribed from your channel and the net change in subscriptions on that day. The table beneath the chart shows countries with the biggest net change in subscriptions over the selected time period and geography.

Friday: Figure Out a Video's Hot Spots

On September 30, 2008, YouTube added a new feature to Insight called Hot Spots. With Hot Spots, you can figure out which scenes in your videos are the "hottest" so you don't have to guess what viewers are watching. Insight also shows which parts of your videos are "coldest" so you can learn where you lost your audience.

You can find this new feature under the Hot Spots tab within the Insight dashboard.

What does *hot* mean? *Hot* shows that compared to other YouTube videos of similar length, your video has fewer viewers leaving at that point, and many viewers may even be rewinding on the control bar to see a particular sequence in your video again. *Cold* means that compared to other YouTube videos of similar length, your video has many viewers moving to another part of it or leaving it entirely.

Figure 9.8 shows an example of Hot Spots in action. The Hot Spots tab in Insight plays your video alongside a graph that shows the ups and downs of viewership at different moments within the video. YouTube determines the "hot" and "cold" spots by comparing your video's abandonment rate at that moment to other videos on YouTube of the same length and incorporating data about rewinds and fast-forwards.

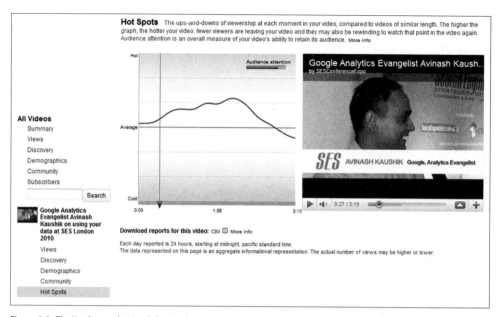

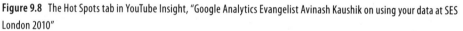

Figure 9.8 The Hot Spots tab in YouTube Insight, "Google Analytics Evangelist Avinash Kaushik on using your data at SES London 2010"

So what does that mean? Well, when the graph goes up, your video is hot: Few viewers are leaving, and many are even rewinding on the control bar to see that sequence again. When the graph goes down, your content's gone cold: Many viewers are moving to another part of the video or leaving the video entirely.

You can see that viewers seemed to enjoy my interview with Kaushik—until he gets to the 2:23 mark, where he talks about the challenge of attribution, or who gets credit for conversions in different scenarios. The low point near the end is where I mention that I'm a Wolverine from the University of Michigan while Kaushik got his MBA at The Ohio State University.

Now, what can you do with this feedback?

You cannot edit a video that has already been uploaded, and it isn't advisable to delete it and repost a new version that includes only the "hottest" scenes. However, you can add annotations to the "coldest" scenes or apply what you've learned about what worked and what didn't to your next video.

Tracy Chan and Nick Jakobi are the YouTube product managers who cooked up Hot Spots. If either one of you read this, consider letting me compare my video to other videos of the same length *in the same category*. That way, I can use other 3-minute, 19-second videos from other reporters as my benchmark instead of videos of the same length in all categories.

Week 2: Verify with TubeMogul

YouTube Insight provides you with information that helps you better understand your audience: who they are, where they come from, what they watch, and when. However, if a significant percentage of your video content views comes from other online video properties, then you will also want to analyze your overall marketing efforts—both on and off YouTube.

To do that, you can use TubeMogul, which not only distributes videos to almost 30 video hosting sites (including blip.tv, Dailymotion, Metacafe, Myspace, Veoh, Vimeo Plus, and YouTube), it also provides in-depth tracking and analytics for online video.

Founded in 2006, TubeMogul is a video advertising and analytics platform that connects advertisers with targeted audiences. In October 2010, the company closed $10 million in Series B funding led by Foundation Capital.

As Figure 9.9 illustrates, I've visited TubeMogul's offices in Emeryville, California, and talked with Brett Wilson, the company's cofounder and CEO, who leads the strategic direction for TubeMogul.

Figure 9.9 Greg Jarboe (left) and Brett Wilson (right) at TubeMogul's offices in Emeryville, California

Wilson previously worked as a consultant for Accenture and has founded two successful Internet companies. He is undefeated at Risk, the reigning foosball champion at TubeMogul, and an aspiring windsurfer and sailor. He received his MBA from UC Berkeley where he met John Hughes, TubeMogul's other cofounder and president of products, and Mark Rotblat, the company's VP of sales.

TubeMoguls has a variety of clients:

Agencies like Digitas, 360i, Crispin Porter + Bogusky, and DigiSynd

Broadcasters like PBS, HBO, CBS Interactive, and the WB

Corporations like Symantec, Red Bull, the Home Depot, and Microsoft

Government organizations like the US Army, NASA, the White House, and Obama '08

Magazine and newspaper **publishers** like the *New York Times*, Marvel, Condé Nast Digital, and Tribune

New media companies like Mondo Media, Howcast, and Revision3

Nonprofits like CATO Institute, Greenpeace, American Solutions, and the National AIDS Fund

Record labels and musicians like EMI, Warner Music, Interscope Records, and Century Media

Video bloggers like Fred, iJustine, Philip Defranco, and Household Hacker

Video sites like blip.tv, Brightcove, Dailymotion, and Metacafe

Although you can trust YouTube Insight, let's take a closer look at how you can use TubeMogul to verify the information and track far more than the traditional metric of video "views."

Monday: Learn what TubeMogul measures

Tuesday: Review the features of InPlay

Wednesday: Revise your ad revenues upward

Thursday: Start a video cattle drive

Friday: Check out TubeMogul Research

Monday: Learn What TubeMogul Measures

You can't tell what TubeMogul measures without a program.

TubeMogul launched its first cross-platform online-video analytics tool in March 2007. The free service aggregated video-viewing data from the top sharing sites to give video creators improved understanding of when, where, and how often videos were watched and to track and compare what was hot and what was not, measure the impact of marketing campaigns, gather competitive intelligence, and share the data with colleagues.

In January 2008, the company introduced Premium Products. Starting at $500 a month, Premium Products offered advanced data analytics, demographic and geographic reporting, video transcoding, scheduled video deployment, multi-campaign functionality, and reports that aggregate viewership information based on keywords.

In October 2008, TubeMogul acquired Flash player analytics firm Illumenix. This extended the company's product offering through a suite of patent-pending tools. At an individual video level, Illumenix was able to track viewer engagement, including how much of a video is actually watched, what the most popular segments of a video are, when a viewer clicks away, and much more. At a sitewide level, Illumenix was also able to track minutes viewed by category and viewer behavior around the content as a whole. And in a world where video was embedded everywhere, Illumenix was also able to report on where video views were coming from, including referring sites and search terms.

In June 2009, TubeMogul announced the launch of TubeMogul 2.0, giving away for free tracking capabilities that were previously available only to large advertisers and top video destinations. This gave video publishers access to a single, standardized set of rich, census-based analytics that could be seen and compared in a single dashboard, aggregating data from 15 of the Web's top video sites.

In March 2010, TubeMogul introduced PlayTime, its "100 percent transparent" video ad network. PlayTime lets advertisers see and control exactly what they're buying by using TubeMogul's InPlay analytics. This allows advertisers to compare performance metrics across placements within social media, such as Facebook games and apps, and on comScore 250 publisher sites in real time. Advertisers can know what sites views are coming from and in what numbers, whether views are click to play or auto-play, how long viewers watch before clicking away, what search terms they are using to find a video, and whether the video is shared or embedded.

In July 2010, TubeMogul launched a free suite of video player analytics. InPlay easily integrated in minutes with any site and could be activated for every major video player on the Web.

In September 2010, TubeMogul launched a free suite of HTML5 analytics. The plug-in, part of TubeMogul InPlay, offered the very same reporting already counted on daily by thousands of top media companies and brands. As Figure 9.10 illustrates, HTML5 video analytics also offered new tools for comparing different video platforms and devices.

On February 11, 2011, TubeMogul added demographic reporting to PlayTime. This gave PlayTime's advertising clients access to free, real-time demographic information on the people who view their video ads, all easily shared and exported. Metrics available included age, gender, household income, marital status, home ownership, and number of children.

Figure 9.10 HTML5 analytics

Tuesday: Review the Features of InPlay

Since the features of TubeMogul InPlay have changed over the past few years, let's review some of the major ones:

Total views and viewed minutes TubeMogul provides an aggregated report of total views for each of your videos across all of the sites that they are hosted on. In addition, total viewed minutes are calculated for each of your videos.

Top videos InPlay lets you see which videos have received the most total views and viewed minutes across your own site and across the Internet overall.

Engagement InPlay lets you see how long users are viewing each individual video, down to the second. This data is presented beside the playing video so content creators can understand where viewers are dropping off most dramatically, insights you can use to develop more engaging creative assets.

Attention span InPlay helps you understand how long your audience is engaged with your content on an aggregated basis across all of your videos. You can see the percentage of users that are viewing for 10 seconds, 20 seconds, 30 seconds, and so on. You can customize the time frame analyzed to determine how your videos are holding your audience's attention over time.

Geographic tracking InPlay lets you determine where your viewers are located around the world. Data is available at the country, state, and city level. You can track total viewed minutes at these geographic levels as well.

Syndication tracking InPlay lets you see which sites across the Internet have embedded your videos and helps you track total views and viewed minutes generated by each of these sites.

Search terms Learn which search terms are being used to locate your videos. See which terms are generating the most views and viewed minutes for each of your videos.

Traffic sources InPlay helps you learn which sites are driving views of your videos. You can see total views and viewed minutes by referring site for each of your videos.

Stream quality InPlay lets you track the quality of your video delivery from the perspective of the viewer. You can see the total number of rebuffers, the percentage of rebuffers of the total views served, the number of viewers lost, and the average start delay in seconds.

Campaign reporting TubeMogul's advertising clients can use InPlay to see all of the analytics previously mentioned as well as detailed insight into the performance of their campaigns. As Figure 9.11 illustrates, TubeMogul provides data on total impressions, views, completion rates, and social actions.

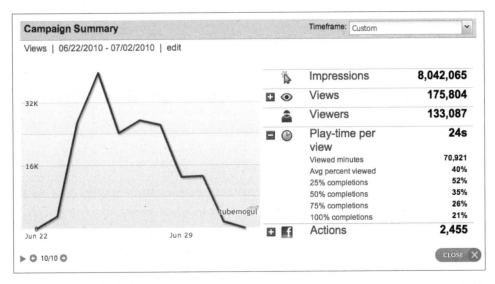

Figure 9.11 TubeMogul InPlay's campaign summary

TubeMogul also enables you to track buzz in the world of user-generated content or compare your brand to your competitors' by tracking videos and viewership across the Internet based upon selected keywords. This is a significant timesaver for anyone manually collecting keyword statistics.

For example, the chart in Figure 9.12 illustrates what happened when the "Hillary 1984" attack video was posted on YouTube by an unknown party in March 2007. As you can see, the unanticipated consequence was a huge spike in daily views of the official videos by Democrats.

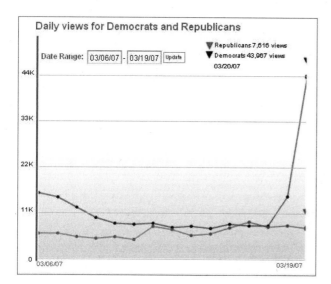

Figure 9.12 Daily views for Democrats and Republicans 03/06/07–03/19/07

The "Hillary 1984" attack video was widely distributed and had over 1.5 million views as of March 22, 2007. However, the buzz spilled over to the response videos officially put out by the Barack Obama and Hillary Clinton campaigns. The chart shows an aggregate of video views on YouTube of the top three Democrats (Obama, Clinton, and John Edwards) versus that of the top three Republicans at the time (Rudy Giuliani, John McCain, and Mitt Romney).

Wednesday: Revise Your Ad Revenues Upward

TubeMogul InPlay has helped Revision3, an Internet television pioneer, to make several data-driven production decisions. This in turn has enabled Revision3 to revise its ad revenues—upward—year after year.

Effective measurement of video performance became much more important as the economy contracted in late 2008 and ad spending worsened. Few companies knew this better than Revision3, the TV network for the Internet generation, which posted record revenues amid industry projections of declining ad spending.

Revision3 used TubeMogul to syndicate many of its shows to YouTube, MySpace, Yahoo!, Metacafe, and other sites as well as track the results, as Figure 9.13 illustrates.

According to a case study on TubeMogul's site, Revision3 also utilized TubeMogul InPlay for its own video player, tracking rich data on viewer behavior that occurs on its site. Using InPlay, Revision3 was able to track typical viewers' experiences, including per-stream data for how much of a video is actually watched, where in the world people are watching, and average download speeds.

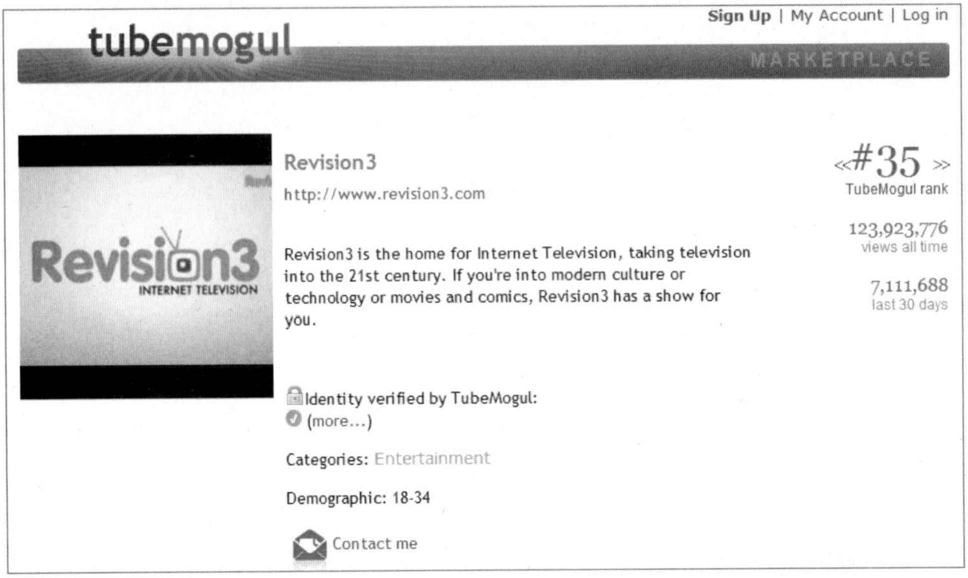

Figure 9.13 TubeMogul profile of Revision3

"Knowing which shows are the most engaging to viewers is helpful in selling advertising and devoting resources," Jim Louderback, CEO of Revision3, noted at the time.

This knowledge enabled Revision3 shows to garner a record number of views for 2008, catapulting its hit programs—including *Diggnation*, *The Totally Rad Show*, and *Tekzilla*—into the stratosphere of Internet superstardom. Views of Revision3's programs increased more than 140 percent year over year to over 46 million views in 2008 from 19 million views in 2007. In addition, the network reported a whopping 129 million segments viewed and nearly one billion minutes of engagement in 2008.

In a press release distributed on January 28, 2009, Louderback said, "Year after year, Revision3's viewer engagement continues to rise, more than doubling in the past year alone. This fact, and our viewer numbers, are especially impressive when you consider that our viewers spend nearly an hour engaged in our long-form programming, such as *Diggnation* and *Tekzilla*."

A year later, Revision3 announced its growth results for 2009. Show viewership across the network climbed to nearly 1.5 billion minutes of viewer engagement, while the company grew its revenue 30 percent. On the ad sales side, Revision3 increased its average deal by 50 percent and added major brands including Klondike, Ford, Adidas, Coors, Patron, Nokia, and Panasonic to its brand advertising roster.

In a press release distributed on February 2, 2010, Louderback said, "We're coming off a tremendous year in 2009, with impressive gains in viewership, advertising and distribution." He added, "What's even more amazing is that we achieved this success during what's now being called 'The Great Recession.' I'm proud of how our entire team worked together to deliver such an amazing performance, and am even more excited about our outlook for 2010—which will be huge!"

A year later, Revision3 announced its growth results for 2010. Total views across the network increased nearly 165 percent year over year, with more than 42 million views in the month of December. The company reached profitability in Q4 of 2010 and grew its revenue 80 percent year over year, while increasing its blue-chip roster of advertising sponsors to more than 60, including Fortune 500 companies such as Verizon, Ford, HP, EA, Sony, HP, and Old Spice.

In a press release distributed on February 1, 2011, Louderback said, "We had another incredible year in 2010, with impressive gains in revenue, viewership, advertising and distribution." He added, "We are thrilled to be leading the reinvention of television as we head to a world where the majority of new TVs will be sold with Internet access, and where tablets and phones are increasingly allowing viewers to enjoy video on any available screen."

Who said, "The way of the pioneer is always rough"?

Thursday: Start a Video Cattle Drive

TubeMogul PlayTime has run hundreds of leading video advertising campaigns to date, spanning over 36 million monthly unique viewers in the United States, according to comScore Actual Reach. PlayTime averages 56.4 seconds of viewing time per ad, 46 percent longer than a typical 30-second TV spot at about one-third the price.

Here is a closer look at one of the PlayTime case studies on TubeMogul's site: Symantec's video cattle drive.

With the release of Microsoft Windows 7, many midsized to large businesses started looking for an easy, effective, and efficient way to migrate to this new operating system. With this in mind, Symantec launched its "7 Steps to Windows 7" kit and services.

The primary audience was IT professionals at companies as well as strategic IT businesses. Conventional marketing to such professionals would typically include proven direct-response mediums like search engine marketing and email. In addition to these, Symantec decided to try something new—video advertising.

Symantec used a cattle drive motif in a video entitled "Moving to Windows 7" (www.youtube.com/watch?v=NnGev1M16Tw). During the video, cowboys described the challenges and benefits of migrating operating systems and of using Symantec as a small crew moved a lot of desktops and laptops to Windows 7. Two versions were created—a 1-minute version for targeted outreach and a 2-minute version for Symantec's site.

Leveraging TubeMogul's PlayTime network and both YouTube's embedded player and TubeMogul's player for video delivery, the video was served as a stand-alone ad within Facebook applications and display ad units on targeted technology sites.

A banner overlay clicking off to Symantec's "7 Steps to Windows 7" microsite was included so that users would not have to wait to the end of the video to get the call to action.

With TubeMogul's help in embedding its YouTube video into ad units targeted at a per-stream level, Symantec achieved the following results:

- 1,057,477 views in the campaign's first week, including over 500,000 YouTube views. It outpaced even Microsoft's *Family Guy* campaign, receiving 38.7 percent more views than Microsoft did in its first week.

- A 2.79 percent click-through rate on overlays and a link in the video's description.

As Figure 9.14 illustrates, viewers watched "Moving to Windows 7" longer than a benchmark of 10 top tech campaigns TubeMogul was tracking.

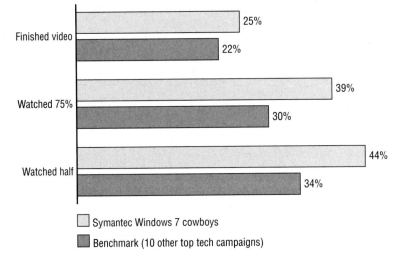

Figure 9.14 Completion Rates: Symantec vs. Other Top Tech Campaigns

Not bad, not bad for a cowboy.

Friday: Check Out TubeMogul Research

Given that TubeMogul is tracking billions of monthly streams, the company is also able to provide industry analysis based on macro-level trends it is seeing in the data.

For example, on February 18, 2011, Brightcove and TubeMogul published the "Online Video & the Media Industry Quarterly Research Report" for the fourth quarter of 2010. The report examined online video discovery, usage, and engagement data from an anonymous sample of more than 200 media companies representing media industry verticals, including broadcast networks, magazine publishers, newspaper publishers, and pure-play Web media properties.

Here are some notable findings:

- Google was the top referral source in driving traffic to online video content for media companies and brands.

- Facebook, which ranked second, was responsible for over one in ten referred video views, a number growing by 11.17 percent per month. Viewers also tended to watch longer when coming from Facebook across categories.

- Both viewing time and video completion rates were up across categories compared to the previous quarter. Completions were up 5.7 percent per category on average.

- Broadcasters led in total minutes streamed in 2010.

- Newspapers uploaded 147 percent more videos than the previous quarter as they continued to ramp up production.

- Brands saw a 98 percent jump in average viewing time, reaching 2:03 minutes on average, higher growth than any other category. Overall views also grew significantly, as brands more than doubled viewers.

- Interestingly, brands exhibited significantly higher engagement rates across all referring sources than other content, which seems to suggest that videos discovered both with SEO and through social sharing are resulting in increased engagement for brand viewers.

As Figure 9.15 illustrates, the average minutes watched per view increased dramatically in Q4 for brands and also hit new highs for broadcasters, newspapers, and online media.

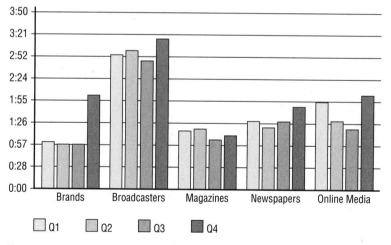

Figure 9.15 Average minutes watched per view

Check back frequently to view TubeMogul's growing list of reports at www
.tubemogul.com/research, or subscribe to its Analyst List to receive an email with
the latest reports. You can also check out the blog at www.tubemogul.com/blog/ or the
Twitter feed (@tubemogul).

Week 3: Verify with Google Analytics

Another tool that can help you analyze your overall marketing efforts—both on and
off YouTube—is Google Analytics.

In Chapter 5, you learned that Google Analytics can be used for more in-depth
tracking, reporting, and analysis on brand channels. This week, we will go into more
detail.

Google Analytics gives YouTube brand channel owners a comprehensive view
of how visitors access and interact with their channels. Analytics reports provide data
such as traffic referral patterns, repeat visitation, user demographics, and much more.

Google Analytics integration on YouTube is available only for brand channels.
Although, I've heard rumors that YouTube may offer it to partner channels in the
future.

Google Analytics can also be installed on your website—and it is absolutely free.
There are several benefits that come with installing it:

- AdWords advertisers can make Analytics available right in their AdWords
  account as a separate tab through a simple linking process. Marketers can
  review extra data for their online campaigns by tracking landing page quality
  and conversions (goals) and pick out their highest-performing ads.

- You can see which pages drive the most page views on your site from the Top
  Content report. This report can answer questions you have about your most or
  least effective pages. For example, a high bounce rate indicates a landing page
  that should be redesigned or tailored to the specific ad that links to it.

- You can learn which groups of visitors became customers or did something else
  important to the success of your business. You can get key insights by setting up
  goals.

There are over 80 reports with customizable, drag-and-drop interfaces. You
can create the segments you want to see with Advanced Segmentation or look at mul-
tidimensional views of your data with Motion Charts. As Figure 9.16 illustrates, you
can also create your own reports with Custom Reporting after watching "Custom
Reporting in Google Analytics" (www.youtube.com/watch?v=NGg1137x3Yw).

Figure 9.16 "Custom Reporting in Google Analytics"

Let's get started.

Monday: Set up Google Analytics

Tuesday: Access Analytics reports

Wednesday: Interpret Analytics reports for websites

Thursday: Understand Analytics reports for channels

Friday: Use additional tracking options

Monday: Set Up Google Analytics

Setting up Google Analytics for your brand channel is a four- or five-step process depending on whether you do it yourself or have a YouTube sales rep help you. Here are the steps:

1. You can sign up for a Google Analytics account at www.google.com/analytics. If you already have an existing Google Analytics login, you can create a new account by selecting Create New Account. While it's possible to create a new profile within an existing account by selecting Add New Profile, I recommend that you create a new account so that the data from your YouTube channel doesn't impact the data summaries from your other websites.

2. Then, fill in all of the required fields for your account. I recommend that you enter your YouTube brand channel URL as the website URL for the Google Analytics account. After you complete the setup process, Google Analytics will display code that includes a profile ID in the form of UA-#######-#. This can be found while you're in the Overview section of the account. You'll need this value in step 3.

3. Next, log in to your YouTube account and go to your channel page. Click the **Branding Options** tab in the channel editing menu and then locate the **Google Analytics account ID** field in the **Tracking and Redirects** options. Enter your Google Analytics profile ID in the field and click the **Save Changes** button. Data about your brand channel will begin populating your Google Analytics reports as soon as you save your profile ID.

4. Finally, save your changes. Once you've done that, it can take up to 24 hours for data to appear in your account. If you don't see any data a day later, then you should read "Why isn't Google Analytics tracking my Website?" at http://bit .ly/hM8aAr.

5. You also have the option of letting your YouTube rep assist you, if you've got any questions about your account. To do this, go your Google Analytics account settings page and click the User Manager link in Figure 9.17. Click the Add User link and then add brandchanneltracking@gmail.com as a user for your account. This optional step allows the YouTube team to view your account to help troubleshoot any issues in your program.

Figure 9.17 User Manager link

Tuesday: Access Analytics Reports

Accessing the Google Analytics reports for your website or YouTube brand channel is fairly straightforward:

1. Log in to www.google.com/analytics and select the account that you've created for your brand channel.

2. If you've got multiple profiles in your Google Analytics account, then click the View Report link to select the appropriate profile.

3. From here, you can access all of the data collected on your channel through the navigation on the left and right side. For example, the Pageviews report in Figure 9.18 is accessible via either the left dashboard (Visitors > Visitor Trending > Pageviews) or the **Pageviews** link in the **Site Usage** section.

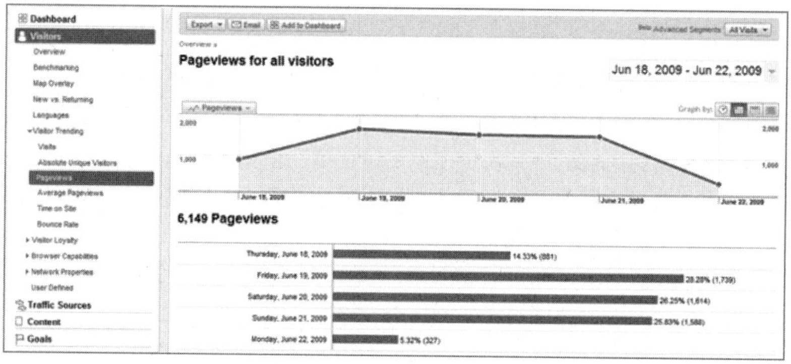

Figure 9.18 Pageviews for all visitors

Here are some of the reports that you might find useful:

Map Overlay (Visitors > Map Overlay) explains where your viewers came from geographically.

Languages (Visitors > Languages) identifies the language preferences of your viewers.

Visitor Trending (Visitors > Visitor Trending) shows the size of your audience over time.

Visitor Loyalty (Visitors > Visitor Loyalty) identifies the number and percentage of repeat visitors to your channel.

Traffic Sources tells you how users interact with your channel after reaching it from a link on a particular site or a search for a particular keyword.

For more information about the types of Google Analytics reports that are available, you can visit the Google Analytics Help Center at www.google.com/support/analytics.

Wednesday: Interpret Analytics Reports for Websites

Although accessing Google Analytics is fairly straightforward, interpreting the data takes "blood, toil, tears, and sweat," as Churchill once said.

Let's start with the basics of Google Analytics for websites. Figure 9.19 shows 21 of the features available to Analytics users.

1. You can click this link to navigate back to your Google Analytics Settings page so you can get an overview of all your accounts and profiles and edit them. From there, you can navigate to the Profile Settings page, where you can view your tracking code and create goals and funnels.

2. You can also navigate to any of your accounts using this drop-down menu.

3. You can click Settings to set the email address associated to your account, your account language, and your email notification settings.

4. The My Account link takes you to a page listing all of your Google Accounts.

5. You can click Help to go to the Google Analytics Help Center.

6. You should remember to sign out of your account when you're done.

7. Visitors provides information on visitor interaction with your channel, the type of visitors, and information about how they are viewing your channel.

8. Traffic Sources lets you find out how different offline or online sources sent traffic to your site. You can view which sources are driving the most traffic to your channel and spot trends from the provided graphs and charts.

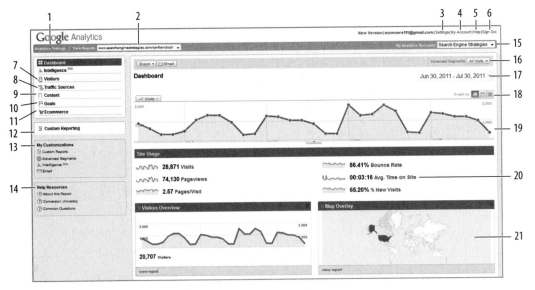

Figure 9.19 Google Analytics dashboard

9. Content reports are all about the pages in your channel and how visitors interacted with each one. You can use the data to find time spent on a page, see landing and exit page information, and get a navigation summary for pages.

10. Goals enables you to set goals for your Google Analytics account and then see data in these reports.

11. Ecommerce reports provide helpful information on the revenue, transaction, and e-commerce activity on a channel.

12. You can design a custom report using whatever metrics you want to see.

13. Settings enables you to slice and dice your data any way that you want to see it. You can click Advanced Segments to segment your audience and apply these to your reports. You can click Email to manage scheduled email reports.

14. You can click on any of these help resources to find information on the specific report you're viewing, get tips on how to interpret and use the information for your campaign, or learn about other people's common questions.

15. You can select from this drop-down menu to jump to another Google Analytics account.

16. You can apply the advanced segment that you've created to a report and then compare it side by side with other graphs.

17. You can select a date range using a calendar or timeline slider to graph your report data by clicking on the arrow. You also have the option to compare current data to past data in this section.

18. You can graph your report by month, week, day, or hour (where available).

19. The selected date range, graph by view, advanced segment, or metric appears here.

20. You can get at-a-glance views of your account's key metrics here.

21. You can add or delete report snapshot modules to your dashboard. To add a module, go to the desired report and click Add To Dashboard at the top of your report. To delete one, click the X in the upper-right corner of every module of your dashboard report.

Thursday: Understand Analytics Reports for Channels

If you've already learned the basics of Google Analytics for websites, you've still got to learn the variations in Google Analytics for channels. Hopefully, the following information will help you to understand the data in the Google Analytics reports for your channel:

• Google Analytics tracks your brand channel as well as pages within the channel, such as ones that show all of your subscribers or favorite videos.

However, it doesn't track activity on video watch pages on your brand channel. Google Analytics doesn't track activity that takes place within gadgets on your channel, either. You'll need to set up a separate Google Analytics ID if you would like to track activity on a custom gadget. As I mentioned earlier, YouTube's Insight tool provides viewing metrics and user information for your video watch pages.

- Because YouTube Insight and Google Analytics use different reporting methodologies, they may provide different numbers for the same statistic. For example, YouTube Insight tracks channel views from the time that you create your account, while Google Analytics tracks views only after you've added your Google Analytics account ID.

- The **Traffic Sources** reports identify referral information. In these reports, any data that results from clicks within the www.youtube.com domain is reported under **direct/none**. This classification also includes visits resulting from a user typing your channel URL directly into their browser. And it includes visits for referring information that was blocked or not detected.

- The **Traffic Sources** reports provide data about the keywords used to reach your channel page from external search engines, such as Google, Yahoo!, and Bing. The keywords don't include data from searches on YouTube.

- Clicks on Promoted Videos don't appear as a campaign in the AdWords traffic reports, but you can track them via the **Top Content** report as long as the ads drive traffic directly to your brand channel. To do this, use the search field at the bottom of the report to filter for URLs containing the string "pyv". In each of those URLs, the **"kw"** parameter contains the keyword that led to the visit.

- The number of pageviews that Google Analytics provides for Promoted Video URLs may differ from the number of clicks in your campaign reports.

That's the bad news. The good news is there's a channel on YouTube where you can watch more videos about Google Analytics. The official Google Analytics channel (www.youtube.com/googleanalytics) features more than 75 videos on topics from "Google Analytics Basics: Finding your tracking code" to "Advanced Segments in Google Analytics" (Figure 9.20).

Figure 9.20 Google Analytics channel

Friday: Use Additional Tracking Options

In addition to Google Analytics, YouTube supports tracking options for brand channels that are not available on standard channels. And I encourage you to use these features:

> **Tracking ad units** are 1×1-pixel third-party tracking tags that brand channel owners can provide. They let you use view-through tracking to better understand a user's behavior after the user leaves your channel page. This tag runs for the length of your media campaign. YouTube brand channel owners generally use standard ad tags and conversion tracking tags. I recommend using a standard ad tag if you want to see how users engage with your website after viewing your brand channel. But I recommend using a conversion tracking tag if you want to test media placements or different creative to determine the most effective ways to drive traffic to your YouTube channel.

> **Survey tags** are 1×1-pixel tags that track control and test groups. YouTube has certified the following vendors for research: comScore, FactorTG, Insight Express, Nielsen, Nielsen IAG Research, and Safecount/Dynamic Logic.

Click-command tags let you track users who click from your brand channel to other websites as well as any post-click data associated with those users. You can implement click tags on any links in the channel banner, channel side column image, and branding box. You can also use a click tag in the website address shown in your channel information box, but that link will be publicly visible. If you're using a standard ad tag, then I recommend that you set up click-command tags in the same campaign as your 1×1-pixel ad tag so that you can properly track conversions.

Tracking image URLs specify the URL for a tracking pixel that you can use to collect statistics for views of your channel or video pages. While tracking tags can drop cookies to track behavior, this simple pixel can only count impressions.

Learning to use YouTube Insight, TubeMogul InPlay, Google Analytics, and the tracking options mentioned in the preceding list can take "many, many long months of struggle and of suffering," as Churchill once said. But you won't win any "flaring battles" in video marketing or tally any "glittering achievements" on YouTube unless you know how to analyze "statistics, diagrams, and curves" that are "incomprehensible to the public."

As Figure 9.21 reminds us, it took from 1939 to 1945 to overcome the U-boat peril. But as Churchill stated later, "The Battle of the Atlantic was the dominating factor all through the war. Never for one moment could we forget that everything happening elsewhere, on land, at sea, or in the air, depended ultimately on its outcome."

Figure 9.21 Officers on the bridge

Week 4: Master Web Analytics 2.0

You should use YouTube Insight to count what is countable. And you should use TubeMogul InPlay or Google Analytics to measure what is measurable. But what can you do to make measurable what is not measurable by these tools?

The answer is to master what Kaushik calls "Web Analytics 2.0." What's that? In his book *Web Analytics 2.0: The Art of Online Accountability & Science of Customer Centricity* (Wiley, 2010), Kaushik says, "Clickstream data is great at the *what*, but not at the *why*."

He adds, "It's important to know what happened, but it is even more critical to know why people do the things they do on your site."

As Kaushik says, I've expanded on, and Figure 9.22 illustrates, Web Analytics 2.0 is

- the analysis of qualitative and quantitative data from *your channel*, your website, and the competition;
- to drive a continual improvement of the online experience that your *audience*, customers, and potential customers have;
- which translates into your desired outcomes (online and offline).

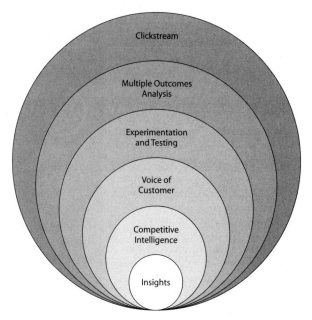

Figure 9.22 The updated paradigm of Web Analytics 2.0

This week, we'll look at some social media monitoring tools, video metrics, competitive intelligence tools, market research, and a Kick Butt Index that make measurable what is not measurable by YouTube Insight, TubeMogul InPlay, or Google

Analytics. This insightful elixir can help you discover the solutions for the hardest challenges, including multichannel analytics and multitouch campaign attribution analysis.

Monday: Monitor social media with Radian6

Tuesday: Look at Visible Measures

Wednesday: Tap into competitive intelligence from Hitwise

Thursday: Visit the Pew Research Center

Friday: Get KDPaine's KBI Development System

Monday: Monitor Social Media with Radian6

One of the missing pieces of the puzzle is finding out who's talking about your brand in the online communities that surround the YouTube community. There are a number of solutions, including Jive and Trackur. But I'm currently using Radian6, the industry's leading social media monitoring platform.

Founded in 2006, Radian6 is the leading social media monitoring, engagement, and insights platform with over 2,400 customers, including more than half of Fortune 100 companies. Radian6's technology captures hundreds of millions of conversations every day across YouTube, Facebook, Twitter, LinkedIn, blogs, and online communities and provides actionable insights in real time.

Radian6's products include a monitoring platform designed to help companies track and analyze their social media efforts as well as an engagement platform to help companies connect with individuals and communities online. The intelligence gained from these conversations has become critical in helping companies better market and sell to prospects, service customers, and understand what's being said about their brand, products, competitors, and services.

Radian6 was chosen as a "leader" by Forrester Research in the independent research firm's "The Forrester Wave: Listening Platforms, Q3, 2010" report, which was released in 2010. In the report, Radian6 ranked above other platforms for functionality and was the only company to receive a 5.00 out of 5.00 score for product strategy and leading scores in market presence in both customers and financials.

On May 2, 2011, Salesforce.com acquired Radian6. The combination of these organizations has the potential to bridge the conversations taking place on Chatter (salesforce.com's private, secure social corporate social network) and public social networks.

As Figure 9.23 illustrates, I interviewed Amber Naslund, director of community of Radian6, at SES New York 2009. I asked her why it is important for small businesses to use social media monitoring tools. She said the cost of these tools is relatively low and using social media is a great way to connect with smaller communities.

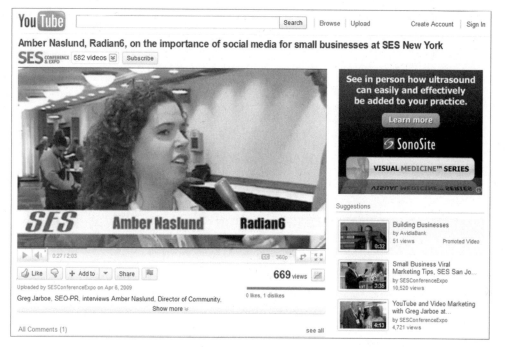

Figure 9.23 "Amber Naslund, Radian6, on the importance of social media for small businesses at SES New York"

Tuesday: Look at Visible Measures

Another company that you will want to look at is Visible Measures, the independent third-party media measurement firm for online video advertisers and publishers.

Founded in 2005, Visible Measures provides several capabilities and metrics that allow Internet video publishers and advertisers to understand audience behavior and analyze the success of Internet video programs. They accomplish this by capturing and measuring every video interaction in every video from every viewer, from play to pause to rewind to forward to a friend, and more.

Visible Measures provides advertisers and their agencies with an integrated view of campaign performance across paid, owned, and earned media. The patented Visible Measures platform shows both how online viewers interact with video content and how that content spreads across more than 300 video sites, including AOL Video and YouTube.

Industry charts powered by Visible Measures include *Advertising Age*'s Top 10 Viral Video Ads, iMedia Connection's Top 10 Brands in Video, *Variety*'s Top 10 Online Film Trailers, and *Motor Trend*'s Top 10 Auto Ads. And as Figure 9.24 illustrates, the Visible Measures 100 Million Views Club, which is updated monthly, lists the most-watched viral videos of all time.

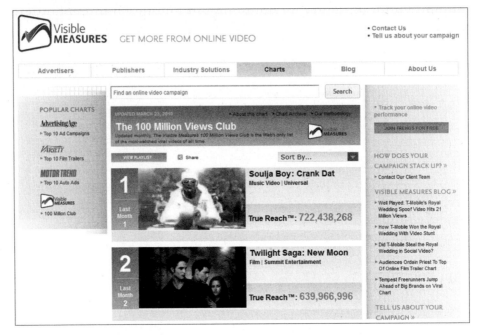

Figure 9.24 The 100 Million Views Club

Visible Measures also shares its perspective on Internet video measurement in the Viral Video Research Blog.

For example, the blog reported on July 29, 2011, that Fabio, the new Old Spice Guy, had driven the deodorant's latest campaign straight to No. 1 on the Visible Measures Viral Video Chart with 3.5 million views. And the blog predicted that Isaiah Mustafa, the old Old Spice Guy who challenged Fabio to a duel, would generate even more views the following week "fueled by the promoted tweets the company is sending out to increase viewer interest."

Wednesday: Tap into Competitive Intelligence from Hitwise

Another one of the missing pieces of the puzzle is finding out what your key competitors are doing online. There are several good services that provide this information, including comScore Video Metrix and Nielsen Online. But the one that I keep going back to for more competitive insights is Hitwise.

Each day, Hitwise provides insights on how 10 million American, 8 million British, and 100,000 Canadian Internet users interact with more than 1 million websites across more than 160 industries. And Hitwise clickstream data provides extensive reports on the upstream traffic to and downstream traffic from a specific website, industry, or custom category.

Founded in 1997, Hitwise is now an Experian company. Instead of monitoring a sample of 10,000 to 50,000 Internet users, Hitwise works with ISP networks to monitor millions of Internet users. As a result, while many other measurement companies have data on the top 1,000 websites, Hitwise has data on over 1 million online businesses.

Hitwise offers a range of products and services that help marketers improve their online performance. The Hitwise flagship product is its online Competitive Intelligence Service.

Although Hitwise doesn't publish the cost of its service on its website, a typical subscription costs from $20,000 to $50,000 a year, depending on the features purchased. Veteran marketers will want to evaluate the benefits as well as the cost of Hitwise. However, new YouTubers might agree with Rebecca Kelley, who posted a review to the SEOmoz blog on March 2, 2007, entitled, "Hitwise: Damn Expensive, but Damn Cool."

There are a couple of less-expensive alternatives. First, you can go to the Hitwise Research Store (http://researchstore.hitwise.com) and purchase a report on your competitor starting at $695 per report. Second, you can subscribe to the free monthly Hitwise newsletter to receive industry statistics, market trends, and other competitive intelligence data.

In addition, I strongly recommend reading the Hitwise Intelligence Analyst Weblogs, shown in Figure 9.25. I do. You'll find posts like "Rebecca Black fastest moving search term in social sphere" by Robin Goad and "Hulu and the Older Early Adopter" by Bill Tancer.

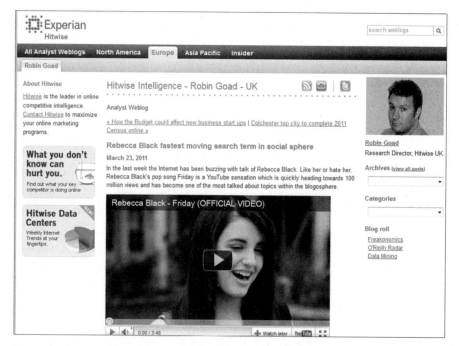

Figure 9.25 Rebecca Black fastest moving search term in social media

Rebecca Black is the name of a 13-year-old girl who made a famously atrocious music video, "Friday," on March 14, 2011, one that was so bad that it went viral in real life, spreading by word of mouth, which resulted in people searching for her by name. Or, go to the Hitwise Press Center. Yes, there's plenty of good data there too, including the press releases "Facebook was the top search term in 2010 for second straight year" and "Lil Wayne Top Search Term on YouTube December 2008."

Thursday: Visit the Pew Research Center

There is a lot of market research available about online video. For example, eMarketer aggregated, filtered, and organized data from 30 sources for its report *The Video Viewing Audience: Trends for Marketers*, which was published in February 2011 and costs $695.

But I find that I get far more than an insight per fortnight by visiting the Pew Research Center's Internet & American Life Project at www.pewinternet.org.

The Pew Internet & American Life Project is one of seven projects that make up the Pew Research Center, a nonpartisan, nonprofit "fact tank" that produces reports exploring the impact of the Internet on families, communities, work and home, daily life, education, health care, and civic and political life.

The Pew Internet Project was initially conceived in the late 1990s when the staff and officers of the Pew Charitable Trusts observed that many of the debates about the impact of the Internet lacked reliable data. The foundation hired Lee Rainie to fashion a grant proposal and the board of directors approved an initial grant in December 1999.

In its early days, the Project team focused on two strains of research. This included who was using the Internet and what they were they doing as well as several dimensions of social life that were not studied by other firms.

The Pew Trusts also told Project staffers to be opportunistic in their studies. If something new, important, and interesting was happening online, the Project was encouraged to pursue it, even if the subject had not been previously mentioned in grant proposals.

In March 2005, the Project published a report titled "Music and Video Downloading." In July 2007, it published the report "Online Video," which was cited extensively in the first edition of this book. In January 2008, the Project published the report "Increased Use of Video-Sharing Sites."

In July 2009, the Project published the report "The Audience for Online Video-Sharing Sites Shoots Up." In June 2010, it published a report called "The State of Online Video," which I cited in Chapter 2. And in July 2011, it published a report that found "71% of online adults now use video-sharing sites," which I mentioned in the introduction to this book.

As Figure 9.26 illustrates, I've also found insights into the growth in online video consumption by voters in reports like "The Internet and Campaign 2010," which the Project published on March 17, 2011.

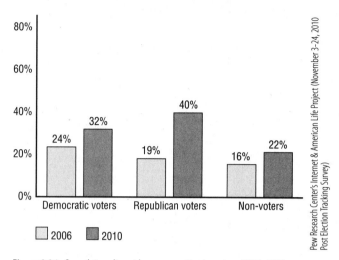

Figure 9.26 Growth in online video consumption by voters, 2006–2010
(based on % of Internet users in each group who watch political videos online)

How does the Pew Internet Project decide which subjects to study and how to frame that research? The new topics it explores emerge from its observations of technology trends, discussions with its funders, and good-spirited arguments among staffers. They always have to make assumptions about which Internet activities are important enough to ensure that they'll capture evidence of them in the big, national phone surveys that they conduct.

But, based on what I've read over the years, the Project has done a pretty good job of trying to make the right guess about which technologies are emerging or showing a trend—up or down—in usage. And it does a great job of exploring and explaining the meaning of its survey data.

I urge you to visit the Pew Research Center, early and often.

Friday: Get KDPaine's KBI Development System

The final missing piece of the puzzle is a new system that helps organizations define social media and marketing success. And to get one, you will want to beat a path to the door of KDPaine & Partners at www.kdpaine.com.

Katie Delahaye Paine is the founder and CEO of KDPaine & Partners, a New Hampshire–based research consultancy. She is the author of the recently published *Measure What Matters, Online Tools for Understanding Customers, Social Media, Engagement, and Key Relationships* (Wiley, 2011) as well as the popular textbook *Measuring Public Relationships* (KDPaine & Partners, 2007). She is also the publisher of KDPaine's PR Measurement Blog at http://kdpaine.blogs.com/ and The Measurement Standard at http://kdpaine.blogs.com/themeasurementstandard/.

And back in 1986, she was the director of corporate communications for Lotus Development Corporation. Yep, she was my immediate predecessor at Lotus, which may explain why we both got interested in measuring the effectiveness of marketing.

In July 2010, KDPaine & Partners announced the KBI Development System, which provides organizations with a systematic methodology to achieve consensus on the key metrics by which to measure their success.

In a press release, Paine explained, "We call it the KBI—for Kick Butt Index, since there's never been a marketer who hasn't heard the words 'we're really getting our butt kicked' and longed for his/her boss to say 'Congratulations, we really kicked butt this time.' The problem is that no one ever stops and says, 'Hey, what exactly do you mean by "kick butt"?'"

KDPaine's KBI helps companies decide what to measure and how to measure it. "Everyone agrees that the most important part of any measurement program is getting started correctly," explained Paine.

"Far too many marketing decisions are made without consensus around the definitions of success and failure, which is why two-thirds of CEOs consistently express dissatisfaction with marketing metrics. When there is no consensus, success can mean anything from accumulating more Facebook friends or more headlines, to increasing web traffic or lead generation," she said.

"With consensus, measurement becomes a continuous quality improvement tool, rather than just a ruler to beat people up, or a justification to spend more money. The KBI system will help organizations eliminate internal conflicts, reduce resistance to metrics, leverage existing research and save thousands in wasted measurement costs," Paine added.

KDPaine's KBI Development Process begins with a tutorial on measurement tools, strategy, and techniques by Paine herself. That workshop is followed by a simple 7-minute survey of everyone involved in making marketing decisions.

Once all the data is collected, it's benchmarked against KDPaine's historical database of marketing performance measures for hundreds of companies. KDPaine then delivers the top three to five personalized goals and three to five metrics accompanied by company-specific recommendations for measurement methodologies and tool selections plus a sample dashboard based on those metrics and goals.

Prices for KDPaine's KBI Development Process start at $7,500. Clients also have the option of working with KDPaine & Partners to identify and implement the necessary measurement tools.

One of KDPaine's clients is SAS, the leader in business analytics software and services. As Figure 9.27 illustrates, Paine and Mark Chaves of SAS spoke about SAS Social Media Analytics at the eMetrics Marketing Optimization Summit in May 2010.

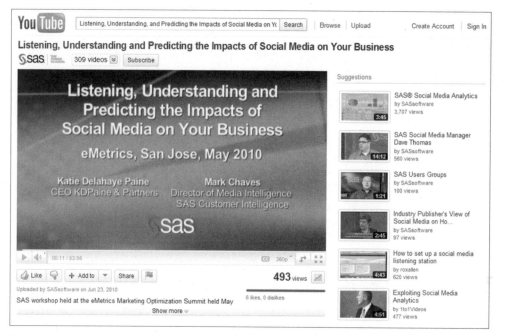

Figure 9.27 "Listening, Understanding and Predicting the Impacts of Social Media on Your Business"

In November 2010, KDPaine & Partners and SAS won the New Communications Award of Excellence in the Social Data Measurement/Measurement Innovation division for their work transitioning traditional PR measurement to an integrated, consistent, and comprehensive communications measurement program.

The research program gathered information from thousands of traditional and social media outlets, including YouTube, Facebook, and social bookmarking sites as well as internal and external blogs. Each item was analyzed to determine the nature of the conversation, content of the posting, engagement level, and how the author positioned the company.

In a press release, Paine said, "This program demonstrated both the opportunities and the challenges of communications and marketing measurement in the 21st century. It's not just about measuring results in different media; it's about adopting an entirely new mindset and taking a holistic view of priorities."

This sort of research is a perfect example of making measurable what is not measurable. It's a perfect example of Web Analytics 2.0.

Study YouTube Success Stories

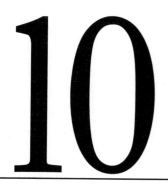

Although it is useful to measure views and ratings, how many of these outputs *do you need to make the cash register ring? In this chapter, we'll study four YouTube success stories to learn how organizations have used video marketing to generate measurable outcomes. And I'll interview the key individuals who were willing and able to tell me more about their YouTube success stories.*

Chapter Contents:

The Story behind the Story

I learned the difference between measuring outputs and outcomes over 20 years ago. Back in 1986, I became the director of corporate communications at Lotus Development Corporation. Actually, I was the company's 13th director of corporate communications, and that was when Lotus was only four and a half years old.

After my first month on the job, I took a very thick report on about 700 magazine and newspaper clippings that we'd generated, walked down the short hall to Jim Manzi's office (he was the chairman, president, and CEO), and casually dropped it on his desk.

My clipping report measured PR success in advertising value equivalency (AVE), which is calculated by measuring the column inches (in the case of print) or seconds (in the case of broadcast media) and multiplying these figures by the respective medium's advertising rates (per inch or per second). The resulting number was what it would have cost Lotus to place advertisements of that size or duration in those media.

But Manzi took a quick look and said, "Jarboe, these are just little pieces of paper. If I could deposit them in a bank, they'd be worth something. So, until you can measure the value of PR in cold, hard cash, don't waste my time with these so-called reports."

Although I'd worked in high-tech public relations at Wang Laboratories, Stratus Computer, and Data General for five years before joining Lotus, I'd never encountered this lack of faith in PR before. But then I'd never worked for a CEO who was a former journalist as well as a former McKinsey consultant before.

And I had to admit, Manzi was right. He was focused on outcomes.

Around that time, my father was the director of marketing at Oldsmobile. His ad agency, Leo Burnett, had created the memorable TV commercial, "It's not your father's Oldsmobile."

The folks at Leo Burnett were measuring the success of their ad campaign in gross rating points (GRPs), which represents the percentage of the target audience reached by an advertisement. If the advertisement appears more than once, the GRP figure represents the sum of each individual GRP. In the case of a TV commercial that is aired five times reaching 80 percent of the target audience, it would have 400 GRPs = 5 × 80%.

But sales of Oldsmobiles were falling from 1.2 million in 1986 to 800,000 in 1988 and then to under 600,000 in 1990. At one point, my dad asked his ad agency, "How many GRPs do we need to sell a car?"

My dad was asking the right question. He was focused on outcomes.

But the folks at Leo Burnett were focused on outputs. And with 20/20 hindsight, it's now clear the ad campaign was "unselling" Oldsmobiles every year it ran by informing older customers the brand wasn't targeted at them anymore and reminding younger prospects the brand had been driven by old fogies for a generation. This had a negative impact on the brand preference of Olds.

So, as I started writing this book, I also started looking for case studies of video marketing campaigns that did more than create lots of views and generate measurable outputs. I looked for YouTube success stories about creating a positive impact on brand preference and generating measurable outcomes.

And then, like the little girl in Figure 10.1, I also interviewed the key individuals who were willing and able to answer the question, "And what's the story behind the story?"

CARTOONBANK.COM

"And what's the story behind the story?"

Figure 10.1 "And what's the story behind the story?" (Cartoon by Arnie Levin in *The New Yorker*, February 8, 1993.)

Here is what I learned from George Wright, Arun Chaudhary, John Goldstone, and Michael Kolowich about Will It Blend?, the Barack Obama 2008 presidential campaign, Monty Python's channel, and the PiperSport launch.

Deliver 700 Percent Increase in Sales: Will It Blend?

Let me start by telling the story of Blendtec, a division of K-TEC that makes high-performing, durable blenders for commercial use and a newer line of home appliances. Although you may not have heard of this small, Utah-based manufacturer, there's a good chance you've had a smoothie, cappuccino, milkshake, or other frozen drink made with a Blendtec blender.

Tom Dickson, the company founder, describes himself as a "geek." And Kate Klonick of *Esquire* described him as "an otherwise bland grandfatherly-type from Utah" in an article on May 3, 2007. In other words, the star of Blendtec's videos isn't as exciting and dynamic as Barack Obama, whom we'll look at later in this chapter.

 Note: Brad O'Farrell, the technical editor of this book, thinks the star of the videos isn't Dickson, it's the Total Blender. So, maybe Blendtec's videos are as exciting and dynamic as "no-drama Obama."

George Wright, Blendtec's first director of sales and marketing, created a YouTube and video marketing campaign called "Will It Blend?" Wearing the white lab coat and safety glasses, Dickson takes everything but the kitchen sink, sticks it in a blender, and says, "Will it blend? That is the question." While the item is blended, he smiles and waits for the process to end. When it does, he empties out the contents, provides a warning not to breathe in the item they just blended ("iPod smoke, don't breathe this!") and the subtitle "Yes, it blends!" appears. In other words, Blendtec's video content isn't as compelling as the classic comedy of Monty Python, which we'll talk about later in this chapter.

When Blendtec hired Wright in January 2006, the company relied on demonstrations at trade shows and word-of-mouth referrals. On October 30, 2006, Wright created Blendtec's YouTube channel and spent $50 creating the first five "Will It Blend?" videos. He bought a white lab coat, the URL, and a selection of items to be blended, including marbles, a rake, a Big Mac Extra Value Meal, a "cochicken" (12 oz. can of Coke and half a rotisserie chicken), and some ice. In other words, Wright had a bare-bones budget.

"Will It Blend?" has since been called "the best viral marketing campaign ever." It's been featured on the *Today* show, *The Tonight Show*, and The History Channel (now called History).

The 101 videos on Blendtec's channel on YouTube (Figure 10.2) have more than 135.4 million views, making it the #60 most viewed of all time in the Directors category. The channel also has over 323,000 subscribers, making it the #33 most subscribed to of all time in the Directors category.

And as Figure 10.3 illustrates, this doesn't count some of the views on or subscribers to the official Will It Blend? site, which has additional Blendtec videos that don't use the YouTube player (www.willitblend.com).

Figure 10.2 The Will It Blend? channel

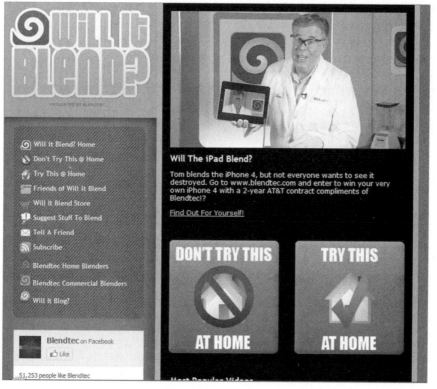

Figure 10.3 The Will It Blend? site

As Figure 10.4 illustrates, the most viewed and most discussed video in the series, "Will it Blend? - iPhone," has more than 8.9 million views. It also has more than 23,400 ratings and almost 12,200 text comments and has been favorited over 22,500 times.

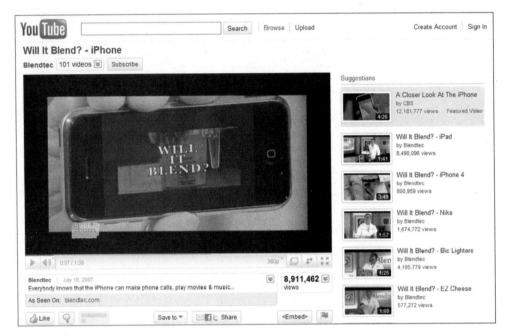

Figure 10.4 "Will It Blend? - iPhone"

I first met Wright on October 3, 2008, at the Digital PR Next Practices Summit in New York City. At the *PR News* conference, he talked about building community and reputation online with social media tools, and I discussed improving your search engine marketing and PR.

I'd already seen "Will it Blend? - iPhone." And I'd already written, "Unless you are one of the Blendtec guys, don't try using their humorous viral marketing techniques at home."

But, before Wright spoke, I still wasn't sure if he had been lucky or good. Slide 3 of his presentation outlined the critical components of his "Will it Blend?" viral marketing campaign. It clearly showed me that Wright was good. Here's a quick idea of what he said about each critical component:

Entertaining "A viral video doesn't have to be funny, but it has to be worth watching! You gotta check this out! That's the test."

Business objective "'Will it Blend?' generates revenue. Nike has offered to pay us money to blend one of their new shoes."

Honesty in claims "When we said we'd blended neodymium magnets, we got email telling us they were ceramic magnets."

Keep it real "We try to be ourselves and our videos are not overproduced. We try to be a little bit edgy, but not too slick."

Interactivity "People suggest things to blend, like the new iPhone. They aren't just viewers; they're engaged."

Simple user subscription "We have more than 200,000 subscriptions to our YouTube channel and our own 'Will it Blend?' website."

Then Wright said, "This new form of marketing has delivered a 700 percent increase in sales for Blendtec." During the network break between our presentations, I asked Wright if he would be interested in providing one of the case studies for this book. And he asked me, "Have you read the profile on Blendtec in Michael Miller's new book, *YouTube for Business*?" (*YouTube for Business* was published by Que in August 2008.)

As a matter of fact, I had read the book. But I wanted to interview Wright a year after Miller had, hoping that there would be new developments or more details to share with my readers. Wright agreed to be interviewed six months later and then headed out to the lobby to blend a wooden rake handle for all the other conference attendees.

In the spring of 2009, I called Wright at his office in West Orem, Utah. As I had hoped, there were new developments and more details for us to talk about. At that point, Wright was Blendtec's vice president of marketing and sales.

And as Figure 10.5 illustrates, Blendtec has used YouTube and video marketing in the past year to transform itself from being focused on business-to-business (B2B) to being focused business-to-consumer (B2C) sales.

Figure 10.5 Blendtec

Q&A with George Wright, Vice President of Marketing and Sales, Blendtec

Here are my questions and his answers.

Jarboe: What's your background? What did you do before joining Blendtec? How did you first get the idea for "Will It Blend?"

Wright: My background is in heavy industry. Before joining Blendtec, I handled PR at a steel mill and marcom for a major pump and valve manufacturer. My budget was huge at these other companies. But that was different at Blendtec, which had a wonder product but no marketing. However, we did have a video producer and equipment already to create instructional videos for our commercial customers. Then I happened upon owner Tom Dickson feeding a 2x2-inch wooden board into a commercial blender as part of a destructive test and found it fascinating. I thought that others might get a kick out of watching the process, and the idea for creating a video was born. I wrote a marketing strategy entitled "Blending Marbles." Then, as I said last October, I spent $50. The most expensive things I bought were half a rotisserie chicken and 12 ounces of Coke. At the time, I said, "Dang, this is good cochicken. This is the best I ever tasted." But then a month later, we transmogrified half a dozen oysters in the whole shell. It was better than anything else (Figure 10.6).

Figure 10.6 "Will It Blend? - Oysters"

Jarboe: Who is your target audience? Is it opinion leaders in the YouTube community or customers who also watch online video? Has your target audience changed from when the channel was launched to now?

Wright: Our target audiences were existing customers, potential customers, and employees. We needed to explain complicated pieces of equipment to both B2B and B2C market segments. Although our target audience now includes homemakers as well as our wholesale dealer network and key accounts, all these people are already interested in our product.

Jarboe: Do you optimize your videos for YouTube? Are there search terms that you put in the title, description, and tags of your videos on YouTube? Are there search terms that you use to optimize videos for Google?

Wright: We have optimized around our product. We created the "Will It Blend?" brand name. But blending an iPod was also part of our search engine optimization strategy (Figure 10.7).

Figure 10.7 "Will It Blend? - iPod"

Jarboe: What is the most compelling video content on Blendtec's channel? Is it one of the most viewed or most discussed videos? Is it your playlist?

Wright: I'm always blown away by "Will It Blend? - Marbles." That was the question I asked in my original marketing strategy. We put a bag of 50 marbles into a Blendtec blender. And yes, it blends! Blending a dozen glow sticks was also fun. When we turned the lights off for effect, our 12-hour lantern was engaging. For live blends, we always blend a rake with a wooden handle because it is visual from a distance. Blending a baseball was funny. But some of the best videos we have done to date are in our playlist (Figure 10.8).

Figure 10.8 Cream of the Crop

Jarboe: What is your channel strategy? How much effort is focused on Blendtec's channel on YouTube versus www.willitblend.com? Has this changed since the channel was launched? Will it change going forward?

Wright: We are focused on our own Will It Blend? website, which we control. The analytics are better. And our website gets more views than our YouTube channel. Now, YouTube is a great place to reach new people. But, the website has links to our e-commerce website, so they [customers] can buy our product.

Jarboe: In addition to creating compelling video content, have you engaged in any outreach effort with the YouTube community or bloggers? Do you give opinion leaders a "heads-up" when a new video is uploaded?

Wright: We have more than 200,000 subscribers. They automatically get a "heads-up" whenever we upload a new video. Although we did let the folks at Nike know when we decided to remix their Air Max 90 Current (Figure 10.9). But they'd asked us to do that.

Jarboe: What production challenges have you faced and overcome? Are there any tips or tools that you used to get videos uploaded?

Wright: Keep it real, keep it short, and get to the point. "Will It Blend?" That's as complicated as it gets. On blending day, we won't let Tom know what we're blending. That keeps it real.

Jarboe: Have you taken advantage of any video advertising opportunities? Have you used Yahoo! Video ads, InVideo Ads, contests, or other high-profile placements?

Wright: We haven't taken out any ads. We did put up a billboard on the side of our factory, but YouTube is a social channel. So, we let it work its magic.

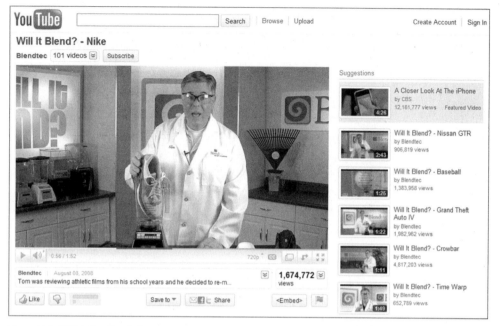

Figure 10.9 "Will It Blend? - Nike"

Jarboe: How do you measure your video campaign? Do you use YouTube Insight, TubeMogul, or other analytics for online video? Do you use web analytics on www.willitblend.com? What feedback have these tools given you that may have led you to change anything you were doing?

Wright: It's hard to pay for fancy analytics when you only spend $50 to start with. So, on our Will It Blend? website, we use Google Analytics because it's free.

Jarboe: I've already got the Will It Blend - The First 50 Videos *DVD. What else should I get?*

Wright: You could get a Will It Blend? T-shirt, which you can wear while pondering life's important questions. What is the purpose of life? What is the airspeed velocity of an unladen swallow? And, of course, Will It Blend?

In March 2010, Wright became executive VP of marketing at Traeger Wood Pellet Grills. He emailed me to say, "Today is my last day at Blendtec... I have accepted an amazing new opportunity to help build a fun company that manufactures wood pellet BBQ grills. If you have never tasted food cooked/smoked on a Traeger Grill, you are missing out!"

He added, "Leaving Blendtec was a difficult decision. Creating the *Will It Blend?* video series was a complete blast and I will certainly miss it. I will continue to provide keynote addresses on social media using the inside story of Blendtec and will actively work to add Traeger success to the continuing story."

Win the Presidency of the United States: Barack Obama

On November 4, 2008, at 9:27 p.m., Barack Obama won the state of Ohio and the outcome of the presidential election became crystal clear. Sean Quinn of FiveThirtyEight.com observed, "That's the ballgame folks. He will be the next president of the United States. Barack Obama will be the next president of the United States."

Today, the whole world knows that Obama won the Democratic Party's nomination after a close campaign against Hillary Rodham Clinton in the 2008 presidential primaries and caucuses. Obama then defeated Republican candidate John McCain in the 2008 general election to become the first African-American elected president. And we also know that the 1,800 videos on BarackObamadotcom's channel on YouTube had been viewed over 110 million times as of November 4, 2008. But did the videos impact what happened next? Obama won 69.5 million popular votes and 365 electoral votes.

To understand the impact of YouTube and video marketing on candidate preference and election outcomes, the person I wanted to interview for this book was Arun Chaudhary. He's been called "Obama's auteur" by Aswini Anburajan of *National Journal Magazine* (April 19, 2008) and "Obama's video guru" by Michael Learmonth of Silicon Alley Insider (July 17, 2008).

Chaudhary's official title on the campaign was new media road director of Obama for America (OFA). Today, he is the White House videographer (Figure 10.10).

Figure 10.10 "Online Video Production Best Practices - A Discussion with Arun Chaudhary from Obama for America"

Barack Obama started using YouTube and video marketing even before officially announcing his candidacy for the presidency of the United States on February 10, 2007.

On January 16, 2007, Obama announced via video on YouTube and his website that he had formed a presidential exploratory committee. As Figure 10.11 illustrates, the 3-minute, 7-second video has more than 1.9 million views.

Figure 10.11 "Barack Obama: My Plans for 2008"

The video also has over 11,100 ratings and almost 4,500 comments. It has also been favorited 1,360 times.

The fact that a preannouncement video could create such an impact indicates that an "invisible caucus" may have been held a month before the "invisible primary."

What's an invisible caucus? And what is an invisible primary?

As Linda Feldmann of the *Christian Science Monitor* reported on February 26, 2007, there was a lot of media buzz about "what's come to be known as the 'invisible primary'—the early jockeying for money, top campaign staff, and high-profile endorsements that winnow the presidential field long before any caucuses or primaries are held."

So, I'm calling the early jockeying for opinion leaders in YouTube's news and politics category an "invisible caucus." And it is worth asking, Did winning it help a former community organizer's presidential campaign take off?

If there is an answer to this question, it's buried in the list of close to 73,000 friends and more than 194,000 subscribers to BarackObamadotcom's channel.

Although you can find out when someone made a campaign donation or public endorsement, YouTube doesn't give you the ability to see the exact date they became a friend or subscriber to a YouTube channel. Yes, the earliest friends and subscribers are on the last page, but no, I don't have the time to go through 73,000 friends and 194,000 subscribers. So, like the chicken and the egg, let's just say we don't know which came first.

We do know that Chaudhary, a 32-year-old New York University film-school professor, took a leave of absence in the summer of 2007 to work for OFA.

In his April 19, 2008, cover story, "Obama's Auteur," Anburajan wrote, "Before Obama, Chaudhary—the son of an immigrant Indian father and a Jewish mother, both scientists—had tried to interest New York-area politicians in his scripts for political ads and Internet videos but to no avail. Then came the senator from Illinois."

Chaudhary lobbied hard for a position in the Obama campaign. He even interrupted both his wedding rehearsal dinner and his wedding day in May 2007 to sell himself to Joe Rospars, OFA's director of new media.

Rospars decided to hire a pro with real film experience to add something fresh to Obama's YouTube and video marketing campaign. "There's a lot of open space to be creative in a campaign and people don't take advantage of it," Rospars told Anburajan.

So Chaudhary became the full-time $40,000-a-year director of field production for the campaign, crisscrossing the country alongside the candidate with two other videographers, making videos that sought to pull supporters into the campaign by letting them peer through his lens.

"Why do you need to see someone with a mike in their hand telling you what Barack Obama said today when you can see for yourself what Barack Obama said today?" Chaudhary told Anburajan.

Chaudhary also told Anburajan about a Chinese-American rapper named Jin the Emcee, who decided to join the Obama campaign after spending a night viewing all of the candidate's campaign videos on his computer.

This provides at least anecdotal evidence for my "invisible caucus" theory.

Of course, the campaign was also being waged offline as well as online. On November 21, 2007, Obama announced that Oprah Winfrey would be campaigning for him. As word spread that Oprah's first appearance would be in Iowa, polls released in early December revealed Obama taking the lead in that critical state. Although celebrity endorsements typically have little effect on voter opinions, the Oprah-Obama tour drew record-setting crowds in Iowa and dominated political news headlines.

On January 3, 2008, Obama won the Iowa Democratic caucus, the first contest in the Democratic nomination season. Obama had the support of 37.6 percent of Iowa's delegates, compared to 29.7 percent for John Edwards and 29.5 percent for Hillary Clinton.

In his remarks to his followers that evening, he said, "On this January night, at this defining moment in history, you have done what the cynics said we couldn't do." He added that in the future, Americans will look back on the 2008 Iowa caucuses and say, "This is the moment when it all began."

This brings us to Obama's "Iowa Caucus Victory Speech" on January 3, 2008. As Figure 11.4 illustrates, the 14-minute, 7-second video has close to 2.4 million views; it also had over 9,400 ratings.

This was the #2 most discussed video on BarackObamadotcom's channel, with more than 5,300 text comments as of April 2009. It had also been favorited more than 1,600 times.

Although news and political junkies could watch the entire speech live at 11:04 p.m. EST, opinion leaders could also share the entire speech with their followers the following day. This means the medium enabled the YouTube community to get a more complete message than you could get from the typical "sound bite," which had dominated political discourse for more than 40 years.

Figure 10.12 "Iowa Caucus Victory Speech"

Now, this didn't shorten the Democratic nomination process, which continued until June 7, 2008. But it did change it.

On July 16, 2008, frog design, *Fast Company*, and NYU's Tisch Interactive Telecommunications Program hosted an event at NYU entitled "Obama and Politics 2.0: Documenting History in Real-Time." It featured a conversation with Chaudhary and Ellen McGirt, a senior writer for *Fast Company*.

The following day, Learmonth posted a story on Silicon Alley Insider about the event entitled "Obama's Video Guru Speaks: How We Owned the YouTube Primary." According to Chaudhary, Obama's organization took online video seriously from the outset, which put them ahead of previous efforts. The Clinton campaign would have had just one staffer videotaping an event; Obama's had between two and four people shooting, editing, and posting video in order to get multiple camera angles. They were fast in getting video posted (as fast as 19 minutes from shoot to post) and fast in alerting voters when new video was up. Wrote Learmonth:

> *Obama's YouTube and web site metrics show that his online viewers aren't pups. The average viewer is 45 to 55 years old, Chaudhary said, a fact he found "shocking." And while Chaudhary made plenty of humorous clips, they weren't the most popular. Invariably the videos that got the most views were long clips of speeches, unscripted moments, or, say, an appearance on "Ellen" or "Oprah." The viewing reflects a hunger not to be entertained, but to know something about the candidate.*

This brings us to the "Obama Speech: 'A More Perfect Union.'" As Figure 10.13 illustrates, the 37-minute, 39-second video has almost 6.5 million views.

Figure 10.13 *"Obama Speech: 'A More Perfect Union'"*

This video also has 29,300 ratings, generated more than 10,000 comments, and was favorited 3,225 times.

Obama spoke in Philadelphia on March 18, 2008 at the National Constitution Center on matters not just of race and recent remarks made by the Reverend Jeremiah Wright but of the fundamental path by which America can work together to pursue a better future.

Just nine days later, the Pew Research Center called the speech "arguably the biggest political event of the campaign so far," noting that 85 percent of Americans said they had heard at least a little about the speech and that 54 percent said they heard a lot about it.

On June 15, 2008, a report by the Pew Internet & American Life Project found 35 percent of Americans said they had watched online political videos—a figure that nearly tripled the reading the Pew Internet Project got in the 2004 race.

The report also found that Obama supporters outpaced McCain supporters in their usage of online video.

Aaron Smith, a research specialists, and Lee Rainie, director of the Pew Internet Project, said, "The punch-counterpunch rhythms of the campaign are now usually played out online in emails and videos rather than in faxed press releases and 30-second ads."

So, what impact did online video have on the outcome of the 2008 presidential election?

BarackObamadotcom's channel on YouTube had been launched on September 5, 2006 (Figure 10.14). It had just over 113,000 subscribers and more than 18 million channel views as of November 1, 2008. And the 1,760 videos on the channel had 93,929,314 total upload views.

Figure 10.14 YouChoose '08

JohnMcCaindotcom's channel on YouTube had been launched on February 23, 2007. It had 28,000 subscribers and over 2 million channel views on that date. And the 327 videos on the channel had over 24 million views all time.

Overall, Obama's videos on YouTube had almost a 4-to-1 lead over McCain's videos in total views and a 9-to-1 lead in channel views the Saturday before Tuesday's presidential election.

In the previous month, Obama's videos had more than 16 million views compared to under 4 million views for McCain's. In the previous week, Obama's videos had over 4 million views compared to 633,000 views for McCain's.

So what impact did YouTube and video marketing have on candidate preference and election outcomes?

On November 7, 2008, Claire Cain Miller posted a story entitled "How Obama's Internet Campaign Changed Politics" on the Bits blog at NYTimes.com. In it, she quoted Joe Trippi, who had run Howard Dean's campaign in 2004.

Trippi said Obama's campaign took advantage of YouTube for free advertising and Trippi argued that those videos were more effective than television ads because viewers chose to watch them or received them from a friend instead of having their television shows interrupted.

"The campaign's official stuff they created for YouTube was watched for 14.5 million hours," said Trippi. "To buy 14.5 million hours on broadcast TV is $47 million."

On November 14, 2008, Jose Antonio Vargas wrote an online column for the *Washington Post* entitled "The YouTube Presidency." In it, he quoted Steve Grove, head of news and politics at YouTube.

Grove said, "The Obama team has written the playbook on how to use YouTube for political campaigns. Not only have they achieved impressive mass—uploading over 1,800 videos that have been viewed over 110 million times total—but they've also used video to cultivate a sense of community amongst supporters."

On April 15, 2009, the Pew Internet & American Life Project reported on the Internet's role in campaign 2008. Here are the findings of its postelection survey of 2,254 adults conducted by Princeton Survey Research Associates International from November 20 to December 4, 2008:

- Forty-four percent of online Obama voters had watched video online from a campaign or news organization, compared to 39 percent of online McCain voters.

- Thirty-nine percent of online Obama voters had watched video online that did not come from a campaign or news organization, compared to 35 percent of online McCain voters.

- Twenty-one percent of online Obama voters shared photos, video, or audio files online related to the campaign or election, compared to 16 percent of McCain voters.

Aaron Smith, a research analyst with the Pew Internet Project, said in the report, "Due to demographic differences between the two parties, McCain voters were actually more likely than Obama voters to go online in the first place. However, online Obama supporters were generally more engaged in the online political process than online McCain supporters."

He added, "Among Internet users, Obama voters were more likely to share online political content with others, sign up for updates about the election, donate money to a candidate online, set up political news alerts, and sign up online for volunteer activities related to the campaign. Online Obama voters were also out in front when it came to posting their own original political content online—26 percent of wired Obama voters did this, compared with 15 percent of online McCain supporters."

Smith also observed, "In 2008, nearly one in five Internet users posted their thoughts, comments, or questions about the campaign on a website, blog, social networking site, or other online forum." He called this group "the online political participatory class." I'd call them opinion leaders. They helped Obama win the presidency of the United States.

Q&A with Arun Chaudhary, New Media Road Director of Obama for America (OFA)

In spring 2009, I got my opportunity to ask Chaudhary questions about OFA's YouTube and video marketing campaign. We conducted the interview via email.

Jarboe: You took leave from NYU to become Barack Obama's director of video field production. How did you first get involved in the campaign?

Chaudhary: An old friend of mine, Kate Albright-Hanna, had taken the position of director of video for the OFA New Media Department. She thought that I might be a good fit to join the team, which was lucky for me because as a film academic and primarily a maker of fiction, I may not have looked like an obvious choice on paper. Video production on the campaign developed very organically as according to need more than by grand design, so the separation of the "Road Team," which I led as the new media road director, wasn't something that was anticipated when I joined the campaign. I was more of the short, funny, creative things guy.

Jarboe: After two years on the campaign trail, you've posted more than 1,000 videos on the BarackObama.com website and on YouTube. What are your most memorable ones?

Chaudhary: There are two videos that always stand out to me.

One I shot on the eve of the Iowa Caucuses (Figure 10.15). President (then Senator) Obama wanted to visit a caucus location, so we went about 45 minutes north of Des Moines to Ankeny, Iowa, not taking any press with us. It was a magic moment, not a single vote of any kind had been cast in the election and we had been campaigning for almost a year, hoping and trusting the American people were hearing the campaign's message. The air was full of anticipation, and when Barack walked in and everyone flocked to him and said they were caucusing for him, we knew that something serious had begun. The little video we made of this visit was posted to YouTube within minutes of it happening but was drowned out in all the attention of the Iowa victory speech that was posted almost immediately afterward. There is a lesson in there somewhere.

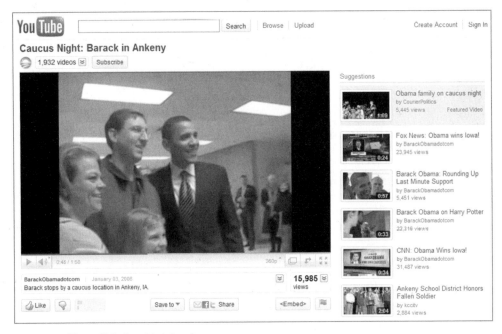

Figure 10.15 "Caucus Night: Barack in Ankeny"

The second video would be our online response to the Clinton campaign's "3 a.m. Girl" ad (Figure 10.16). Senator Clinton had made a political ad about a 3 a.m. phone call that occurred "while your children are asleep." In a strange turn of events, the child in the stock footage the ad used had grown up to be an Obama supporter. The young woman was actually an Obama precinct captain in Washington State. I went to Tacoma to see her, and within 20 hours, travel included, we had a response piece up in YouTube. It was really fun and interesting to do it as a web piece because we had screen time enough to really play around with the material. The final product was as much of a deconstructing of the typical negative ad as it was the young girl's story.

Jarboe: Who was your target audience? Was it opinion leaders in the YouTube community or political activists who also watched online video? Did your target audience change from 2007 to 2008 or from the primaries/caucuses to the general election?

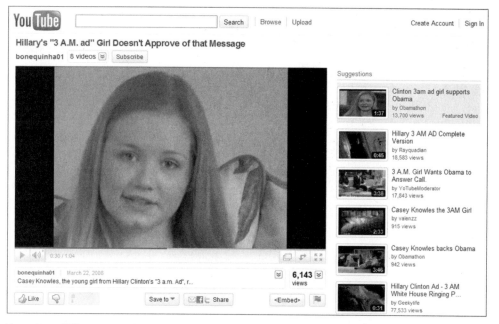

Figure 10.16 "Hillary's '3 A.M. ad' Girl Doesn't Approve of that Message"

Chaudhary: Our target audience was voters, all kinds of voters. While YouTube community folks and political activists were probably vocal commenters on our work, I don't think it would make sense to think of them as a target audience. We wanted to appeal to a wide variety of folks. When you have a candidate as exciting and dynamic as Barack Obama was, the most important thing you can do is get him in front of as many people as possible. We used to say the YouTube or live stream hits of his speeches were like adding thousands of extra seats in the room. Especially in the early states, the sort of people you want to watch an event are folks who couldn't physically make it for some reason. Rather than fishing for viral success, you'd rather have real prospective voters see your candidate make his or her case.

Jarboe: Did you optimize your videos for YouTube? Were there search terms that you put in your title, description, and tags of your videos on YouTube? Were there search terms that were used to optimize videos for Google?

Chaudhary: We tried to be very specific. Location and date of the speech was very important because you really hope that folks who weren't physically able to make the rally are able to find the footage. Topic is very important as well, because a lot of folks looking for political content online are hoping to find answers to their specific questions (what is the candidate's position on health care?) in that way; the candidate's websites are very much a modern update of campaign literature, or maybe even a bit like the voting guides various groups used to publish close to election times (Figure 10.17). You really can't be too specific with your titling, though of course there are only so many words you can actually have in the title itself. I also think it's important to include information in the piece itself. With emerging technologies and when posting videos on many different platforms, you never quite know what will happen. One of the format rules for BarackObama.com that was designed and enforced by Kate Albright-Hanna was that the opening card for every video would be the date and location. I remember thinking that it was maybe a little too austere, but she was absolutely right. If you lived in Keokuk, Iowa, and a friend forwarded you a video link, the first thing you would see when you clicked on it would be November 20th, 2007, Keokuk, Iowa, and you would immediately know why it was relevant to you.

Figure 10.17 "Barack Obama on Health Care"

Jarboe: What was the most compelling video content of the campaign? Was it "Yes We Can - Barack Obama Music Video" or "Obama Speech: 'A More Perfect Union'"?

Chaudhary: I think I better leave the awarding of superlatives to folks who were the audiences of these movies, but between the two you mentioned, I would have to go with "A More Perfect Union." The Will.i.am piece (which was not produced by the campaign; it was made by the artists themselves) was really great, and I think a lot of people found it very inspiring and accessible, but we had consistent calls from the public to put up speeches in their entirety. As time went on, we found that some of the effort of finding specific clips and producing them with cut shots was better spent trying to get entire speeches and town halls online. Folks really seemed to respond to being allowed to see the candidate unedited. In a sense they wanted to see the candidates in the raw and make their own decision, not to feel like they were being fed media. With a candidate as compelling as Barack Obama was, it made a lot of sense to let them see him in this manner. The more people actually saw him speak and heard his views, the more likely they were to vote for him. With a different candidate one might need to take a different strategy, but for us, Barack Obama was always the star; we were just the backup singers.

Jarboe: What was your channel strategy? How much effort was focused on BarackObamadotcom's channel on YouTube versus BarackObama.com/tv/? Did this change from 2007 to 2008 or from the primaries/caucuses to the general election?

Chaudhary: There was a change. As we began seeing that the strongest case we could make for Barack Obama was being made by Barack Obama himself, we spent more time and video resources on the road with the candidate. The team that I led, the Road Team, consisted of six folks who did all the videotaping, still photography, and blogging from the trail itself, putting up YouTube clips from every event, whether it be a speech, a town hall, or even a visit to a local diner.

There was another video team (the one led by Kate Albright-Hanna) who made video content from headquarters, often the more produced pieces. The YouTube channel ended up being dominated by material from the Road Team simply because of the huge volume of videos we produced, although everything was on it. BarackTV was curated by Kate Albright-Hanna (using a higher-quality player than YouTube) with an eye toward the more produced content (Figure 10.18). It was meant to be a complete viewing experience rather than campaign literature.

Figure 10.18 Organizing for America

Jarboe: In addition to creating compelling video content, did you engage in any outreach effort with the YouTube community or bloggers? Was there any effort to give opinion leaders a "heads-up" when a new video was uploaded?

Chaudhary: There was some effort put into blog outreach, mostly from the HQ side; I can't really speak to it, because I wasn't involved with it, nor was it something we thought about much on the road.

Jarboe: What production challenges did you face and overcome? Was video produced in the field but uploaded from headquarters? Are there any tips or tools that you used to get videos uploaded on a daily basis?

Chaudhary: The production challenges were immense. We would often arrive at events with about 10 minutes to go before a speech would start and need to set up our cameras and live-streaming computer as fast as we could. If everything went right, it was just about possible. Editing was just as challenging. The Road Team edited in the field on laptops and uploaded with aircards. On an airplane you can only upload to about 30,000 feet before losing all signal, so time was always of the essence. The watch-word on our team was "workflow." Because we were doing so many events and traveling so constantly, we had a lot of opportunity to improve the workflow; see what order things should be done in, what tasks the computer could handle doing at the same time, figure out how to fill what little time we had to its fullest. Redundancy also helped. Every Road Team member had a camera, a laptop, and an aircard. That way we weren't reliant on any one person to get the job done; we were all able to do what we needed to do. It was definitely a process. By the end of the campaign, it was taking us minutes to upload what was taking hours at the beginning. There was no magic formula, it was just experience. The thing about doing a process over and over and over is that eventually you get better. A tip I would definitely offer others is to always worry about the audio first; once you have that everything else is fixable. Bad video can seem like a choice while bad audio is always a mistake.

Jarboe: Did you take advantage of any video advertising opportunities?

Chaudhary: This isn't really anything I can speak to directly; Joe Rospars and our online ad guys Michael Organ and Andrew Bleeker did a lot of amazing things, even putting up Obama posters in video games, but it wasn't something the Road Team got involved with other than providing footage—something we did for the television folks as well.

Jarboe: How did you measure your video campaign? Did you use YouTube Insight, TubeMogul, or other analytics for online video? Did you use web analytics on BarackObama.com? What feedback did these tools give you that led you to change what you were doing?

Chaudhary: We did pay attention to the analytics. In fact, there was an entire section of the New Media Department devoted to analyzing all the data.

On a personal level, I was never quite sure how accurate the metrics of YouTube Insight or TubeMogul were, but I think it can show you some general trends and that can be quite useful. Seeing that folks would actually watch entire speeches and not just clips was very useful, especially as it is slightly counterintuitive. Also finding out that our core audience was much older than the 18–25 demographic was very interesting. According to the YouTube Insight tool, our main audience was 40 to 50, which is what you would expect from normal political media but not necessarily online. It has certainly reinforced my notion that online political video was essentially the modern replacement for the printed campaign guides of the past. I think a lot of folks went to all the websites to compare and contrast the candidates' views and make an informed decision.

Jarboe: I see President Obama using YouTube (Figure 10.19) as effectively as President Roosevelt used radio when it was still a new medium. How do you see President Obama's use of online video?

Chaudhary: Without getting into specifics, I will say that President Obama has said that he is committed to the idea of a more open, more transparent administration and that online video can certainly be an effective means to achieve that end.

Figure 10.19 Whitehouse's channel

So, did the Barack Obama 2008 presidential campaign use video marketing to generate measurable outcomes?

As Figure 10.20 illustrates, *Fast Company* named Obama's presidential campaign team #1 in the Fast Company 50 for 2009. The magazine said, "This year's most successful startup took a skinny kid with a funny name and turned him into the most powerful new national brand in a generation."

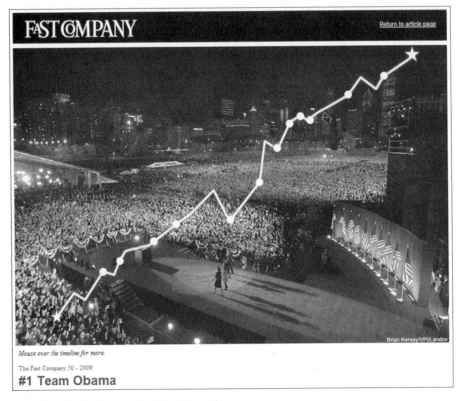

Figure 10.20 The Fast Company 50 - 2009: #1 Team Obama

Fast Company said, "The team has become the envy of marketers both in and out of politics for proving, among other things, just how effective digital initiatives can be." It added, "The community that elected Obama raised more money, held more events, made more phone calls, shared more videos, and offered more policy suggestions than any in history. It also delivered more votes."

There's one additional lesson to learn from the former community organizer's presidential campaign. In Steve Garfield's book, *Get Seen: Online Video Secrets to Building Your Business* (Wiley, 2010), Thomas Gensemer, managing partner of Blue State Digital, shared his thoughts on how video played a role in the Obama campaign for president in 2008.

Gensemer said, "Some 11,000 videos were produced over the course of 22 months, fewer than 10 percent of them probably actually featured the candidate, fewer than 2 percent actually took time from the candidate."

He added, "The story of (the campaign) was about people like you going to events with your video camera, or someone going with a clipboard to sign people up—that became the excitement around this campaign."

Gensemer concluded, "It wasn't about technology. It was about a candidate and an inner circle who understood that one neighbor knocking on the next was more important than flooding the airwaves, and putting things in the mail, that was the essence of the campaign."

Increase Sales of DVDs 23,000 Percent: Monty Python

"And now for something completely different."

It's Monty Python, another group that has used YouTube and video marketing to generate measurable outcomes—yes, yes, the six comedians: Graham Chapman, John Cleese, Terry Gilliam, Eric Idle, Terry Jones, and Michael Palin.

The group created *Monty Python's Flying Circus*. I saw their first show on the BBC when it aired on October 5, 1969. I was a student at the University of Edinburgh back then. Some of my favorite sketches are "Dead Parrot," "The Spanish Inquisition," and "The Ministry of Silly Walks."

The Pythons went on to make such movies as *Monty Python and the Holy Grail* (1975), *Monty Python's Life of Brian* (1979), and *Monty Python's The Meaning of Life* (1983). And Idle wrote *Monty Python's Spamalot*. I bought a T-shirt at the musical that says, "I'm not dead yet."

But I never expected to see the Pythons in this book until January 21, 2009. That was the fateful day the YouTube Blog mentioned, "When Monty Python launched their channel in November, not only did their YouTube videos shoot to the top of the most viewed lists, but their DVDs also quickly climbed to No. 2 on Amazon's Movies & TV bestsellers list, with increased sales of 23,000 percent."

That was exactly the kind of success story that I knew you, the reader, would want to read. But, I didn't know how to contact Cleese, Gilliam, Idle, Jones, or Palin. (Chapman is deceased.)

So, I poked aimlessly about MontyPython's channel (shown in Figure 10.21) on YouTube hoping to find a way to connect with one of the comedians.

I have a YouTube account, so I could have sent them a message. But I thought that would make me look like just another fan of their sketch comedy.

Then, I discovered that, as Figure 10.22 illustrates, one of the most viewed videos on their channel was entitled "The Monty Python Channel on YouTube." That didn't seem right.

Figure 10.21 The Monty Python Channel

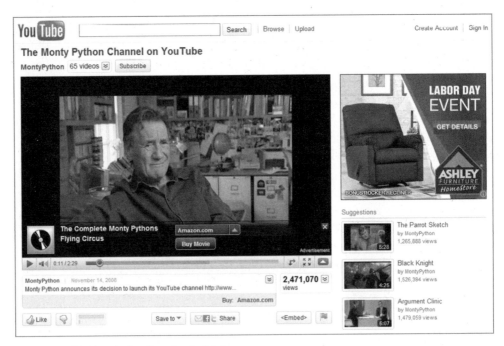

Figure 10.22 "The Monty Python Channel on YouTube"

I watched the 2-minute-and-29-second video and then read the channel information box. One was a close imitation of the language and thoughts of the other.
Based on my extensive research, I concluded that the Pythons had created the YouTube

channel in November 2008 to stop YouTubers from ripping them off. Here's an edited transcript "lovingly ripped off" from their remarks:

> *For three years, you YouTubers have been ripping us off, taking tens of thousands of our videos and putting them on YouTube....*
>
> *We know who you are....*
>
> *We know where you live....*
>
> *We could come after you in ways too horrible to mention....*
>
> *But being the extraordinarily nice chaps we are, we've figured a better way to get our own back....*
>
> *It's time for us to take matters into our own hands....*
>
> *By launching our very own Monty Python channel on YouTube....*
>
> *No more of those crap-quality videos you've been posting. We're giving you the real thing—high-quality videos delivered straight from our Monty Python vault....*
>
> *What's more, we're taking your most viewed clips and uploading brand-new high-quality versions....*
>
> *And what's even more, we're letting you see absolutely everything for free....*
>
> *But we want something in return....*
>
> *We want you to click on the links and buy our movies and TV shows....*
>
> *Only this will soften our pain and disgust at being ripped off all these years.*

As you can see in Figure 10.22, "The Monty Python Channel on YouTube" has almost 2.5 million views. It also has more than 6,000 ratings and over 2,500 text comments. In addition, it has been favorited more than 4,000 times and has generated 35 video responses.

Meanwhile, Aaron Zamost in Google Corporate Communications put me in touch with John Goldstone, who is Monty Python's producer. In fact, Goldstone has been collaborating with the Monty Python team since 1974.

I emailed Goldstone some questions and he promptly emailed me back some answers. His email included an image of the Python mascot, Mr. Gumby (Figure 10.23), so I knew it was authentic.

Figure 10.23
Monty Python's Mr. Gumby

Q&A with John Goldstone, Producer of *Monty Python and the Holy Grail*

Although I was tempted to ask at least one question that was "far too silly," I didn't want to be stopped by a member of the "Anti-Silliness Patrol." So, I asked Goldstone questions that were similar to the ones I'd asked Wright and Chaudhary.

Jarboe: What's your background? How did you first get involved in Monty Python's channel on YouTube?

Goldstone: I have been working with Monty Python over the last 35 years. I produced the three movies—*Monty Python & the Holy Grail*, *Life of Brian*, and *The Meaning of Life*—and because we were able to keep the copyright in the movies and the 45 episodes of *Monty Python's Flying Circus*, I was able, when DVD became the primary format for home entertainment, to revisit the movies and TV shows and give them a whole new life both technically and with a considerable amount of new content. As the power of DVD started to recede last year, it was time to review our digital strategy, and apart from initiating a program of making the titles available for digital download, we felt the time had come to deal with the "YouTube problem." On the one hand, we were surprised at the number of clips that had been uploaded to YouTube in clear infringement of our copyright, and while we didn't want to be spoilsports, it was getting pretty much out of control and we could see no real benefit. So I arranged a trip to meet the YouTube guys on the Google campus in San Jose and discovered that they had a program that would enable us to have our own Monty Python channel on YouTube where we could put up clips from the movies and TV shows of far greater quality and order that might also encourage viewers to want to see whole movies or TV episodes via links to Amazon and iTunes and expand our Monty Python fan base.

Jarboe: Who was your target audience? Was it opinion leaders in the YouTube community or Monty Python fans who also watched online video? Did your target audience change from when the channel was launched to now?

Goldstone: Because Monty Python has been around for almost 40 years (October 2009 is the 40th anniversary of the first broadcast on BBC TV of *Monty Python's Flying Circus*), there are possibly now six generations of Monty Python fans around the world, so it wasn't a question of targeting but more about letting YouTube do its miraculous thing and bring its very wide audience into our net.

Jarboe: Did you optimize your videos for YouTube? Are there search terms that you put in the title, description, and tags of your videos?

Goldstone: We gave each clip as much cross reference as possible to make the search that much easier.

Jarboe: What is the most compelling video content on MontyPython's channel? Is it one of the most viewed or most discussed videos? Is it one of your playlists?

Goldstone: Certainly the most compelling, viewed, and discussed is the new introduction video we created for the launch of the channel. I had written the mission statement for the channel, which became the commentary for the introduction video, and we drew on interviews with the Pythons to tell the story. We used the playlist option as a way to create themes, which we continue to populate with new videos.

Jarboe: What is your channel strategy? How much effort was focused on Monty Python's channel on YouTube versus http://pythonline.com? Has this changed since the channel was launched? Will it change going forward?

Goldstone: We have been developing PythOnline, which Eric Idle started in 1996, from its original form into a more interactive, user-generating platform and are about to go for a full launch of the MashCaster, which the folks at New Media Broadcasting Company who manage PythOnline for us have developed as a down-loadable software program that enables Terry Gilliam–type animation to be created, shared, broadcast, and uploaded on PythOnline and of course YouTube. User-generated content is therefore a big part of our future direction. *(Figure 10.24 shows the PythOnline site home page.)*

Jarboe: In addition to creating compelling video content, have you engaged in any outreach effort with the YouTube community or bloggers? Do you give opinion leaders a "heads-up" when a new video is uploaded?

Goldstone: So far we have preferred to provide new content on a regular basis to which YouTube subscribers to the Monty Python Channel are automatically alerted.

Figure 10.24 PythOnline

Jarboe: What production challenges have you faced and overcome? Are there any tips or tools that you used to get videos uploaded?

Goldstone: Maintaining high-definition quality has been the biggest challenge. Our mission statement criticized the inferior quality of so many of the clips that had been uploaded before the launch of the Monty Python Channel and we wanted to show how good they could and should be.

Jarboe: The YouTube Blog says your "DVDs quickly climbed to No. 2 on Amazon's Movies & TV bestsellers list" when you launched your channel, "with increased sales of 23,000 percent." Why did you take advantage of YouTube's click-to-buy platform? Did you also use Yahoo! Video ads, InVideo Ads, contests, or other high-profile placements?

Goldstone: The click-to-buy ability was exactly what we were looking for to make the link from video to the right Amazon page much more effective than the URL by the side of the video description. We are only now beginning to address premium advertising, which is only possible when you can show the size, composition, and consistency of your viewers.

Jarboe: How did you measure your video campaign? Did you use YouTube Insight, TubeMogul, or other analytics for online video? Did you use web analytics on http://pythonline.com? *What feedback did these tools give you that may have led you to change anything you were doing?*

Goldstone: The analysis tools have been very useful for identifying where in the world our viewers are, although, because our DVDs have been available in many countries of the world, we have known for some time where our major audience bases are.

Jarboe: I've been a fan of the Pythons since Monty Python's Flying Circus *first aired on the BBC. Did the Pythons create a YouTube channel just to stop their content from being released illegally on the Internet, or is this the beginning of a new chapter in the quest for Global PythoNation?*

Goldstone: It certainly started as a way to control what was going on, but the extraordinary response we got to launching our own channel has opened up broader ideas to reach and expand our audience.

That is serious advice from a man who has been producing comedy films in England since the mid-1970s. But, perhaps I should make an appointment with the Argument Clinic (Figure 10.25), because I'd like to have a five-minute argument with Goldstone about one of his statements.

He said, "There are possibly now six generations of Monty Python fans around the world." But that's highly unlikely for a group that's been around for only 40 years, unless those fans are baboons. According to *Wikipedia*, a new generation of baboons comes along every five to eight years. So, it's possible that six generations of baboons have been born since 1969.

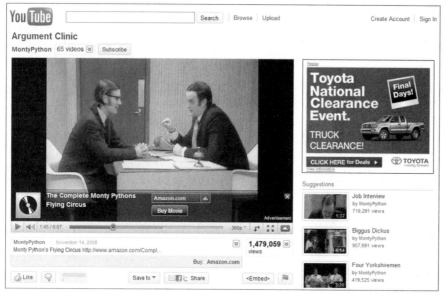

Figure 10.25 "Argument Clinic"

But let's not bicker and argue over who begat who. If you close your eyes and just listen to the sound that a 23,000 percent increase in DVD sales is making, you can hear the cash register ring.

Generate $2.1 million in Sales: PiperSport Launch

Can you use YouTube to sell a $140,000 product?

I asked Michael Kolowich that question for Search Engine Watch's channel on Feb. 2, 2010 (Figure 10.26).

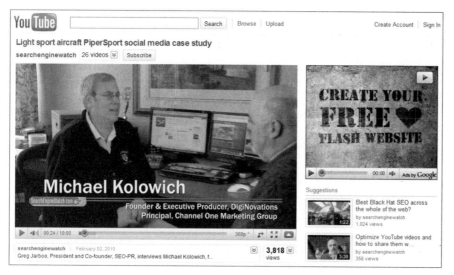

Figure 10.26 "Light sport aircraft PiperSport social media case study"

I've known Kolowich for more than 30 years. Early in his career, he was a reporter at **WGBH-TV** in Boston, where he won an Emmy Award for outstanding news reporting. From 1985 to 1988, he was corporate vice president of marketing and business development of **Lotus Development Corporation**. From 1988 till 1991, he was the founding publisher of *PC/Computing.*

Kolowich is currently president and executive producer of **DigiNovations**, which he founded in late 2001. During the 2008 presidential election campaign, he was architect and producer of **Mitt TV**, the acclaimed video website for the Mitt Romney presidential campaign.

In the past three years, DigiNovations has also produced major projects for Genzime, Harvard Business School, MIT, the Museum of Science, and Piper Aircraft.

On Thursday, January 13, 2010, the Piper Aircraft marketing team faced a dilemma.

The good news was that Piper management had just inked a licensing deal that would allow the company to bring a game-changing personal aircraft to the market, the PiperSport.

The bad news was that launch day for the PiperSport would be just eight days later, on January 21, at a major sport aircraft show in Florida.

The eight-day timeline would be short even for a traditional launch. But PiperSport seemed to be a product tailor-made for social media: a hip new personal transportation product targeted at young pilots at a price point roughly double that of a luxury car. With the timeline tight and the budget even tighter, Piper decided that a digital marketing campaign would be the quickest way to build awareness and excitement about a new airplane.

Commissioning DigiNovations to take the lead, Piper quickly assembled a tightly integrated program on Facebook, YouTube, and Twitter that produced strong awareness, eye-popping sales results, and many turned heads in the aviation marketing field. Piper turned a budget of less than $50,000 into presales of more than a dozen $140,000 aircraft, more than half of which were ordered via $10,000 deposits made through a PayPal web link.

This is the story of that campaign.

With time short and resources scarce, Piper and DigiNovations settled on several objectives:

- Create broad awareness of the new PiperSport within two weeks of launch, as measured by search inquiries, website visits, and social media engagement.
- Steal the thunder from a major competitor, Cessna Aircraft, whose entry in the same class had suffered a major manufacturing delay.
- Create strong interest in the aviation press, fueled by a sense of market interest and momentum, sufficient to earn a major aviation magazine cover.

- Build a communications channel with at least 5,000 "fans" via a social media channel, feeding enthusiasts and evangelists with a steady stream of news and updates.

- Create at least three aircraft sales directly attributable to social media channels, more than amortizing the full cost of the social marketing program with margins on the sold aircraft.

The time horizon of the first phase of the campaign would be January 21 through mid-April, when the first PiperSport would be delivered to the first customer at a major air show in Florida.

The Video

The longest lead-time item would be creation of a marketing video to introduce the PiperSport to the public. Making it trickier was that the initial aircraft were in a secret location and had not yet been certified and insured to fly. The DigiNovations team settled on a highly personalized, informal approach to introducing the PiperSport, featuring key Piper executives taking the viewer on a video "tour" of its features, Piper's chief pilot discussing detailed flying characteristics, and a young woman taking her first lesson in the aircraft.

As Figure 10.27 illustrates, "Inside the PiperSport - the New Light Sport Aircraft from Piper (HD)," has more than 115,000 views. It also has over 100 ratings and 11 comments. And it has been favorited over 160 times.

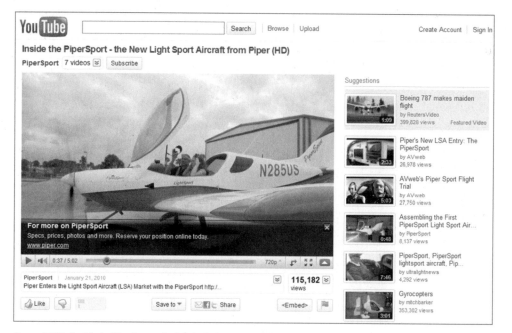

Figure 10.27 "Inside the PiperSport - the New Light Sport Aircraft from Piper (HD)"

The YouTube Channel

A custom-designed YouTube channel would host not just the main video but also shorter, supplemental "tell me more" pieces built from outtakes as well as video reviews from aviation journalists when they became available. A mechanism was set up to scan for new videos twice a day so that all new independently produced video material could be discovered and "favorited" for inclusion in the PiperSport channel.

PiperSport's channel (Figure 10.28) has more than 84,000 channel views, almost 150,000 total upload views, and over 500 subscribers.

Figure 10.28 PiperSport's channel

The Facebook Fan Page

The team created a Facebook fan page (facebook.com/PiperSport) and began loading it with useful content so that it would look vibrant and "full" even to the first visitors who arrived. The team took advantage of the fact that there was a small but very enthusiastic cadre of fans of a predecessor to the PiperSport in the United States who could be attracted and cultivated to enthusiastically review and post about the aircraft, even before the official PiperSport would fly in April. This provided plenty of photographs, stories, and personal videos to keep the anticipation high even before the first delivery in April. The Facebook page was launched simultaneously with the announcement and seed-promoted with pay-per-click ads on Facebook targeted at pilots and aviation enthusiasts. The Piper team posted several times a day during the first two weeks, daily for the following month, and even now posts every two to three days (and comments daily).

As Figure 10.29 illustrates, the PiperSport Light Sport Aircraft fan page has almost 11,900 fans, or people who like it. It also has 10 photo albums and has embedded four YouTube videos.

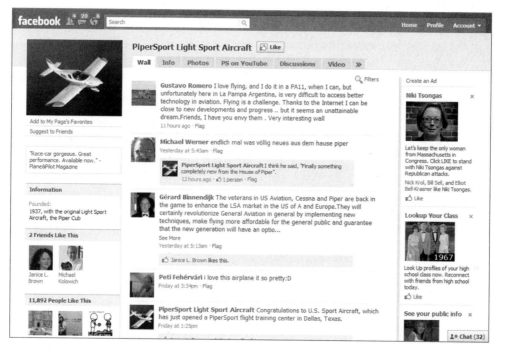

Figure 10.29 PiperSport Light Sport Aircraft

The Twitter Feed

While the Facebook page was targeted at enthusiasts, a Twitter feed (twitter.com/ PiperSport) was more narrowly targeted at aviation journalists and opinion leaders. The objective here would be quality, not quantity, to keep opinion leaders well-informed about every event and milestone, new material, and so on. The team measured success here by retweets by opinion leaders to their respective audiences.

As Figure 10.30 illustrates, the PiperSport Twitter feed has more than 400 followers. These include almost 100 percent of a targeted list of aviation journalists, bloggers, and opinion leaders.

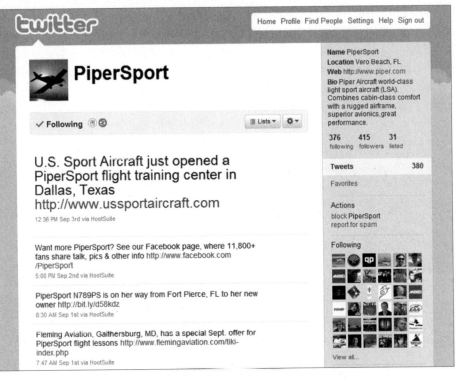

Figure 10.30 PiperSport Light Sport Aircraft on Twitter

Here are some of the important results milestones for the social media launch of
the PiperSport:

- On January 20, 2010, a Google search for "PiperSport" turned up zero results;
  it now returns more than 106,000 results. What's more, the company's official
  channels—website, Facebook page, YouTube videos, Twitter feed, and other
  materials—occupy 4 out of the top 10 search results.

- The PiperSport program has been cited by Technorati and Search Engine Watch
  as a groundbreaking program in social media marketing effectiveness. Market
  enthusiasm inspired *Flying Magazine* to put PiperSport on its May 2010 cover.

- By late April, at least 15 new PiperSports had been ordered at an average order
  size of nearly $140,000 each. Eight of these had been bought via $10,000 deposits made through PayPal; Facebook had been credited by at least four buyers
  publicly as influencing their sale. PiperSports are being sold much faster than
  they can be made.

Q&A with Michael Kolowich, President and Executive Producer, DigiNovations

I interviewed Kolowich about launching the PiperSport. Here are my questions and his
answers.

Jarboe: What's your background? How did you get involved with the PiperSport launch?

Kolowich: I am a marketing advisor to Piper Aircraft, the 73-year-old small airplane manufacturer that brought the PiperSport to market in 2010. Before the launch, the Piper marketing team asked me to review their market-launch plan and to come up with ideas to spice up the introduction of this very cool, sexy airplane that they feel will be a game-changer.

Jarboe: Who is your target audience? Is it opinion leaders in the YouTube community or customers who also watch online video? Did you have different target audiences for YouTube, Facebook, and Twitter?

Kolowich: Pilots—and people who want to be pilots—are heavy users of the Internet and social media. We know this by the traffic on aviation-related websites, blogs, bulletin boards, and online communities. We can also see that pilots post and consume a huge number of YouTube videos. So we believed we could reach potential buyers directly on YouTube and Facebook through a combination of SEM, SEO, and targeted Facebook ads. Twitter, on the other hand, has an extremely active group of influencers—aviation journalists, bloggers, and pundits; our Twitter strategy, therefore, was aimed principally at influencers who could seed and accelerate our direct-to-customer approaches in YouTube and Facebook.

Jarboe: Do you optimize your videos for YouTube? Are there search terms that you put in the title, description, and tags of your videos on YouTube? Are there search terms that you use to optimize videos for Google?

Kolowich: It's important to optimize videos for YouTube—especially in an environment where there are so many pilots watching so many videos. We want to make sure we're seen not just when directly searched for, but also under "related videos" when a viewer is done watching another video. So we comb through our competitors' video titles, descriptions, and tags to find appropriate matches. "Light Sport Aircraft" is the name of the new category of airplane to which the PiperSport belongs, so we certainly optimize around that. Our main brand name, Piper, is also quite popular among pilots as a search term. You'll have to guess our other keywords; I don't want to give away ALL our secrets!

Jarboe: What is the most compelling video content on PiperSport's channel? Is it one of the most viewed or most discussed videos? Is it your playlist?

Kolowich: "Compelling" has a lot of dimensions. All of our videos on the PiperSport YouTube channel are well-watched, but we frankly have roles that each of them plays. By sheer viewing volume, "Inside the PiperSport - the new Light Sport Aircraft from Piper (HD)" would have to be considered the most compelling—especially if you look at the Hot Spots analysis under YouTube Insights, showing much higher-than-normal viewer engagement. But another one that seems to get a lot of pass-around action is a 30-second time-lapse, set to "Flight of the Bumblebee," that shows a PiperSport being assembled at high speed (Figure 10.31).

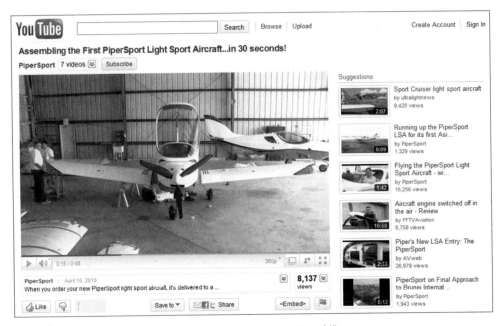

Figure 10.31 "Assembling the First PiperSport Light Sport Aircraft...in 30 Seconds!"

Jarboe: What is your channel strategy? How much effort was focused on PiperSport's channel, website, Facebook page, or Twitter feed? Has this changed since the YouTube channel was launched? Will it change going forward?

Kolowich: Facebook and YouTube have equal but complementary roles in our channel strategy. We've found the level of engagement to be much higher with the PiperSport community on Facebook rather than YouTube. But adding new YouTube videos periodically gives us something to post about in Facebook, and we try to post almost daily.

Jarboe: In addition to creating compelling video content, have you engaged in any outreach effort with the YouTube community or bloggers? Do you give opinion leaders a "heads-up" when a new video is uploaded?

Kolowich: We should do more outreach, but with limited resources we rely on Twitter and Facebook posts to get the word out about our videos. People are paying attention—when we post about a new YouTube video on Facebook, it's not unusual to see the YouTube counter go up by almost 1,000 views within hours.

Jarboe: What production challenges have you faced and overcome? Are there any tips or tools that you used to get videos uploaded?

Kolowich: As someone who's been producing video for 38 years, most of the solutions to production challenges are second nature. And in fact, we developed during the last presidential campaign a production process that goes from raw video to online in hours—even minutes, if necessary. We don't upload raw video—it's simply too big, and I'd prefer to do the first-level compression myself; rather, we've developed a set of presets for Apple Compressor, Adobe Media Encoder, and MPEG StreamClip that produce nice, crisp videos that play on YouTube's high-definition settings. Our only frustration is that YouTube defaults to a low-resolution version, so unless the viewer clicks on the settings button, they won't see our nice, pristine high-def version.

Jarboe: Have you taken advantage of any video advertising opportunities? Have you used Promoted Videos or other ad placements?

Kolowich: Promoted Videos (via AdWords) has been essential to seeding our videos initially for a quick start. We place relatively inexpensive keyword buys against both phrases that are too broad to pick up our videos (e.g., "new light sport aircraft") or that are competitive and wouldn't naturally come up in a search ("Cessna Skycatcher"). This has significantly increased our reach in very short periods of time, at relatively low expense.

Jarboe: How do you measure your video campaign? Do you use YouTube Insight, TubeMogul, or other analytics for online video? Do you use web analytics on www.piper.com? What feedback have these tools given you that may have led you to change anything you were doing?

Kolowich: We watch two things in particular on YouTube Insight: Hot Spots (which helps us determine which scenes work and which ones don't during the course of a video) and Referrals (to watch the progression from Promoted Videos to organic growth). We also track them through to inquiries and conversions on www.piper.com.

Jarboe: How does the launch of the PiperSport compare to other launches by Piper Aircraft? Was anyone at Piper Aircraft surprised that you could use YouTube and video marketing to sell a $140,000 product?

Kolowich: Never before has a Piper aircraft been launched in quite this way. The old approach was to rent space at an air show, hold a news conference, take a lot of reporters and editors up for a flight, and hope for a magazine cover—or at least a favorable review. The combination of Facebook, YouTube, and Twitter fanned the flames of interest in PiperSport to a fever pitch between its announcement in January 2010, and its actual availability 12 weeks later. It was so surprising that the dealer infrastructure, accustomed to a more leisurely ramp-up, was not prepared to handle the volume of inquiries. Fortunately, our website had a way to order the airplane online—and even to place deposits via PayPal. And month by month through the first year, PiperSport continues to exceed all expectations; in 2010, it is expected to outsell all other airplanes in its class.

Now, you can't deposit fans, views, or followers in a bank. But, $2.1 million in sales are worth something. And, if you do the math, generating $2.1 million in sales with a marketing budget of less than $50,000 means that Piper Aircraft got a short-term return on a marketing investment of 42X.

So, you can measure the value of social media and video marketing in cold, hard cash.

However, you'll want to know the epilogue to this story.

On January 12, 2011, Piper Aircraft terminated its business relationship with Czech Republic–based Czech Sport Aircraft to market that company's Light Sport Aircraft, citing differences in business philosophies.

In a press release, Piper CEO Geoffrey Berger said, "After a year working with Czech Sport Aircraft, Piper determined that it is in our company's best long-term interests to discontinue the business relationship which distributed a Light Sport Aircraft manufactured by the Czech company and distributed under Piper's brand by a separate distributor network."

When I asked Kolowich for a comment, he said, "This story is one of those 'be careful what you wish for' stories."

He added, "The breakup had nothing to do with the marketing success of the product; in fact, PiperSport became the best-selling light sport aircraft in the world and succeeded beyond its wildest dreams, based in no small measure on the social media and video marketing buzz. Rather, it was a difference in operating philosophy between the two companies that caused the rift."

He concluded, "Ironically, the fact that the PiperSport had become a social media phenomenon made it that much more difficult for Piper to let go. But the end was announced on—where else?—Facebook. And Piper turned its attention to a much more daunting social media challenge: promoting its $2.5 million PiperJet Altaire, which already has quite a Facebook and YouTube following."

And now you know … the rest of the story.

A Quick Look
at the Future

YouTube has changed dramatically over the last six years, and the rules of video marketing are now radically different too. Today, everyone involved in YouTube marketing feels like they're playing "Calvinball." In this final chapter, we will take a quick look at what has changed at YouTube in just the past year, visit a destination for insight into the zeitgeist of the world's largest video site, identify the new rules of YouTube marketing, and learn how to shape the future of a forum for people that acts like a distribution platform. Finally, it will be time to say, "Enough storyboarding. Let's shoot something."

11

Chapter Contents:
"It's Never the Same! It's Always Bizarre!"
Look at What Has Changed in the Past Year
Stay on Top of the Latest Trends
Play by the New Rules of YouTube Marketing
"Hit 'em Where They Ain't"

"It's Never the Same! It's Always Bizarre!"

This is the last chapter, and I know you are eager to get started. You have already spent an hour a day over several months learning what I can currently teach you about YouTube and video marketing. Like the fellows in Figure 11.1, you are ready to say, "Enough storyboarding. Let's shoot something."

"Enough storyboarding. Let's shoot something."

Figure 11.1 "Enough storyboarding. Let's shoot something." (Cartoon by Leo Cullum in *The New Yorker*, June 4, 2001.)

I hear you. Or, as the Na'vi say in the film *Avatar* (2009), "I see you." But there is one more important lesson you need to learn: There is always more to learn.

New developments at YouTube and continual changes in video marketing mean the mysteries of online video can never be revealed once and for all. So you need to continue asking questions in the days, weeks, and months ahead.

YouTube has changed dramatically over the last six years, and the rules of video marketing are now radically different too. In early 2006, everyone in the field was trying to create viral videos. But, as Figure 11.2 illustrates, Google Insights for Search shows that web search interest in the terms "viral video" and "viral videos" peaked in March 2006 and is currently less than 40 percent of what it was back then.

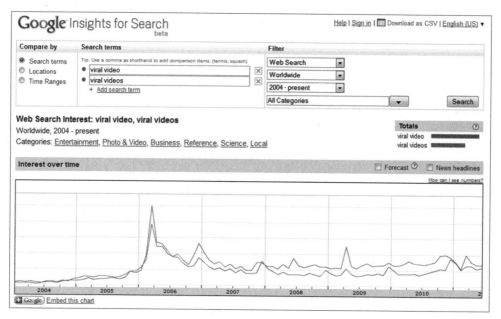

Figure 11.2 Google Insights for Search – Web Search Interest: viral video, viral videos

Today, everyone in YouTube marketing feels like they're playing Calvinball, the game invented by Bill Watterson in his comic strip *Calvin and Hobbes*. According to Hobbes, "No sport is less organized than Calvinball." Or, as the Calvinball theme song says:

> *Other kids' games are such a bore!*
> *They've gotta have rules and they gotta keep score!*
> *Calvinball is better by far!*
> *It's never the same! It's awalys bizarre!*

Key features of various games included the Babysitter Flag, the Bonus Box, the Calvinball Theme Song, the Corollary Zone, the Invisible Sector, the Opposite Pole, the Perimeter of Wisdom, the Pernicious Poem Place, Time-Fracture Wickets, and the Vortex Spot.

Scoring was arbitrary, whimsical, and capricious. In one strip, Calvin observed, "The only permanent rule in Calvinball is that you can't play it the same way twice!" And Hobbes replied, "The score is still Q to 12!"

So, let's start this chapter by taking a quick look at what has been changed, amended, or deleted at YouTube in just the past year. This should help you pick up the nuances of video marketing fast.

Look at What Has Changed in the Past Year

At the end of Chapter 1 of this book, you read how YouTube celebrated its fifth birthday on May 16, 2010.

On that day, the YouTube team said on the YouTube Blog, "Since we never could have predicted all that happened in YouTube's first five years, we certainly can't imagine what the future will look like. But we do know there's a lot more to be done."

That was an understatement.

What follows are thumbnail descriptions from the YouTube Blog of just the 40 most significant things that have changed in the year to follow.

Top Changes: May to November 2010

Google Moderator on YouTube was launched on May 27, 2010. Olivia Ma, YouTube news manager, and Ginny Hunt, product manager, Moderator, said, "Moderator is a versatile, social platform that allows you to solicit ideas or questions on any topic, and have the community vote the best ones up to the top in real-time." Nick Kristof of the New York Times uses it to take questions about his travels around the globe, Howcast uses it to ask for ideas for its next how-to video, and cardiologist Dr. Euan Ashley of Stanford uses it to answer questions about heart disease and other genetic-related disorders.

The **YouTube Video Editor** was introduced on June 16, 2010. Rushabh Doshi, software engineer, said, "The editor is ideal for merging single, short clips into a longer video." You can use it to trim the beginning and end of your videos, add a soundtrack from YouTube's AudioSwap library, and remix Creative Commons videos.

On June 23, 2010, Judge Louis L. Stanton granted Google's motion for summary judgment in **Viacom's lawsuit** with YouTube. Kent Walker, vice president and general counsel, Google, said, "This is an important victory not just for us, but also for the billions of people around the world who use the web to communicate and share experiences with each other." On June 24, 2010, I wrote on Search Engine Watch, "For years, Viacom continuously and secretly uploaded its content to YouTube, even while publicly complaining about its presence there. It hired no fewer than 18 different marketing agencies to upload its content to the site. It deliberately 'roughed up' the videos to make them look stolen or leaked. It opened YouTube accounts using phony email addresses. It even sent employees to Kinko's to upload clips from computers that couldn't be traced to Viacom. And in an effort to promote its own shows, as a matter of company policy Viacom routinely left up clips from shows that had been uploaded to YouTube by ordinary users. Executives as high up as the president of Comedy Central and the head of MTV Networks felt 'very strongly' that clips from shows like *The Daily Show* and *The Colbert Report* should remain on YouTube. Viacom's efforts to disguise its promotional use of YouTube worked so well that even its own employees could not keep track of everything it was posting or leaving up on the site. As a result, on countless occasions Viacom demanded the removal of clips that it had uploaded to YouTube, only to return later to sheepishly ask for their reinstatement. In fact, some of the very clips that Viacom was suing YouTube over were actually uploaded by Viacom itself. Given Viacom's own actions, there is no way YouTube could ever have known which Viacom content was and was not authorized to be on the site. But Viacom thinks YouTube should somehow have figured it out. Yesterday, Viacom said in an emailed statement, 'We believe that this ruling by the lower court is fundamentally flawed.' I disagree. Judge Stanton got it right."

YouTube announced the launch of **"Life in a Day"** on July 6, 2010. Tim Partridge, product marketing manager, said, "On July 24, you have 24 hours to capture a snapshot of your life on camera." As Figure 11.3 illustrates (http://youtu.be/XMxuocCN100), Kevin Macdonald, the Oscar-winning director of *One Day in September*, edited the most compelling footage into a feature documentary film, which was executive produced by Ridley Scott, the director behind films like *Thelma & Louise, Gladiator,* and *Black Hawk Down.*

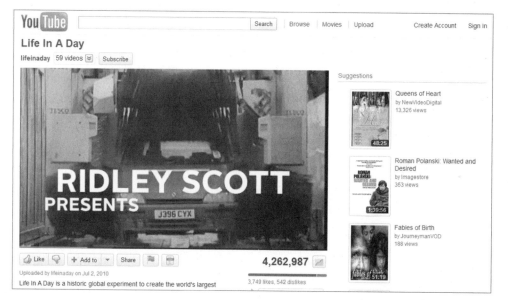

Figure 11.3 "Life In A Day"

An updated version of **YouTube Mobile Website** was rolled out on July 7, 2010. A year later, YouTube Mobile was getting more than 320 million views a day and represented 10 percent of the video-sharing site's daily views.

YouTube announced support for videos shot in **4K** on July 9, 2010. Ramesh Sarukkai, YouTube engineer, said, "To give some perspective on the size of 4K, the ideal screen size for a 4K video is 25 feet; IMAX movies are projected through two 2K resolution projectors." However, watching videos in 4K will require ultra-fast high-speed broadband connections.

A new **embed code style** that uses <iframe> was announced on July 22, 2010. Toliver Jue, software engineer, said, "If you use the new embed code style, your viewers will be able to view your embedded video in one of our Flash or HTML5 players, depending on their viewing environment and preferences." The new embed style also allowed embeds to work on mobile devices, which typically use a built-in player instead of Flash or HTML5.

The **upload limit increased to 15 minutes** for all users on July 29, 2010. Joshua Siegel, product manager, Upload and Video Management, said, "We encourage you to take full advantage of this new time limit by making a video of your '15 minutes of fame.'" On August 12, 2010, I posted "Look Who Is Monetizing their 15 Minutes of Fame on YouTube" to Search Engine Watch. I said, "I found several categories of YouTube partners that were using their extra time to make some extra money. This includes: Beauty Tips, Technology & Electronics, Machinima, Video Blogs, and Gadgets." I added, "Not every beauty tip or gadget demo can be squeezed into 10 minutes. Some need a full 15 minutes to cover every detail. And don't get me started on the time it takes to learn a sound strategy for getting into high rounds on the COD:WaW Zombie Map Shi No Numa."

YouTube began a limited trial of a new **live-streaming** platform on September 12, 2010, in conjunction with four partners: Howcast, Next New Networks, Rocketboom, and Young Hollywood. Joshua Siegel, product manager, and Christopher Hamilton, product marketing manager, said, "This new platform integrates live streaming directly into YouTube channels; all broadcasters need is a webcam or external USB/FireWire camera."

YouTube Leanback on Google TV was launched on October 18, 2010. Camille Hearst, product marketing manager, said, "Leanback offers 10 channels, updated daily, featuring popular and interesting videos in genres like Comedy, Entertainment, News, Science & Technology, How To & Style, and more. You can also watch full-length movies and TV shows rented from youtube.com in the highest quality." As Figure 11.4 illustrates, I interviewed Maile Ohye, developer programs tech lead, Google, at SES Chicago 2010 about optimizing sites for TV (http://youtu.be/eXgqD8tb5Gg). She said, "Current sites should already work, but you may want to provide your users with an enhanced TV experience—what's called the '10-foot UI' (user interface)."

YouTube announced on October 28, 2010, that **Promoted Videos had hit half a billion views.** Jay Akkad, product manager, said, "In the past year, we've seen a more than six-fold increase in the number of times viewers have clicked to watch a Promoted Video." On August 8, 2011, YouTube announced that Promoted Videos had hit a billion views as well as other changes, including placement on Google Video search results, introduction on YouTube Mobile, and inclusion in TrueView video ads.

YouTube also announced on October 28, 2010, that it had over **one billion subscriptions.** Georges Haddad, product marketing manager, said, "Over a billion subscription updates are sent to our users' homepages every week, and 16 YouTube channels have crossed the one million subscriber mark: fred, nigahiga, kassemg, shanedawsonTV, shanedawsonTV2, smosh, universalmusicgroup, machinima, sxephil, mysteryguitarman, davedays, kevjumba, realannoyingorange, raywilliamjohnson, collegehumor and failblog." As this was written, raywilliamjohnson's channel had more than 4.3 million subscribers and nigahiga's had almost 4.2 million.

Figure 11.4 "Introducing Google TV and optimizing sites for TV at SES Chicago 2010"

YouTube partnered with CBS News on November 2, 2010, to **live-stream election results** and highlight election trends on YouTube and Google. Ramya Raghavan, YouTube News & Politics, said, "This approach of examining web trends adds a new level of depth to election reporting and is a model that news organizations can use for any major event or milestone." It's worth noting that 9 of the top 10 searches on Google.com that day were election related—and most of them were queries on where to vote.

As Figure 11.5 illustrates, the company announced on November 10, 2010, that over **35 hours of video was uploaded to YouTube every minute.** Hunter Walk, director of product management, said, "That breaks out to 2,100 hours uploaded every 60 minutes, or 50,400 hours uploaded to YouTube every day."

The company asked users to try out a prototype of **YouTube Topics on Search** on November 10, 2010. Palash Nandy, software engineer, said, "Put simply, we try to identify topics on YouTube and associate videos with them." Go to www.youtube.com/topics to try it out.

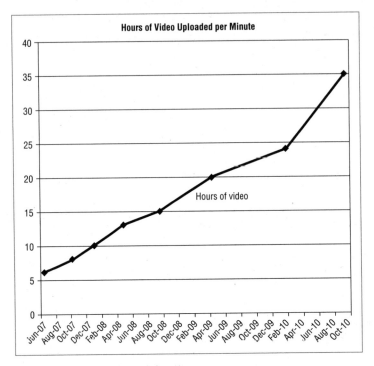

Figure 11.5 Hours of Video Uploaded per Minute

Top Changes: December 2010 to May 2011

YouTube introduced **TrueView Video Ads** on December 2, 2010. Phil Farhi, senior product manager, said, "We think that giving viewers a choice of which ads they want to watch means it's even more likely that they'll be engaged with the ad, and that advertisers will get their messages across to the right person." On the Inside AdWords blog, Gordon Zhu added, "And we charge advertisers only when a viewer has chosen to watch your ad, not when an impression is served." What does this mean to advertisers? You pay only when a viewer watches either 30 seconds of an ad or a 15-second ad to its completion. In June 2011, YouTube reported that 70 percent of users were skipping pre-roll ads. I'll bet this news nugget caused some sleepless nights for the folks at Hulu, where viewers can't skip pre-rolls and advertisers are charged even if 70 percent of viewers don't think their ads are relevant or engaging.

On December 9, 2010, YouTube began allowing selected users with a history of complying with the YouTube Community Guidelines and its copyright rules to **upload videos that are longer than 15 minutes.** Joshua Siegel, product manager, and Doug Mayle, software engineer, Upload, said, "This launch has been made possible in part by the continued advances in our state-of-the-art Content ID system, as well as our other powerful tools for copyright owners." It was also made possible in part by Judge Stanton's decision.

YouTube announced some important **improvements to annotations** on December 9, 2010. Itamar Gilad, product manager, said, "One in five YouTube video views shows annotations and many of these are clickable." This means YouTube had close to 100 million individual annotations at that point in time. And some content creators were getting as much as 20 percent of their views from annotation links placed in their videos. So, annotations aren't geeky. They are effective for content discovery and cross promotion.

YouTube Trends was officially unveiled on December 20, 2010. Kevin Allocca, YouTube Trends manager, said, "YouTube Trends features new algorithmically-generated feeds that highlight which topics and videos are trending right now." I'll say more about YouTube Trends later in this chapter.

A **new YouTube homepage** was launched on January 19, 2011. The YouTube team said, "We removed some of the less-used modules such as 'Videos Being Watched Now.' Then we moved modules like 'Spotlight' and 'Featured Videos' over to the right side." On January 20, 2011, I gave YouTube credit for opening up an experimental homepage for anyone who wanted to try it out. On Search Engine Watch, I said, "Millions of users opted in and now have this new version set as their homepage. Many of the people who tried the experimental homepage filled out YouTube's feedback form." While not everyone loved the new homepage, most people thought it was better than the old homepage.

On January 27, 2011, YouTube live-streamed the world premiere of **"Life in a Day"** from the Sundance Film Festival. Tim Partridge, product marketing manager, said, "The final film contains 1,025 videos that give an honest and compelling glimpse of our world."

On January 27, 2011, **US President Barack Obama** sat down for his second YouTube interview (http://youtu.be/etaCRMEFRy8). Steve Grove, head of News & Politics, said, "The President took the opportunity to respond to the protests in Egypt for the first time, to address your concerns on jobs, the debt, and health care, and to answer a series of more personal questions that you submitted in video and text over the past few days on YouTube." As Figure 11.6 illustrates, the interview took place in the Diplomatic Room in the West Wing, which is the same room where FDR used to deliver his fireside chats.

On February 25, 2011, **UK Prime Minister David Cameron** answered questions from YouTube users. Ramya Raghavan, News & Politics manager, and Jayme Goldstein, UK product marketing manager, said, "Today, in a special interview produced by YouTube World View and Al Jazeera English, you can get to see how the Prime Minister tackles a selection of the questions you voted to the top—including his thoughts on what should be done in Libya, whether banks in the U.K. should pay increased taxes, and what Britain's role is in Afghanistan."

Figure 11.6 "The YouTube Interview with President Obama, 2011"

On March 4, 2011, **US Speaker of the House John Boehner** sat down for his first-ever YouTube interview. Steve Grove, head of News & Politics, said, "It's clear that Americans are still feeling the weight of the recession—a large majority of the questions submitted for Speaker Boehner were on the topics of jobs, the economy, and spending in Washington."

The creation of **YouTube Next**, a new team to turbo-charge creator development and accelerate partner success, as well as the acquisition of **Next New Networks** were both announced on March 7, 2011. Tom Pickett, director of global content operations and YouTube Next, said, "The number of partners making over $1,000 a month is up 300% since the beginning of 2010 and we now have hundreds of partners making six figures a year." Today, only a small percentage of partners can afford to hire editors and producers. So, helping partners to grow enables them to create even more original content.

The **YouTube Creator Institute**, the first initiative from YouTube Next, was announced on March 10, 2011. Bing Chen, YouTube Creator initiatives and product marketing, said, "Participants will learn everything from story arcing to cinematography, money-making strategies to social media tactics." The inaugural classes were held at the University of Southern California School of Cinematic Arts and Columbia College Chicago's Television Department.

YouTube Next's second initiative, **YouTube NextUp**, was announced on March 16, 2011. Heather Wall, new business development, said, "YouTube NextUp is about accelerating the growth of the next big YouTube stars." Initially, 25 partners from around the United States were selected for the development program.

As Figure 11.7 illustrates, TED and YouTube announced the 10 winners of the **Ads Worth Spreading** challenge on March 18, 2011 (`http://youtu.be/WKboBODx1f4`). Mark Sabec, product marketing manager, said, "The winners represent some of the most creative, compelling and out-of-the-box executions of the past year. They embody a new paradigm for advertising creative, pushing the boundaries on what will move audiences and spur action by embracing longer-form storytelling as advertising."

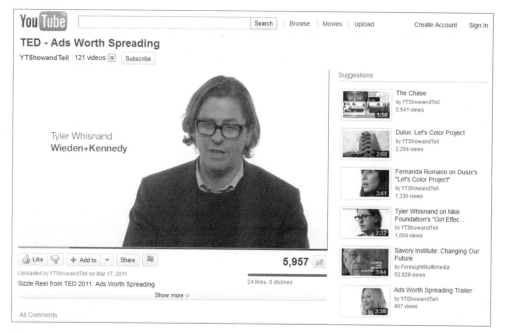

Figure 11.7 "TED - Ads Worth Spreading"

On March 24, 2011, YouTube announced the beta launch of **YouTube.com/create**, where you can use video creation sites to make personal videos or animations and post them directly to YouTube. Stanley Wang, software engineer, said, "No video camera? No problem! Create original videos with your own photos, clips or just an idea." Initially, Xtranormal Movie Maker, Stupeflix Video Maker, and GoAnimate were available. One True Media was added later.

On March 31, 2011, YouTube launched a preemptive **April Fools' Day hoax** by adding a button to the video player that, when clicked, applied a video filter and replaced the audio with piano music to resemble the style of a silent film from 1911. William Howard Taft, who was president in 1911, said in a faux guest post, "I venture to say that there is no other destination on the web which has taken more real steps of … progress than the YouTubes (sic), making its debut today." Go to `http://youtu.be/CNm8ZCJ7Fx8` and watch the "Top 5 Viral Pictures of 1911." They appear to be the lost forerunners of Keyboard Cat, Rickrolling, the FAIL Blog, the Bed Intruder Song, and the Annoying Orange.

The initial rollout of **YouTube Live**, the site's live-streaming beta platform, was announced on April 8, 2011. Joshua Siegel, product manager, and Christopher Hamilton, product marketing manager, said, "The goal is to provide thousands of partners with the capability to live-stream from their channels in the months ahead." Using the same name for its live-streaming platform as the company used for its 2008 event in San Francisco can create confusion, but check out the browse page at www.youtube.com/live and you'll see what YouTube Live now means.

On April 16, 2011, Google sent an email to users of Google Videos letting them know it would be **ending playbacks of Google Videos** on April 29. After receiving feedback about making the migration easier, the April 29 deadline was eliminated. On April 22, Mark Dochtermann, engineering manager, said, "We will be working to automatically migrate your Google Videos to YouTube." Game over.

On April 18, 2011, 10 video ads received *Ad Age* **Viral Video Awards**. Kate Rose, YouTube communications, said, "All of them put the YouTube platform to work in innovative ways and are fantastic examples of how brands can engage viewers." The GEICO video in Figure 11.8 (http://youtu.be/2fXsfAeqimY), which features Andres Cantor, Telemundo's legendary soccer commentator announcing a chess match, was one of the viral videos that won the award for the best "Make a Dull Industry Fun" Campaign.

Figure 11.8 "Andres Cantor - GEICO Commercial"

On April 19, 2011, the Royal Household announced that the **royal wedding** of Britain's Prince William and Miss Catherine Middleton would be live-streamed on their official YouTube channel: www.youtube.com/theroyalchannel. Rachel Ball, partner development associate, said, "More than 50 years ago, the marriage of The Queen's sister, Princess Margaret, and Antony Armstrong-Jones was the first royal wedding to be broadcast on television and had over 20 million viewers. This one is already heralded as the first of the Internet age, where for the first time in thousands of years of royal history, the moment will be captured online and preserved forever."

On April 19, 2011, YouTube announced that all new videos uploaded to the site were being transcoded into **WebM,** an open media file format for video and audio on the Web. James Zern, software engineer, said, "We're also working to transcode our entire video catalog to WebM....So far we've already transcoded videos that make up 99% of views on the site or nearly 30% of all videos into WebM." The move to WebM was less significant than the disclosure that 70 percent of all videos on YouTube get only 1 percent of views.

On May 6, 2011, YouTube announced that the **royal wedding** had been live-streamed 72 million times around the world to 188 countries. Rachel Ball, partner development associate, said, "When it was all said and done, the total streams on April 29, 2011, reached 101 million as romantics around the globe tuned in to watch the fairytale ceremony, the procession and the final balcony kiss."

On May 9, 2011, YouTube announced the addition of thousands of full-length feature films from major Hollywood studios and that they were available to rent in the United States at **YouTube.com/movies.** Camille Hearst, product marketing manager, said, "In addition to the hundreds of free movies available on the site since 2009, you will be able to find and rent some of your favorite films. From memorable hits and cult classics like *Caddyshack, Goodfellas, Scarface,* and *Taxi Driver* to blockbuster new releases like *Inception, The King's Speech, Little Fockers, The Green Hornet* and *Despicable Me.*" I found *Harry Potter and Deathly Hallows – Part 1,* but I couldn't find *The Adventures of Buckaroo Banzi Across the 8th Dimension.*

On May 18, 2011, **YouTube Town Hall** was launched. Will Houghteling, YouTube News & Politics, said, "YouTube Town Hall is an online platform for members of Congress to virtually debate and discuss the most important issues of the day."

On May 18, 2011, Google announced a **Promoted Video pricing change** on Inside AdWords, Google's official blog for news, information, and tips on AdWords. Baljeet Singh, senior product manager, YouTube, said, "Until now, Promoted Videos have been priced on a cost-per-click (CPC) basis; similar to AdWords search ads, you were charged every time a user clicked on a Promoted Video ad. Beginning on May 25th, we're changing the pricing structure of this format to a cost-per-view (CPV) model, shifting the focus to actual viewership." Because this announcement wasn't cross-posted on the YouTube Blog, I missed the news about the change until after it took effect.

YouTube celebrated its **sixth birthday** on May 25, 2011, and thanked the YouTube community for a couple of amazing birthday presents. First, YouTube thanked content creators and partners for uploading more than **48 hours** of video to the site every minute (Figure 11.9). Second, YouTube thanked visitors for driving the site past the **3 billion** views a day mark. The YouTube team said, "You've made YouTube successful because it's a reflection of you and your world. If this is what we've accomplished together in six years, we can only imagine where you'll take us in the next six!"

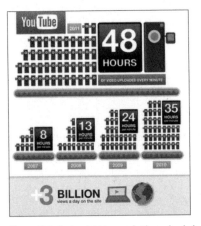

Figure 11.9 Forty-eight hours of video uploaded every minute and 3 billion views a day on the site

These 40 thumbnail descriptions from the YouTube Blog show that as many significant things have changed at YouTube in the past year as in its first five years. The pace of change at YouTube makes Calvinball look like a kid's game.

And I'm not even counting the roll out of the Google +1 button on YouTube, the launch of Creative Commons licensing on YouTube, or the launch of "As Seen On" YouTube pages, which were all announced in June 2011.

"Welcome to the future of video. Please stay awhile."

And I didn't count Salar Kamangar replacing Chad Hurley as head of YouTube on October 29, 2010, because it didn't significantly change things at YouTube. In a statement issued by Google, Hurley said, "For the past two years, I've taken on more of an advisory role at YouTube as Salar Kamangar has led the company's day-to-day operations."

In the spring of 1999, Kamangar was hired out of Stanford as Google's ninth employee. Today, he is the senior vice president of YouTube and Video at Google as well as the head of YouTube.

Douglas Edwards, author of *I'm Feeling Lucky: The Confessions of Google Employee Number 59* (Houghton Mifflin Harcourt, 2011), says, "I didn't know anything about Salar Kamangar when he came up to me in my first month at Google and asked for help. Someone mentioned he had been an intern. On the basis of that single fact, I underestimated him, as I suspect most people did."

Edwards adds, "Salar is a Porsche packaged as a Dodge Dart. Dark haired with large, limpid brown eyes and a shy, infectious grin, he could have stood in for Sal Mineo in *Rebel without a Cause*, but despite his disarming demeanor, he argued his positions with passion, persuasiveness, and persistence. For a thin man, he was very hard to get around."

On May 9, 2011, Kamangar wrote a post on the YouTube Blog entitled, "Welcome to the future of video. Please stay awhile." If you want a quick look at the future of YouTube, his post is worth reading:

`http://youtube-global.blogspot.com/2011/05/welcome-to-future-of-video-please-stay.html`

Six months after becoming the head of YouTube, Kamangar demonstrated that he could do more than lead the company's day-to-day operations. He also had "the vision thing."

Kamangar said, "It's a Saturday and you want to watch your favorite YouTube star's show, a big Hollywood movie, a clip of your friend's weekend in Austin, a newly-released music video, a global sporting event, a live concert and breaking news from Japan. Six years ago, when YouTube first arrived, you'd have to go from TV to laptop, desk to couch, or platform to platform, to do all this. Six years ago, there were also two types of video: video you watched on your TV, and video you watched on your laptop. Today there's increasingly just video, and it's available everywhere: on a phone, a tablet, a laptop or a television screen, in your office, on your couch, in a cab."

He added, "YouTube isn't about one type of device or one type of video. Content from traditional media partners, made-for-web and personal videos all co-exist on the site. Like surfing? You can watch pros shoot barrels, rent your favorite surf movie and check out your friend's upload of his morning session at your favorite local spot. News junkie? YouTube has breaking news uploads from citizen journalists alongside anchored reports and live streams from news partners."

Kamangar concluded, "While six years ago you had to move device, room and platform to get all the video that matters most to you, today you can find it all on YouTube. By expanding our content partnerships worldwide and stimulating the success of budding filmmakers, artists and entrepreneurs, we'll ensure that YouTube remains the best place for the world to see and discover rich talent. So stay tuned—there's much more to come."

So, a lot has changed in the past year. But, I feel things at YouTube are generally going in the right direction.

Stay on Top of the Latest Trends

If all you needed to do to be successful was keep up with the changes at YouTube, then you could visit the YouTube Blog every weekday and read about the latest developments.

But, with 48 hours of video now being uploaded to YouTube every minute, keeping up with the latest goings-on around the site can be a challenge. In other words, video marketing is also changing.

So, I strongly recommend that you also visit YouTube Trends (http://youtube-trends.blogspot.com/) each weekday to stay on top of the latest popular videos and trends on the world's largest video site.

As Figure 11.10 illustrates, YouTube Trends was officially unveiled in December 2010 with a video featuring the Gregory Brothers (http://youtu.be/i__1Z5a9Sak).

Figure 11.10 "Introducing YouTube Trends (Feat. The Gregory Brothers)"

YouTube Trends is a great destination for daily insight into the cultural zeitgeist of the world's largest video site. By using viewership data and aggregating the wisdom of top curators across the Web, YouTube Trends identifies popular videos and provides a sneak preview of broader trends developing in the YouTube community.

The site also offers a number of new tools to help you identify and understand the latest trends across YouTube.

For example, *trending topics* are algorithmically generated by looking at common metadata within a set of videos that are currently rising in popularity. For example, if there is a sudden spike in views for videos that all mention "Boston Red Sox" in the titles, descriptions, and tags, then that may be labeled a trending topic on YouTube.

Trending videos are ones that have become popular because they were embedded in popular blogs or websites and were viewed by a significant number of people externally in addition to being viewed on YouTube.com.

There is also a Trends dashboard that lets you quickly explore what's popular in different cities in the United States or around the world as well as within specific demographic groups.

Let's take a look at the 10 most interesting videos and cultural trends on YouTube during the first half of 2011, according to Kevin Allocca, YouTube Trends manager.

"How Soon Till Spring?"

On January 21, 2011, Allocca posted "How Soon Till Spring?" He said, "According to YouTube data, searches for 'snow' videos generally peak in December, which could mean that while we like to take in the winter weather when it first arrives, we are not excited about looking at more of it after the holidays."

As Figure 11.11 illustrates, a quick look at the popularity of "snow" searches over the last few years appears under the video "NEW YORK SNOW STORM 12/26/2010 BROOKLYN NY HD" (`http://youtu.be/uLnU0Ad6aVA`).

Figure 11.11 "NEW YORK SNOW STORM 12/26/2010 BROOKLYN NY HD"

"The Super Bowl Ad That Went Viral Before It Even Aired"

On February 7, 2011, Allocca took a look at "The Super Bowl Ad That Went Viral Before It Even Aired." He said, "Volkswagen's 'The Force' Super Bowl ad has been seen over 16 million times since it was posted on February 2nd. In the first day, the video was picked up by pop culture blogs and highlighted early by Jalopnik in the U.S., which posted it that morning with the headline, 'The Star Wars Super Bowl commercial everyone will talk about.' By the next day, the video was already atop our Most Shared list. It was viewed over one million times in the first 24 hours and over 5 million times in the first 48."

As Figure 11.12 illustrates, "The Force: Volkswagen Commercial" (http://youtu.be/R55e-uHQna0) was the most-viewed video that week globally. The chart below the video shows that "The Force" saw its highest peak on the Friday before the big game.

Figure 11.12 "The Force: Volkswagen Commercial"

"Keywords of a 'Revolution'"

On February 16, Allocca posted "Keywords of a 'Revolution'" to YouTube Trends. He said, "In an attempt to get a wider snapshot of the events in the Middle East over the past two weeks, we've pulled together some YouTube keyword data to examine which words were tied closest to the dramatic footage coming out of the region."

He took 2,000 videos uploaded to YouTube that included the Arabic word for "revolution" in the title. Then, he looked at the keywords tagged to those videos and translated them into English using Google Translate. As Figure 11.13 illustrates, the "word cloud" below was a visualization of those keywords using the online tool Wordle (www.wordle.net).

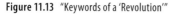

Figure 11.13 "Keywords of a 'Revolution'"

"Which Trailers Saw the Biggest Oscar Bump?"

On March 3, 2011, Allocca posted "Which Trailers Saw the Biggest Oscar Bump?" He said, "Interest in *The Black Swan* saw the biggest bump around Oscar weekend. It was the movie that saw the largest spike in YouTube search interest the day after the Oscars and its most-popular trailer drew over half a million views between Feb 27th and March 1st. In the search department, *Inception*, *Toy Story 3*, *The Fighter*, and *127 Hours* saw spikes as well."

The King's Speech, the Best Picture winner, also drew increased attention, although it saw a smaller spike in YouTube search interest compared to some of the other nominees. The trailer for *The King's Speech* also drew a sharp increase in views the day after the film's victory. As Figure 11.14 illustrates, the chart below "The King's Speech Movie Trailer Official (HD)" (`http://youtu.be/pzI4D6dyp_o`) shows the trailer's views from the previous few months:

Figure 11.14 "The King's Speech Movie Trailer Official (HD)"

"The Most Popular 'Ted Talks'"

On March 9, 2011, Allocca posted "The Most Popular 'Ted Talks,'" He said, "Following last week's TED Conference—Technology, Entertainment and Design—we looked into YouTube search data and have found that searches for 'TED Talk' have gradually been increasing over time and recently have been reaching their highest point ever. TED's channel is also now the #1 subscribed non-profit channel on YouTube and over 200 talks have been posted in the past year alone. Videos from TED, the slogan for which is 'Ideas Worth Spreading,' have been viewed around 60 million times."

The top five most-viewed TED Talk videos have gradually accumulated their high view counts over time. As Figure 11.15 illustrates, at the top of the diverse list is Tony Robbins' 2007 talk (`http://youtu.be/Cpc-t-UwvlI`).

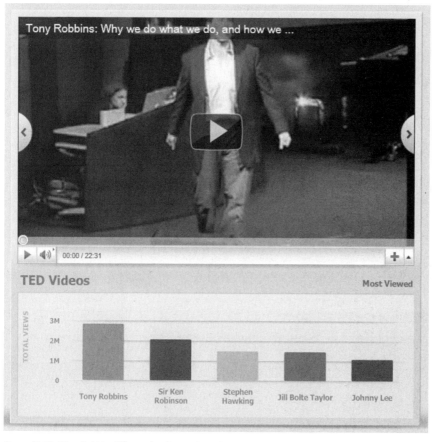

Figure 11.15 "Tony Robbins: Why we do what we do, and how we can do it better"

"Words Do Hurt"

On March 29, 2011, Allocca posted "Words Do Hurt." He said, "Anti-bullying campaigns pushed off in full force last fall with the It Gets Better project created by Dan Savage. That campaign, which began modestly, resulted in hundreds of encouragement videos from celebrities, politicians, and everyday people (including googlers) who wanted to share stories and words of encouragement. Eventually the president of the United States even contributed one."

Some of the most powerful videos are put up by those who are being bullied. One of these, "Words are worse than Sticks and Stones," is shown in Figure 11.16 (http://youtu.be/37_ncv79fLA).

Figure 11.16 "Words are worse than Sticks and Stones"

Alye's simple message—"Words are powerful"—generated video responses and hundreds of comments. YouTube Trends took those comments and created the graphic shown in Figure 11.17 to get a general idea of what "words" had been used by those responding to her video.

Figure 11.17 Words are powerful

"Rebecca Black Hits 100 Million Views"

On April 14, 2011, Allocca posted "Rebecca Black Hits 100 Million Views." He said, "Rebecca Black's 'Friday' video officially crossed the 100 million view mark this week. The video, which was posted in February, really took off in March, roughly a mere one month ago."

By comparison, it took Justin Bieber's "Baby"—the most-viewed music video on YouTube—two months and eight days to hit 100 million views. As Figure 11.18 illustrates, the chart below compares the daily views for "Baby" and "Friday" starting on their posting to the day they hit 100 million.

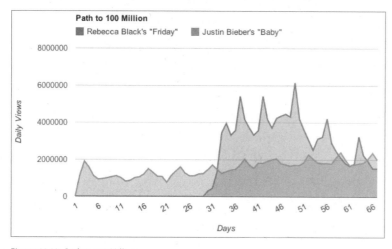

Figure 11.18 Path to 100 Million

"Friday" had amassed more than 167 million views. The video also had more than 3.1 million "dislikes"—87 percent of its total ratings by YouTube users, prompting several critics to call it "the worst song ever."

Her next song, "Rebecca Black – My Moment – Official Music Video" (http://youtu.be/20xWD85Ngz4) had already chalked up more than 23.1 million views as this was written. This video had almost 502,000 "dislikes"—64 percent of its total ratings by YouTube users, prompting one YouTuber to comment wryly, "Leave Rebecca Alone!"

"'Royal Wedding Entrance' Averaging Millions of Views"

On April 20, 2011, Allocca posted "'Royal Wedding Entrance' Averaging Millions of Views." He said, "Though it was only posted late last Friday, T-Mobile's 'Royal Wedding Entrance' video has become one of the top 10 most-viewed videos of the past month on YouTube. The clip, which is a spoof of the now-famous 'JK Wedding' video, has picked up nearly 7 million views since last Friday, and as indicated in the chart below, is still averaging over 1 million views per day."

The video received an early boost from choreographer Louie Spence and generated a lot of tweets. As Figure 11.19 illustrates, "The T-Mobile Royal Wedding" (http://youtu.be/Kav0FEhtLug) had almost 22.8 million views as this was written.

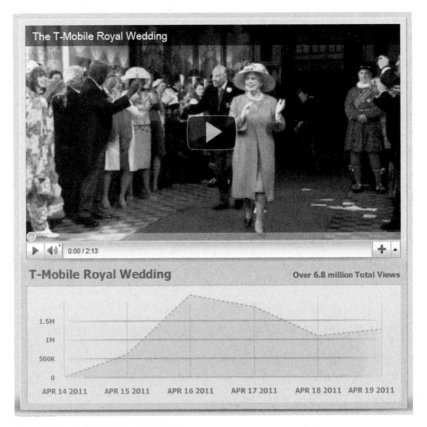

Figure 11.19 "The T-Mobile Royal Wedding"

"Obama's 2011 Correspondents' Speech Draws Millions of Views"

On May 2, 2011, Allocca posted "Obama's 2011 Correspondents' Speech Draws Millions of Views." He said, "President Obama's remarks Saturday evening will go down as the most popular ever for the White House Correspondents' Dinner on YouTube. The speech, which was posted by CSPAN, has been the Most Shared and the top Trending Video for the past two days."

The chart below "President Obama at the 2011 White House Correspondents' Dinner" (http://youtu.be/n9mzJhvC-8E) shows the disparity in views for the CSPAN videos of remarks made by President Obama and President Bush over the past few years (Figure 11.20).

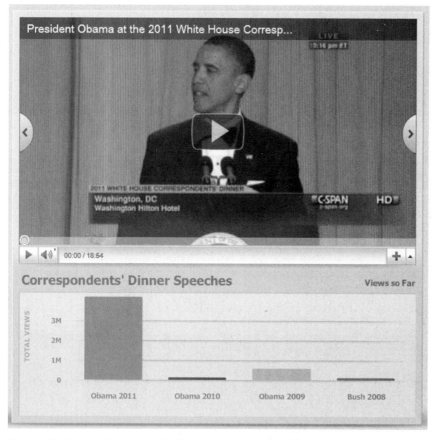

Figure 11.20 "President Obama at the 2011 White House Correspondents' Dinner"

"Inside YouTube Search: Looking Back at a Major News Week"

On May 12, 2011, Allocca posted "Inside YouTube Search: Looking Back at a Major News Week." He said, "Last week was a major week for news involving the President, with Obama delivering two starkly contrasting, yet incredibly popular speeches."

As this was written, Obama's correspondents' dinner remarks had more than 8.8 million views. As Figure 11.21 illustrates, the president's address on the death of Osama bin Laden, which he delivered the following night, had over 6 million views.

Figure 11.21 "President Obama on Death of Osama bin Laden"

Allocca added, "Today, we've gone back and looked at last week's search data for some perspective. Searches around the world for 'Obama' on YouTube so far this month were at their relative highest since January 2009, when the President was inaugurated."

To stay on top of the latest popular videos and trends on the world's largest video site, you need to visit YouTube Trends early and often. Every weekday at 4 a.m. and 4 p.m. Eastern time, YouTube Trends identifies four of the videos generating significant buzz on YouTube as well as on news and culture websites.

Checking out "4 at 4" every morning and every evening Monday through Friday should help you pick up the nuances of video marketing fast.

Play by the New Rules of YouTube Marketing

YouTube is changing daily and video marketing is changing twice a day. So what do you need to do?

David Meerman Scott, author of *Real-Time Marketing and PR: How to Instantly Engage Your Market, Connect with Customers, and Create Products that Grow Your Business Now* (Wiley, 2010), says, "Wake up, it's revolution time!"

He adds, "Gone are the days when you could plan out your marketing and public relations programs well in advance and release them on your timetable. It's a real-time world now, and if you're not engaged, then you're on your way to marketplace irrelevance."

Scott is a friend and neighbor. And as Figure 11.22 illustrates, we've swapped a few marketing video case studies on Search Engine Watch's channel (http://youtu.be/SSsHtR-ov1k).

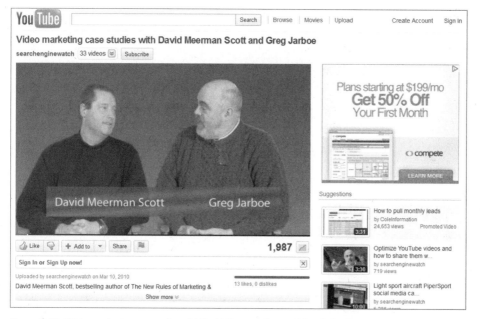

Figure 11.22 "Video marketing case studies with David Meerman Scott and Greg Jarboe"

And we agree: "Real time" means news breaks over minutes, not days. It means ideas percolate, then suddenly and unpredictably go viral to a global audience. Caught up in old, time-consuming processes, too many companies leave themselves fatally exposed by flying blind through this new media environment. You don't have to be among them.

With a tip of my cap to Scott, let me review the nine new rules of YouTube marketing, which look suspiciously like the chapter titles of this book. (Aren't you glad that happened? It's one of the benefits of reading the second edition of this book.)

Map Out Your Video Marketing Strategy

When mapping out your video marketing strategy, you should identify the top opinion leaders in your category on YouTube. And then you should reach out to these opinion leaders to get them to discover your video and share it with their followers.

There are two groups of opinion leaders who can make you or break you.

The inner circle is made up of people with YouTube accounts. They can post comments to your YouTube videos and on YouTube user channels. They can make a video response. They can add your video to their favorites or a playlist. They can flag inappropriate videos.

And most importantly, people with YouTube accounts can click on the yellow Subscribe button and do the following:

- Subscribe to all of your videos and their public activity (i.e., your favorites and ratings).

- Subscribe to only your video uploads.

- Unsubscribe from your channel.

So, how important are subscriptions? At the end of December 2010, Ryan Higa became the first YouTube creator to hit 3 million subscribers to his YouTube channel (www.youtube.com/nigahiga). His path to this milestone dates all the way back to July 2007 when he uploaded his first video.

"How to be Ninja" (http://youtu.be/JdLCEwEFCMU) now has more than 29.4 million views, as you can see in Figure 11.23.

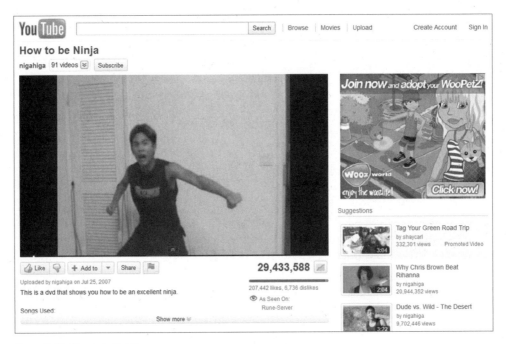

Figure 11.23 "How to be Ninja"

Instead of hoping that his next 90 videos would also "go viral," Higa was able to add a steady stream of new subscriptions month after month until he hit "the big 3-0-0-0-0-0-0." With a growing number of subscribers receiving updates and staying informed when something new occurred on his channel, Higa only needed to upload 91 videos to his channel to get more than 862 million total upload views.

As the chart from YouTube Trends in Figure 11.24 illustrates, new subscriptions to nigahiga averaged over 100,000 a month in 2010.

Figure 11.24 Subscriptions to nigahiga

The outer circle of opinion leaders who can make you or break you are the people who embed videos into their blogs and websites. In February 2009, TubeMogul research found that 44.2 percent of viewers discovered videos embedded on blogs and 45.1 percent discovered videos by going to a video site. More recently, YouTube has made a couple of announcements to strengthen its relationship with this second group of opinion leaders.

On June 9, 2011, YouTube rolled out two new features that take the next step in embedded videos:

HD preview images Any new video uploaded to YouTube in a resolution of 480 pixels or higher will have an HD preview image wherever the player is embedded. YouTube will also automatically give HD preview images to older videos, as long as they're 480 pixels or larger.

Logoless player YouTube also added a version of the YouTube player without a YouTube logo, so the video plays without any branding nearby.

On June 10, 2011, the video sharing site launched "As Seen On" YouTube pages to deepen the connection with content curators who embed YouTube videos on blogs and sites across the Web, often adding their own commentary and perspective.

On the YouTube Blog, Kurt Wilms, product manager, and Nathan Hunt, software engineer, said, "By crawling web feeds of sites that have embedded videos, we've built dedicated pages that highlight your embedded videos. This means that there is now a place on YouTube to find videos mentioned on your favorite blogs and sites."

They added, "Starting today the 'As Seen On' links on our video pages will direct users to these pages to surface more content and commentary. As a blog or site owner, this is another way all that hard work you put into building your readership can pay off and generate even more traffic for your site."

This is something worth mentioning the next time you reach out to blogs like Gizmodo, Boing Boing, and TechCrunch and ask them to consider embedding your new video.

Make Videos Worth Watching

You need to make original videos worth watching. Please note that I didn't say you need to produce videos that are 3 minutes long.

The length of the typical video is 3 minutes long, but the length of a video worth watching can vary depending on the story that it tells. For example, "Dear 16-year-old Me" (http://youtu.be/_4jgUcxMezM) is 5 minutes and 4 seconds long. The video was uploaded on May 2, 2011, by the David Cornfield Melanoma Fund.

"Dear 16-year-old Me" doesn't feature actors. It features real Canadians and Americans whose lives have been touched by melanoma. These people share their stories with viewers.

And as Figure 11.25 illustrates, "Dear 16-year-old Me" had more than 2.6 million views as this was written.

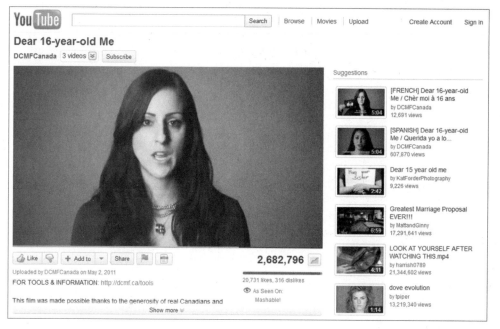

Figure 11.25 "Dear 16-year-old Me"

Create Content Worth Sharing

You also want to create compelling content worth sharing. And even brands and advertisers can create content that people seek out, love, and share with others.

For example, one of the 10 winning ads in TED and YouTube's inaugural "Ads Worth Spreading" challenge was Chrysler's "Born of Fire" created by Wieden+Kennedy. The winning ads were selected by a diverse judging panel made up of 24 artists, business people, and thought leaders, including Robert Wong from Google's Creative Lab and YouTube creative champion Terrence Kelleman of Dynomighty.

"Chrysler Eminem Super Bowl Commercial - Imported from Detroit" was uploaded to YouTube on February 5, 2011, and aired on Super Bowl XLV the following evening.

The judges said, "In this spot, a classic American car-maker repositions the luxury automobile—and, at the same time, re-brands a troubled city. Our judging panel loved the powerful, authentic tone of this love letter to the city of Detroit."

As Figure 11.26 illustrates, "Chrysler Eminem Super Bowl Commercial - Imported From Detroit" (http://youtu.be/SKL254Y_jtc) had more than 12 million views as this was written.

According to the Viral Video Chart, "Chrysler Eminem Super Bowl Commercial - Imported From Detroit" had been shared almost 400,000 times as this was written: more than 383,000 times on Facebook, over 16,000 times on Twitter, and 564 times in blogs.

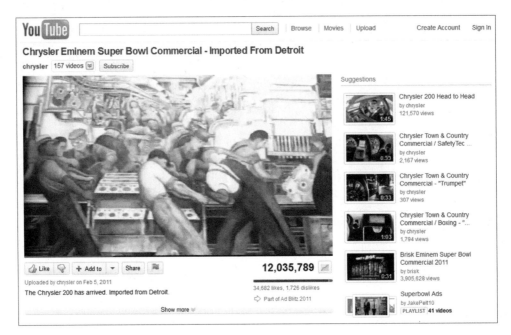

Figure 11.26 "Chrysler Eminem Super Bowl Commercial - Imported From Detroit"

Customize Your YouTube Channel

You have to use YouTube, not Yahoo! Video or Google Videos. But that doesn't mean your YouTube channel can't stand out. You can customize your channel background and theme. You can add an image as your channel's background. I provided four examples of some great new channel designs in Chapter 5. Here are four more:

- LisaNova at www.youtube.com/lisanova

- nalts at www.youtube.com/nalts

- sxephil at www.youtube.com/sxephil

- University of Phoenix at www.youtube.com/UniversityofPhoenix

If you are thinking seriously about creating a brand channel, which allows marketers to customize the look and feel of their presence on YouTube, then visit the video sharing site's Show and Tell Channel (www.youtube.com/ytshowandtell), which is the home of the best creative marketing examples on YouTube.

One of the brand channels featured there is GoProCamera's channel (www.youtube.com/gopro). As Figure 11.27 illustrates, GoPro makes the world's best-selling wearable HD cameras for sports.

On March 16, 2011, Kermit Pattison of the *New York Times* wrote a small business guide entitled "Online Video Offers Low-Cost Marketing for Your Company." One of his tips was "build a brand channel."

Figure 11.27 GoProCamera's channel

He said, "GoPro.com, a maker of small high-definition cameras that can be worn during adventure sports, has built a thriving YouTube presence with customer videos. YouTube allows businesses to establish channels, or a home page that lists videos, playlists and contact information. The GoPro channel features more than 100 videos—including surfing, skiing, motocross, auto sports and flight—which have been viewed more than 24 million times."

Nick Woodman, founder and chief executive of GoPro, told Pattison, "It is the No. 1 most convenient way for us to validate our product to customers." Woodman also said his business was growing 300 percent a year.

Explore YouTube Alternatives

You want to explore YouTube alternatives, but YouTube is the elephant in the room and it's hard to get around it.

According to Experian Hitwise, YouTube was in first place in May 2011 with an 86.9 percent share of U.S. visits to 78 video sites. Hulu was in second place that month with 2.9 percent of U.S. visits, Bing Videos was in third with 2.0 percent, and Yahoo! Video was in fourth with 1.4 percent.

And as this was written, Google was one of about a dozen companies involved in talks to potentially buy Hulu.

On July 2, 2011, Jessica Guynn and Dawn C. Chmielewski of the *Los Angeles Times* reported, "Google Inc., which already rules the Web with the world's most popular search engine and video site, appears poised to take an even deeper plunge into Hollywood with a potential bid for rival online video pioneer Hulu, people familiar with the discussions said."

According to Guynn and Chmielewski, "Google is one of a dozen companies kicking Hulu's tires, said people familiar with the situation who spoke on the condition of anonymity because talks are confidential."

Now, Yahoo!, Amazon, Dish Network, or some other company could end up becoming the next YouTube alternative. But buying Hulu just means acquiring a video site that gets 2.9 percent of U.S. visits. So YouTube will remain the elephant in the room.

Optimize Video for YouTube

You should optimize your YouTube video watch pages—particularly the title, description, and tags—to help your videos be discovered in search results and Related Videos.

What impact can this have?

On February 5, 2010, I taught a customized YouTube and video marketing workshop for Voyage.tv, home of the world's best travel videos. I shared video optimization tips like, "If you want to include your brand name in the title, it should always go last."

Before the workshop, one of their videos was titled "Voyage TV's Renaissance Aruba Resort & Casino Video." It ranked #2 in YouTube search results for the term "renaissance aruba resort & casino."

After the workshop, the title was optimized to read "Renaissance Aruba Resort & Casino Hotel - Aruba, Caribbean - On Voyage.tv." As Figure 11.28 illustrates, the video is now ranked #1 in YouTube search results for "renaissance aruba resort & casino."

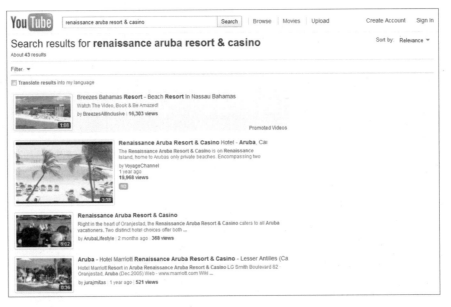

Figure 11.28 Search results for "renaissance aruba resort & casino"

Voyage.tv's channel (www.youtube.com/voyagechannel) had been created on May 18, 2009. Before the workshop was held, the channel had 1,510 total upload views.

Figure 11.29 shows Voyage.tv's channel, which had 1,829,050 total upload views as this was written. In other words, optimizing its videos for YouTube helped Voyage.tv go from an average of less than 6 views a day to an average of more than 3,548 views a day.

Figure 11.29 Voyage.tv's channel

Engage the YouTube Community

You can engage the YouTube community on the video sharing site in a number of ways:

Talk to your audience Break the "fourth wall," the imaginary boundary between the actors on a traditional three-walled set in a proscenium theater and the audience. Do this by using shout-outs, asking questions, or encouraging viewers to "like" your videos and become subscribers.

Enable comments You can delete comments by haters or trolls, but you want to encourage feedback. During the 2010 United States Senate special election in Massachusetts, Republican Scott Brown enabled comments on his YouTube videos, while Democrat Martha Coakley disabled them on hers. As of Election Day, Brown's 58 videos had 774,314 views, while Coakley's 59 videos had 102,389 views. Brown won with 1,168,107 votes, while Coakley lost with 1,058,682 votes. Any questions?

Participate in the YouTube community Comment on other people's videos, upload video responses, subscribe to other channels, collaborate with other content creators, provide feedback when YouTube's staff asks for it, and participate in events like VidCon, 789, and YouTube Meetups (www.meetup.com/youtube/) in 668 cities.

In addition, you should engage the YouTube community beyond the video sharing site by reaching out to blogs as well as encouraging viewers to share your videos using email, Facebook, Twitter, and Google's +1 button. This can generate significant results.

For example, Yell, the international directories business, hired my firm in March 2009 to help promote the launch of stand-alone TV ads for its UK service based on the signature tune of cult Internet cartoon character Magical Trevor.

Magical Trevor is the creation of animator Jonti "Weebl" Pickering, whose distinctive style and animated characters have a worldwide following on the Internet. The commercial was produced through Tomboy Films, which represents Jonti's work for commercials.

Yell's public relations department handled the traditional media relations and generated stories in *Marketing Week*, Mad.co.uk, and *Marketing*. The TV campaign, developed by creative communications agency Rapier, broke on March 20 and ran for a month, with two 10-second variants running for a further two months to the end of May across major terrestrial, satellite, and cable channels. It was supported by a 60-second variant on Yell118247's channel on YouTube (www.youtube.com/yell118247) and 40-second radio ads.

There was also a campaign page at www.118247.com where visitors could see the ads, download a ringtone of the theme tune, and participate in a fun poll gauging whether they love or hate the ad.

As Figure 11.30 illustrates, my firm embedded a YouTube video of the 30-second TV ad into an optimized press release, which was distributed on March 22. We also used PRWeb's TweetIt feature to automatically share the press release through Twitter at the same time it was distributed through PRWeb.

We also conducted a blog outreach and social media marketing campaign. The YouTube video embedded in the press release was also embedded in the blogs Funkadelic Advertising, C64Glen, Welcome to my nightmare, and Your Face is an Advert on March 22, 2009, and it was embedded in the blog Scrambled eggs and mashed bananas two days later.

As Figure 11.31 illustrates, "Yell 118 247 Directory Heaven TV ad by Weebl," the 30-second YouTube video embedded in the press release, tweeted about, and pitched to bloggers, had more than 314,000 views as this was written.

This 30-second video also had 1,439 ratings (1,351 likes and 88 dislikes), 1,548 comments, and five video responses and had been favorited 2,641 times.

On April 16, Camille Alarcon of *Marketing Week* wrote an article entitled, "Yell extends 118 24 7 campaign following success." She said, "Yell, the international directories business, is extending the advertising campaign for its directory enquiries service 118 24 7, after recording a 70 percent increase in call volumes to its UK call centres."

Figure 11.30 Yell Adopts 'Magical Trevor' for First Ever Stand-Alone TV Ads for UK Business Directory Enquiries Service 118 24 7

Figure 11.31 "Yell 118 247 Directory Heaven TV ad by Weebl"

Trust but Verify YouTube Insight

You should trust YouTube Insight to determine where and how people are finding your videos, but you should verify your findings with Google Analytics, if you get the opportunity.

My firm created a channel for the SES Conference & Expo (www.youtube.com/sesconferenceexpo) back on January 29, 2008. But YouTube Insight wasn't introduced until March 26, 2008.

I remember the first time I used YouTube's video analytics tool. I had always wanted to know who was watching our videos. What videos were they watching? Where did they find our videos? Finally, I had some answers.

And I discovered some detailed statistics about the videos that we had uploaded to the site that answered questions I hadn't even asked yet: When did the popularity of a video peak? Why were some of our videos more popular relative to all videos in that market over a given period of time? How long did it take for a video to become popular?

Since then new YouTube Insight features were added:

A Discovery tab in April 2008 that shows how viewers found your video, whether by searching on YouTube or Google, browsing under Related Videos, receiving a link to the video from an email or website, or watching it in an embedded player off YouTube.

A Demographics tab in May 2008 that displays view count information broken down by age group (such as ages 18–24), gender, or a combination of the two, to help you get a better understanding of the makeup of your YouTube audience.

A Hot Spots tab in September 2008 that plays your video alongside a graph that shows the ups and downs of viewership at different moments within the video.

A Community tab in March 2009 that allows you to see how many times viewers have shared, rated, favorited or commented on a video.

Each new feature gave us a better understanding of our viewers and how they engaged with our videos. Whether I wanted to know how old our audience was, how many times our most-viewed video had been rated the previous week, or which minute of a clip was most engaging, YouTube Insight could give me the answer.

Using these metrics, we were able to increase our videos' view counts and improve the popularity on our channel. For example, worldwide views on SESConferenceExpo's channel were 64,512 from April 1, 2008, through March 31, 2009, almost doubled to 124,170 during the next 12 months, and increased again to 165,073 from April 1, 2010, through March 31, 2011.

But I knew that I was measuring outputs, not outcomes. And I understood that increasing our videos' view counts and improving the popularity on our channel weren't major marketing goals of our client, Matt McGowan, the managing director of

Americas for Incisive Media. His key marketing objective was to put "butts in seats" (my words, not his) at SES Conference & Expo events.

So, we started looking at the Google Analytics reports for the SES Conference & Expo website as well as the YouTube Insight data for SESConferenceExpo's channel. (Oh, did I mention that we started looking during the worst recession since the great depression?)

According to *Tradeshow Week* magazine, attendance at conventions and tradeshows fell by 8 percent in the first quarter of 2009 and the number of exhibitors participating at tradeshows dropped 10 percent. Instead of hunkering down, SES and my firm launched a social media marketing campaign. The goal was to listen to and communicate with attendees, exhibitors, speakers, and bloggers in North America and Europe. The key topic of this conversation was the value of attending conferences and expos in a recession.

According to a *Tradeshow Week* survey, executives said that in a challenging economy it was even more important to keep up-to-date with industry trends, see new products and services, and maintain and build relationships. In short, attending the leading conventions and tradeshows during a recession kept them informed and competitive.

One executive said, "If you don't keep up with what is going on in your business, a recession can keep you going down." Another executive added, "We still have to keep up with changes in the industry and be prepared for the upswing."

Despite aggressive budget cuts to get out in front of weak economic trends, 89 percent of *Tradeshow Week* survey respondents said they were going to the most important events in their industry. So, the primary message of our campaign was this: SES Conferences & Expo is "the leading search and social marketing event."

Christian Georgeou, the marketing manager of SES Conference & Expo, handled the social media outreach on Facebook, Twitter, and LinkedIn. My firm handled the social media outreach on YouTube and blogs. Together, we engaged SES speakers, attendees, and exhibitors in discussions about how the conference helped them "keep up-to-date on trends and issues," the expo hall let them "see new products," and the event enabled them to "network."

For example, "Nicholas Fox, Google, on future of search advertising at SES San Jose 2009" (http://youtu.be/ZcYcVI-_rao) looked at one of the latest trends and issues. "Ryan Hupfer, HubPages, and Ren Chin, YieldBuild on exhibiting at SES San Jose 2009" (http://youtu.be/TTMA_FsDcQs) examined new products. "Searching for Santa at SES Chicago 2009" (http://youtu.be/RMcW75JVjT0) was shot at a networking event.

We used Radian6 to monitor the program because it had the broadest coverage of video sharing sites like YouTube, Facebook public discussion forums, micromedia like Twitter, and blogs.

Our analytics efforts generated actionable insights. For example, one of the most viewed videos of the campaign was "SES Chicago 2009 from attendee Kathryn Joy, New England Journal of Medicine" (http://youtu.be/00TCcBCITg8). As Figure 11.32 illustrates, the video had over 3,600 views as this was written.

Figure 11.32 "SES Chicago 2009 from attendee Kathryn Joy, New England Journal of Medicine"

Now, 3,600 views may not qualify as a "viral video," but Joy's candid comments were an effective testimonial to the value of attending conferences and expos in a recession. So, as Figure 11.33 illustrates, Georgeou started embedding playlists of our testimonials on the SES website for upcoming events.

And the SES team discovered that we could do more than increase our videos' view counts. We could also put "butts in seats."

In 2009, our initial campaign helped SES Toronto in June and SES San Jose in August to remain flat in a down economy. (That's back when flat was the new up.) After we started embedding playlists of testimonials on the SES website, SES Berlin in November and SES Chicago in December were up over the previous year's events.

In the first quarter of 2010, conference registrations for SES London and SES New York were up more than 10 percent over the previous year and space in the expo halls sold out for these events.

Figure 11.33 SES London 2010

On June 29, 2010, Incisive Media won the Best Use of Social Media award at the Conference Awards 2010. McGowan and the entire team at SES had been able to demonstrate the following achievements:

- Improved delegate numbers attributable to the use of social media.

- Attracted delegates who would not have been contacted by other traditional marketing channels.

- Improved discussion and networking opportunities before, during, and after the events.

- Increased value for sponsors of the event and exhibitors.

- Received excellent feedback from delegates.

In a press release, McGowan said, "*Social media networks have enabled us to reach attendees in ways which have been difficult in the past.*" He added, "*All measurements from first contact through to client engagement and sales via social channels have showed marked improvement (year over year).*"

Study YouTube Success Stories

The ninth new rule of YouTube marketing is, study YouTube success stories to learn what works, and focus on the ones that measure outcomes, not outputs. Increasingly, these success stories involve video advertising and YouTube.

For example, Kate Rose, who handles communications for YouTube, sent me an email in May 2011 that tipped me off to a new case study about a Fortune 300 insurance company and a full-service media agency with search marketing capabilities. Her tip enabled me to become the first blogger or journalist to interview the key players. My story appeared in Search Engine Watch on June 6, 2011.

Here's the backstory: Headquartered in Madison, Wisconsin, American Family Insurance (www.amfam.com/default.asp) is a multiline property and casualty insurance provider with auto, home, business, and life products. Internally, the company was already utilizing YouTube Promoted Videos to highlight its videos at the top of YouTube search results—a great start to get more video views.

This enabled American Family Insurance to get prominent placement in front of the audience they wanted to reach on YouTube. But the company wanted to improve performance and reached out to Mindshare (www.mindshareworld.com) to implement some search marketing best practices.

Telisa Yancy, American Family Insurance's advertising director, says, "The proliferation of media fragmentation, and the continued growth of consumer consumption of content within the social media hubs presents a challenge for most marketers. Mindshare stepped up to our challenge to help us expand reach by gaining more views on our brand channel and did it in an effective yet efficient way."

Danny Huynh, Mindshare's group search director, says, "In today's world of social media, we were particularly interested in how we can apply our search savvy and data analytics to video. So when American Family Insurance came to us to help increase traffic to their YouTube Brand Channel, we took it as the perfect opportunity to find out."

First, just as with any search campaign, Mindshare looked at which American Family Insurance video ads were performing the best. The agency discovered people weren't searching for YouTube videos using broad terms such as "life insurance" or "car insurance." Instead, they were discovering, watching, and sharing videos about "identity theft," particularly on social networking sites.

Ryan Pedersen, associate search director says, "So, we put more budget behind keywords and video ads that spoke to this consumer concern. On top of this, we could also promote our videos to video categories such as Autos & Vehicles and only promote the videos to our target in the 19 states that American Family Insurance serves. We used this knowledge to refine our keyword and ad group criteria—connecting the right content to the audience who was looking for it."

As Figure 11.34 illustrates, you can see an example of this content by watching "AmFam | ID Theft | Do you know who you are?" (http://youtu.be/g0a6yo2ya3Q).

Figure 11.34 "AmFam | ID Theft | Do you know who you are?"

Second, just as search engine marketers would optimize a landing page, Mindshare looked at where to send people who clicked on a promoted video. Rather than driving users to American Family Insurance's brand channel page to watch more videos, Mindshare directed them to American Family Insurance's website, shown in Figure 11.35.

Figure 11.35 Identity Theft Protection

Finally, video advertising on YouTube provided Mindshare with access to YouTube Insight, a self-service analytics and reporting tool. This tool lets anyone with a YouTube account view detailed statistics about their audience for the videos they upload to the site—and to make adjustments as needed. Using YouTube Insight, Mindshare learned people were watching videos on their mobile phones, which they're definitely taking into consideration for future campaigns.

There were two significant results of this effort. First, video views and organic traffic to American Family Insurance's brand channel dramatically increased from 5,967 in October 2010 to 44,467 in January 2011. This was achieved at the same budget as before by lowering the average cost-per-click (CPC) from $2.11 to $.92.

Second, American Family Insurance reached prospective customers earlier in the consideration cycle—a necessary strategy when you are competing with national insurance companies with much larger advertising budgets.

As search engine marketers, Mindshare found other takeaways to be invaluable:

- There's a huge audience that's searching and browsing for information on YouTube, and search engine marketers have a pivotal role to play in taking advantage of this resource.

- Mindshare applied its data analytics skill set to a new area of marketing—video, one of the fastest-growing formats online.

- Search engine marketers can also support their colleagues in display media planning by honing in on keywords and categories that perform the best in video.

- Using the Hot Spots feature in YouTube Insights, Mindshare's search team found they can feed research with demographic and engagement insights and help their creative team understand who's watching which videos and when.

Expanding the role of search on YouTube proved extremely successful for American Family Insurance, but they are just one example of a YouTube success story, with many more to come.

"Hit 'em Where They Ain't"

Now that you've learned to play by the new rules of YouTube marketing, remember this: The rules can be "changed, amended, or deleted by any player(s) involved." Remember, YouTube didn't become the largest worldwide video sharing community by getting there "firstest with the mostest." As I mentioned in Chapter 1, YouTube's strategy seemed to follow the advice of legendary baseball player Wee Willie Keeler: "Keep your eye clear, and hit 'em where they ain't."

Keeler played right field for four Major League Baseball (MLB) teams from 1892 to 1910. So, in a parallel universe, his last MLB appearance was the year before the debut of "the YouTubes" in 1911. Nevertheless, YouTube partners will want to follow his advice too. Why? There are a couple of reasons.

You need to "keep your eye clear" because YouTube can change, amend, or delete rules at any time.

For example, on July 7, 2011, Noam Lovinsky, product manager, invited YouTube users "to play along with us by participating in one of our latest TestTube experiments: Cosmic Panda."

What is Cosmic Panda? Well, if you follow the cosmic critter over the double rainbow to www.youtube.com/cosmicpanda, you'll see what might be become a future design of YouTube that looks different, including channels, playlists, and videos.

As Figure 11.36 illustrates, I took this experiment for a test drive to see what the SES Conference & Expo channel might look like in the future.

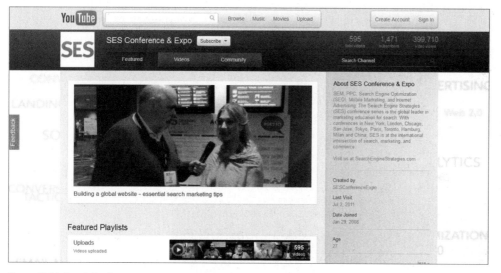

Figure 11.36 Cosmic Panda

The early reaction to Cosmic Panda has generally been positive. On July 7, 2011, Brenna Ehrlich of Mashable said, "When it comes to channels, the new header is a lot more polished looking." She added, "Overall, the whole layout is much cleaner and more professional looking."

Jeremy Scott of ReelSEO said, "I've tried it out, and I must say... it seems pretty cool to me at first glance." He added, "This thing is outstanding in my opinion. Simplified and slick."

And on July 10, 2011, Liz Shannon Miller of GigaOm interviewed some YouTube partners to find out "What YouTube creators think about Cosmic Panda." The response was largely positive. So, I think Cosmic Panda gives all of us a quick look at the future of YouTube.

Now, YouTube isn't the only player who can change, amend, or delete rules at any time. Some of the most successful partners haven't played by the old rules of video marketing. Instead, they created some of the new rules of YouTube marketing. For example, more than 20,000 partners are producing original content for the Web and commanding TV-size audiences for their own brand of programming, including folks like Annoying Orange. The first episode of the *Annoying Orange* series was uploaded to YouTube by Dane Boedigheimer on October 9, 2009. As this was written, his channel (www.youtube.com/realannoyingorange) has 691 million total upload views and close to 2 million subscribers.

The Annoying Orange has become such a recognized YouTube personality that one of the "Top Viral Pictures of 1911" featured in YouTube's 2011 April Fools' Hoax was "The Irksome Citris."

Do you feel like you've just been touched by the Babysitter Flag?

Video advertisers will also want to follow Keeler's advice to "hit 'em where they ain't." As audiences, platforms, channels, and devices continue to fragment into ever-more-specific niches, earning people's attention has become ever more challenging. To find audiences and break through all the noise, brands must create content that people seek out, love, and share with others.

For example, check out the video "NSFW. A hunter shoots a bear!" As Figure 11.37 illustrates, it had 17.3 million views as this was written.

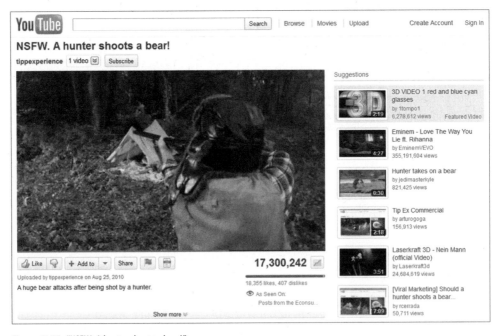

Figure 11.37 "NSFW. A hunter shoots a bear!"

This campaign for correction tape product Tipp-Ex hands control of the story to the user and offers dozens of funny outcomes that reward experimentation and discovery. Ben Parr of Mashable called it "one of 2010's greatest examples of interactive ads."

So, if I'm in the Perimeter of Wisdom, then I get to make a decree.

In addition to visiting the YouTube Blog every weekday as well as YouTube Trends every morning and every evening, you'll want to do a couple of other things. You need to keep your eye clear to see trends before everyone else has spotted them too.

One of these things is to use MyAlltop (http://my.alltop.com) to create a "personal, online magazine rack" of your favorite websites and blogs. You can create a personal collection from over 32,000 information sources—if you're interested in YouTube and video marketing, they have it covered.

Another website to visit is ReelSEO (www.reelseo.com), the online video marketer's guide. It's the world's leading resource for valuable news, research, analysis, tips, and trends for the online video and internet marketing industries, and I recently became a contributor.

Finally, you will want to visit Search Engine Watch (http://searchenginewatch.com). I write frequently about YouTube and regularly about video marketing.

Remember, "The only permanent rule in Calvinball is that you can't play it the same way twice!" And "the score is still Q to 12!"

So pick up the nuances of this game fast; this is fun!

Index

Note to the Reader: Throughout this index **boldfaced** page numbers indicate primary discussions of a topic. *Italicized* page numbers indicate illustrations.

C

R

rack focus camera technique, 78
Radeon Direct X11 video card, 298
Radian6 social media monitoring, **358**, *359*
Raghavan, Ramya, 415, 417
Rainie, Lee, 362, 383
Rajaraman, Shiva, 21, 94
"Rampage III Extreme 24GB RAM Core i7 980X
    SUCCESS!! Linus Tech Tips" video, 298
"Randy Pausch Last Lecture: Achieving Your Childhood
    Dreams" video, 104–106, *105*
rankings, search, **249–250**
Ransom, Diana, 153
Rao, Leena, 234
Raptor Resource Project, 220
ratings, allowing and asking for, **257–258**, *258*
Reagan, Ronald, 195
*Real-Time Marketing and PR: How to Instantly Engage
    Your Market, Connect with Customers, and Create
    Products that Grow Your Business* (Scott), 435
"Really Achieving Your Childhood Dreams" lecture
    (Pausch), 104
"Rebecca Black fastest moving search term in social
    sphere" post (Goad), 361, *361*
"Rebecca Black Hits 100 Million Views" post (Alloca),
    431–432
"Rebecca Black - My Moment - Official Music Video"
    video, 432
Recent Activity module, **172**
red/cyan glasses, 90
ReelSEO guide, 455
referrers in Insight, 333
Reid, Antonio, 150
Reider, Suzie, 31, 133–134
relationships in Paul Revere's ride, **278–281**, *278–280*
relevance, ads, 95
*Remix: Making Art and Commerce Thrive in the Hybrid
    Economy* (Lessig), 177
remixing videos, 178
"Renaissance Aruba Resort & Casino Hotel - Aruba,
    Caribbean - On Voyage.tv" workshop, 442
Rentals program
    description, 176, **179**
    launching, **23**
Reporters account type, 169
Reporters category for brand channels, 265, *265*
reports in Google Analytics, **351**, *351*
Republican Debate, **13–14**, *14*
research from TubeMogul, **346–348**, *347*
responses
    posting, **284–286**, *285–286*
    video, 257, **284–286**, *285–286*
Revere, Paul, ride of
    history, **278–281**, *278–280*
    message relaying, **310–311**, *311*
    routes, **301–302**, *302*
Revision3, **343–345**, *344*
Reyes, Ricardo, 15
Rice, Scott, 76
Ricketts, Camille, 224
"Rivalry" campaign, 283
Robbins, Tony, 429, *429*
Robertson, Hal, 80–82
Rocketboom, 197

Rogers, Everett M.
    communication models, 29
    on early adopters, 38–39
    interpersonal relationships, 278, 280
    on opinion leaders prudent judgment, 49, 51
    overview, **31–32**, *32*
    S-shaped diffusion curve, 35
    two-step flow model, 29, 32, 60
"Roller Babies" video, 136
rollerskating video, **135–137**, *135*
Romney, Mitt, 54–56
Roosevelt, Franklin Delano, 57
Rose, Kate, 420, 450
Rosen, Emanuel, **42–44**, *43–44*
Rosenblatt, Richard, 231
Rospars, Joe, 380, 390
Ross, Andy, 111–112
Ross, Bob, 64
Rotblat, Mark, 338
Rothman, Julia, 144
Rountree, Ellie, 160, *160*
Roy, Sumantra, 248
Royal Channel, The, 14, 29, *29*
royal wedding, 29, *29*
    live streams, 220, 421
    views, 432, *432*
"'Royal Wedding Entrance' Averaging Millions of Views"
    post (Alloca), **432**
RSS feeds, **306–307**
rumors, 49
Rushfield, Richard, 107
Russian nesting dolls technique, 251, *251*
"Ryan Hupfer, HubPages, and Ren Chin, YieldBuild on
    exhibiting at SES San Jose 2009" video, 447

S

S-shaped curve, 32, *32*, 35
Sabbagh, Dan, 127
Sabec, Mark, 97, 138, 419
Sacerdoti, Tod, 236
Salesforce.com, 358
Samberg, Andy, 40, 160
Sandler, Ali, 129–130
Sandoval, Greg, 229
Sarno, David, 286
Sarukkai, Ramesh, 413
Savage, Dan, 430
ScanScout company, 234
Schaller, Brian, 77–78
scheduling live events, **199**
Schlosberg, Jason, 115
Schmidt, Charlie, 159–160
Schmidt, Eric, 10
Schönberg, Claude-Michel, 128
Schor, Elana, 16
Scott, David Meerman, 435
Scott, Jeremy, 453
Scott, Ridley, 413
Scott, Zack, 292, **296–297**, *297*
"SCRIPT COPS Episode #1: Drop the Script - Pilot
    episode" video, 76, *76*
Script Wizard program, 75
ScriptWright program, 75